THE MINNESOTA ARCHAEOLOGIST

VOLUME 65	2006

Publications Committee

Managing Editor: Deborah Schoenholz
Editor: Chuck Diesen
Proofreader: Anna Morrow

Executive Board of the Minnesota Archaeological Society

President: Rod Johnson
Vice President: Pat Emerson
Secretary/Treasurer: Paul Mielke
Directors: Jim Cummings, Chuck Diesen, Rhoda R. Gilman,
Joe McFarlane, Ron Miles, Anna Morrow, Debbie Pommer,
Deborah Schoenholz

The Minnesota Archaeologist is published annually by the Minnesota Archaeological Society. Subscription is by membership in the Society. For information on membership and on the Society's other activities, go to www.mnarchaeologicalsociety.org.

Copyright © 2007 by the Minnesota Archaeological Society. All rights reserved.
Requests to reprint should be addressed to Anna Morrow, 612-922-7006 or anmorrow@earthlink.net.

Publication of The Minnesota Archaeologist is supported in part
by a generous bequest from the estate of William Lundquist.

Published by The Minnesota Archaeological Society
and
Prairie Smoke Press
PO Box 439
Champlin, MN 55316

THE MINNESOTA ARCHAEOLOGIST

VOLUME 65   2006

Contents

IN MEMORIAM

In Memorium: Tim Ready
Deborah Schoenholz..7

ARTICLES

The Savanna Portage: An Archaeological Study
Guy Gibbon 9

The Lower Rice Lake Site, 21CE5
Kent Bakken..31

Investigations at the Sucker Lakes Site
Andrea K. LeVasseur and William J. Yourd..79

Photospread: Minnesota Archaeological Society: Playing with Prehistory
Debbie Schoenholz..87

Animal Remains and Bone Tools from the North Twin Lake Site (21MH5),
Mahnomen County, Minnesota
David Mather..93

Lead Round Ball and Shot from a Fur Trade Post on Horseshoe Bay, Leech Lake
Matthew J. Mattson 113

Archaeological Remains of Two Mid-Nineteenth-Century Dakota Homes Associated
with the Riggs Hazelwood Mission Site (21YM11/YM-MNF-007)
Richard E. Berg and James E. Myster..129

The Rock Art of Big Room Cave
Rebecca Sprengelmeyer..175

Notice to Authors

The Minnesota Archaeologist accepts submissions of original research by professional or avocational archaeologists on the anthropology and archaeology of this region. Authors should submit papers in accessible electronic formats (word processing files and digitized images). Acceptable file formats include .doc or .rtf text and tables and .jpg, .bmp, or .tif graphics. Files in .pdf format will be accepted fpr initial review but must be replaced before production. These should be submitted on CDs and sent to the address below. Internet submissions are also encouraged, with files sent as email attachments or via web download. However, please contact the editor by email at the address below before sending such submissions, in order to arrange for the most efficient transfer.

Note that figures should be scanned at a resolution of no less than 300 dots per inch (dpi) at 100 percent (full size as printed) or submitted as high-resolution, camera-ready hard copy. Figures and tables should not be embedded in word processing files. For further information on electronic formats and file preparation, please contact the managing editor, who would be happy to entertain your questions because it saves so much time and work in the long run.

Managing Editor
schoe030@tc.umn.edu

Manuscripts will be edited for content only with the consent of the author. Style will conform to the journal's style, which is based on the Society for American Archaeology's *Style Guide for American Antiquity and Latin American Antiquity* and on the *Chicago Manual of Style*. Copies of the *Style Guide for The Minnesota Archaeologist* are available from the editor or may be downloaded from our website at www.mnarchaeologicalsociety.org. Send materials or inquiries to

Editor
c.diesen@att.net

The Minnesota Archaeologist
Minnesota Archaeological Society
Fort Snelling History Center
St. Paul, MN 55111
www.mnarchaeologicalsociety.org

Letter from the Editor:

I would like to thank the Executive Board of the Minnesota Archaeological Society for asking me to act as editor of this volume of *The Minnesota Archaeologist*. The experience has been interesting, educational, and entertaining.

We believe the current volume to be a valuable mix of pre- and post-contact subjects with something of interest to a wide audience, from spelunking adventures in the southeast corner of the state to a comprehensive survey of the fur trade era use of the Savanna Portage. Because of the generosity and at the suggestion of Dr. Guy Gibbon, this volume also includes a CD containing a large amount of additional data related to his Savanna Portage article. The CD can be found at the end of the volume inside the back cover.

I hope everyone enjoys this latest volume of *The Minnesota Archaeologist* as much as I did in helping to put it together.

Chuck Diesen
Editor

In Memorium: Tim Ready

by Deborah Schoenholz

Tim Ready was my friend and cohort at the Science Museum of Minnesota for six years. He worked at the museum for more than 25 years until 2005, when the staff was restructured. When he died unexpectedly on October 5, after an aneurism put him in a coma, he was again working on a project for the Science Museum, an institution into which he put his whole heart.

Tim studied archaeology with Eldon Johnson and Guy Gibbon at the University of Minnesota in the exciting early 1970s, where he helped conduct the first systematic statistical survey of the Minnesota River. Later he worked the Mountain Lake site with Joe Hudak and Scott Anfinson and eventually moved into the Science Museum Anthropology Department with Hudak, staying on as Curator Orrin Shane's assistant after Joe moved on.

Tim's many artistic skills found an outlet with the anthropology collections, and he turned his hand to casting, making models, and what became his first professional love, photography. Among many other projects, he reconstructed the famous Link Vessel from the Bryan site in Goodhue County, (see sidebar), which we have featured on the cover of this journal and from which the Minnesota Archaeological Society has taken its logo, the thunderbird. The photograph, taken for the museum catalogue, is also Tim's.

The Science Museum initiated and maintains anthropology collections from Hmong culture as part of its ongoing interest in local populations, and Tim not only helped with the nine-year project "Hmong Odyssey: Tradition in Transition," he became an unofficial ambassador to the local community, a fixture in their cultural celebrations and a friend in their homes. The exhibit, which opened in 1990, headlines a complete Hmong house that Tim and a group of Hmong men built using traditional handmade tools.

When I asked for pictures of Tim for this memoriam, Ed Fleming, also from the Science Museum, sent me what he had. There were astonishingly few, given Tim's many years with the institution. Most were shots of Tim doing demonstrations for children and visitors, and I realized that of course, Tim was almost always the one behind the camera, which was where he truly wanted to be. And so I was grateful for the wonderful photo of him that I have used here, behind the camera at Catalhoyuk, Turkey, where he travelled with Orrin Shane in the late 1990s. This field work was a great adventure for Tim, a highlight of his career as a photographer, and he was very pleased that some of his photos from the world heritage site were included in the 2005 book *The Goddess and the Bull: Catalhoyuk, An Archaeological Journey to the Dawn of Civilization*.

Tim was only 56 years old, and he left many people to miss him besides the family to whom he was so dedicated. Rock on, Tim, wherever you are now; I promise to plant that weeping willow tree.

CURATOR'S CORNER: Rare Thunderbid Preserved
By Tim Ready
Curatorial Assistant for Anthropology

This past year the museum was fortunate to add a unique pottery vessel to its collection of prehistoric ceramics. The vessel was donated by Mr. Adolph W. Link, a member of the Minnesota Archaeological Society, who found the fragmented pot at the Bryan site near Red Wing, Minnesota. Upon assembling a large section of the vessel from the 376 pieces of "prehistoric jigsaw puzzle" he had found, Mr. Link discovered that this pot had been decorated in a unique way. In place of the abstract geometric and curvilinear designs common to pottery from the site, he found representations of birds with outstretched wings. Four such birds had been placed around the vessel, and projecting from the head of each was a wavy line enclosed by two parallel lines. After examining the archaeological literature for information on other similar artifacts and finding no direct counterparts, Mr. Link realized that this was indeed an unusual specimen. With this in mind, the vessel was offered as a donation to SMM in order to assure its preservation and accessibility, both for scientific study and public appreciation.

Although Mr. Link had successfully pieced together a large portion of the vessel, over 60 percent of it was still missing or could not be assembled from the remaining small fragments. Clearly a complete restoration, which would flesh out the missing areas with plaster, was in order. This involved a lengthy process, but it's a good example of the conservation, preparation, and restoration routinely performed behind-the-scenes in order to properly maintain the museum's collections.

In this case the first step in the restoration process was, ironically, to carefully take apart those pieces which Mr. Link had assembled. This was necessary because white glue had been used which under humid conditions may release its grip. The original pieces were reassembled using a solvent-based cement.

Next, a clay model of the original size and shape of the pot had to be constructed. To accomplish this, the curves of the rim, neck, and shoulder areas of the reassembled section were projected to calculate the original diamers of those areas. A full-size profile drawing of the pot was then made according to these measurements. Based on this profile, a full-scale clay model was sculpted. The assembled original vessel section was then positioned and incorporated into the clay model.

A mold was constructed by covering the model with layers of latex and cheesecloth. The clay was then dug out of the mold, leaving the original vessel section in place.

The final step in the process was accomplished by pouring a plaster mix into the mold and rotating it to completely coat the inside. When dry, the mold was peeled away leaving the finished restoration. All that remained was to paint the areas of plaster.

This vessel is now on display in a new exhibit on Mississippian ceramic art in the Anthropology Hall. Between 900 and 1600 A.D. inhabitants of the Mississippi Valley region achieved the highest level of cultural development in the prehistory of eastern North America. The Bryan site was a Mississippian village occupied from about 1100 to 1400 A.D. The size and shape of the vessel are typical for pottery of this culture. The design may represent the Thunderbird, a common deity in native North American religions. Storms were attributed to Thunderbirds; their eyes produced lightning and their wings caused thunder. This may explain the wavy line (lightning) enclosed by the two parallel lines (thunder) which project from the head of the bird.

One of Tim Ready's images: The Adolf Link vessel.

Reprinted from the Science Museum of Minnesota's Encounters, January, 1980

The Savanna Portage: An Archaeological Study

Guy Gibbon
Department of Anthropology
University of Minnesota

Portages in heavily forested areas represent a largely ignored site type that presents historical archaeologists with unique problems of survey and excavation. Because of their length, fragile nature, and neglect, they are increasingly being destroyed by contemporary activities such as camping, hiking, and the construction of paths and access roads. Portages are often long, usually invisible, and nearly always crosscut by a myriad of more recent trails. In heavily forested areas, portions of the trail are often difficult to reach, and handy datum points are generally absent. As a result, their survey and sample excavation can be time and labor intensive. The survey and test excavations of the Savanna Portage in Aitkin County present trial solutions to these problems. In reading this report, it is important to recall that the Savanna Portage archaeological survey project was a special purpose, ad hoc survey, whose objective was the location of the main route or routes of the Savanna Portage at the least possible cost. The search strategy adopted and the structure of this report were guided by that objective. An accompanying CD-rom includes detailed supplemental information, including detailed descriptions of the recovered artifacts. The CD contains:

> *Narrative Clues to the Route of the Portage*
> *Retracing the Route of the Portage*
> *Pose 1*
> *Pose 5*
> *Pose 9*
> *References Cited*
> *Portage Illustrations*
> *Portage Illustration Captions*

Preface and Acknowledgments

Although numerous portages once connected waterways in Minnesota, the Savanna Portage was of special importance, for it connected the two great travel routes of Lake Superior and the Mississippi River. The Mississippi swings far to the east in this part of the state before it winds back to Brainerd and eventually southward through the Twin Cities, making it a watery highway to both northern and southern Minnesota. The archaeological explorations of the Savanna Portage summarized in this report were carried out as student training exercises in the 1980s, and for many years afterward the recovered materials were used in training classes at the University of Minnesota. Special thanks to Bob Barry, the manager of Savanna Portage State Park during the early years of the project, and David Radford, State Parks Head Archaeologist, for the opportunity to undertake this project on State of Minnesota land. Special thanks as well to Eugene Willms, who conducted the 1982-83 survey of the portage, and Scott Jacobson, who helped excavate Poses 5 and 9. This report is dedicated to Bob Barry in recognition of his genuine interest in the route of the Savanna Portage.

Because of its fame and heavy use, I have included more extensive descriptions than usual of the portage and of the artifacts recovered during the project on an accompanying CD-rom. Besides these descriptions, the CD-rom contains extensive tables of artifact proveniences and measurements, and additional illustrations. While we would all agree that data tables make more than boring reading, they will be of interest to specialists who require detailed information on artifact locations and characteristics in their studies. A deep debt of gratitude to Deborah Schoenholz and Chuck Diesen of the Minnesota Archaeological Society for making this publication and CD-rom opportunity possible.

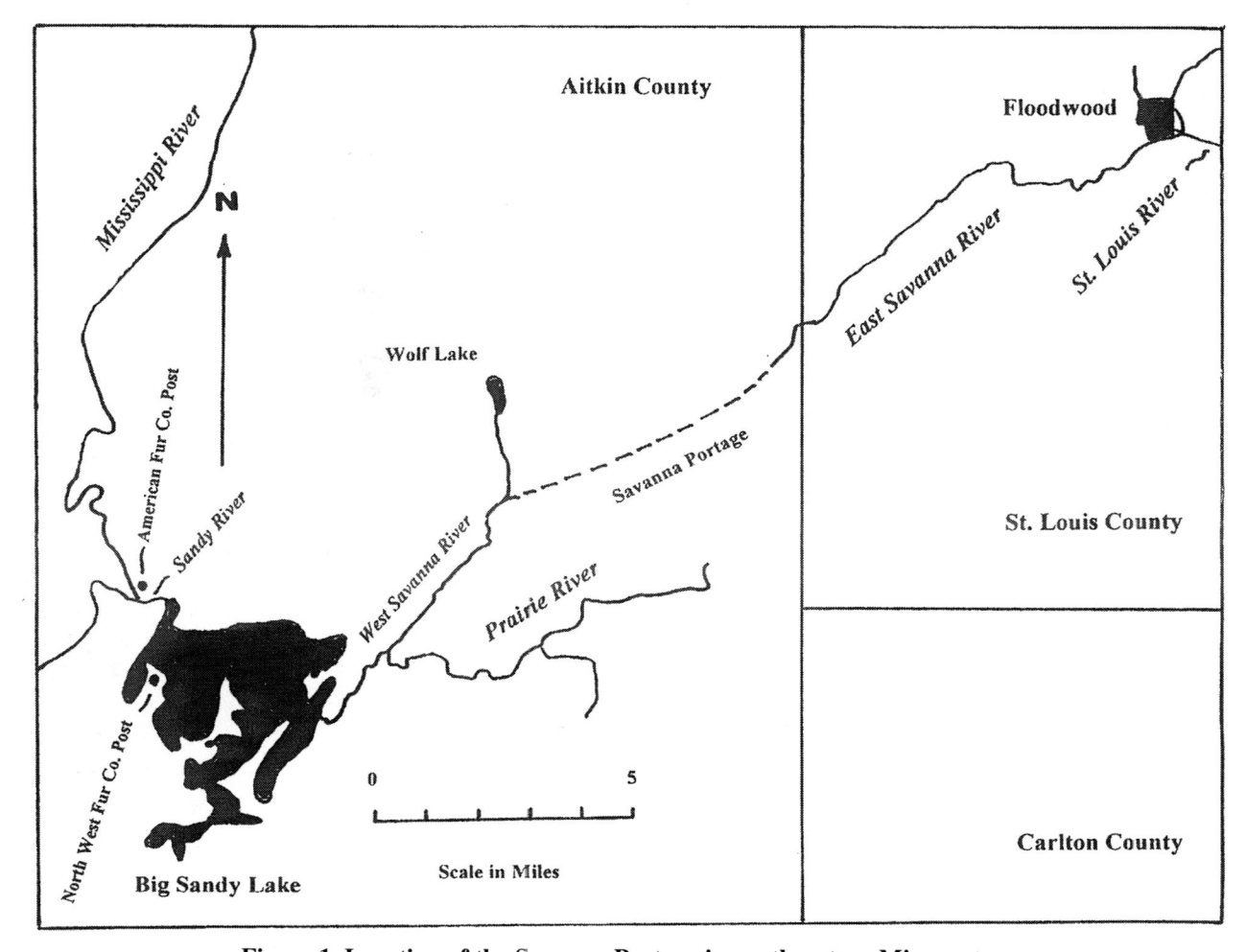

Figure 1. Location of the Savanna Portage in northeastern Minnesota.

The Savanna Portage

The site focus of this study is the Savanna Portage, the heavily used six-mile-long dry land route that was the main link between the Great Lakes and the Upper Mississippi River until the late nineteenth century (Figure 1). Although the earliest French entrepreneurs to cross the Savannah Portage may have done so as early as 1679, it was probably a well-used Indian route long before the first Europeans entered the western Great Lakes. Continued aggression between the Ojibwe and the Dakota effectively slowed the passage of European explorers and traders across the portage from the 1730s until 1775, when the passage of the Quebec Act and the establishment of the Mississippi River as a boundary between the two warring nations opened the route to a free flow of travelers once again.

From 1780 to 1870 the portage was a busy throughway, traveled first by members of the North West Company and their competitors and later by employees of the American Fur Company, missionaries, Indian agency employees, military personnel, politicians, and tourists. Many of these travelers were headed to or coming from Big Sandy Lake, a center of fur trade and missionary activity, and many others were merely passing through from one transportation network to another. Though rarely mentioned in diaries and reports, there was most likely a steady passage of Native Americans across the portage at this time as well.

According to most accounts, the portage was six miles long and contained 13 poses (canoe and/or pack rests) spaced one-half mile apart. Since the pose at the beginning of the crossing was not counted as a resting place, travelers actually counted 12 poses as they crossed the portage. Various poses and special features along the route were also occasionally described in written records. For instance, there was at least one section of log walkway in the marshy east end and a small stream in the same general area that had been artificially enlarged so that canoes could be dragged along it.

A military road built between St. Paul and Duluth in 1858 diverted traffic from the portage, and its usefulness as a transportation route was diminished still further in 1870, when the Northern Pacific Railroad reached the nearby town of McGregor. These events and the construction of additional roadways led to the abandonment of the portage as a regular route of transportation in the 1870s. The portage assumed its present role as an historic tourist attraction when it was incorporated in the Savanna Portage State Park in 1961.

Relocating The Route Of The Portage

It is perhaps surprising that the Savanna Portage, a prominent and heavily traveled route, could be lost, but it was-for a variety of reasons. Perhaps the most obscuring factor was logging of much of the route between 1888 and 1912, during which the landscape of the western two-thirds of the route was especially disturbed and altered. Logging trails that can be easily mistaken for the path of the portage were formed at this time, too. "Judicial ditches" dug between 1905 and 1931 to drain the region for farming also changed the configuration of the landscape on the east end of the route by lowering the water level. The establishment of small farms in the area early in the twentieth century undoubtedly resulted in the appearance of still other worn paths and disturbed ground, and the encroachment upon the trail of brush and trees after its abandonment further disguised its route.

The search for the original route of the Savanna Portage began in 1926, when local historians attempted to retrace its path (Hart 1927). Other attempts were initiated in the 1940s and the 1950s (Gibbon and Willms 1985:2-3), but the real route of the portage remained in doubt for several reasons. First, the reconstructed trail varied from one search to another. Second, no systematic verification of any of the proposed routes was ever attempted. And, third, the routes as reconstructed ran through several low-lying marshy areas when apparently higher and drier routes were available. In 1981 the manager of the park at the time, Bob Barry, piqued my interest in helping find the route of the portage by pointing out these discrepancies.

Research Plan

The present study of the portage was shaped by a number of clearly defined goals and by one constraint. It was designed to (1) relocate the physical and cultural features of the portage mentioned in primary sources (mostly diaries and expedition reports); (2) locate the precise path or paths of the portage; (3) locate all 13 of the poses; (4) excavate portions of the path or paths and the poses to verify their existence; (5) recover artifacts that could be displayed for tourists in the park; (6) identify highly visible physical and cultural features of the portage that could be identified by signs that would make an informative walk along the route; and (7) formulate a plan to preserve any portion of the portage threatened by destruction. The constraint was limited funding; whatever search strategy was adopted had to maximize the attainment of the project's goals at the least possible cost.

The strategy adopted involved both survey and test excavations. Exploratory field research began in 1981 with an attempt to locate a pose and a portion of the trail. The purpose of this exploratory phase in the project was to gain sufficient information about the archaeological "signature" of the trail and poses to design a comprehensive but cost-effective survey of the entire route of the portage. One individual conducted this survey during the summer months of 1982 and 1983.

Working Assumptions

In approaching the archaeological survey of the route of the portage, four working assumptions were adopted to structure the investigation. The first assumption was that the idea of a single path stretching from one waterway to another was, possibly, too simple. The main route of the portage could have

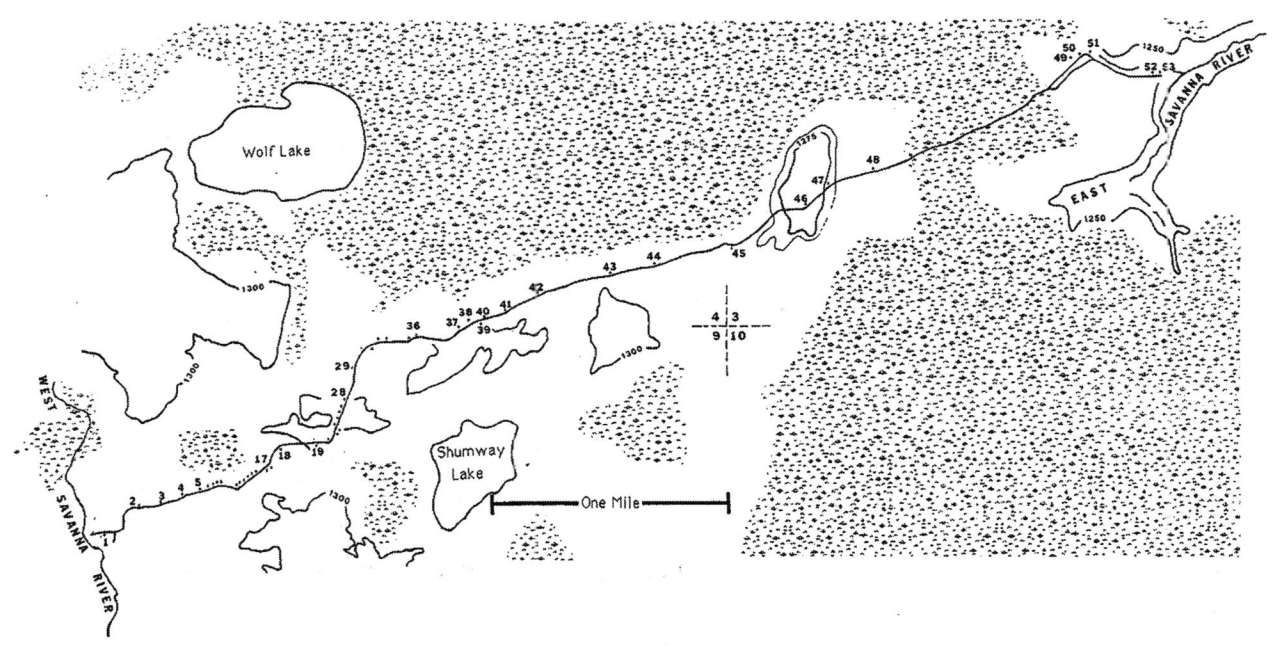

Figure 2. Reconstructed route of the Savanna Portage with locations of metal reference posts (north at top of figure).

changed over the years as the landscape was altered by natural and cultural factors. For example, dry years could have made some usually marshy but more direct links along the route accessible to travelers. The second assumption was that of the many paths and other cultural features visible along the apparent route of the portage, probably only a few were associated with the original trail; that is, no existing paths or other features should be assumed to be associated with the portage and its use without confirming evidence. As mentioned above, logging skid routes and cow paths almost certainly crosscut and parallel the Savanna Portage.

The third assumption was that the search would be more efficient if it was guided by the eyewitness accounts of those who actually crossed the portage during its period of active use. Although numerous discrepancies exist among accounts, they contain many clues to the general route of the portage (see "Tracing the Route of the Portage" in the CD-rom). They also mention specific physical and cultural features along the route that would confirm a reconstruction if they could be relocated. They mention, too, when and why the portage was crossed and what was carried across. These clues together provide a set of expectations concerning the kinds and amounts of artifacts that might be encountered along the route during the survey. For example, most of the travelers were males, and the greatest volume of traffic was connected with the fur trade, by the French prior to 1760, then by the English from about 1760 to 1810, and finally by the Americans from about 1816 to 1840 (the date when the Aitkin American Fur Company post on Big Sandy Lake apparently fell into disuse).

The final assumption was the unexpected result of trial field tests conducted as field school exercises in 1981. Systematic survey began by shovel testing along transects that crosscut the probable routes of portage trails. This traditional approach was quickly abandoned for several reasons. First, shovel testing proved inadequate in locating the small numbers of widely spaced artifacts that represent the route of the portage today. In fact, two parallel transects through a major pose with test holes spaced 8 yards apart failed to encounter any artifacts. Second, shovel testing was too time-consuming given the constraints of the survey, especially when the fill from tests was screened through ¼ inch mesh. Experiments indicated that testing without screening fill was twice as rapid and rarely failed to indicate the presence of artifacts. Although 10-30 percent of all artifacts in the fill were overlooked in nonscreened shovel-tests, this was considered a reasonable tradeoff in an exploratory survey. But even this more rapid procedure proved too time consuming when compared with the option described below. And third, when artifactual material was recovered in a shovel test, the absence of easily accessible reference points to which it could be tied dictated the selection of a ground-search technique that did not require the immediate removal of artifacts from the ground.

Because of the inadequacies of traditional shovel testing in this particular situation, another ground-search strategy was adopted. This strategy was based on the assumption that the portage should be represented by a corridor or corridors of metal that could be inexpensively and accurately located by systematic transect sweeps with a sensitive metal detector. Poses should be represented too by more diffuse distributions of lost or discarded metal objects.

The Survey

Long transect sweeps were made across the narrower eastern half of the route the first season and the broader western half the second season (Figure 2). In general a zigzag route was followed back and forth across the peninsula until portions of the trail were encountered (see "Retracing the Route of the Portage" in the CD-rom). The trail was then traced as far as possible from that juncture. This search procedure ensured that long stretches of the trail would be efficiently located and that multiple, parallel trails along the peninsula would be discovered if they existed. During sweeps, when the metal detector (a Garret Deep Seeker with a large disc) indicated the presence of a metal object, the location was recorded in a daily log and marked by tying bright orange flagging to an overhanging twig or limb of a tree. In less forested areas a flagged marker stuck in the ground served a similar purpose. An occasional artifact was uncovered, examined *in situ*, and then left in place to ensure that the flagged metal objects were associated with the use of the portage rather than with more recent logging and farming activities. By the end of the survey a single intermittent but clearly defined narrow track of orange flagging stretched from one end of the portage to the other. In addition, concentrated scatters of flags along the route marked the possible location of five of the 13

Figure 3. Metal reference post with inscribed aluminum tag.

poses (which were numbered 1 through 13 beginning on the west end).

Establishing a Datum-Reference System

The survey phase of the project concluded with the establishment of a datum-reference system. Fifty-three metal pipes were spaced along the reconstructed route of the portage (Figure 2). Each pipe was tagged with a numbered aluminum marker and driven securely into the ground about 10 yards from the trail (Figure 3). The location and distance between each pipe was recorded using a transit and the entire reference system was tied into a permanent field datum established during the first year of the project and USGS section markers. Besides providing an essential frame of spatial reference for the project, the pipes provided accurate reference points for future projects along the trail.

Physical Features of the Portage

Figure 4. Spring view of the path of the portage in the east savanna.

Actual traces of the trail and other features mentioned by travelers were relocated during the survey. Although discontinuous, a single trail is still visible in many areas, especially along the relatively undisturbed east end. For instance, a clearly defined 8-12 inch wide and ½-1 foot deep path runs from the easternmost pose (No. 13) to the first pose in the savanna (No. 12) one-half mile to the west (Figure 4). Pose 12 was associated with a large clump of raspberry bushes, possibly the result of the disturbance of the ground at that pose by fur traders; a platform may have been built at the pose to protect packs from getting wet from water in the savanna when the traders stopped for a rest. The enlarged "canal" along which canoes were dragged, sections of log walkway, a pond mentioned by travelers, and other features of the physical context of the portage were relocated as well. Perhaps not unexpectedly these features closely paralleled the track of orange flagging.

Test Excavations

The next phase of the project involved limited test excavations. Tests were conducted for two reasons: to substantiate the reconstructed route of the portage and to explore the form and content of poses. Except for the westernmost pose (No. 1), where larger excavation units were used within the context of field school training, the unit of excavation was a standard 1x1 foot shovel test centered on a flagged metal object. The assumption was that metal and nonmetal artifacts co-vary in their distribution and that the location of metal artifacts was an efficient and accurate way to locate nonmetal artifacts.

Tests along the trail

Very few of the metal artifacts flagged along the trail were removed from the ground. The goal of this phase of the project was to demonstrate that the flagged items dated for the most part to the period when the portage was in active use without causing extensive damage to the path. "Retracing the Route of the Portage" in the CD-rom provides a formal description of the historic artifacts recovered along the trail between poses. In brief summary, the kind and number of these artifacts is described below using four functional categories, though in wilderness settings, material objects were frequently used for unintended purposes (Table 1). Some pieces of logging and farming equipment, which were more widely scattered throughout the park than fur trade-related material, were also taken from the ground (See Table A in "Retracing the Route of the Portage"). Figures 5-7 illustrate some of these artifacts, and many more of these artifacts are illustrated in the CD-rom.

Personal Objects: Items that were most likely associated with individuals include 10 metal buttons, a plain brass ring with no face, a bracelet made from a round brass rod with transverse grooves filed around the exterior surface, a silver-plated brass brooch, a locket with an oval brass frame enclosing a glass set within a convex outer surface, two tinkling cones, four strike-a-lights, and the tomahawk section of a tomahawk pipe with ornamental etchings and a dull blade.

Table 1. Artifacts Found Along the Portage Trail and in Poses 1, 5, and 9

	P	1	5	9		P	1	5	9
Buttons	3	21	7	9	Candle Holders	1			
Hooks and Eyes		2			Cast Iron Kettle Piece		1		
Hair Pipes		3			Tin Cup Piece		1		
Lead Spacers		2			Nails	50	63	47	25
Pendant		1			Hinges and Pintles		1		
Earrings		2			Rivets		2		
Rings	1	3	1	1	Window Glass Pieces		25		
Bracelets	1				Gunflints	1	36		
Broochs	1				Gun Mainsprings	1	1		
Lockets	1			1	Lead Balls	39	4	9	5
Tinkling Cones	1	13	2		Lead Shot	20	1		
Buckles			2	2	Gun Butt Plate			1	
Glass Necklace Beads		26			Gun Worms	1		2	
Glass Seed Beads		129			Trigger			1	
Flagstaff Tip				1	Musket Barrels	4		2	
Religious Medallions		1			Ramrod Thimbles	1			
Strike-a-Lites	3		1	2	Flintlock				1
Jew's-Harp				1	Harpoons	2	1	3	
Tomahawk-Pipes	1				Ice Chisels	1			
Kaolin Pipe Bowls		14			Traps	4			
Kaolin Pipe Stem Pieces		60	2		Fishhooks	1			
Slate Pencils		1			Scabbard Components	1			
Spy Glass Lens		1			Projectile Point		1		
Ceramic Items (e.g., cup)	1	14		1	Harness Rings, etc.	5	2		
Brass Kettle Fragments	7	1			Baling Needles	1			
Kettle Bail Handles	2	1			Coins		1		
Kettle Lugs	3	2			Punches	1	1		
Glass Container Pieces	1	84			Awls	6		6	2
Mirror Fragments		3			Trade Axes	8		3	3
Spoons	2		1	1	Sheet Copper Tags	2			
Corner Brackets		2			Trunk Locks		1		
Skillet Handle				1					
Pot Holder			1	2					
Keys		1	1	1	Stone Projectile Points		2		
Barrel Hoops		1	1		Bone Weaving Shuttles		1		
Knives	12		8	7	Native Potsherds	15	88	19	
Forks			2		Chipped Stone Flakes	3	49		
Candlemold			1		Stone Knives		1		

Household Items: Artifacts considered household items include two pieces of whiteware plate, 12 brass kettle parts (including two wire bail handles, three kettle lugs, and a complete kettle), a piece of clear medicine bottle glass, two pewter spoons (one of which is a large serving spoon), 12 knives (three clasp, seven case, and two unidentified), and the top of a brass candleholder.

Construction Items: The only construction items found along the trail were nails, 12 of which were hand wrought and 38 of which were machine cut.

Craft/Activity Items: Items that fall in this category include 68 firearm elements (one English Brandon flint gunflint, an iron mainspring from a flintlock, 39 lead balls, 20 pieces of "buckshot," a coiled gun worm, three musket barrels, a ramrod thimble, and two pieces of lead), three "muskrat" harpoons, one skew-pointed ice chisel, parts of five traps, one fishhook, the metal top of a knife scabbard, five harness elements (a brass horse bell, a brass harness ring, an iron safety clip, and two harness buckles), a steel baling needle, a metal punch, six iron awls, eight trade axes, and two sheet copper "tags."

Figure 5. Sample of artifacts from the trail: clasp knives (A and B); case knives (D, G, and H); ice chisel (C); spoon bowl (E); metal awls (I); iron objects of unknown function (F and J).

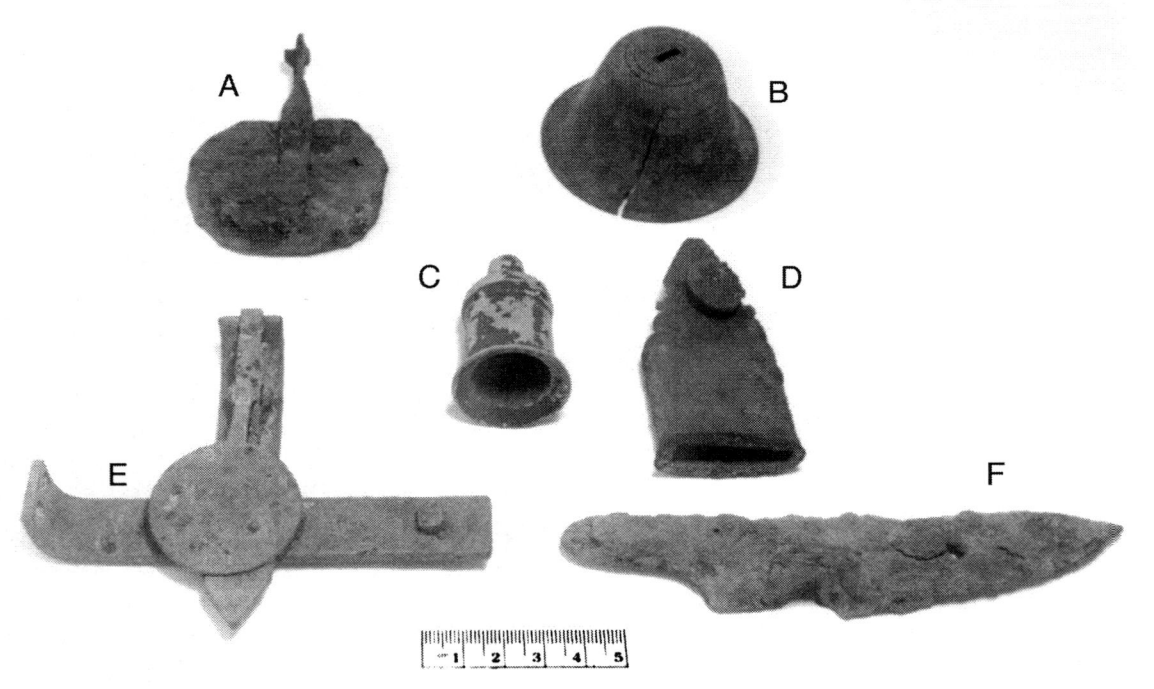

Figure 6. Sample of artifacts from the trail: trap parts (A and E); harness bell (B); candle holder (C); scabbard tip (D); irregular piece of iron (F).

Eighteen Native American artifacts were also found along the trail. These include 15 pieces of shell-tempered, late prehistoric Sandy Lake pottery and three quartz flakes, one of which has use marks on it.

The Westernmost Pose

Portions of the westernmost Pose 1 and Poses 5 and 9 were also tested. The westernmost pose was located next to the West Savanna River, while Poses 5 and 9 were interior rest stops along the route of the portage within forested areas. Although poorly documented in written records, a structure referred to in local oral tradition as a "trader's cabin" was apparently erected as early as 1794 on the westernmost pose, possibly to intercept travelers before they reached the trading post on Big Sandy Lake. This structure was not located during our excavations, but an array of building hardware (the strap element of a pintle hinge, hand wrought and early machine-cut nails, several iron rivets, most of the historic ceramics, and the only pieces of clear window glass found on a pose) lend support to the tradition that a structure connected in some way with fur trade activities was present at this site as early as the 1790s.

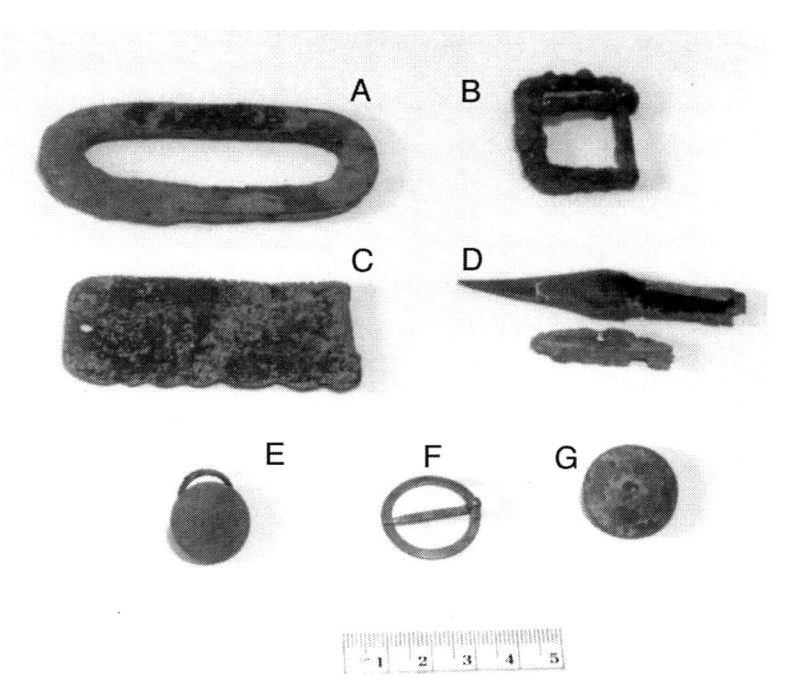

Figure 7. Sample of artifacts from the trail: strike-a-light (A); harness buckle (B); brass "tag" (C); brass kettle scrap (D); buttons (E and G); brooch (F).

The westernmost pose seems to have been the major stopping place when the portage was crossed, for an equally large camping/rest stop was not found along the trail or at the east end of the portage in the wet savanna. Presumably, travelers crossing from the east camped on the west end before starting the winding and arduous journey down the West Savanna and Prairie rivers, and those coming from the west camped at the first pose before carrying their equipment over the six-mile-long trail. The presence of a trader's cabin or rest shelter would have made this an attractive pose as well. At any rate, the number and variety of artifacts and the size of their scatter greatly exceed those of the other poses located during the survey. Table 1 lists the general categories of artifacts recovered from the pose, which are summarized by kind and number below. Figures 8-10 illustrate some of these artifacts. "Pose 1" in the CD-rom provides a formal description of all artifacts recovered from this pose as well as a description of the excavation itself.

Personal Objects: Items that an individual person might have been associated with include 21 buttons (15 brass, four iron, one glass, and one bone), two hook and eyes (one three part gold clothes hook and an iron eye), 153 glass trade beads (139 drawn and 14 simple wound), one bone bead, a French St. Mary religious medallion, three finger rings (a gold ring with a white spidel stone, a brass ring with a blue spidel stone, and a brass band ring), 13 tinkling cones (seven brass, three iron, one copper, and two thimble tinklers), two trade silver earring bobs, a cut glass black gemstone pendant, two lead spacers, three hair pipes, a flat strip of trade silver, 98 clay smoking-pipe bowls and 60 pipe stem pieces, one roughly rounded slate pencil, and two pieces of a spyglass lens.

Household Goods: Artifacts usually associated with household contents include 215 pieces of household ceramics (204 pieces of whiteware, 10 pieces of pearlware, and one piece of stoneware), four kettle parts (two iron kettle lugs, one iron bail rod, and a fragment of brass kettle with a single lug hole), 77 pieces of beverage bottle (34 pieces of clear, curved, thick bottle glass; 18 pieces of thick olive green bottle glass; three pieces of an olive green ribbed whiskey flask; 12 pieces of clear medicine bottle glass, including at least one Essence of Peppermint bottle; eight fragments of a clear square to rectangular bottle with a floral design; one piece of light green bottle glass; and a piece of pale blue bottle glass), two fragments of clear glass drinking tumblers, seven pieces of an olive green fruit jar, three pieces of mirror, a section of a cast iron kettle, the flat handle of a tin cup, two metal corner furniture brackets (one iron, one brass), an iron trunk lock, the round bow and part of the round shaft of an iron key, and a flat piece of broken barrel hoop. Besides these artifacts, small amounts of plant (seeds, pits, nutshell, and charcoal) and animal remains were found, as well as a few fragments of mussel shell (see Tables K and L in "Pose 1" in the CD-rom).

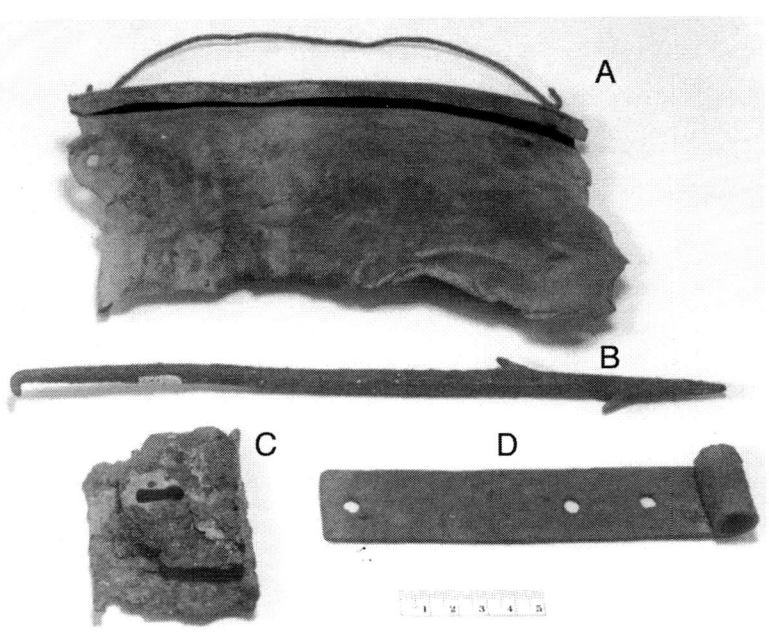

Figure 8. Sample of artifacts from Pose 1: brass kettle fragment and bail (A); muskrat harpoon (B); trunk lock mainplate (C); pintle hinge (D).

Construction Items: Items that are normally used in construction include the strap element of a pintle hinge, 87 nails (41 hand wrought, 40 machine cut, and six unidentifiable shank fragments), two iron rivets, and 25 pieces of clear window glass.

Craft/Activity Items: Items in this category include 48 artifacts associated with firearms (13 blade gunflints, four spall gunflints, 21 small gunflint fragments, the iron mainspring of a flintlock, an iron gun worm, four lead balls, a piece of "buckshot," a .22 cartridge with H.P. stamped on the head, and two miscellaneous pieces of iron), a stemmed brass projectile point, an iron "muskrat" harpoon, a U.S. "seated liberty" dime with a date of 1883, a harness buckle and ring, an iron punch, and 21 miscellaneous pieces of metal (three lead, eight brass, and 10 iron).

A relatively small number of Native American artifacts were scattered across the pose. There are 31 grit-tempered body sherds (23 with cord-marked exterior surfaces, six with eroded exterior surfaces, and two with a fabric-impressed exterior surface finish), 58 shell-tempered bodysherds (36 with cord-marked exterior surfaces, 13 with a carved-paddle surface finish, and two with plain exterior

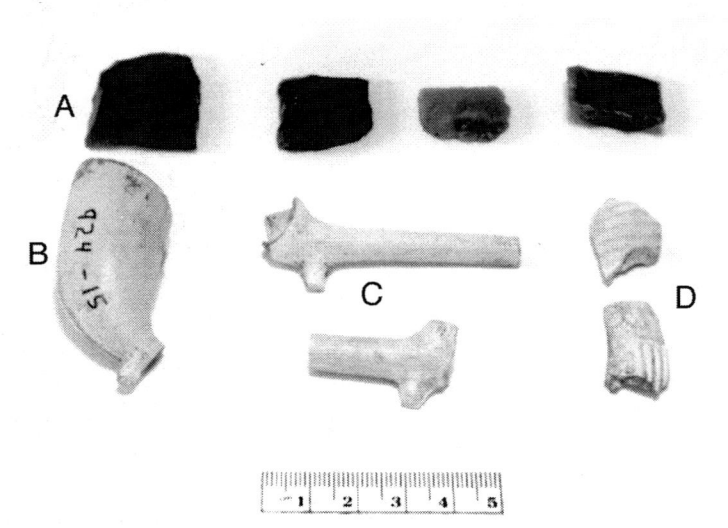

Figure 9. Sample of artifacts from Pose 1: gunflints (A); clay pipe bowl (B); pipestems with spurs (C); pieces of pipe bowl (D).

Figure 10. Sample of artifacts from Pose 1: Historic ceramics.

surfaces), and two rim sherds (one dating to the Initial Woodland period and the other to the Terminal Woodland [Sandy Lake] period). There are also 101 stone flakes (quartz, chert, chalcedony, slate, and agate), a quartz core, a small piece of fire-cracked rock, a quartz knife, two broken quartz Madison triangular projectile points, and a broken bone weaving shuttle.

In contrast to the abundance of modern artifacts along the portage trail, the only modern artifact found *in situ* during excavation was a small length of plastic-coated wire.

Interior Poses

Poses 5 and 9 are represented by more concentrated distributions of artifacts and a narrower range of functional and material types than at Pose 1 (Table 1). As on the trail itself, clay pipes, glass beads, and ceramics are rare, while gun parts, metal trade goods, and nails dominate the assemblages. The large numbers of nails found along the trail and at poses remain somewhat of a surprise and are still not adequately explained. Also of interest is the presence of unused trade items apparently hidden but never recovered (pairs of trade axes and muskrat spears, an unused gun barrel). Whether they represent fur trade larceny or a practice common at the time of caching goods and provisions along the trail for later retrieval remains unclear.

If there were 13 poses spaced about one-half mile apart along the portage trail, then Pose 5 was the fifth from the west end, for the pose is near metal post 38 about two miles from Pose 1. The pose is situated on a dry ridge between a small pond and a steep ravine. The distribution of artifacts recovered from Pose 5 is illustrated in Figure 11 by context of utilization. The position of each artifact or artifact cluster is recorded by artifact number in Table C in "Pose 5" in the CD-rom, which also contains a formal description of the artifacts and the excavation of the pose. Figures 12 and 13 illustrate some of these artifacts. The recovered artifacts are summarized by kind and number below.

Personal Objects: Objects normally associated with individual people found in Pose 5 include four brass buttons, two small buckles, two brass tinkling cones, a plain brass ring, a brass Jew's harp, two pieces of kaolin smoking-pipe stem, and what is most likely a Prince Albert tobacco can.

Household Items: Artifacts usually considered household items include a pewter spoon, two composite forks, two identical brass pot handle holders, six iron awls, and an iron barrel hoop.

Construction Items: Items normally associated with a structure include an iron key, 49 nails (12 hand wrought, 25 machine cut, one wire nail, and several nail fragments), three spikes, and two bolts.

Craft/Activity Items: Craft/activity items include 17 objects associated with firearms (nine lead balls, two gun worms, two musket barrels [one with the mark PHILA and the faint letters–RINGER above it], a musket trigger, a butt plate with an etched design, a cartridge casing with WRA CO 38 WCF impressed on the head, and the butt of a Peters 12-gauge shotgun shell), three "muskrat" harpoons, seven knives (two clasp, four case [one is a Cross-L knife], and one blade fragment), a cast iron ring the size of a shower ring, three trade axes, a candle mold, and 14 miscellaneous pieces of metal.

Nineteen pieces of Native American grit-tempered Woodland pottery were also found in the area. Eight are plain, nine are cord-marked on the exterior surface, and two have exfoliate exterior surfaces.

Pose 9 is the small knoll that the portage runs through as one leaves the marshy, eastern end of the portage. It was frequently cited in journals as a resting area after the wet savanna had been traversed when traveling westward. Formal descriptions of the excavation of Pose 9 and the artifacts recovered are included in "Pose 9" in the CD-rom. The distribution of artifacts recovered from Pose 9 is illustrated in Figure 14 by context of utilization; as Figure 14 illustrates, the artifacts in Pose 9 were concentrated in a surprisingly small circular area. From the frequent mention of this pose as a place of rest, a larger and

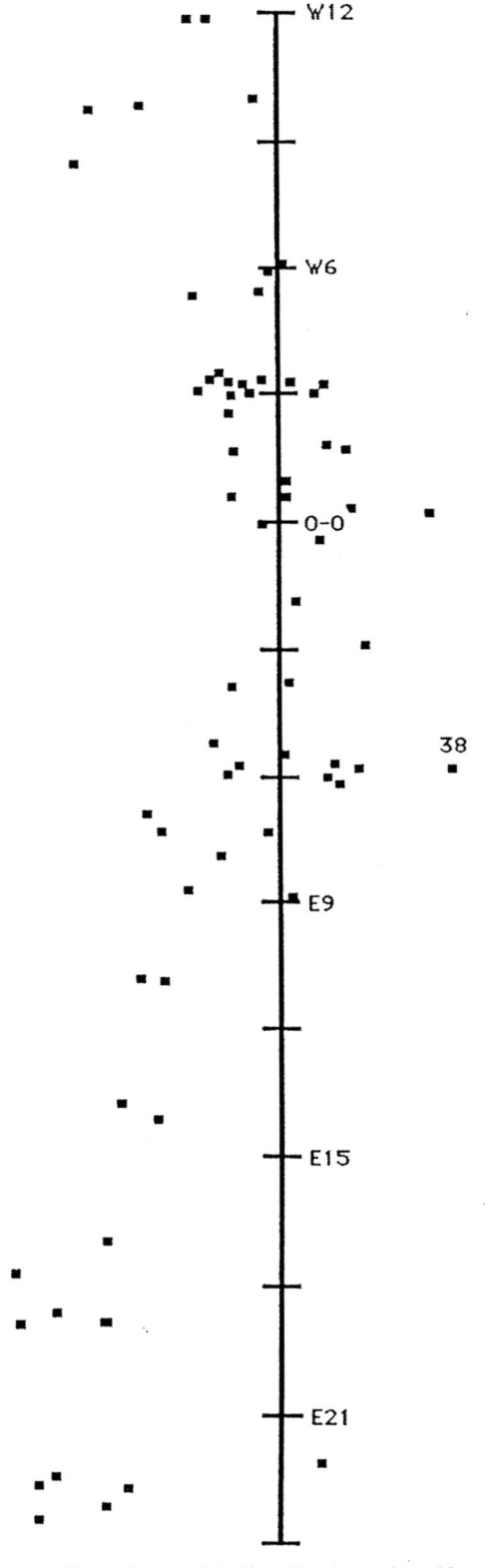

Figure 11. Pose 5: spatial distribution of artifacts related to the utilitarian context of utilization (e.g., knives, beads, buttons, ceramics, gunflints; distance between 0-0 and W6 is 48 feet).

Figure 12. Sample of artifacts from Pose 5: knives (A, C, D, F, H-K); spoon (B); forks (E and G).

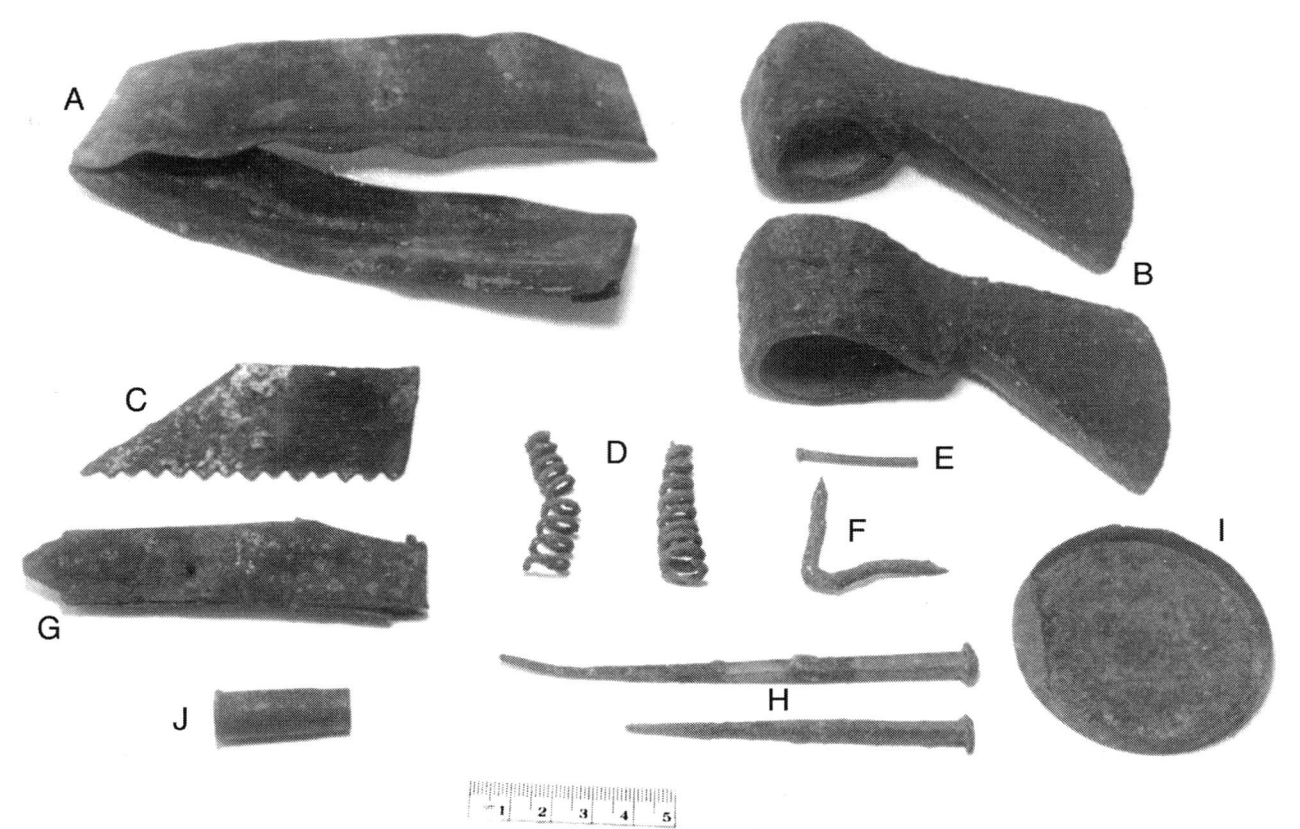

Figure 13. Sample of artifacts from Pose 5: folded piece of metal (A); trade axes (B); piece of brass with saw edge (C); gun worms (D); machine-cut nail (E); hook (F); section of barrel hoop (G); hand-wrought rose-head nails (H); tin top (I); cartridge (J).

denser scatter of artifacts was expected. Figures 15 and 16 illustrate some of these artifacts. The recovered artifacts are summarized by kind and number below.

Personal Objects: Artifacts in this category include 10 brass buttons, two metal buckles, a brass ring with a mounted cut piece of glass in the shape of a half sphere, a brass egg-shaped "spoon locket," and the decorated brass top of an umbrella (a floral and scroll design).

Household Items: Items typically associated with household contents include the bottom of a ceramic container, part of the handle of a pewter spoon, two strike-a-lights (a complete and an open elongated oval), two pot holders (one brass, one iron), an 80 cm long skillet handle, an iron bucket top, a can shaped like a sardine can, two iron awls, and an iron key.

Construction Items: Items considered associated with construction include 39 nails (four hand wrought, 25 machine cut, one wire, and the rest fragments), the round shank of a spike, a metal washer with 3 stamped on one side, and an iron object that may be a bracket.

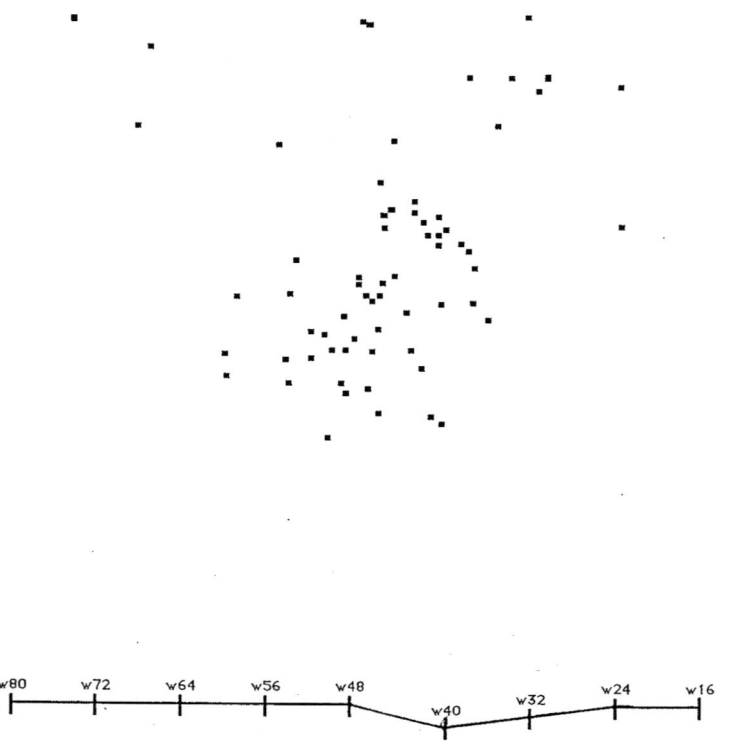

Figure 14. Pose 9: spatial distribution of artifacts related to the structural content of utilization (e.g., nails, hinges, rivets, window glass; distance between W40 and W48 is 8 meters).

Craft/Activity Items: Artifacts in this category include 13 objects associated with firearms (five lead balls, a flintlock with the word Barnett impressed on the right side, and seven cartridge casings [with U.M.C. S H 38 55, WRA CO 30 WCF, or the letter U impressed on the head]), seven knives (three clasp, two case, and two fragments), three trade axes, an iron handle, small pieces of scrap metal (one copper, seven brass, 11 iron), and three miscellaneous metal items (two pieces of steel wire, a flattened brass tube).

Of interest, too, are discrepancies between the locations of interior poses as described in written records and as relocated during the survey. Of all the clues to features of the portage provided by written records, the greatest inconsistencies are associated with the location of poses. One possible answer is that the described rest areas were ephemeral or alternative stops used for a very brief period of time at which metal objects were not lost in number.

Conclusions

The primary goal of the Savanna Portage project was the relocation of the portage for Savanna Portage Park management. Nonetheless, the results of the project also provide a base for the cultural resource management (CRM) of this historic site and for historical interpretation. This final section briefly examines the use of the portage through time and summarizes the search method developed in the project.

Figure 15. Sample of artifacts from Pose 9; razor (A): knives (B-E).

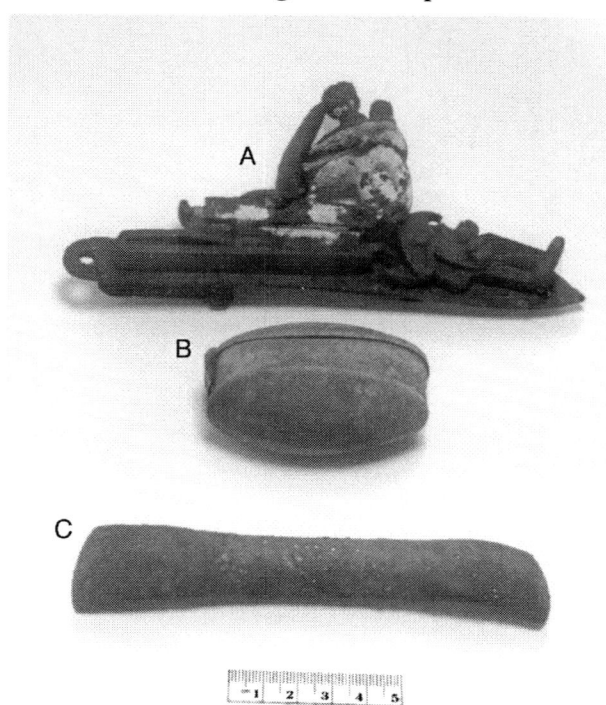

Figure 16. Sample of artifacts from Pose 9: Barnett flintlock with gunflint (A); "spoon locket" (B); possible iron handle (C).

Pattern in the Use of the Portage through Time

In exploring the presence of pattern in the use of the Savanna Portage, we confined our analysis in this part to the question, How did the kinds of artifacts lost or discarded along the portage change through time? The previous section reached general conclusions about differences in the use of Pose 1 and Poses 5 and 9, the two interior poses examined.

Providing precise and accurate dates for when an historical artifact was actively used can be a subtlety complex process. Catalogues and company records can, for example, provide a *terminus ante quem* date, that is, the date of the first manufacture before which the artifact could not have been in circulation. Determining a *terminus post quem* date, that is, the date after which an artifact could not have been in use, is more complex, as antique stores and my grandmother's kitchen clearly show. The process is further complicated by problems of cultural lag, the

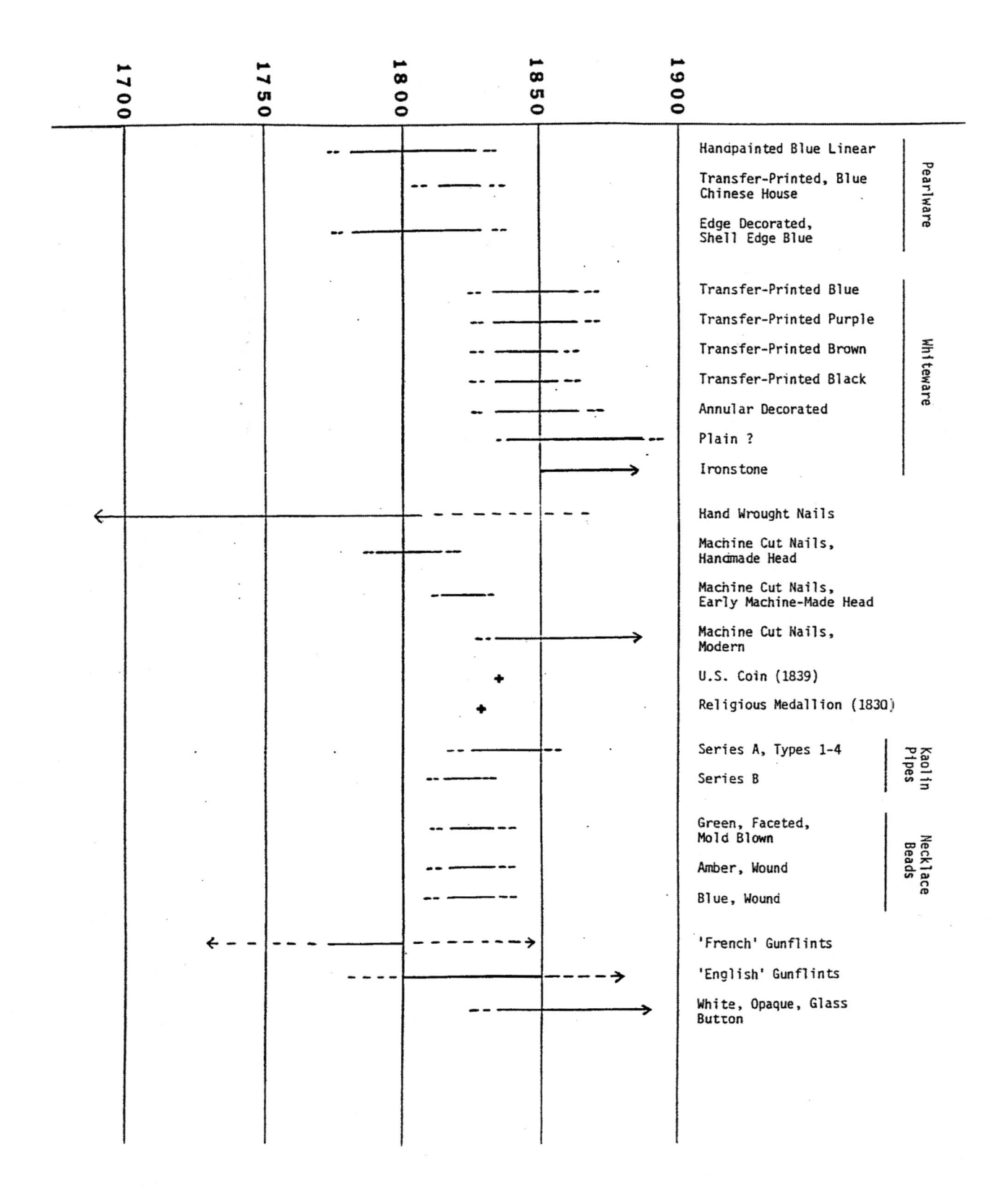

Figure 17. Temporal distribution of datable artifacts from Pose 1.

Table 2. Suggested Life-spans of Historic Earthenwares from the "Trader's Cabin" Site on the West End of the Savanna Portage

<pre>
Pearlware

    Handpainted
        Blue
            Linear (Floral?)   1780-1830   1805

    Transfer-Printed
        Blue
            Chinese House   c.1810-1830   1820   (*1830)

    Edge Decorated
        Shell Edge
            Blue   1780-1830   1805   (*1830)

Whiteware

    Transfer-Printed
        Blue   1830-1860   1845   (*1830)
        Purple   1830?-1860   1845
        Brown   1830-1850   1840
        Black   1830-1850   1840

    Annular Decorated
        All Types   1830?-1860   1845

    Plain?   1840-1890?   1865

    Ironstone   appeared in 1850s
</pre>

(* Suggested modal date of popularity for the Midwest; modal dates of popularity and life-spans of earthenware types taken from Lofstrom, Tordoff, and George 1982)

ability of wilderness folk to pay for new fashions and better equipment, unequal access to market centers, and so on. Early historic Minnesota was not a monolithic market throughout which innovations spread evenly. We might anticipate finding, then, that large, active settlements, such as Fort Snelling, were innovative centers whose artifact life spans were not coincident with those found in a backwater trapper's cabin near Big Sandy Lake.

With these cautions firmly in mind, a variety of post-contact artifacts from this site can be assigned approximate dates of expected use in this area of the Midwest (Figure 17). Although many more items can be dated than are dated here and some items can be more precisely dated than is done here, the emerging temporal framework is sufficient to establish the time periods when most of the material in our artifact sample was discarded or lost. Some items, like tinkling cones, metal projectile points, seed beads, brass kettles, and bone buttons, were present throughout the historic period considered here (c.1650-1840). Though they had periods of particular popularity (e.g., seed beads are present in much greater numbers in the last 75 years or so of this period than they are in earlier periods), they are not diagnostic as an item for a period and so are not discussed here.

Of all the classes of material found along the portage without actual dates stamped on them, historic earthenware ceramics have been most carefully dated (Lofstrom, Tordoff, and George 1982). Table 2 contains suggested life spans and mean or modal dates of popularity for most of the earthenwares recovered from Pose 1, that part of the portage with the greatest amount of historic ceramics. A comparative study of the temporal distribution of clay smoking pipes has not yet been completed in Minnesota. However, some suggested dates for some of the categories found along the portage can be cautiously put forward. Class I, Series A clay pipes with heavy raised lines seem to occur fairly late in the historic period (Bradley 2000). Type 1 dates between c.1835 and 1841 at Fort Snelling and may, more broadly, date between the 1820s and the 1850s in this area. Type 2 pipes are very similar to a bowl found at Fort Renville that dates between 1826 and 1846. Types 3 and 4 also seem fairly late, dating to the 1840s and 1850s in the officer's latrine at Fort Snelling. Series B pipes with stamped and/or impressed marks or designs are similar to the oldest pipes at Grand Portage (c.1780-1803), but they could date as late as the 1820s. These suggested dates should be used with caution until a firmer temporal framework for clay smoking pipes is established in Minnesota.

In the western Great Lakes region, hand-wrought nails are not particularly useful dating tools, for they were used in this area in the seventeenth century, for most of the eighteenth century, and well into the nineteenth century in more remote areas. In 1790, the first cut nails were produced, although the heads were still shaped individually by hammering (Wells 2000). By 1815, the heads of machine-cut nails were also machine-made, though these particular nails can be identified by the presence of a slight waist below the head. This characteristic disappeared in the 1830s, when the modern machine-cut nail that is abundant in Pose 1 came into general use. The modern wire nail that is in general use today began to be manufactured in New York in the 1850s but probably did not reach this area until the 1860s or even later. Because of their superior clinching ability, hand-wrought nails were often used in small numbers well into the nineteenth century.

French blond-colored gunflints were used in small numbers from c.1660 throughout the remainder of the seventeenth century; they became a dominant type in the last quarter of the eighteenth century (Kenmotsu 2000). Dark English blade gunflints were available during the last quarter of the eighteenth century. They reached their peak of popularity during the nineteenth and early twentieth centuries. French gunflints still predominate at Fort Atkinson in Nebraska, which dates between 1820 and 1827; they are also present at Possey, Oklahoma, where they seem to date between c.1830 and 1840.

The dating of necklace beads is still in its infancy in this area. However, based on similarities with beads from the Black Dog site near Minneapolis, which was analyzed by Roderick Sprague for Gordon Lothsom, the green faceted mold blown beads date to the 1820s+, the amber wound beads to c.1820, and the blue wound beads to c.1820-1825. Quimby (1966:88-89) has also suggested that all multifaceted cut glass beads date at least to c.1760-1820. Opaque cylinder white and black beads, and white opaque wire wound beads with a barrel form, are also present at Grand Portage (c.1780-1803). Undoubtedly, the dates for these and other beads found in Pose 1 will be more firmly dated in the future.

What are the implications of these suggested dates for the use of the portage? Some of the pearlware, hand-wrought nails, metal buttons with wedge-shaped shanks, and French gunflints could be evidence for the Euroamerican use of the portage before about 1780. Traffic across the portage increased rapidly after that date, especially between c.1793 and c.1840 (when the Aitkin American Fur Company post on Big Sandy Lake supposedly fell into disuse), as employees of the North West Company and the American Fur Company repeatedly crossed the portage. The use of the portage seems to have gradually ebbed after this period of intense use to about 1870, when the first passenger train reached the nearby town of MacGregor. This scenario is not inconsistent with the c.1790-1850 peak use of the portage suggested by written records from the period. Phrased another way, the Savanna Portage seems to have been used more frequently by British (c.1760-1810) and American (c.1810-1870) travelers than by earlier French (c.1650-1760) travelers.

Project Summary

According to one popular account, historical archaeology encompasses five different pursuits, or avenues of inquiry: historical supplementation, reconstruction of past life ways, processual studies, archaeological science, and cognitive studies (Deagan 1982). Not considered are the strategies of field survey and excavation that underlie all of these approaches, that in fact make a study an example of historical archaeology rather than, say, of ethnohistory or history *sensu stricto*. There are many reasons why strategies of field survey and excavation are a legitimate and fundamental avenue of inquiry in historical archaeology. For instance, it is usually not immediately apparent what form a particular type of historical activity will take in the archaeological record, what the artifactual content of that activity might be, and what field strategy or strategies are most appropriate in recovering both the form and artifact content of that type of site. Trial surveys and excavations provide a fund of experience that indicates what these strategies are for particular types of sites, and that experience potentially enriches all other avenues of inquiry.

The study presented in this report is an example of this avenue of inquiry in historical archaeology. It summarizes a trial survey and excavation of a portage and a type of site whose archaeological examination has been largely ignored in historical archaeology. Since contributions within this avenue of inquiry are methodological, the emphasis is on the general rather than on the specific, on survey and excavation strategies and the reconstructed form of the site rather than on the study of the recovered material, though the last two sections summarized general temporal and spatial trends in the use of the portage. The extensive descriptions of the recovered material in the accompanying CD-rom are included to facilitate more detailed artifact studies by other individuals.

In brief recapitulation, the approach presented here for the location and sampling of an historic portage can be divided into four phases: (1) a preliminary reconstruction of the route of the portage and its physical setting based on written accounts, and some initial reconnaissance to familiarize planners with the survey area; (2) a comprehensive and systematic survey of the route with a metal detector to flag metal artifacts (with an occasional peek at an artifact to verify that it dates to the target time period), and the establishment of a series of connected reference points; (3) limited test excavations to confirm the route of the portage and the location of poses and to pursue specific research/preservation objectives; and (4) the preparation of reports and CRM proposals.

The core of this particular approach is the location of metal artifacts and the establishment of a reference system *before* excavation. Although limited excavation was carried out during the project to verify the presence of the route and a few poses, this procedure can be employed as a nondestructive search technique, for it requires only limited checking of flagged material to confirm that you are tracing a portage rather than the frequently used path of a later settler or logger.

It has been assumed throughout this report that it is worth our time, energy, and money to excavate or at least relocate the route of portages. A skeptical reader might ask, Why? In the case of the Savanna Portage, the answer is fairly straightforward: in a park named Savanna Portage State Park, it is important for interpretive and conservation purposes to know what the route of the portage was. Instructional signs along the portage can highlight poses and historical events that occurred along the route, such as the burning of the east end savanna, the now sunken presence of boardwalks, the location of poses and the canoe canal, and the presence of the logging dam that changed the route of the West Savanna River. For many visitors to the Park, these details of everyday life in early historic Minnesota are more interesting than the webs of political intrigue that fill history books. For conservation purposes, it is important to know where the portage ran before the next park road or public camping grounds is put in.

On a more abstract level, knowledgeable students of early historic Minnesota are as interested in the network of routes that connected homesteads, fledging towns, and centers of commerce, such as mines and sawmills, as they are in the homesteads, towns, and sawmills themselves. The study of pathways of intercommunication tell us who was connected to whom, the ranked importance of routes of flow of goods and information, and how these pathways changed through time. Our daily lives depend on a constant flow of goods, information, and people from one location to another. Studies that focus only on places and that neglect the interconnections among them misrepresent the dynamics of daily life today and in the past.

On a still more abstract level, the interconnections among places are essential elements of a landscape archaeology that connects human behavior with particular places and times (Anschuetz et al. 2001; Deetz 1990; Rossignol and Wandsnider 1992; Yamin and Metheny 1996). A portage is not simply a feature in a physical environment, but a cultural product within cultural systems that structure and organize peoples' interactions within natural environments. As cultural products, portages are meaningful places whose cultural meanings change through time. The vestige of these changing meanings is the archaeological record. This perspective raises an interesting question: Did the Savanna Portage remain the same meaningful place when used by pre-contact Native Americans, the French, the British, and early Americans? The answer is, Not likely! Landscapes are dynamic constructions, with various groups of people imposing their own cognitive map on the physical environment. Archaeology is well suited for applying an interpretive landscape approach because of its combined anthropological perspective and time depth. The Savanna Portage report is, besides a methodological contribution, a fledgling step in this interpretive direction.

Bibliography

Allen, Lt. J. and H.R. Schoolcraft
   1832 A Map and Report of Lieut. Allen and H. R. Schoolcraft's Visit to the Northwest Indians in 1832. U.S. House of Representatives, 23rd Congress, 1st Session, Document No. 323. Washington, D.C.

Anschuetz, K.F., R.H. Wilshusen, and C.L. Schick
   2001 An Archaeology of Landscapes: Perspectives and Directions. *Journal of Archaeological Research* 9(2):157-211.

Boutwell, Rev. W.T.
   1832 Diary in the Manuscript Department of the Minnesota Historical Society, St. Paul.

Bradley, C.S.
   2000 Smoking Pipes for the Archaeologist. In *Studies in Material Culture Research*, ed. by K. Karklins, pp. 104-133. The Society for Historical Archaeology, Tucson, Arizona.

Brunson, Rev. A.
   1879 *A Western Pioneer*, Vol. 2. Hitchcock and Walden, Cincinnati.

Cherry, J.F.
   1983 Frogs Around the Pond: Perspectives on Current Archaeological Survey Projects in the Mediterranean Region. In *Archaeological Survey in the Mediterranean Area*. ed. by D.R. Keller and D.W. Rupp pp. 394-397, International Series, No. 155, British Archaeological Reports, Oxford.

Cherry, J.F., J.L. Davis, A. Demitrack, E. Mantzourani, T.F. Strasser, and L.E. Talalay
   1988 Archaeological Survey in an Artifact-Rich Landscape: A Middle Neolithic Example from Nemea, Greece. *American Journal of Archaeology* 92:159-176.

Cherry, J.F., J.L. Davis, and E. Mantzourani
   1991 *Landscape Archaeology as Long-Term History: Northern Keos in the Cycladic Islands from Earliest Settlement until Modern Times*. Monumenta Archeologica Vol. 16, UCLA Institute of Archaeology, Los Angeles.

Coues, E. (editor)
   1965 *The Expeditions of Zebulon Montgomery Pike*. Ross and Haines, Minneapolis.

Deetz, J.
   1990 Landscapes as Cultural Statements. In *Earth Patterns: Essays in Landscape Archaeology*, ed. by W.M. Kelso and R. Most, pp. 2-4. University Press of Virginia, Charlottesville and London

Ely, E.F.
   1833-34 Diary in the Manuscript Department of the Minnesota Historical Society, St. Paul.

Gaylord, G., E. Baratt, and L. Eagen
   1954 Traverse of Savannah Portage Trail Between East and West Savannah Rivers as Made with Hand Compass and Chain, December, 1954. Unpublished manuscript

on file at Savanna Portage State Park, McGregor, Minnesota.

Gibbon, G., and E. Willms
1985 The Savanna Portage: An Archaeological Study. Manuscript submitted to the Minnesota Department of Natural resources, St. Paul.

Glover, R.
1962 *David Thompson's Narrative*. Champlain Society, Toronto.

Hart, I.H.
1927 The Old Savanna Portage. *Minnesota History* 8:129-130.
1964 Savanna Portage Expedition–1964. *Conservation Volunteer*, March-April, p. 49. Minnesota Department of Conservation, St. Paul.

Holmquist, J.D.
1951 Louis LeConte's Geological Excursion. *Minnesota History* 32:95

Houghton, D.
1832 Diary in the Manuscript Department of the Minnesota Historical Society, St. Paul.

Jacobson, S.
1989 Undergraduate Thesis. Unpublished undergraduate thesis on file in the Wilford Laboratory of Archaeology, University of Minnesota, Minneapolis.

Lewis, L.
1844 Letter of Lucy M. Lewis to James R. Wright, May 29, 1844 William Lewis Papers, Manuscript Department of the Minnesota Historical Society, St. Paul.

Lofstrom, E.U., J.P. Tordoff, and D. George
1982 A Seriation of Historic Earthenwares in the Midwest. *Minnesota Archaeologist,* 41(1):3

Kenmotsu, N.
2000 Gunflints: A Study. In *Approaches to Material Culture Research for Historical Archaeologists*, comp. by David Brauner, pp. 340-372. The Society for Historical Archaeology, Tucson, Arizona.

Nicollet, J.N.
1836 Maps of 1836, Nos. 1-53, Microfilm. Manuscript Department, Minnesota Historical Society, St. Paul.

Nute, G.L.
1923-24 A Description of Northern Minnesota by a Fur Trader in 1807. *Minnesota History* 5:35-36.

Oliphant, L.
1855 *Minnesota and the Far West*. William Blackwood, London and Edinburgh.

Owen, D.D.
1852 *Report of a Geological Survey of Wisconsin, Iowa, and Minnesota*. Lippincott, Grambo, Philadelphia, Pennsylvania.

Quimby, G.I.
1966 *Indian Culture and European Trade Goods: The Archaeology of the Historic Period in the Western Great Lakes*. University of Wisconsin Press, Madison.

Rossignol, J., and L. Wandsnider (editors.)
1992 *Space, Time, and Archaeological Landscapes*. Plenum Press, New York.

Schoolcraft, H.R.
1821 *Narrative Journal of Travels from Detroit Northwest in the Year 1820*. Hosford, Albany New York.

Stone, L.
1974 Need Citation

Watrall, C.
1969 An Archaeological Survey of Savanna Portage. Unpublished manuscript, Minnesota Historical Society, St. Paul.

Warren, W.
1957 *History of the Ojibway Nation*. Ross and Haines, Minneapolis.

Wells, T.
2000 Nail Chronology: The Use of Technologically Derived Features. In *Approaches to Material Culture Research for Historical Archaeologists*, comp. by D. Brauner, pp. 318-339. The Society for Historical Archaeology, Tucson, Arizona.

Woodbridge, D.E. and J.S. Pardee (editors.). 1910 *History of Duluth and St. Louis County, Past and Present* C. F. Cooper and Co., Chicago.

Woolworth, A.
1975 Personal Communication

Woolworth, N. and Alan Woolworth
1969 Savanna Portage Southwest. Unpublished manuscript on file at the Savanna Portage State Park.

Yamin, R. and K.B. Metheny (editors.)
1996 *Landscape Archaeology: Reading and Interpreting the American Historical Landscape*. University of Tennessee Press, Knoxville.

The Lower Rice Lake Site, 21CE5

Kent Bakken
Department of Interdisciplinary Archaeological Studies
University of Minnesota

The Lower Rice Lake site (21CE5) is a habitation located on a ridge overlooking Lower Rice Lake, in northwestern Minnesota. During at least part of the period of habitation, a focal activity was harvesting and processing of wild rice. Typological evidence suggests repeated occupations, including multiple Woodland components. This paper provides descriptions of the site and its geography, of research conducted at the site, and of the artifacts recovered. The evidence reviewed comes from several surface collections and from limited test excavation conducted in 1965.

Background and Introduction

The Lower Rice Lake site, 21CE5, is a prehistoric habitation located in northwest Minnesota. The University of Minnesota collections contain materials from this site, including surface collections and materials from formal excavation in 1965. These materials had not, however, been analyzed and reporting on the site was limited (Evans 1960; Johnson 1969a, 1969b). I undertook an analysis of the site for a master's thesis project. This report is a summary of the resulting M.A. thesis (Bakken 1994), which includes additional detail on the fieldwork and collections.

The site initially appeared to have considerable research potential. Unfortunately, problems with stratigraphy and excavation records limit the usefulness of the results. The analysis did produce potentially useful comparative data, however, which is presented here.

Site Description

The Lower Rice Lake site, sometimes called the Ponsford Landing site, is located on a ridge along the southeast edge of Lower Rice Lake (Figs. 1, 2). The lake is drained by the Wild Rice River, a tributary of the Red River. The site itself is located only 11 km (7 miles) west of the major divide separating the Red River drainage from the Mississippi River drainage; the Mississippi Headwaters lie approximately 20 km (12 miles) to the southeast.

The ridge on which the site is located runs southeast to northwest at an elevation of about 16 m (50 feet) above the lake. Vegetation now blocks any view of the lake. The immediate site area is wooded with both deciduous and coniferous species and has dense understory vegetation. The soil at the site is a well drained, slightly acidic, sandy to gravelly loam (Agricultural Experiment Station 1980:37).

Site maps by Garland (1959) and Schissel and Anfinson (1977) indicate an "almost impassable" dirt road leading from the clearing and running generally northward along the ridge. This road was not observed during an inspection of the site in 1990, and apparently has become overgrown and obscured.

No mounds or other surficial archaeological features were visible during the 1990 inspection. A gravel road leading to the lake had been cut through the site from east to west. On either side of the road, the ridge crest was leveled to create a clearing. A small remnant of the natural land surface was left in the middle of this clearing, apparently to avoid a large oak tree and a hand operated water pump, indicating that a half meter to a meter of soil was removed. The clearing unfortunately coincides with the central and richest part of the site. The soil removal cut to a depth that would have removed the entire archaeological stratum over most of the leveled area. At least two, and possibly several, of the excavation units described below were removed by this alteration. Margins of the site should be preserved beyond the limits of the clearing, however.

History of Site Investigation

Area residents have known about and collected artifacts from the Lower Rice Lake site since at least the 1930s. The University of Minnesota collection (now housed at the Minnesota Historical

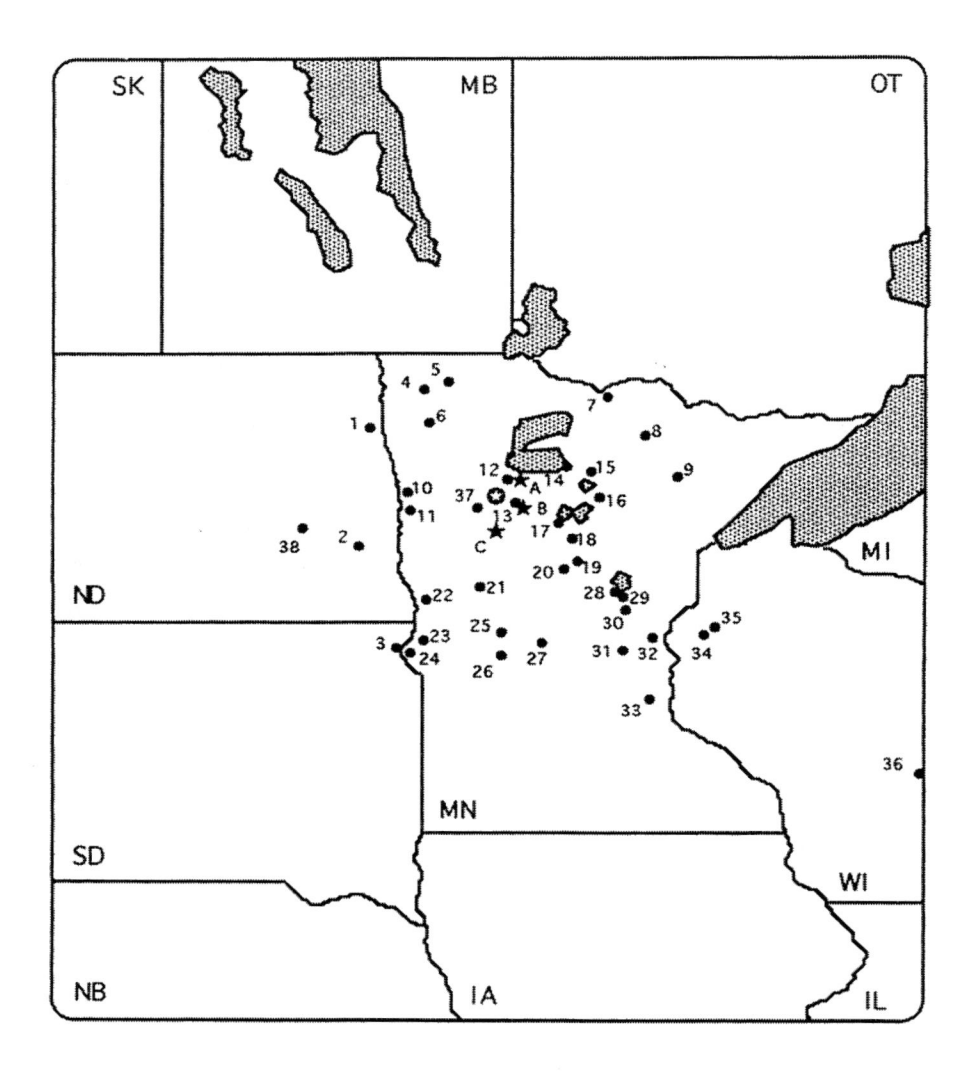

○ Lower Rice Lake Site
• Other Archaeological Sites
★ Pollen Core Locations

Figure 1. Location of Lower Rice Lake site, 21CE5, and other sites discussed in text.

Society) includes artifacts collected during this period and donated to the University in 1967 by a "Mr. Gagne." In 1952, University archaeologists were contacted by local residents Robert H. Littlewolf and David Littlewolf, who had been "digging for arrowheads" at the site and sought information on the artifacts they had found. These and other artifacts were viewed in the following year at the Littlewolf home by Lloyd Wilford (1953).

In 1959 a party from the University of Minnesota visited the site. Garland (1959) recorded that "collectors had taken 'tubsfull' of materials from Ponsford where cuts had been made in the 'bank' of the landing." Garland also noted that "The site has been freely 'potted,' and there is much picnic and camping debris about. But the amount of materials exposed and the extent of their scattering indicates a continued rich site." It was during this visit that Robert Littlewolf gave materials he had collected from the Lower Rice Lake site, including human remains, to the University of Minnesota.

Archaeological Sites					
			Langer	21CA58	20
			Mooney	21NR29	10
Altern	47BT50	35	Naze	32SN246	38
Arvilla	32GF1	1	Nett Lake	21KC1	8
Bartke	21PO1	26	Neubauer	21PN7	32
Basswood Shores	21DL90	25			
Berscheid	21TO3	27	North Twin Lake	21MH5	37
			Norway Lake	21CA22	18
Big Rice	21SL163	9	Old Shakopee Bridge	21ML20	28
Bradbury Brook	21ML42	30	Onigum Marina	—	17
Browns Valley	21TR5	24	Osufsen	21IC2	15
Canning	21NR9	11			
Christensen Mound 1	21SH1	31	Petaga Point	21ML11	28
			Sanders Site 3	47WP70	36
Cooper Mound	21ML16	28	Schocker	21BL1	14
Crosier	21ML33	29	Scott	21CA1	16
Dead River	21OT51	21	Shea	32CS101	2
De Spiegler	39RO23	3			
Dunn Farm	20LU22	—	Smith	21KC3	7
			Stumne	21PN5	32
Femco	21WL1	22	Upper Rice Lake	21CE4	12
Fickle	47BT25	34	Wilson	21TR2	23
Ft. Poualak/Hays Lake	21CW14	19			
Greenbush Borrow Pit	21RO11	5			
Gull Lake Dam	21CA37	20	Pollen Core Locations		
Haarstad	21MA6	6	Bog D		A
Itasca Bison Kill	21CE1	13	Marquette Pond		B
King Mound	21CW2	19	Rice Lake		C
Lake Bronson	21KT1	4			
Lake Phalen	—	33			

Figure 1b. Key to Figure 1.

In 1965 the University conducted further investigations at the site, under the direction of Elden Johnson with fieldwork supervised by Gordon Lothson. This work included additional mapping, surface collection, and the excavation of six formal test units. Five units yielded artifacts; one was sterile. Approximately 4,500 artifacts were recovered, including lithics, ceramics, worked and unworked bone, and charcoal samples. The results of these investigations, which constitute the bulk of the systematic research conducted at the site, are discussed in further detail below.

Artifacts were also noted at the site by representatives of the Office of the State Archaeologist in or about 1985, subsequent to severe disturbance to the site caused by work on the access road. This work involved leveling part of the ridge crest on either side of the access road. This activity destroyed what appears to have been the central and densest part of the site, including at least the two most productive units from the 1965 excavations. The disturbance exposed habitation-related artifacts, including numerous ceramic body sherds, a few pieces of lithic debitage and a few animal bone fragments. Human remains were also disturbed by the construction activity. These were assembled and reburied on site (L. Peterson, personal comm. 1992). The artifacts were not studied or documented because of their possible association with human burials.

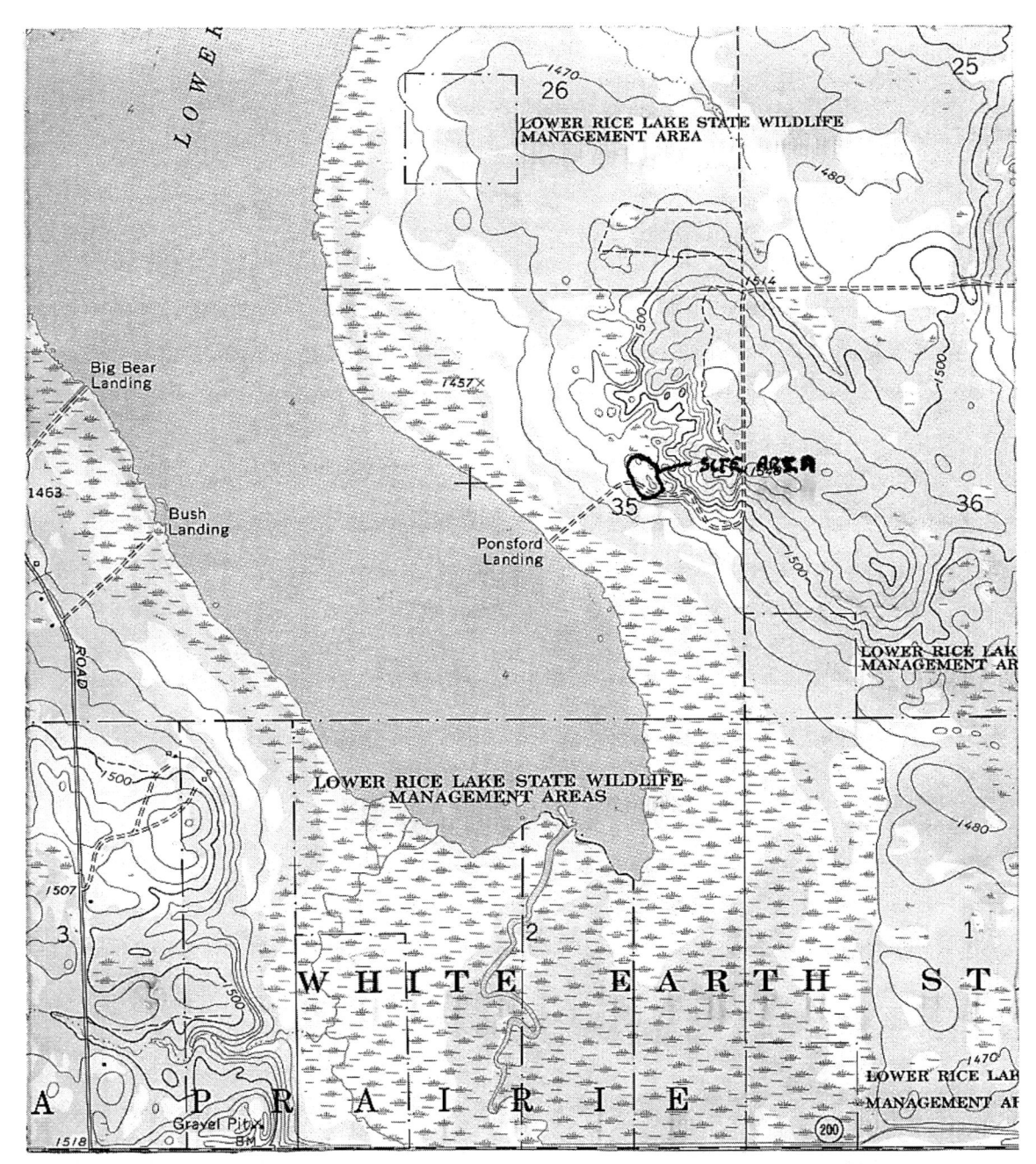

Figure 2. Landscape context of the Lower Rice Lake site, 21CE5 *(From USGS Zerkel Quadrangle,*

A brief report on this and the nearby Upper Rice Lake site (21CE4) was published by Evans (1960). The site was mentioned in Johnson's (1969a, 1969b) overviews of archaeological evidence for prehistoric use of wild rice. In 1978 the Lower Rice Lake site was entered into the National Register of Historic Places.

The 1965 Excavations

This study of the site included the excavation of six units, of which one measured 1 by 1 m and the others 2 by 2 m, for a total of 21 square meters (Fig. 3). The units were excavated in 10 cm levels. Excavated soil was screened; the size of mesh was not specified but was presumably 1/4 inch, based on known University practices at that time. Prove-

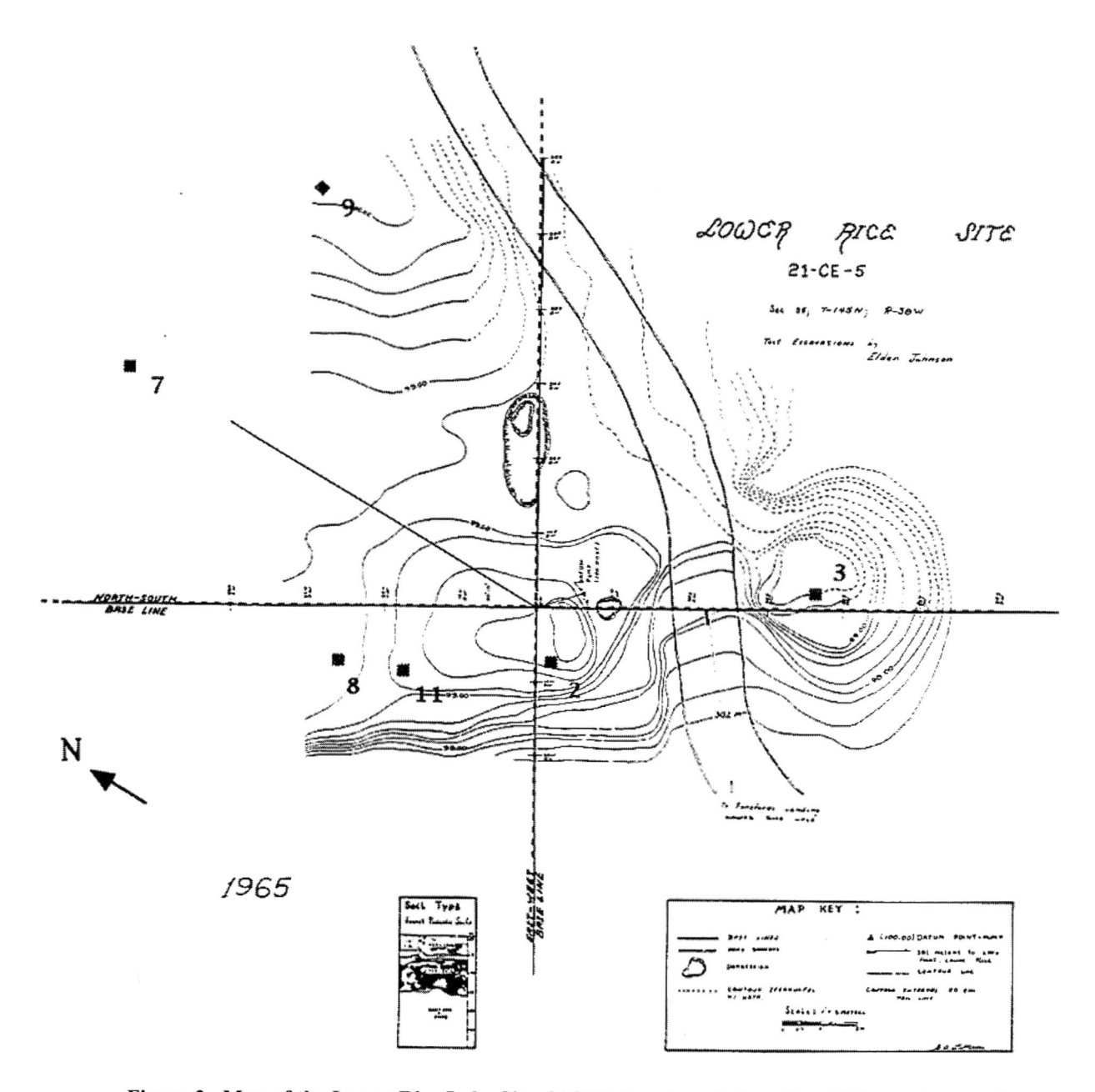

Figure 3. Map of the Lower Rice Lake Site, 21CE5, based on University of Minnesota records.

nience was maintained by unit (rather than individual 1 x 1 m area) and by level, or by feature and level.

The present study of the materials from this excavation is complicated by several factors. The information provided in field notes is limited, and the excavation techniques are occasionally puzzling. The field notes contained little information on the stratigraphic placement of features; whatever could be inferred regarding vertical location of features is discussed below in connection with each feature. The site map (Fig. 3) included good information on topography and landscape features, although it did not show the location of excavation units. The location of the units has been interpolated based on information in field notes. The provenience of a few artifacts has been lost. This is because of artifact breakage in storage, or illegible accession numbers. These artifacts have been tallied with items from the surface collections.

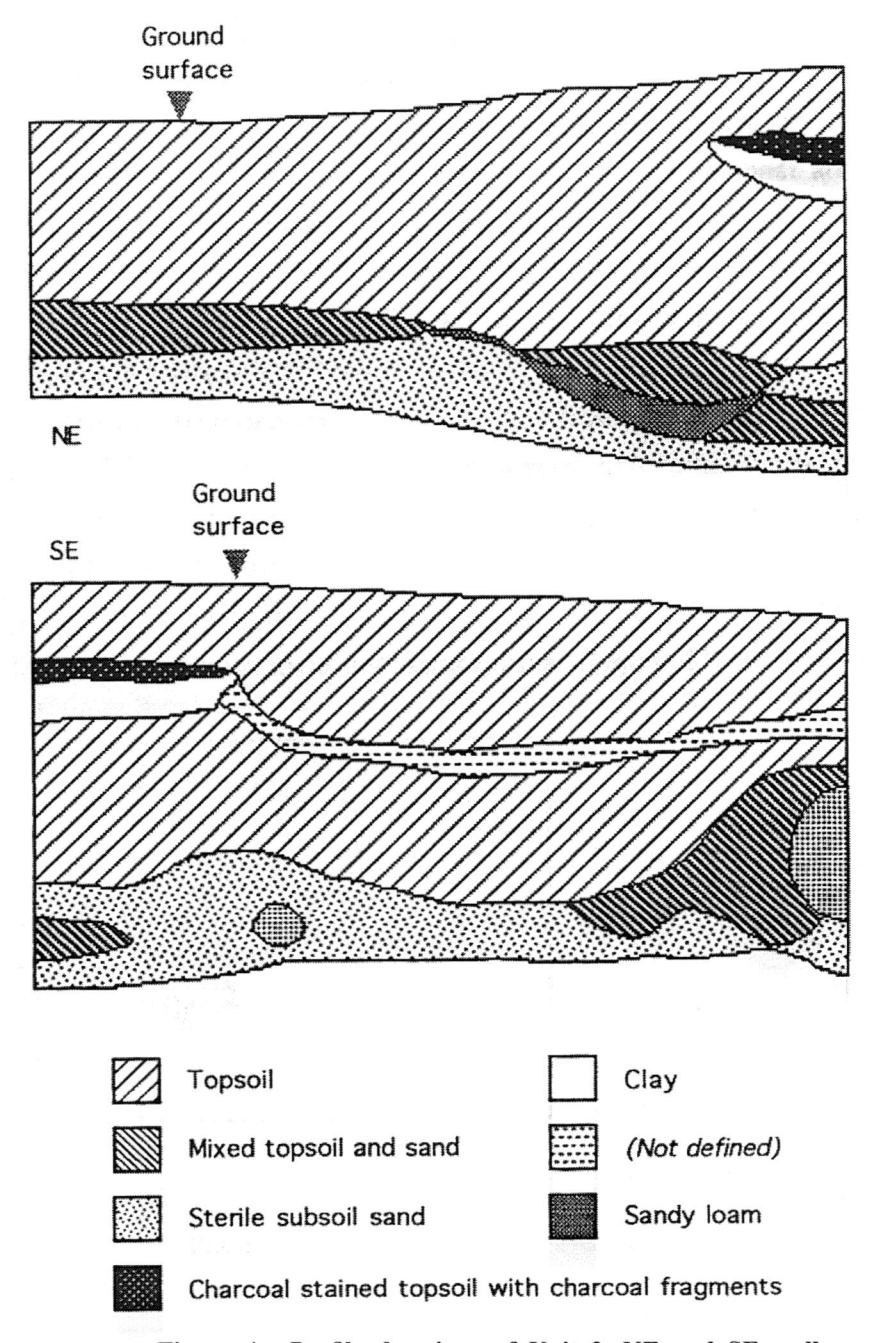

Figure 4. Profile drawings of Unit 2, NE and SE walls.

Finally, the accession records for the excavated materials are incomplete and contain errors. In most cases it has been possible, by comparing field notes, artifacts, and photographic documentation, to make corrections to the accession record with a high degree of confidence. In a few cases probable corrections are made, although with less confidence. In one instance no provenience could be determined. The problems with provenience, and the attempted solutions, are discussed in detail in the manuscript version of this report (Bakken 1994). The following summary of excavation units and features from the 1965 investigations is based on field notes and photos. The description of artifacts is based on new cataloging and analysis.

Four units were excavated along the ridge crest. From north to south, these are Units 8, 11, 2 and 3. The interval between units varied from about 10 m to over 30 m. Units 7 and 9 were excavated 30 to 50 m east of the ridge crest. The nonconsecutive unit numbers require a note of explanation. The site itself, each excavation unit, as well as any cultural features as commonly understood, were all called features. Feature 1 was the entire site, Feature 2 was an excavation unit, Feature 4 was a ricing jig, and so on. Excavation units are called units rather than features in this report, but the original "feature" numbering is retained.

Twelve features were encountered during excavation, including 5 ricing jigs, 3 fire pits or hearths, two other pits and two possible post molds. Eight were designated as features (numbers 4, 5, 6, 10, 12, 13, 14 and 15; see note above about nonconsecutive numbering), while four others were noted but not designated as features.

Unit 2

This unit was located in the clearing where the road crosses the ridge, north of the road (Fig. 3). The 2 by 2 m unit was excavated in 10 cm levels to a general depth of 60 cm. Field notes indicate that the general 50 to 60 cm level contained no artifacts. Excavation of Feature 10, a "pit" underlying part of the unit, continued to a final depth inferred from profile drawings to be between 80 and 100 cm below surface. A total of five features were encountered in Unit 2, including the pit, a hearth, a clay ricing jig bowl and two possible post molds. There are no photos of Unit 2. Soil profiles of two walls are reproduced in Figure 4.

Unit 2 was the most productive excavation unit, accounting for 48 percent of the excavated artifacts. The unit was especially productive in terms of ceramics, including both grit and shell-tempered sherds with a variety of surface treatments. There are 42 defined vessels from Unit 2, including Blackduck (n=8), Brainerd Horizontally Corded (n=1), Northeastern Plains Village ceramics (n=2), Sandy Lake Smooth (n=2), Sandy Lake Stamped (n=1), Sandy Lake Cordmarked (n=14), and unidentified wares (n=14). The unit also produced a fragment of a grit-tempered clay elbow pipe. Lithic artifacts included small triangular projectile points (n=2), two scrapers, other chipped stone tools (n=6) and flaking debris (n=81). All lithic raw materials present at the site were represented in the unit, with the exception of Knife River Flint (KRF). Swan River Chert and Red River Chert were the most common. The unit also contained a hammerstone or roughly formed basalt ax. Manufactured bone artifacts included three conjoining fragments of a possible bone arm band (which also conjoin a fourth piece found on the surface), and another fragment from a second bone arm band. Faunal remains included bird, mammal, fish, reptile and unidentified vertebrate bone fragments. Over half were mammalian. Identified species include white-tailed deer (*Odocoileus virginianus*), cottontail rabbit (*Sylvilagus floridanus*), coyote (*Canis latrans*) and canvasback duck (*Aythya valisineria*). One charcoal sample was taken from the unit; it was not dated. Three historic artifacts (one piece of sheet steel and two sawn bone fragments) were found in the top excavation level. Other materials from the unit include five pieces of burned clay, a spall of basaltic rock, and a burned pebble fragment.

The highest artifact densities occurred in Levels 2 and 3, each of which contained several hundred artifacts. Level 4 also had high artifact density, although only a quarter to a third of the density in the overlying levels. Levels 1 and 5 contained relatively small numbers of artifacts. The unit profiles (Fig. 4) suggest that the fire hearth and clay ricing jig are associated with the densest layer of sherds and other artifacts.

There are three Sandy Lake vessels, one Blackduck vessel and one unidentified ware vessel that have fragments in more than one level of this unit. There are also four mends that establish connections between Feature 10 (see below) and the general unit stratigraphy (of which two are Sandy Lake, one is Blackduck, and one is an unidentified ware). The only level that is not connected to the rest of the unit stratigraphy in this way is Level 1. This is in contrast to the rest of the excavation units at the site, which raises questions of whether there may be unresolved problem with the accession record reconstruction, or if Level 1 may represent fill that was deposited over the top of the previous

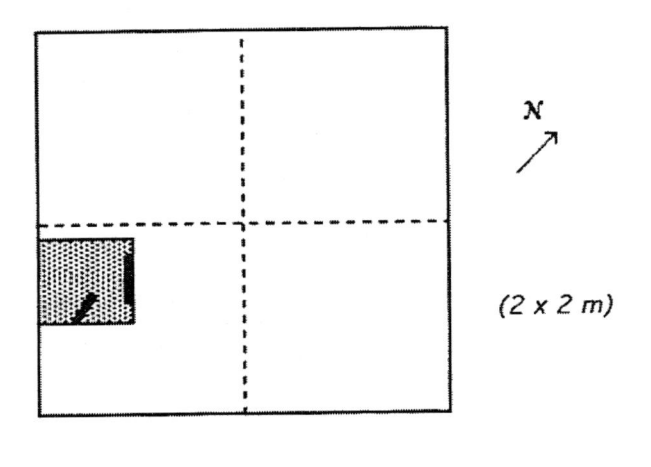

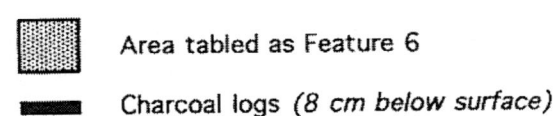

Figure 5. Plan view drawing of Feature 6, Unit 2, 21CE5.

■ Area tabled as Feature 6
■ Charcoal logs *(8 cm below surface)*

stratigraphy. Without more complete information these questions cannot be satisfactorily answered.

Feature 6, according to the field notes, was a hearth or "fire pit with charcoal logs and abundant fragments of charcoal" and ash, located between 8 and 18 cm (Figs. 4, 5). The top of the feature was defined by a charred log at 8 cm, and the bottom by a "charcoal lens 3 cm thick, 18 cm below surface." This places the feature principally in Levels 2 and 3, the levels with the highest artifact density. A charcoal sample was collected from the feature; it was not dated.

Only seven artifacts are directly associated with Feature 6: a Blackduck rim sherd; a shell-tempered, smooth surface body sherd; three grit-tempered, cordmarked body sherds one of which was burned; a Swan River Chert flake; and a burned mammalian bone fragment. The field notes state that some charred bone and burned potsherds from the feature are also bagged with the artifacts from Levels 2 and 3 of the unit. Apparently this resulted from the feature being excavated as a square measuring approximately 20 to 25 cm on a side, rather than by following its natural outline and stratigraphy (Fig. 5).

Feature 10 was defined in the field notes as a "pit dug into the layer of sterile subsoil sand, possibly the burial pit of a mound. The pit fill was darker sand, due in part to staining by carbon; but mostly probably due to being mixed with topsoil." No reasons are given to support the suggestion that the pit may be "the burial pit of a mound."

In a plan view of the unit at 40 cm (Fig. 6), the pit appears to have a well-defined, slightly irregular edge and to occupy most of the east half of the unit. The profiles of this unit (Fig. 4), however, suggest that the pit was not necessarily so well defined. The angle at which the excavation levels intersected the stratigraphy may have exaggerated the definition. The feature could alternately be interpreted as a depression 20 to 30 cm in depth and having sloping sides.

The excavation of Feature 10 proceeded in a curious fashion. Apparently the natural stratigraphy and outline of the feature were disregarded in favor of a completely arbitrary but metrically tidy procedure. The western portion of the unit, generally outside of but possibly including parts of the feature, was excavated to 60 cm. Subsequently a square measuring about 1 by 1.2 m was excavated in the eastern part of the unit. This square was located completely or substantially within the feature. According to the field notes, the square (i.e., "feature") was excavated to 60 cm, materials from the 40 to 50 cm and 50 to 60 cm were bagged together, and the bottom of the pit varied from 50 to 55 cm below the surface. This is difficult to reconcile with the unit profile, which would appear to indicate that the bottom of the pit was somewhere between 80 and 100 cm below the surface. Without further information, it is difficult to interpret the feature adequately.

Most of the artifacts in Feature 10 were grit-tempered, cordmarked sherds. There were also a few shell-tempered and indeterminate-temper sherds, and sherds with smooth surfaces, net impressions or horizontal cordmarking. Defined vessels include Sandy Lake Cordmarked (n=2), Blackduck (n=1), and unidentified wares (n=3). Each of the Sandy Lake and Blackduck vessels, and one of the unidentified ware vessels, have fragments in the upper levels of the unit. The only manufactured bone item in the feature was a segment of an arm band. About half of the other bone fragments were identified as mammalian. The mammalian bone included a frag-

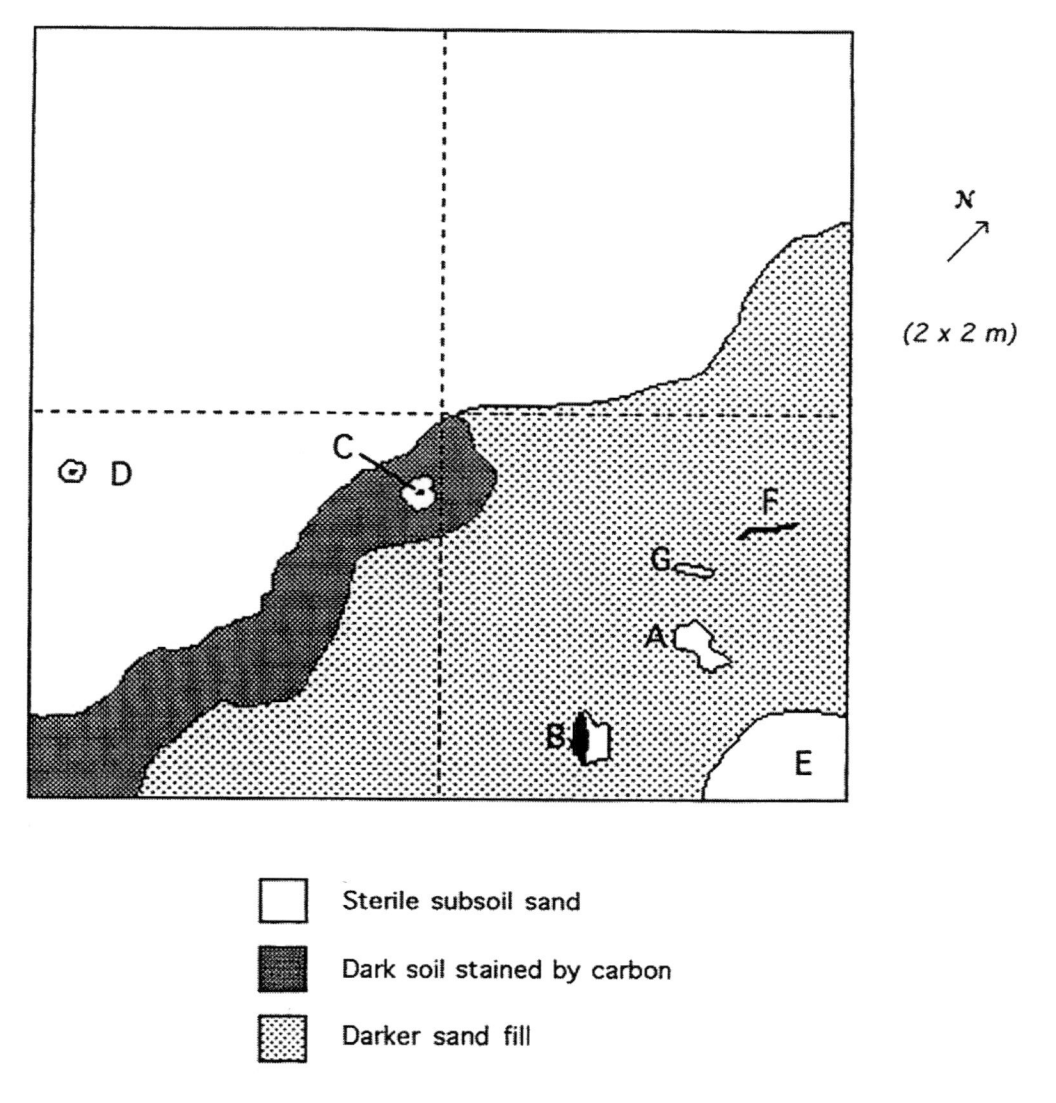

A Fire cracked rock, 40 cm below sod surface
B Fire cracked rock, 38 cm below sod surface
C Possible post mold with clay, 30 cm below sod surface
D Possible post mold, 40 cm below sod surface
E Possible ricing jig bowl, 23 cm below sod surface
F Charred fragment of wood, 40 to 43 cm below sod surface
G Bone fragment, 47 cm below sod surface

Figure 6. Plan view drawing of Feature 10, Unit 2, 21CE5.

ment of a coyote (*Canis latrans*) maxilla (including the two back molars on the left side), and two fragmentary beaver (*Castor canadensis*) incisors. Avian, reptilian and unidentified vertebrate specimens were present in smaller numbers. The feature contained one stone knife, two utilized flakes, and 20 pieces of flaking debris. Swan River Chert was the most common raw material, with a few other materials present in small amounts. The feature also contained two pieces of burned clay. According to field notes, the feature contained pieces of fire-cracked rock, but these apparently were not saved.

Other Features. The field notes provide information on three other features in this unit, none of which were formally defined. The first is a "pos-

Figure 7. Photograph of Features 4 and 5, Unit 3, 21CE5.

sible ricing jig bowl" located in the east corner of the unit. This is shown in the profile (Fig. 4) and plan (Fig. 6) drawings for the unit. A lens of dark, charcoal stained soil was found resting on top of a clay disk appears to be fairly uniform in thickness, with the edges tapering or beveling up. Although the feature was not completely exposed, it appears to be no less than 50 cm in diameter and approximately 10 cm in thickness. The top was located 23 cm below the surface. No information is available on specific artifactual associations.

The other two undefined features are a "possible post mold with clay" located within and near the edge of Feature 10 at a depth of 30 cm, and a "possible post mold" located outside Feature 10 at a depth of 40 cm (Fig. 6). Both were cross sectioned and "found to be recent." The evidence for these features being modern is not discussed.

Unit 3

This unit was the southernmost unit excavated on the ridge crest. It was located in the clearing where the road crosses the ridge, to the south of the road (Fig. 3). The unit measured 2 by 2 m, and was excavated in 10 cm levels to a depth of 70 cm. The unit contained two features, both ricing jigs. There was no profile drawing for this unit.

Artifact density in Unit 3, while still high, was substantially lower than in Unit 2. The ceramic sherds were typically grit-tempered and either cordmarked or smooth-surfaced. There was also a smaller percentage of shell-tempered sherds; other surface treatments include net impressing, horizontal cordmarking, and stamping. A total of 24 defined vessels are represented in this unit including examples of Blackduck (n=6), Northeastern Plains Village (n=1), Onamia/St. Croix (n=2), Sandy Lake Smooth

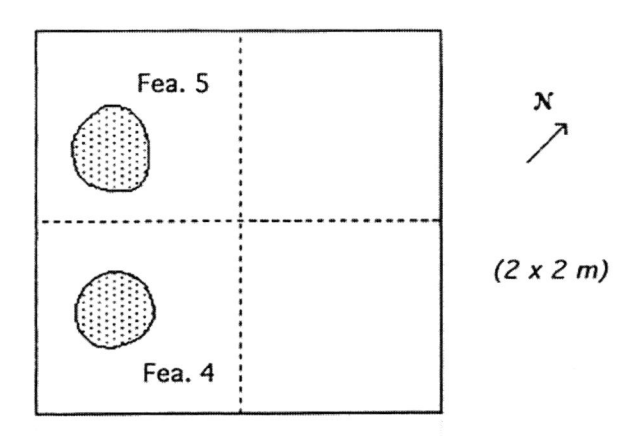

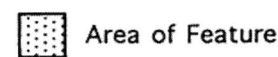

Figure 8. Plan view drawing of Features 4 and 5, Unit 3, 21CE5.

(n=1), Sandy Lake Cordmarked (n=7), unidentified wares (n=6), and a substantially complete miniature vessel. Lithic artifacts included a side-notched projectile point, scrapers (n=6), a knife, other bifaces (n=4), a retouched flake, and flaking debris (n=30). Swan River Chert and Red River Chert were the most common lithic raw materials, with other materials present in smaller amounts. Two manufactured bone artifacts come from this unit, a carved rib fragment and a phalange that appears to have been carved to a point. A bear canine was also found. Other faunal remains are primarily mammalian, with small percentages of reptilian, avian and piscine remains present. Taxa identified include canvasback duck (*Aythya valisineria*), Canada goose (*Branta canadensis*), muskrat (*Ondatra zibethicus*), bear (*Ursus* sp.), possibly bison (*Bison bison*), and weasel or mink (*Mustela* sp.). Eight pieces of burned clay occurred in the unit. There were also two historic artifacts (pieces of steel) present in the first excavation level.

Most of the artifacts from this unit were contained in the upper three excavation levels. There is a slight increase in total number of artifacts from the first to second and second to third levels. Below this point, artifact density drops off quickly. Level 4 is almost sterile.

Features 4 and 5 were located in the western portion of the unit, approximately a meter apart (on center) (Figs. 7, 8). Their depth below surface is not clearly recorded. The arbitrary depth below datum indicates that both are at the same level. Based on general elevation information provided for the site, it is estimated that they begin near the top of Level 2 (10-20 cm) and continue into Level 3 (20-30 cm).

Feature 4 was a ricing jig pit measuring 43 by 44 cm in diameter and approximately 11 cm deep. The pit was lined with clay up to 6 cm thick. A smooth surfaced Sandy Lake rim sherd with interior rim notching was associated with this feature. A few other sherds, bone fragments and pieces of lithic debitage were also recovered. Field notes indicate that the feature contained charcoal; a sample was not collected.

Feature 5 was also a ricing jig pit. It measured 41 by 46 cm in diameter, and was approximately 11 cm thick. The pit was lined with clay up to 6 cm deep. A few sherds, bone fragments and a single quartz flake were associated with the feature. Field notes indicate that the feature also contained charcoal; a sample was not collected.

Unit 7

This unit was located approximately 50 m northeast of the other units, off the ridge crest (Fig. 3). It measured 2 by 2 m, and was excavated in 10 cm levels to a depth of 30 cm. Only five artifacts were recovered from this unit, all from the 0 to 10 cm level. These were three grit-tempered, cordmarked body sherds, a fragment of a Swan River Chert biface, and a mammal bone fragment. No features were encountered in the unit.

Unit 8

This unit was the northernmost unit on the ridge crest (Fig. 3). It measured 2 by 2 m, and was excavated in 10 cm levels to a depth of 50 cm. This unit contained three features -- two ricing jigs and a truncated pit dug into the subsoil. Although the depth below surface for the ricing jigs was not recorded, they appear to have been located in Levels 2 and 3, between 10 and 30 cm. There is no profile drawing for this unit.

Artifact density in Unit 8 was comparable to that in Units 3 and 11. Almost all the ceramic sherds from this unit were grit-tempered. Cordmarking was the most common surface treatment, and horizontal cordmarking was much more common in

Figure 9. Photograph of Features 12, 13 and 15, Unit 8, 21CE5.

this unit than in any of the other excavation units. Smooth-surfaced, net-impressed, and stamped sherds are also present. There were 24 defined vessels associated with Unit 8, including examples of Blackduck (n=10), Brainerd Horizontally Corded (n=2), Brainerd Net Impressed (n=2), Sandy Lake Smooth (n=1), Sandy Lake Cordmarked (n=4), and unidentified wares (n=5). The relatively small count of Sandy Lake vessels is worth noting, and correlates well with the relative scarcity of shell-tempered sherds in this unit. Faunal remains were primarily mammalian and reptilian, with one fragment of mollusc shell also occurring. Avian bone is conspicuously absent. None of these faunal remains could be identified by genus or species. Lithic artifacts included scrapers (n=3), a biface, and flaking debris (n=28). Swan River Chert and Red River Chert were the most common lithic raw materials, with other raw materials present in smaller amounts. A charcoal sample collected from this unit was dated to 710 ± 60; the significance of this date is examined below. It is not believed to accurately date the context from which it was collected.

Most artifacts in Unit 8 are concentrated in Levels 1 and 2 (0-20 cm). Artifact density drops off quickly in the next three levels, and picks up slightly in the pit feature which constitutes the lower portion of unit stratigraphy. Sherds from Brainerd Horizontally Corded Vessel 27 were found in every level of the unit except Level 4. This includes Feature 15.

Feature 12 was a ricing jig pit measuring 46 by 48 cm in diameter and approximately 6 cm in depth (Fig. 9). The depth below surface for this feature was not recorded, but appears to have been between 10 and 30 cm. It was located in the northeast quadrant of the unit. The only artifacts re-

Figure 10. Photograph of Feature 15, Unit 8, cross section, 21CE5.

covered in association with the feature were four grit-tempered sherds. According to the field notes, charcoal also occurred in association with the feature. There were no plan view or profile drawings.

Feature 13 was a circle of solid clay indicating the location of a ricing jig pit, located in the northwest quadrant of the unit (Fig. 9). The depth below surface was not recorded, but appears to have been between 10 and 30 cm. The arbitrary depth below datum of Features 12 and 13 indicates that they are at about the same level. There are two artifacts associated with this feature, a Red River Chert scraper and a rim sherd from a Sandy Lake Smooth vessel. The field notes also indicate that there were "scattered flecks of charcoal on top" of the feature. There were no plan view or profile drawings.

Feature 15 was the lower part of a circular pit, apparently truncated by disturbance of the overlying soil. It measured approximately 97 by 99 cm, 18 cm in depth, and was located in the southwest quadrant of the unit (Figs. 9-11).

It is described in the field notes as being a "pit of sandy humus intrusive in sub-soil." The feature was apparently discerned at the bottom of the 40 to 50 cm level. It contained sherds, turtle remains and charcoal. Field notes also indicate that presence of fire-cracked rock. All the sherds from the feature are grit-tempered, and either horizontally cordmarked or net-impressed. This includes six rim sherds, representing two Brainerd Horizontally Corded vessels and one Brainerd Net Impressed vessel. The only faunal remains in the pit were fragments of turtle shell (plastron) and long bones. There were no lithics or other artifacts. Because this

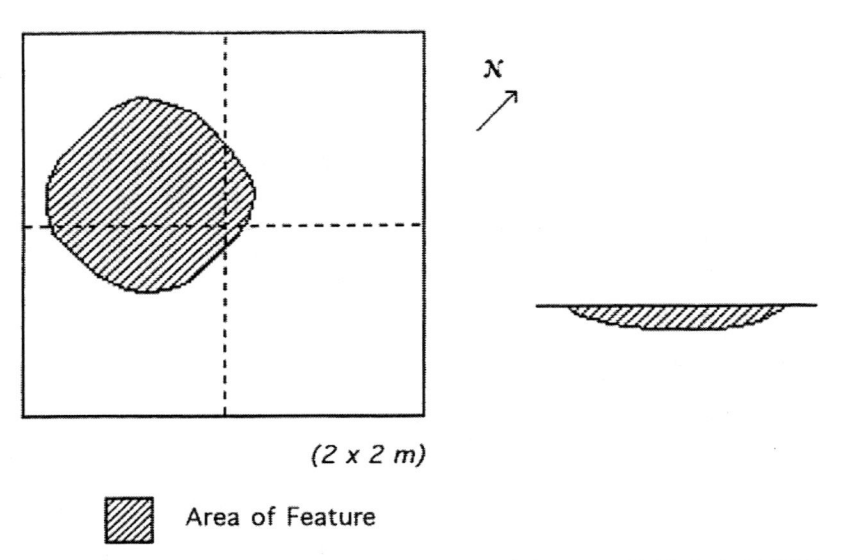

Figure 11. Plan view and profile drawings of Feature 15, Unit 8, 21CE5.

bottom part of the pit appeared to be intact, and because the feature was clearly associated only with Brainerd ceramics, a small charcoal sample from the pit was dated in hope that it would provide a date on the Brainerd utilization of the site. (Because the sample was small, the AMS method was used.) The resulting date of 710 ± 60 B.P. (A.D. 1240) (Beta-60259, CAMS-5372) is discussed further below.

Unit 9

This unit was located east of the ridge crest (Fig. 3). It measured 1 by 1 m, and was excavated to a depth of 30 cm. The unit contained no artifacts or features. This provides the only direct evidence of site limits.

Unit 11

This unit was located on the ridge crest, between Units 2 and 8 (Fig. 3). It measured 2 by 2 m, and was excavated to a depth of 40 cm. The unit contained two features, both fire hearths. One of these features, visible in a profile drawing of one wall of the unit (Fig. 12), was not formally designated. Field notes indicate that the wall in which this feature was visible was covered with a sheet of plastic before the unit was backfilled, in order to preserve the profile.

Artifact density in Unit 11 was comparable to that of Units 3 and 8. The ceramics were primarily grit-tempered and either cordmarked or smooth-surfaced.

Shell-tempered sherds did occur, and other surface treatments included stamping, net impressions and horizontal cordmarking. A total of 12 defined vessels for this unit include examples of Northeastern Plains Village (n=1), Onamia/St. Croix (n=1), Sandy Lake Smooth (n=1), Sandy Lake Stamped (n=1), Sandy Lake Cordmarked (n=4), and unidentified wares (n=5). Lithic artifacts included a corner-notched projectile point, a small triangular projectile point, a scraper, a knife, and flaking debris (n=24). Swan River Chert, Red River Chert and Tongue River Silica were the most common lithic raw materials. Faunal remains from the unit were primarily mammalian bone fragments, with small amounts of avian and piscine bone and a single fragment of mollusc shell. Identified taxa included pintail duck (*Anas acuta*), Canada goose (*Branta canadensis*) and possibly weasel or mink (*Mustela* sp.). One charcoal sample was collected from the unit; it was not dated.

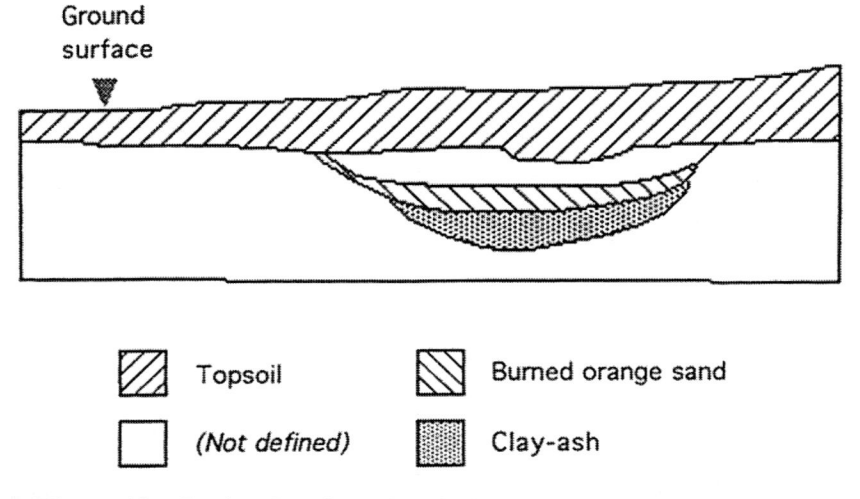

Figure 12. Profile drawing of Unit 11, SE wall, including undesignated feature, 21CE5.

Figure 13. Photograph of Feature 14, Unit 11, 21CE5.

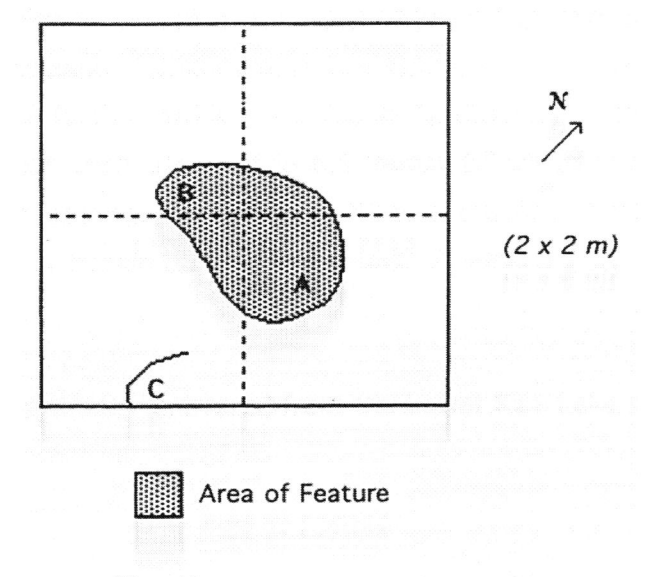

Area of Feature

Elevations
A 10 cm below surface
B 20 cm below surface
C 30 cm below surface

Figure 14. Plan view drawing of Feature 14, Unit 11, 21CE5.

The unit contained one historic artifact (a piece of steel), for which the level is not known. There were two burned chert pebble fragments in Level 1, and three pieces of burned clay in Level 2. A tube-style catlinite pipe was also recovered from this unit.

Feature 14 was a fire pit that contained ash, rock and charcoal (Fig. 13). According to the field notes, the feature "seems to have been lined with clay." In plan view (Fig. 14), the feature had an irregular, teardrop shape. It measured approximately 50 cm in length and 35 cm in maximum width. The vertical location of the feature was not recorded and cannot be determined based on the available information. Feature 14 contained a number of grit-tempered sherds, with cordmarked, stamped, smooth, net-impressed, and horizontally-cordmarked surface treatment. This includes one rim sherd which is a Sandy Lake Stamped vessel. The feature also contained avian, mammalian and piscine bone fragments. Pintail duck

Table 1. Summary of Materials Recovered from 21CE5

Ceramic	**4441**
Partial Miniature Vessel	1
Rim Sherd	203
Handle Sherd	1
Body Sherd	4,235
Elbow Pipe Fragment	1
Lithic	**201**
Projectile Point	4
Other Biface	8
Scraper	10
Utilized and Retouched Flake	6
Flaking debri	170
Nonchipped Stone Tool	1
Faunal	**462**
Faunal Artifacts	20
Faunal Remains *(totals include faunal artifacts)*	442
Avian	*27*
Mammalian	*209*
Molluscan	*2*
Piscine	*6*
Reptilian	*31*
Unidentified Vertebrate	*167*
Bontanical *(Charcoal)*	**3**
Historic	**6**
Bone	2
Metal	4
Other	**26**
Burned Clay	-
Burned Pebbles	3
Rock Spall	1
TOTAL	**5,139**

Table 2. Faunal Species Identified, 21CE5

Taxonomic Name	Common Name		Element
Bison bison	Bison	n = 1	phalange
Canis latrans	Coyote	n = 1	maxilla
Castor canadensis	Beaver	n = 3	incisor (3)
Cervus elaphus	American Elk, Wapiti	n = 1	phalange
Odocoileus virginianus	Whitetail Deer	n = 1	phalange
Sylvilagus floridanus	Cottontail Rabbit	n = 1	mandible
Anas acuta	Pintail Duck	n = 1	scapula
Aythya valisineria	Canvasback Duck	n = 5	humerus; coracoid (4)
Branta canadensis	Canada Goose	n = 4	humerus; caracoid; tibiotarsus; scapula
Esox masquinongy	Muskellunge	n = 1	dentary

n = number of identified specimens

(*Anas acuta*) was specifically identified. A charcoal sample was taken from the feature; it was not dated.

Another feature noted in a sketch of the southeast wall profile (Fig. 14) was not given a formal feature designation. The feature was a fire pit having a lenticular cross section. It measured approximately 1 m in width and 25 to 30 cm in depth. The top of the feature appears to be located between 10 and 20 cm below the surface.

Materials Recovered

The materials recovered from the Lower Rice Lake site were grouped into six categories for this analysis: ceramics, lithics, faunal materials, botanical materials, historic objects and other objects. The ceramics category includes only sherds from ceramic vessels; lumps of burned clay and a fragment of a ceramic pipe are included under the category "other." The lithics category includes only artifacts relating to flaked stone technology; stone objects that are carved or ground, including a catlinite pipe, are included in the category "other." The faunal materials were further divided into faunal artifacts, or deliberately formed objects of bone, antler, shell, etc., and faunal remains, which were not modified except as a result of food processing. In addition to these categories of artifacts, remains from an unknown number of human burials were found. A summary of all these materials is given in Table 1.

A majority of the artifacts recovered from the Lower Rice Lake site are ceramic, including rim sherds, other decorated sherds, and undecorated body sherds. They represent several Middle and Late Woodland ceramic wares. Lithic artifacts, including tools and debitage, are much less common. The few typologically diagnostic lithic tools also indicate Middle and Late Woodland affiliation. The faunal sample includes a number of utilitarian and ornamental artifacts made from bone or antler. The rest of the faunal remains are bone and shell fragments representing various mammalian, avian, reptilian and molluscan taxa. Although most of the faunal sample was badly fragmented, six mammalian, three avian and one piscine species could be identified (Table 2). Charcoal samples (one of which was dated), a few pieces of burned clay and a few historic period artifacts constitute the remainder of the sample from the site. Although most of the human remains

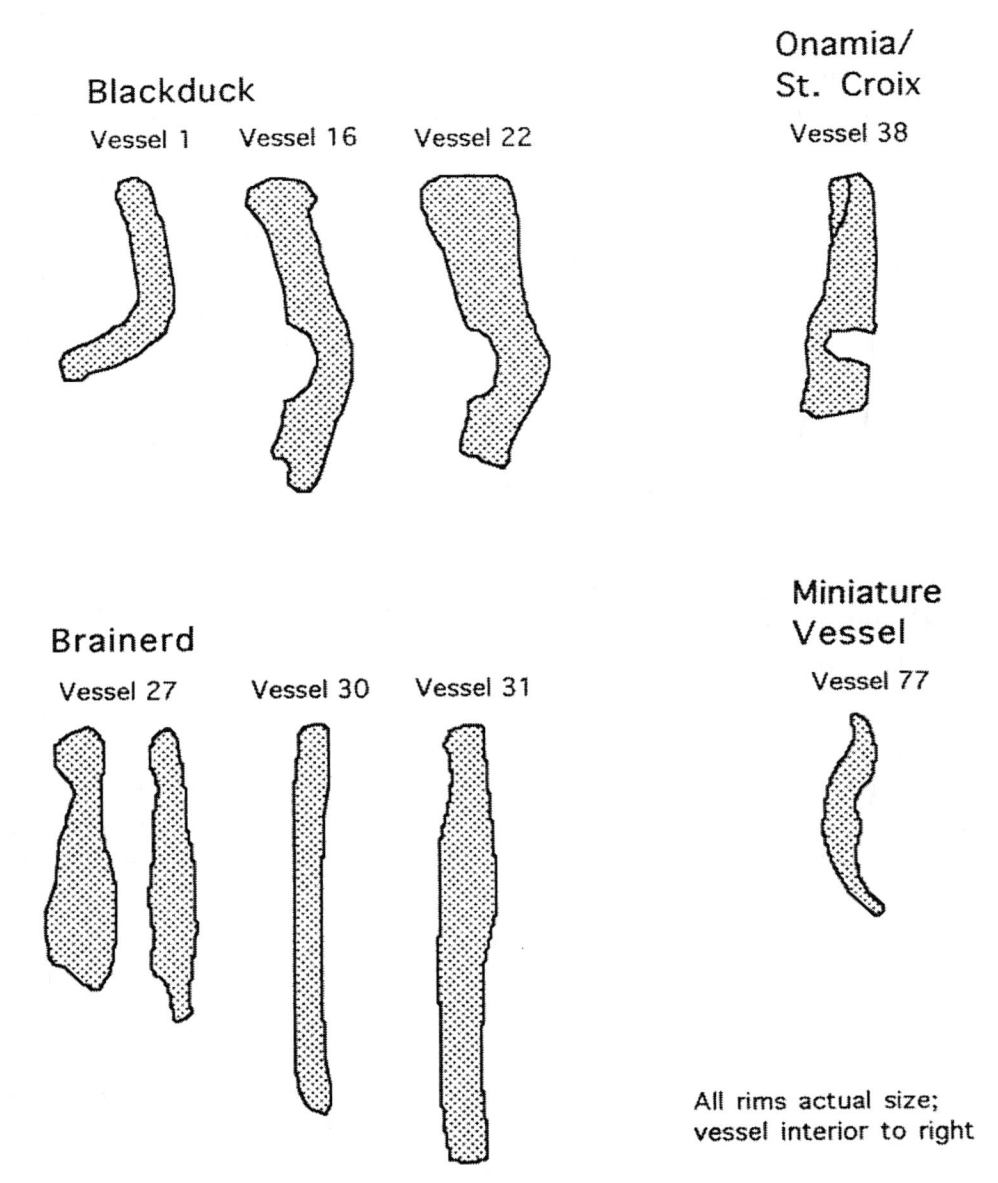

Figure 15. Selected rimsherd profiles, 21CE5.

Blackduck: Vessel 1, Vessel 16, Vessel 22
Onamia/St. Croix: Vessel 38
Brainerd: Vessel 27, Vessel 30, Vessel 31
Miniature Vessel: Vessel 77

All rims actual size; vessel interior to right

from the site were never studied, the partial remains of one subadult individual are described below.

Ceramic Artifacts

Ceramics artifacts constitute the largest set of materials from the site (n=4,441, %=86.8). They include part of a miniature vessel, 203 rim sherds, a handle, and a few dozen other decorated sherds. The rest of the ceramic artifacts are undecorated body sherds. The analysis of these artifacts consisted of three basic steps: refitting; inventorying; and defining vessels, which were then assigned to specific ceramic wares and ware varieties. Based on this analysis, Sandy Lake and Blackduck wares are the most common; Brainerd and Onamia/St. Croix wares are also well represented. A Northeastern Plains Village ware or wares, not specifically identified, constitutes a minor component. Miniature vessels are also present. Some rims and decorated sherds and most of the undecorated body sherds could not be assigned to any specific ware. (Note that "vessel" in the following discussion is used in a conceptual rather than literal sense.)

Figure 16. Blackduck rimsherds, 21CE5 *(Top: Vessels 1, 2, 13; Middle: Vessels 3, 4, 21. Bottom: Vessels 5 [two*

Figure 17. Blackduck rimsherds, 21CE5 *(Top: Vessels 8, 23, 22, 10; Bottom: Vessels 16, 24, 15).*

Blackduck (n=26): The Blackduck ceramics from the Lower Rice Lake site are not well enough preserved to give a good indication of vessel form. All the Blackduck rim sherds are broken at or above the neck, and no mends were found between rim and body sherds. This also means that in most cases only partial decorative motifs are represented.

The lips on the Blackduck rims were flattened, and most lips were thickened. Many rims were also thickened. Lip orientation is difficult to establish in most cases because rim orientation is unclear. However, the lips seem to vary from outwardly beveled to straight. The rims are generally outflaring; rim angles could not be determined (Figs. 15-17). All the Blackduck vessels were grit-tempered.

The most common decorative elements on the Blackduck rim sherds were cord-wrapped object (CWO) impressions (n=26, %=100.0), punctates (n=16, %=61.5) and vertical brushing (n=4, %=15.4). Only 2 of the 26 vessels displayed other decorative elements. One vessel had a series of shallow, round impressions ("dimples") along the rim interior at the edge of the lip. The rim exterior was decorated with a series of marks impressed upward and into the rim just below the lip. The implement used to create these impressions does not appear to be a CWO. This vessel is also unusual in that the lip was partly smoothed and partly treated with oblique CWO impressions. On another vessel, the thickened part of the lip on the rim interior was impressed with a series of drag or push marks. The tool used to create these marks apparently had a straight, irregular edge; the striations created by the lateral movement of the object are clearly visible.

Decoration on the rim interior was observed on only five vessels. The lip was smooth and undecorated on three vessels. The remaining vessels all had some form of CWO decoration on the lip. Decoration to the rim exterior consisted most commonly of oblique over horizontal CWO impressions. In 15 vessels this also included a row of punctates. In addition, there were a number of decorated sherds that were not substantial enough to permit definition and description of a separate vessel, but that appeared to be from Blackduck vessels.

Blackduck ceramics are found throughout the site, although no vessels were defined for Unit 11 and only four characteristic Blackduck sherds were found in the unit. Blackduck was also more common in Unit 8 than in the rest of the site, constituting close to half the defined vessels in that unit.

Brainerd Ware (n=5): The Brainerd vessels identified at the Lower Rice Lake site are not well enough

Figure 18. Brainerd rimsherds and decorated bodysherd, 21CE5 *(Top Row: Vessel 27 [all sherds]; Middle Row: Vessels 27 [two sherds], 28, decorated body sherd; Bottom Row: Vessels 30, 31).*

preserved to give a good indication of vessel form. The Lower Rice Lake vessels thin toward the lip; the point of maximum thickness or the degree of variation in thickness of the vessel wall cannot be determined (Figs. 15, 18). All vessels are grit-or sand-tempered. Both varieties of Brainerd Ware - Horizontally Corded and Net Impressed - were represented by rims, decorated sherds and body sherds. In Feature 15, both varieties of Brainerd Ware were found in a common context in association with turtle remains. Out of a total of 401 Brainerd sherds, 62 percent (n=249) were net-impressed and 38 percent (n=152) were horizontally corded. This includes 3 net-impressed and 11 horizontally cordmarked rim sherds. Altogether, Brainerd sherds account for about 9 percent of the sherds from the site.

There appear to be some differences between the vessels of the two Brainerd Ware varieties at the Lower Rice Lake site, both in terms of vessel construction and decorative treatment. All three of the defined Brainerd Horizontally Corded vessels share a casual lip treatment. Lip finishing appears to be limited to cursory flattening or smoothing, with little attention given to producing a regular, consistent form. The lip is generally thicker than the adjacent body wall, onto which it overlaps in an irregular fashion. The lip may be beveled, rounded or flattened, apparently all on the same vessel. Observed thickness ranges from 3 mm (just below the lip) to 8 mm. Cordmarking on these vessels is horizontal to oblique in relationship to the lip. The exact orientation seems to vary somewhat on a single vessel. Of the three horizontally corded vessels, two are undecorated. The other is decorated with a row of angular punctates placed a little more than a centimeter below the lip. A decorated body sherd preserves part of a broad trailed line.

The two net-impressed vessels represented give the impression of being more carefully made than the horizontally cordmarked vessels. The lips are more carefully finished and the body wall thickness more uniform. In addition, the decoration on one vessel is carefully executed and more complex than the extant motifs on the horizontally corded vessels. The decoration occurs just below the lip. There is first a series of impressions created by pushing a small, round object (possibly a stick) upward and diagonally toward the lip. These impressions are round in cross section, approximately 2 mm wide, and spaced 6 to 7 mm apart. Below each diagonal mark, a circle has been impressed onto the

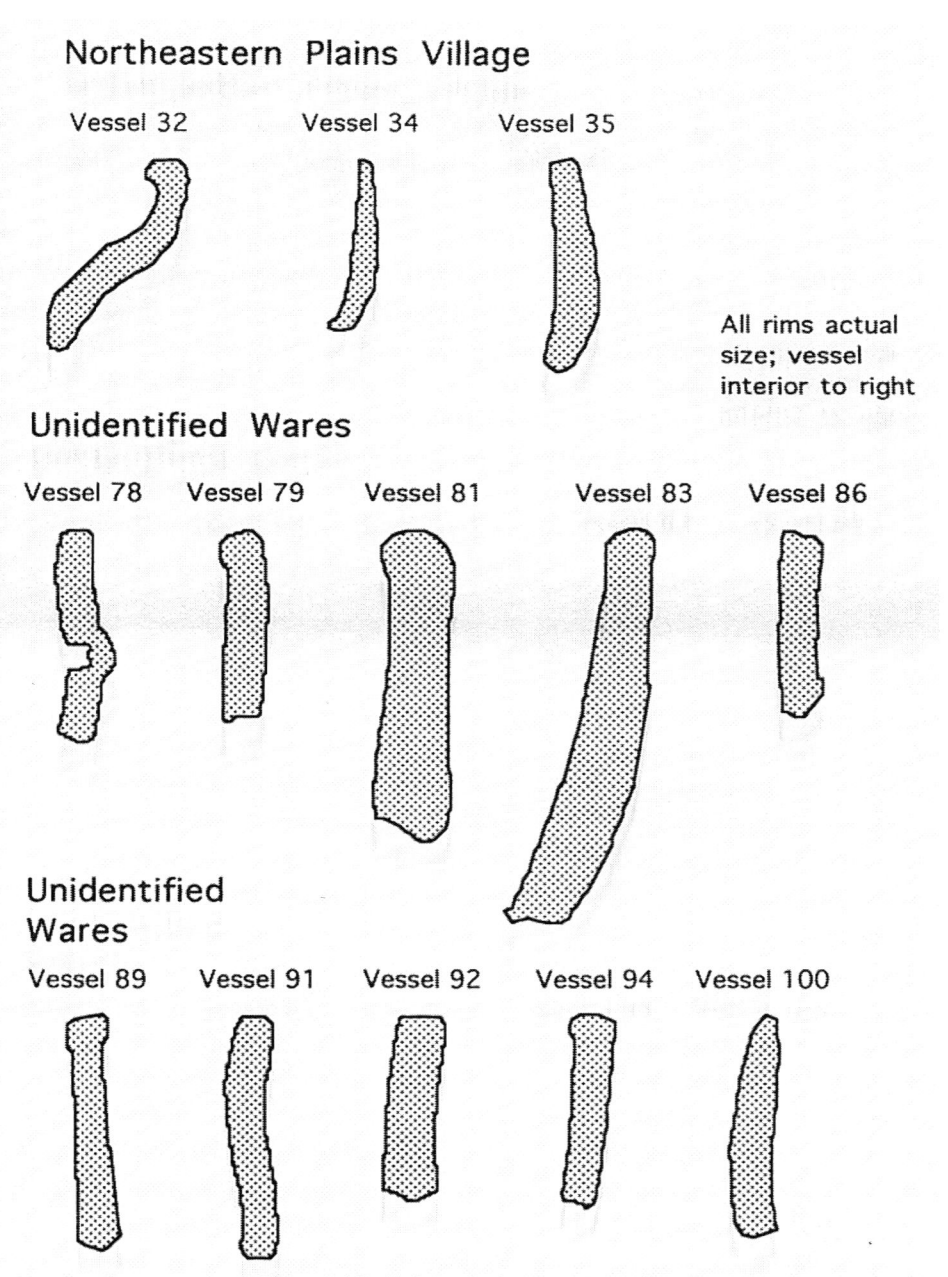

Figure 19. Selected rimsherd profiles, 21CE5.

vessel surface. These marks appear to have been created with the end of a hollow tube, such as a small bone or a reed. The circles are approximately 4 mm in diameter and spaced 6 to 7 mm apart.

Defined Brainerd Ware vessels are found only in Units 2 and 8, although horizontally cordmarked and net-impressed sherds occur throughout the site (except Unit 7, where only three sherds were found). The Brainerd Ware body sherds are fairly evenly distributed across the site, except in Unit 8, where horizontally cordmarked sherds are relatively more abundant.

A number of rims from the site resemble Brainerd vessels in terms of form and paste but are smooth-surfaced. These may still be from Brainerd vessels, given the fact that the upper part of the rim on the Langer site vessel appears to have been smoothed (Neumann 1978:60). This association is not, however, strong enough to allow these rim sherds to define Brainerd Ware vessels.

Figure 20. Northeastern Plains Village rimsherds, 21CE5 *(Top: Vessels 32, 36, handle; Bottom: Vessels 35, 34).*

Figure 21. Northeastern Plains Village bodysherds, 21CE5 *(Decorated bodysherds - vessels not defined).*

Northeastern Plains Village Ceramics (n=5): The Northeastern Plains Village vessels identified at the Lower Rice Lake site are not well enough preserved to give a good indication of vessel form. It may be noted that the lip on one vessel is rolled to the exterior at an abrupt, near 90 degree angle; the juncture between rim and shoulder is also sharp (Figs. 19-21). There is also a loop handle.

Decorative elements on the defined vessels included broad trailed lines, narrower incised lines, possible fingernail impressions and broad, shallow punctates. On some sherds, these lines intersect at a 90 degree or near 90 degree angle. Three sherds have fragments of compound motifs consisting of chevrons of small, shallow punctates or impressions (2 to 3 mm across) combined with lines or other design elements (cf. Peterson 1979:42-43; Anfinson 1979b:160). Another sherd has a compound design consisting of multiple impressions of an unidentified tool in a row-and-column array. The loop handle has at least two parallel, incised vertical lines. It is also interesting to note that the interior of one vessel preserves a partial fingerprint. It is not possible to determine the ratio of shell to grit tempering in this ware at Lower Rice Lake. Shell temper also occurs in smooth-surfaced Sandy Lake Ware, and there does not appear to be any way to assign undecorated, smooth-surfaced sherds to one ware or the other.

Some of the decorated, shell-tempered, smooth-surfaced ceramics included in this category could be more closely related to Oneota ceramics. They do not, however, seem to resemble the predominantly shell-tempered Ogechie series, which "represent the farthest northern known extent of Oneota ceramics in Minnesota" (Ready and Anfinson 1979:143). Therefore the ceramics of this type that occur at Lower Rice Lake are grouped under a Northeastern Plains Village ceramic category, which includes both grit- and shell-tempered vessels.

The distribution of these sherds across the site is unclear, because of the overlap in characteristics with smooth surfaced Sandy Lake sherds. Clear examples of Northeastern Plains Village sherds were found, however, in Units 2, 3, 8 and 11.

Onamia / St. Croix (n=3). There were only three definable Onamia/St. Croix vessels at the Lower Rice Lake site, together with three decorated body sherds that could not be assigned to any of the defined vessels (Figs. 15, 22). The vessels come from Units 2, 3 and 11; the other sherds come from Unit 3 and the surface collection. The Onamia/St. Croix vessels from the Lower Rice Lake site are fragmentary. Little can be deduced about vessel form, overall sur-

Figure 22. Onamia/St. Croix rimsherds and decorated bodysherds, 21CE5 (Top: Vessels 39, 38, 37; Bottom: Decorated bodysherds, vessels not defined).

face treatment, or total decorative motif. Decorative elements include large dentate stamping, comb stamping, and use of a CWO. All three of these vessels exhibit rows of horizontal impressions; two also exhibit "crimping" of the lip created by making impressions on both the lip interior and exterior.

The defined Onamia/St. Croix vessels come from Units 3 and 11. Decorated Onamia/St. Croix body sherds come from Unit 3 and the surface. The complete distribution of Onamia/St. Croix body sherds across the site cannot be tracked because it is not possible to consistently distinguish undecorated sherds of this ware from other undecorated, grit-tempered and cordmarked body sherds originating with other wares.

Sandy Lake Ware (n=35). At the Lower Rice Lake site, surface treatment on Sandy Lake sherds included examples of cordmarking, smoothing and stamping. On the defined vessels cordmarking was most common (n=30), with a few examples of smooth-surfaced (n=5) or check-stamped vessels (n=2). Simple-stamped body sherds also occur, but the sample was not adequate to define any vessels. The cordmarking on Sandy Lake vessels ranged from fine, generally parallel cordmarking to broad, parallel cordmarking, to indistinct patterning where individual cords could not be discerned. The latter surface treatment might be called "fabric impressions" by some investigators.

Undoubtedly many of the cordmarked and smooth-surfaced body sherds from this site come from Sandy Lake vessels. With the exception of shell-tempered, cordmarked body sherds, it is essentially impossible to associate most of these sherds with Sandy Lake.

The stamped sherds from the Lower Rice Lake site include examples of both checked and simple-stamped treatment, although the latter predominates. A total of 151 stamped sherds were found. They constitute 1 to 4 percent of the total ceramics everywhere in the site except Unit 11, where they constitute 11 percent.

In general, the Sandy Lake vessels are more complete than vessels of the other wares. In the case of the cordmarked variety, some substantial portions of vessel profiles were reconstructed. These include rims that provide a profile for the entire upper portion of a vessel, and large sections from the body of a shell-tempered, cordmarked vessel that do not articulate with shoulder or rim (e.g., Figs. 23-29). Although the evidence is not conclusive, it appears to support a globular shape for these vessels, as seen in more complete vessels from other sites. Two

Sandy Lake

Vessel 40 Vessel 44 Vessel 46 Vessel 61 Vessel 71 Vessel 72 Vessel 73

Sandy Lake

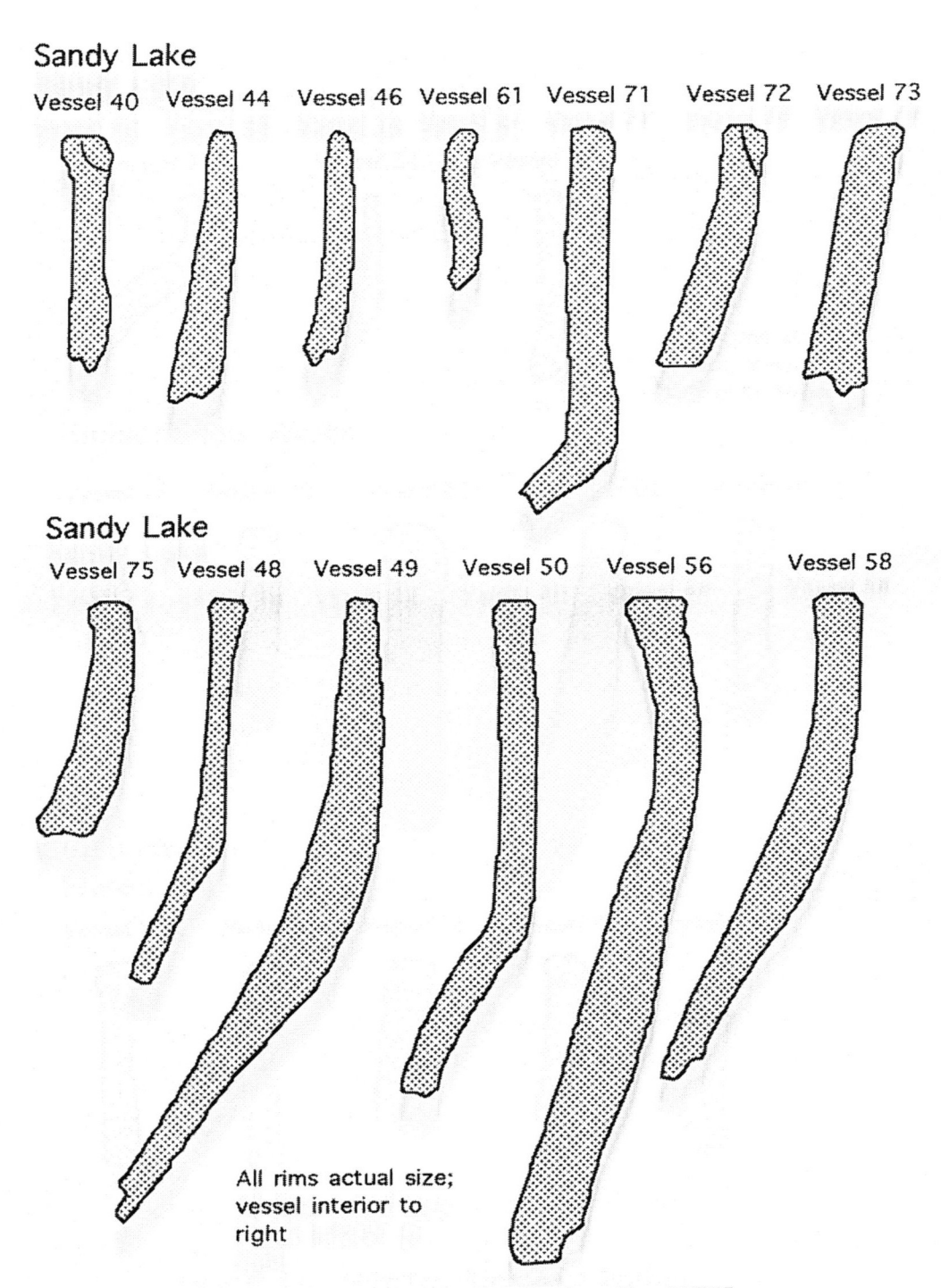

Vessel 75 Vessel 48 Vessel 49 Vessel 50 Vessel 56 Vessel 58

All rims actual size; vessel interior to right

Figure 23. Selected rimsherd profiles, 21CE5.

variations on the globular form are indicated by rim sections. In the first, the rim is generally short (up to 3 cm) and contracts slightly toward the lip. It meets the body of the vessel in a smooth curve. The vessel wall is often thickened at this point, producing a distinct ridge on the vessel interior. This is the "classic" Sandy Lake vessel form. In the second variation, the rim is straight, has a vertical orientation, and is relatively high. It meets the body of the vessel in a distinct angle, and the vessel wall thick-

Figure 24. Sandy Lake Smooth and Stamped rimsherds, 21CE5 *(Top: Vessels 40 [two sherds], 44; Bottom L: Vessel 46 [five sherds]; Bottom R: Vessel 45).*

Figure 25. Sandy Lake Cordmarked rimsherds, 21CE5 *(Top: Vessel 47 [three sherds]; Middle: Vessel 47 [four sherds]; Bottom: Vessel 48 [five sherds]).*

ness is more uniform. This vessel form is reminiscent of Onamia/St. Croix. In addition, bowl-shaped Sandy Lake vessels may also be present (cf. Cooper and Johnson 1964:477). Such vessels can constrict slightly toward the lip, but lack a shoulder or neck. The evidence for this latter vessel form is somewhat tenuous, consisting of small rim sherds with a clear inward curvature. However, some more substantial sections of Sandy Lake rims indicate that such a curvature may also occur on larger, necked vessels.

One vessel displays a variation on rim form, a compound, s-shaped curve (Figs. 23, 29). In this vessel, the upper rim portion is somewhat convex, and the lower rim portion is slightly concave (defined in reference to the exterior). Cooper and Johnson, in their original definition of Sandy Lake Ware, note the occurrence of "what may best be termed an incipient S-curvature" in the sample of Sandy Lake rims from the Scott (21CA1) and Fickle (47BT25) sites (Cooper and Johnson 1964:475-476). Another example occurs at the Mooney site (21NR29) (Michlovic 1987:50).

Decoration on the Sandy Lake vessels from this site consists almost exclusively of notching applied to the lip interior or, less commonly, directly onto the lip. Most of these notches are plain-surfaced and relatively broad; in a few cases, these notches were made with a CWO. Eleven of the cordmarked Sandy Lake vessels have interior lip notching, and three have notches impressed onto the lip surface. Of these, two vessels have CWO notches, both on the lip interior. All the smooth surfaced Sandy Lake vessels are decorated with smooth notches impressed onto the lip interior. None of the stamped Sandy Lake vessels have any decoration.

Vessel 71 has decorations applied to the rim interior some distance below the lip, just above the juncture of rim and body. These consist of linear impressions arranged to form upward pointing triangles (∧ ∧). This vessel also has a crenelated lip, created by deep notches impressed downward into the lip. The rim is tall and straight, the paste more massive and friable, and there is an angular juncture between rim and body (Figs. 23, 28). Although none of these characteristics is unusual for Sandy Lake Ware, the total effect is quite unlike typical Sandy Lake.

Both grit and shell temper occur in the Sandy Lake ceramics at the Lower Rice Lake site. Their relative

Figure 26. Sandy Lake Cordmarked rimsherds, 21CE5 *(Left: Vessel 49; Right: Vessel 50 [two sherds, exterior and interior]).*

Figure 27. Sandy Lake Cordmarked rimsherds, 21CE5 *(Left: Vessel 56; Right: Vessel 58).*

abundance cannot be determined, however. In part this is because the shell has apparently been leached out of many sherds, at least near the surface. In most cases, shell tempering could only be seen in sherds with a fresh break; as discussed above, sherds were only called "shell tempered" where this characteristic could be directly observed. In addition, shell temper also occurs in smooth-surfaced Northeastern Plains Village vessels, and there does not appear to be any way to assign undecorated, smooth-surfaced sherds to one or the other ware.

Defined Sandy Lake vessels occur throughout the site, although they are relatively less common in Unit 8. The total distribution of Sandy Lake body sherds through the site is difficult to determine. Although shell-tempered, cordmarked sherds are probably associated with Sandy Lake, they are difficult to track because of the often stated difficulty in accurately discerning shell temper. Check- and simple-stamped sherds, presumed to be Sandy lake, are more easily tracked. They also occur in small percentages throughout the site, except for Unit 11, where they constitute over 10 percent of all sherds.

Miniature Vessels (n=1): One partial miniature vessel was recovered from 21CE5 (Figs. 15, 30). It has an estimated height of 32 to 34 mm and a maximum diameter (on the body below the shoulder) of 25 to 30 mm. Thickness varies from 1 to 4 mm. The surface is smooth, and there does not appear to be any temper. The vessel is undecorated. It has a globular shape, gradually rounded shoulder, and a slightly outflaring rim. It appears to be pinched out of a lump of clay.

Other fragments that appear to be from similar miniature vessels were found in Units 2 and 3.

Unidentified Ware Vessels (n=31): A number of vessels were defined and described, but could not comfortably be assigned to established ceramic wares (Figs. 19, 30, 31). Some of these definitions were based on small or poorly preserved sherds. In a few cases, however, the remains were more complete but did not seem to fit within established ceramic categories. They vary in form, and include one possible bowl. Decorations include punctates,

Figure 28. Sandy Lake Cordmarked rimsherds, 21CE5 *(Left: Vessel 71; Center: Vessel 51; Right: Vessel 73).*

Figure 29. Sandy Lake Cordmarked rimsherds, 21CE5 *(Top: Vessel 74 [two sherds], 75 [two sherds]; Bottom: Vessels 52, 61, 72).*

bosses and CWO impressions. Additional detail is provided in the full length report (Bakken 1994).

Body Sherds (n=4,237): Body sherds were categorized by surface treatment and type of temper. Grouped by surface treatment, the majority were cordmarked (n=2,331, %=55.0), with smaller amounts of smooth-surfaced (n=694, %=16.4), net-impressed (n=247, %=5.8), horizontally cordmarked (n=141, %=3.3), stamped (n=147, %=3.5), and indeterminate-surface (n=677, %=16.0) sherds. Considered by temper, grit was the most common (n=3,392, %=80.1), followed by shell (n=332, %=7.8). Indeterminate temper sherds account for the rest of the sample (n=513, %=12.1). As discussed above, many of these were probably shell-tempered, although the shell was not directly observable. It is unlikely, however, that all the indeterminate temper sherds were shell-tempered. Thus the occurrence of shell tempering in ceramics at the Lower Rice Lake site can be said to be somewhere between 8 percent and 20 percent; an estimate of 15 percent is proposed.

Three surface treatments can be identified with specific wares: net-impressed (n=249, %=6) and horizontally cordmarked (n=141, %=3.3) sherds are associated with Brainerd Ware, and stamped sherds (n=147, %=3.5) are associated with Sandy Lake. Correlating surface treatment and temper allows a few other sherds to be associated with specific wares. Cordmarked, shell-tempered sherds (n=280, %=6.6) most likely come from Sandy Lake Ware vessels. This accounts for a little more than 12 percent of the body sherds. The remaining 88 percent cannot be associated with any specific wares. This information is summarized in Table 3.

Lithic Artifacts

Lithic artifacts constitute a relatively small percentage of the materials from the site (n=204, %= 3.9). Of this total, 34 pieces are tools, ranging from formal patterned tools such as projectile points to nonpatterned, expedient tools such as retouched flakes. Only six of these, all projectile points, could be considered diagnostic. The remainder of the lithic artifacts are pieces of flaking debris. In terms of raw materials the sample displays a typical diversity for the region, including at least a dozen different local and nonlocal silicates. Analysis of the flaking debris suggests some procurement and reduc-

Figure 30. Unidentified ware rimsherds and miniature vessel, 21CE5 *(Top: Vessels 91, 86, 80; Center: Vessels 88, 90; Bottom: Vessels 81, 92, 77 [two sherds]).*

Figure 31. Unidentified ware rimsherds, 21CE5 *(Top: Vessels 78 [two sherds], 98, 100; Middle: Vessels 89 [two sherds], 108, 83; Bottom: Vessels 79, 94.)*

tion of cobbles at the site, probably on an opportunistic basis. This may have included heat treatment.

Projectile Points (n=6): Four of the six projectile points are the small, triangular form typical of those found in Late Woodland sites throughout Minnesota and the upper Midwest (Fig. 32). Three are made of Swan River Chert and one of Red River Chert. They range in length from 15 to 22 mm (although the tip is missing from two specimens). The sides are convex and the bases are slightly concave.

The fifth projectile point is a small, corner-notched specimen made of rhyolite. The point is 25 mm in length. The tip is blunt and the sides are convex. The notches are broad, relatively shallow, and taper to the corner of the base. The neck width between the notches is 12 mm. The base, though damaged, appears to be straight, has been thinned on one side, and is almost as wide as the proximal end of the blade. Except for the lack of basal grinding, this point generally resembles the Besant points described by Kehoe (1974) for the Northern Plains and adjacent woodlands. (This type is also known as Anderson Corner Notched [MacNeish 1958].) In the plains sites that Kehoe (1974:109) examined, this type of point was dated "from probably the time of Christ to about A.D. 400." Similar points, from Middle Plains Woodland sites in southeastern North Dakota, are illustrated by Gregg and Picha (1989:43, 51, 54). The dates for these components range from 2035 $\pm$ 70 to 1760 $\pm$ 200 B.P. (85 BC to A.D. 190). The sixth projectile point is a small side-notched specimen made of Red River Chert. The sides are convex and the base may be slightly convex. It measures 32 mm in length, 17 mm in width and 4 mm in thickness. Damage to this point has obscured the diagnostic details of its morphology, and no typological comparison is attempted.

Knives (n=2): There are two stone knives from the site, both made of Swan River Chert. The smaller specimen, measuring 33 mm in length, has one concave and one strongly concave side. The larger specimen, measuring 45 mm in length, has one slightly convex and one strongly convex side (Fig. 32).

Generalized Bifaces and Biface Fragments (n=6). : There are also six generalized bifaces or biface fragments. Raw materials include Red River Chert (n=3), Swan River Chert (n=2) and Knife River Flint (n=1).

Scrapers (n=12): A total of 12 scrapers or scraper fragments were found at the site (Fig. 33). These include side scrapers (n=2), end scrapers (n=5), double side scrapers (n=1), side-end scrapers (n=2), an irregularly shaped scraper, and a fragment of a scraper edge. One of these pieces has a moderate amount of bifacial retouch. The other nine scrapers have a plano-convex cross section; four have minor bifacial retouch on the ventral surface. One is manufactured from a cortical spall from a pebble. Raw materials represented include Red River Chert (n=5), silicified wood (n=2), Knife River Flint (n=1), Swan River Chert (n=2), and unidentified chert (n=2). In addition, there is a single, irregularly shaped piece of Knife River Flint with a short section of steep retouch on one side (Fig. 33). This edge may have been used for scraping.

Utilized and Retouched Flakes (n=6): The debitage sample included six flakes showing modification on one or more edges, either deliberate or resulting from use. Raw materials represented include Knife River Flint (n=2), rhyolite (n=2), Red River Chert (n=1), and Swan River Chert (n=1).

Lithic Debitage and Raw Materials: Only 170 pieces of lithic debitage were recovered from the Lower Rice Lake site. This is a small sample, considering that over 4,000 ceramic sherds were recovered. Because the sample is small, appeared to be generalized, and came from a number of components that could not be separated, a general analysis was applied to the assemblage. Each piece of debitage was characterized according to lithic raw material, presence or absence of cortex (the natural weathered surface of a cobble), and whether or not it had been heat-treated. This kind of analysis can provide a basic indication of what types of lithic reduction was carried on at the site, to what degree local materials were utilized, and how individual raw materials fit into this scenario.

The small size of the assemblage is in itself a significant point. This suggests that lithic procurement and initial reduction, a process that produces an abundance of debitage, was not a significant activity at the site. Instead, it would be expected that most of the flintknapping occurring at the site related to tool maintenance, or possibly to production of finished tools from preforms (partly completed, stylistically undistinguished tools). However, cortex was detected on 60 pieces of debitage, or 35 percent of the total. This is more than would be expected in an assemblage that was exclusively the result of tool maintenance; some element of procurement and initial reduction must be represented. Only three raw materials provide a large enough sample to make a significant comparison of the relative amount of cortex. For Red River Chert, 63 percent of the debitage exhibits cortex, for Swan River Chert this figure is 33 percent, and for Tongue River Silica 36 percent. These figures are all high enough to indicate that a few cobbles of all three of these materials may have been collected nearby and reduced at the site, probably on an opportunistic basis.

Heat treatment was detected on 81 pieces of debitage, or 48 percent of the total. Heat treatment could be dependably detected on four raw materials -- Red River Chert, Swan River Chert, Tongue River Silica and unidentified chert. The percentage of heat treatment varies among the materials. Swan River Chert (n=54, %=61.4) and Tongue River Silica (n=10, %=71.4) were highest; Red River chert was substantially lower (n=13, %=34.2). The sample of unidentified chert was too small to yield a significant percentage. Swan River Chert and Tongue River Silica are both marginal quality materials with difficult working properties; heat treatment was apparently frequently used to improve their working quality to an acceptable level. Red River Chert is generally a moderate to good quality material, not necessarily requiring heat treatment.

Locally available raw materials present include Swan River Chert (n=88), Red River Chert (n=38), possibly Tongue River Silica (n=14), quartz (n=17), quartzite (n=2), rhyolite (n=6), chalcedony (n=4), basalt (n=1) and silicified wood (n=2). These comprise about 85 percent of the total sample. Of this, Swan River Chert and Red River Chert alone comprise about 64 percent. These materials are also the most abundant of the locally available silicates (Bakken 1985). Nonlocal materials include Knife River Flint (n=4) and Gunflint Silica (n=4), totaling about 4 percent of the total sample. The primary source of Knife River Flint is in west central North Dakota (Clayton, Bickley and Stone 1970; Gregg 1987), although scattered, small cobbles are found

Table 3. Summary of Ceramic Bodysherds and Rimsherds by Surface Treatment and Temper, 21CE5

	Grit n	Grit %	Shell n	Shell %	Indet n	Indet %	Total n
Bodysherds							
Cordmarked	1,770	41.8	267	6.3	293	6.9	2,330
Smooth	626	14.8	22	0.5	46	1.1	694
Net Impressed	241	5.7	-	-	5	-	246
Horiz. Cordmark	138	3.3	1	-	2	-	141
Stamped	121	2.9	5	-	21	0.5	147
Indet.	494	11.7	37	0.8	146	3.4	677
Total	3,390		332		513		4,235
Rimsherds							
Cordmarked	55	27.1	13	6.4	19	9.4	87
Smooth	29	14.3	3	1.5	4	2.0	36
Net Impressed	3	1.5	-	-	-	-	3
Horiz. Cordmark	11	5.4	-	-	-	-	11
Stamped	2	1.0	1	0.5	1	0.5	4
Indet.	56	27.6	-	-	6	3.0	62
Total	156		17		30		203

Three ceramic objects are not included in these totals: a handle sherd, a partial miniature vessel, and a fragment from a clay elbow pipe.

Figure 32. Projectile points and other bifacial chipped stone tools, 21CE5.

Figure 33. Unifacial chipped stone tools, 21CE5.

in the southern half of Minnesota and in other parts of the Upper Midwest. KRF circulated widely in prehistory (cf. Clark 1984), and is common on sites in northwestern Minnesota. Gunflint Silica is available in northwestern Ontario and northeastern Minnesota, from both bedrock and drift sources (Romano 1991; A. Romano, personal communication 1993).

Lithic materials whose local availability is unclear include Knife Lake Siltstone (n=9) and unidentified cherts and other unidentified silicates (n=11), totaling about 12 percent of the sample. A previous survey of lithic raw material availability in northwestern Minnesota concluded that "siltstone" was locally available in the till (Bakken 1985). How-

ever, further study showed that the material was actually rhyolite. The availability of siltstone in northwestern Minnesota needs to be re-evaluated.

Faunal Artifacts

Although the collections at the site yielded a relatively small set of faunal remains, artifacts manufactured from bone, antler or other faunal elements were relatively abundant. This abundance may not truly be characteristic of the site. Over half of these objects come from a surface collection that was compiled over years, and that likely targeted such noticeable and interesting objects. The collection include both utilitarian and ornamental objects.

Of the 20 faunal artifacts from the site, 12 are made from split large mammal ribs and 1 from a large mammal rib that is not split. One artifact is a large mammal phalange that appears to have been carved to a point. A harpoon and two conical tools are carved from antler. One artifact is made from a bird long bone. The remaining object is fashioned from what may be a section of mammalian long bone. In addition, there was a bear canine that does not display obvious signs of deliberate modification. It is described in this section, however, because its presence on the site was likely related to its symbolic value; i.e., it is not believed to be the remains of a meal.

Awls (n=2): The first example is curved from end to end. It tapers evenly from base to point. Polish is apparent for 2 cm back from tip. There are lines incised on the dorsal (bone exterior) surface, but these appear to be incidental. The base does not appear broken, but is unfinished. The awl measures 140 by 9 by 2 mm. It is made from a section of split large mammal rib, and comes from the surface collection (Fig. 34). The second awl is almost flat end to end. One end is broken. There is damage to the tip, and the ventral (bone interior) surface is spalling off near the tip. Polish is apparent along about half of one edge. The awl measures 121 by 10 by 3 mm. It is made from a section of split large mammal rib, and comes from the surface collection (Fig. 34). Awls of this form are not uncommon on Late Woodland sites in this region.

Arm Band Fragments (n=5): Five fragments of carved band, such as might be worn around the wrist, were recovered at the site. Four of the fragments conjoin. They represent most of a tapered band that has been bent at a relatively sharp angle toward one end. The band has a uniform width of 17 mm near the middle and tapers to 7 mm at the intact end. One end is broken; the other end is straight rather than curved, and bent downward. A small hole (2 mm) has also been drilled through the band near this end. The extant, reconstructed portion of the band measures 92 by 17 by 2 mm. It is made from a split large mammal rib. One of the fragments came from Unit 3, Level 2, and three from the surface collection (Fig. 35). The fifth band fragment is apparently part of a different band. Part of a small drilled hole is preserved on one broken end. It is generally similar to the band described above. The band measures 27 by 12 by 2 mm. It is made from a split large mammal rib (Fig. 35). This fragment came from Unit 3, Feature 10. More complete examples of this kind of bone band are seen at the Haarstad (21MA6), De Spiegler (39RO23), Wilson (21TR2) and Arvilla (32GF1) sites (Johnson 1973:76). *Conical Tools (n=2).* One of the semiconical tools has a flattened facet on one side at the tip. The facet measures 50 mm back from the tip, with a maximum width of about 18 mm. The entire tip of the tool, including the facet, shows polish. The other end is unfinished or possibly broken. This object is 104 mm long, has a diameter of 26 mm, and is made of antler (Fig. 34). It came from the surface collection. The second conical tool may be an antler tip. Deterioration of the specimen, however, makes this identification uncertain. Most of the surface has spalled off, precluding any observation of wear patterns. The base may be socketed. This object is 107 mm long, and has a diameter of 16 mm (Fig. 34). It came from the surface collection. Conical antler tools are occasionally found in sites in the region, although they are not common. Johnson (1973:78 - Plate 28f) describes examples from the Lake Bronson (21KT1) and Arvilla (32GF1) sites, which he considers to be flaking tools.

Harpoon (n=1): This unilaterally barbed harpoon is carved from antler. There are six barbs along one side, and a notch carved near the base on the same side. The entire surface appears to have been carved. The base and tip are slightly damaged. This object measures 122 by 11 by 6 mm (Fig. 35). It came from the surface collection. Antler harpoons have been found at a number of sites in the region (e.g., Johnson 1973:11, 63-64, 78; Stoltman 1973:106). None of the examples that were noted, however, bear a strong resemblance to this piece.

Shaft Straightener (n=1): This is a fragment of a large mammal rib, broken at both ends, with a hole 11 mm in diameter drilled through the rib. Both ends are damaged. This object measures 244 by 29 by 11 mm (Fig. 36). It came from the surface collection. Such implements are sometimes called "shaft straighteners," based on the interpretation that they were used as "wrenches" for straightening arrow shafts.

Spatulate Tool (n=1): This flat tool may be divided into blade and tang. Approximately one-third of the length is blade; the remainder is tang. The blade is broadest near its base, and has an slightly excurvate taper to the tip. The back edge is straight for the entire length of the tool. The edges are damaged but both ends are present. This object measures 151 by 25 by 2 mm, and is made from a flat section from the side of a split large mammal rib (Fig. 34). It came from the surface collection.

Decorated Bone Objects (n=3): Several worked bone objects were not sufficiently complete to indicate their overall shape and function. The first is incised with four diagonal lines spaced 11 to 22 mm apart. One end is rounded, the other missing. The width is uniform for most of the length but tapers near the ends. This object measures 76 by 9 by 2 mm (Fig. 35). It is made from split rib, and came from the surface collection. A second object has two adjacent points or crenelations on one side, near the midpoint. There are X marks incised across the surface of the band near each end, followed by diagonal lines nearer the end. The width is uniform except for tapering near the end. One end is angled and beveled, the other end is missing. This object measures 126 by 10 by 3 mm (Fig. 35). It is made of split rib, and came from the surface collection. Another fragment has two notches carved into one edge, spaced 3 mm apart, and three notches carved into the other edge, 2 and 3 mm apart. This object measures 21 by 12 by 2 mm. It is made of split rib, and came from Unit 3, Level 2.

Other Worked Bone (n=4): The first object is a flat piece of bone, one side of which shows the cancellous interior. One edge is roughly finished, and one end is rounded and polished. This object measures 137 by 20 by 5 mm. It may be a section from a mammalian long bone. It came from the surface collection. A second object is a carved bone "band," which has a uniform width along most of its length, then tapers near the ends. The ends are rounded. There is intermittent polish along one edge. This object measures 236 by 13 by 2 mm. It is probably a split section of mammalian rib. It came from the surface collection. A third object appears to be some kind of mammalian phalange that has been carved to a point (Fig. 35). This object measures 41 by 17 by 10 mm. It came from Unit 3, Level 3. There is also part of a large avian long bone that has been carved (Fig. 35). Both ends are broken. This piece is comparable in size and morphology with the unmodified possible swan long bone also found at the site. The modified long bone measures 57 by 15 by 1 mm. It came from the surface collection.

The fragments of turtle plastron that were recovered from Feature 15, most of which articulate, are probably worked. There are striations on the external surface, running longitudinally (front to back), that appear to be deliberate. In addition, the absence of the carapace suggests that this was deliberately placed, rather than being a natural taphonomic assemblage.

Bear Canine (n=1): A single bear canine was recovered from Unit 3, Level 5. There are no obvious signs of alteration, such as drilling or grooving to facilitate mounting or suspension. Bear canines are not uncommon in sites in this region, although they are usually modified with notches or perforations so they could be suspended from a cord (e.g., Johnson 1973:81; Wilford 1970:30). A possible occurrence of other unmodified bear canines comes from a burial context at the De Spiegler site (39RO23) (Johnson 1973:56).

Faunal Remains

A total of 442 bone, antler, tooth or other faunal remains were collected from the Lower Rice Lake site (including the 20 faunal artifacts discussed above). Most of these pieces were badly fragmented. As a result, only a few could be identified to the level of genus and species. In many cases it was possible to determine whether these fragments were mammalian (n=209, %=47.3), avian (n=27, %=6.1), reptilian (n=31, %=7.0) or piscine (n=6, %=1.4). In other cases even this marginal identification was not possible; these fragments are classified only as vertebrate (n=167, %=37.8). In addition, two fragments of clam shell were recovered. No diagnostic morphology was present on the shell fragments, and identification of genus and species was not possible.

Species that could be confidently identified are listed in Table 2. A minimum number of individuals was not calculated because the sample of identifiable elements was so small. Other types of animals that could not be as specifically identified included swan (n=1), weasel or mink (*Mustela* sp.) (n=1), rat or gopher (n=1), bear (*Ursus* sp.) (n=1), unidentified species of turtle (n=2), unidentified species of duck (n=2), and possibly muskrat (*Ondatra zibethicus*) (n=1). Identifications were made using the comparative osteological collection at the Minnesota Historical Society.

Even though *Ursus americanus* is the only species of bear known to be native to the area, the bear canine is not assigned to this species. Jones and Birney (1988:302) say that although the grizzly bear "does not now occur in the north-central states and perhaps never did," they note that "there is, however, a questionable record from the Sandhill River, Polk County, north-western Minnesota, dating from 1807. *U. arctos* is known certainly to have occurred in adjacent North Dakota." In addition, *U. arctos* has been identified at archaeological sites in this part of the state (e.g., Anfinson, Michlovic and Stein 1978:33).

Some bone from the site was burned (n=54) or calcined (n=48). This amounts to 23 percent of the faunal remains. Considered by class, 16 percent of mammalian, 16 percent of avian and

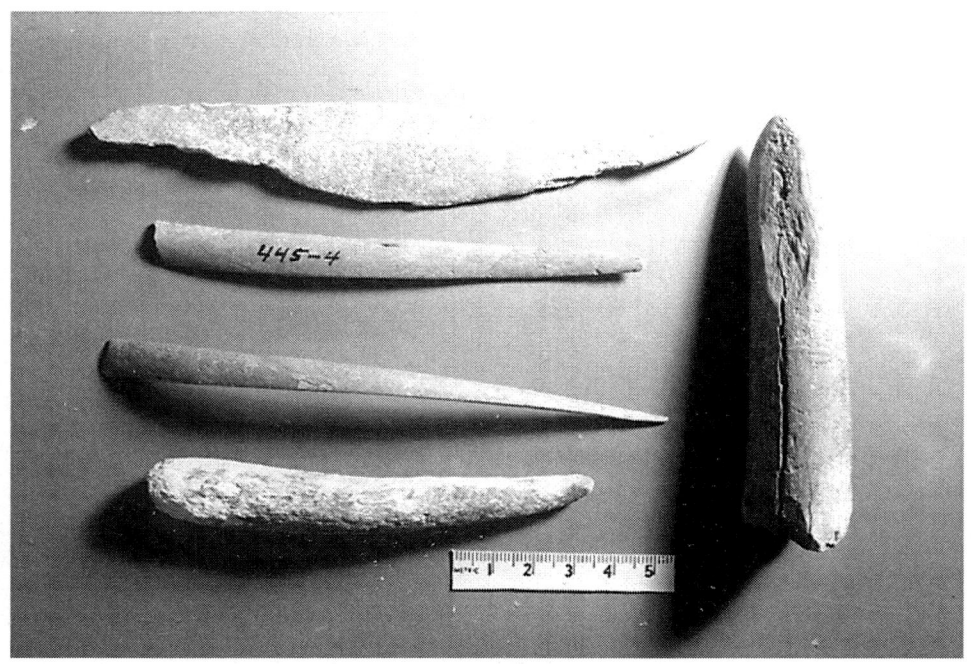

Figure 34. Faunal artifacts, 21CE5.

38 percent of vertebrate bone fragments were burned or calcined. None of the identified reptilian or piscine bone was burned or calcined.

There was no clear pattern to the general stratigraphic or horizontal disposition of identified faunal elements. The lack of bird bone in Unit 8 may be significant, although given the size of the sample from the unit (n=49) this cannot be stated with confidence. The only clear association of faunal remains with other artifacts was in Feature 15, where fragments of turtle shell and bone were found in a pit with fragments of at least three Brainerd Ware vessels.

Botanical Samples

The botanical samples from the site consisted exclusively of charcoal samples recovered from excavated contexts (Features 6, 14, and 15). No taxonomic identification was attempted. Only one sample, found in Feature 15 in association with Brainerd ceramics and turtle remains, had a context that was felt to justify the expense of radiocarbon dating. The results of this assay are examined below. Although dates on the remaining charcoal samples could help to delimit the period of site habitation, their contexts do not provide clear associations with specific components.

Historic Artifacts

Only six historic period artifacts were identified in the collection from the site. These included four pieces of steel and two bone fragments that had flat, striated ends indicating they had been cut with a modern saw. These six artifacts were used primarily to evaluate stratigraphy and recent disturbance. Because the site is actively utilized up to the present time, these artifacts could date anywhere in the period from initial Euroamerican settlement to the time they were collected in 1965. No other interpretation of these historic artifacts is advanced.

Other Materials

Clay Elbow Pipe (n=1). A fragment of a clay elbow pipe was recovered from Unit 3. This portion comes from near the elbow, displays parts of both the interior and exterior surfaces, and has no decoration. The elbow of the pipe appears to be curved rather than angular (Fig. 37). The overall form cannot be reconstructed from this fragment. It may have resembled the pipe from Christensen Mound 1 (21SH1) (Wilford, Johnson and Vicinus 1969:14-15, 58), which also has a rounded elbow.

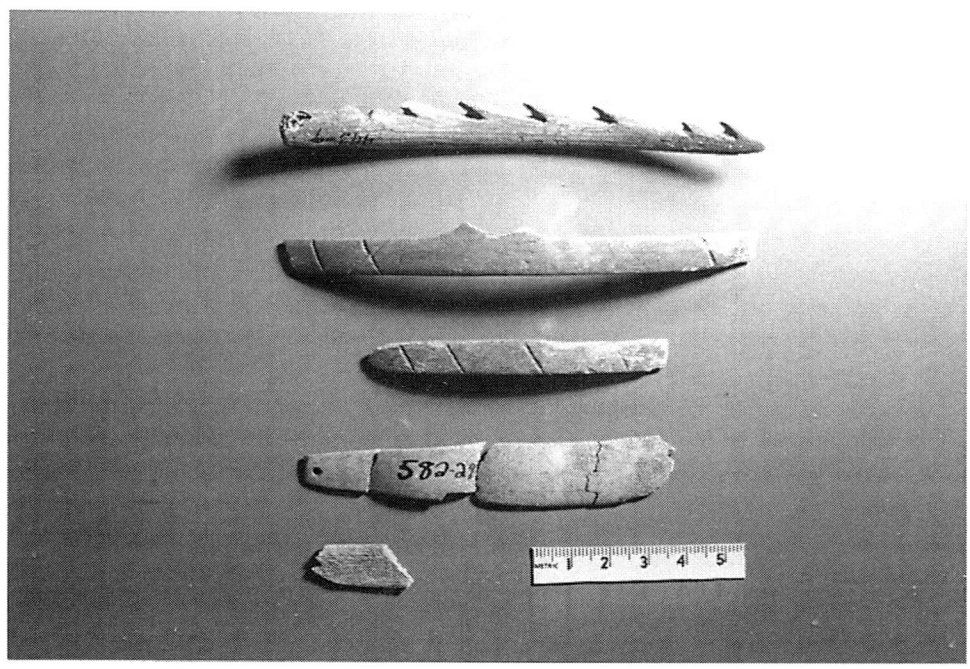

Figure 35. Faunal artifacts, 21CE5.

Pipestone Tube Pipe (n=1). A complete pipestone pipe was recovered from Unit 11, Level 4. This pipe is in the form of a straight tube 41 mm in length (Fig. 37). The diameter is 17 mm at both ends. The pipe contracts to a diameter of 13 mm at a point approximately one-third of the way along its length. The bore also narrows at this point. The pipe is very symmetrical and carefully thinned. The entire exterior surface exhibits longitudinal striations, understood to be carving marks. It generally resembles an ethnographic example illustrated by Murray (1962:plate 1, no. 2).

Hammerstone (n=2): The remaining stone tool from the site is a modified basalt cobble. It is either a hammerstone that has been damaged in such a fashion as to have a crude bifacial edge, or it is a roughly formed ax. This piece is broken near the midsection. It has an extant length of 57 mm, width of 42 mm, and a maximum thickness of 24 mm. There is also a spall of basaltic rock that may have resulted from breakage of a hammerstone.

Miscellaneous (n=25): Excavation also produced 22 small pieces of burned clay that do not appear to be ceramic sherds. They came from Units 2, 3 and 11. These may be pieces of clay that were incidently baked in a fire hearth. Similar pieces of "clay waste" were noted by Gibbon (1976:21) at another ricing site, Old Shakopee Bridge (21ML20). Three fragments of burned chert pebbles, showing no evidence of deliberate reduction, were recovered. These were probably also incidentally burned in a fire hearth.

Human Remains

The total number of individuals interred at the site remains unknown, but is probably at least two. The partial remains of one individual, collected at the site in or before 1952 by Robert Littlewolf and subsequently delivered to the University of Minnesota, were examined by Myster. She describes the remains as

> those of a single incomplete subadult individual. An inventory of the skeletal material present identified three thoracic vertebral arches, two right ribs, the right first metacarpal and approximately 75 percent of the cranium, including the frontal, right and left parietal and occipital bones, as well as the bones of the face. The right maxillary deciduous first and second molars are present. The mandible is not present....

A determination of sex cannot be made due to the young age at death of this individual. At this

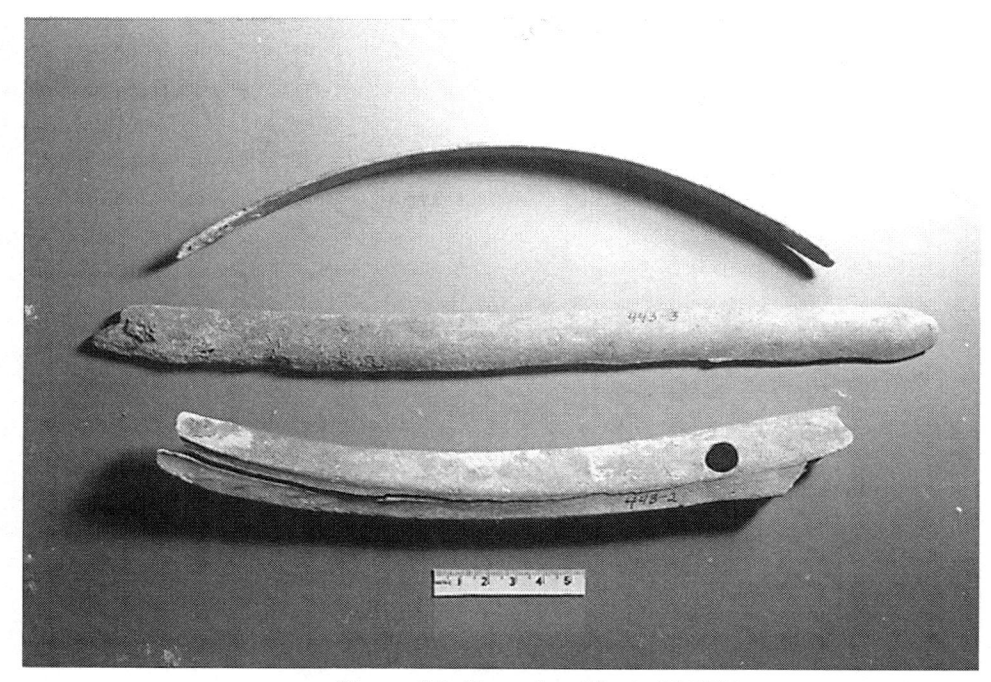

Figure 36. Faunal artifacts, 21CE5.

time there are not reliable techniques available to determine sex of subadult individuals.

The age at death of the individual is determined to be between four and five years of age +/- 12 months and is based on dental eruption patterns and development of the alveoli (tooth sockets).

No skeletal or dental pathologies or anomalies were observed.

Because these remains were collected with no control for provenience or associated artifacts, no evaluation can be made of burial mode or grave goods. At least one additional individual is probably represented by the human remains discovered in or about 1985. These remains were not studied or described, and no information on burial mode or grave goods is available.

Discussion

As previously mentioned, because of problems with site documentation and condition this paper concentrates on description of the site and material found at the site. Therefore the following interpretive discussion of the site is summary rather than detailed. Additional detail can be found in the original version of the site report (Bakken 1994).

Site Structure

The total size of the site is difficult to estimate because its limits are unknown. An estimate of minimum size can be attempted based on known distribution of artifacts and limits imposed on site expanse by the landscape. The northernmost and southernmost artifact-bearing units are separated by 95 m. The northern unit produced few artifacts, suggesting it might be near the site limits, and the southern unit is near a steep slope that is likely to be the site edge. This suggests that the site may not be much larger than 100 m along a north-south axis. The easternmost and westernmost artifact-bearing units are separated by 40 m. The eastern unit produced few artifacts, and the western unit is near a steep slope. In addition, an excavation unit that contained no artifacts is located 20 m farther east, indicating that the site limits have been passed. This suggests that the site may not be much more than 50 m along an east-west axis. This reasoning assumes a somewhat regular and compact shape for the site, which may not be the case. Nonetheless, it represents the best estimate that can be made based on available evidence. Given that the distribution of artifacts is

Figure 37. Ceramic elbow pipe fragment and pipestone tube pipe, 21CE5.

not likely to conform to a 50 by 100 m rectangle, but occupy an irregular area within these limits, the site is estimated to occupy less than 5000 square meters.

The Lower Rice Lake site lacks either true vertical stratification or discernible general trends in vertical stratification. The distribution of ceramic surface treatment (Fig. 38) provides an example of the lack of stratification. The distinctive Brainerd net impressed and horizontally cordmarked ceramics should be earlier in age than most of the cordmarked ceramics which, to judge by the relative abundance of rimsherds, are associated primarily with Blackduck and Sandy Lake. Yet the stratigraphic distribution is the same for each of these ceramic categories. All of the present surface treatments occur in all levels, and the distribution of each type of surface treatment also peaks in the same levels. The same pattern is seen with the distribution of temper (Fig. 39). Grit temper is characteristic of all the ceramic wares from the site. Shell temper, however, is associated only with the late Sandy Lake and possibly the Northeastern Plains Village wares. If the site were stratified, shell temper should be relatively more abundant in the upper levels. This is not the case.

One explanation for the lack of stratification would be that this site, located on a high ridge, has not received significant deposition of sediments since before the beginning of its human utilization. It would certainly not be receiving alluvial deposits, and the prospects for eolian deposits also seem limited. This assumption of an essentially stable land surface means that habitation occurred on the same surface during the entire period of site utilization. The subsurface location of artifacts would thus result from their incorporation into the soil rather than from the accumulation of sediments over the artifacts. Two potential factors would have contributed to this process. The first is pedoturbation. The second is soil movement resulting from human activity. The construction of ricing jigs, fire hearths, pits and other features certainly accounts for a great deal of soil disturbance and circulation. More recent "potting" and construction would also contribute a degree of stratigraphic mixing.

There may be some partial horizontal separation of components. Part of the evidence for this is the distribution of defined ceramic vessels. In Units 2, 3 and 11, the three southernmost units, Sandy Lake accounts for the majority of the vessels. The percentage varies from 45 percent to 86 percent; absolute count varies from 6 to 15. In contrast, Sandy Lake accounts for only 16 percent of the vessels in Unit 8, the northernmost unit. In Unit 8, vessels from the earlier Brainerd and Blackduck components are more abundant. In addition, fewer than 1 percent of the sherds from Unit 8 are shell-tempered, in comparison with 5 to 12 percent in the other units and 8 percent for the site overall (Fig. 40). Shell tempering should be associated with the later Sandy Lake and Northeastern Plains Village ceramics. Thus Unit 8 seems to be more strongly associated with the earlier period of site utilization. In the case of Unit 11, 11 percent of the sherds have stamped surfaces, compared with 1 to 2 percent in the other units and 3 percent for the site overall (Fig. 41). Unit 11 contains only Sandy Lake vessels and one Northeastern Plains Village vessel. In addition to suggesting that Unit 11 is more strongly associated with the later period of site utilization, this also would to support the association of stamped surface treatment with Sandy Lake.

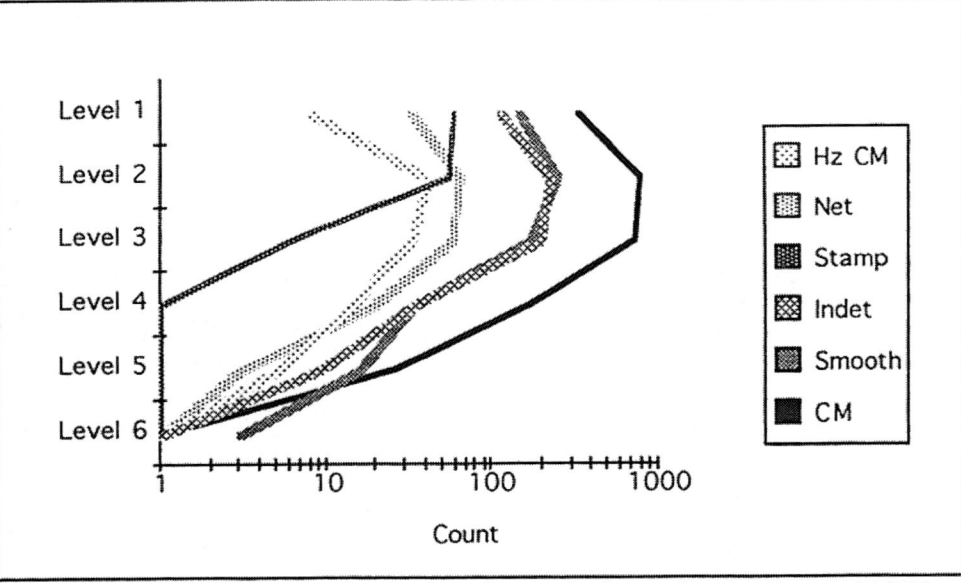

Figure 38. Stratigraphic distribution of ceramics by surface treatment, 21CE5.

Site Function

For at least part of the period of utilization, the Lower Rice Lake site has served as a wild ricing camp. This is indicated primarily by the presence of ricing jigs. Unfortunately, the available evidence does not clarify whether the site was used for ricing through all or only part of its history; aside from the ricing jigs, there is a lack of functionally diagnostic features. In addition, there are no clear associations between the ricing jigs and temporally or culturally diagnostic artifacts.

Although harvesting wild rice was the focal activity at the site, at least during certain periods other lacustrine resources were also utilized. These included waterfowl, turtles, fish and clams, all of which are represented in the sample of faunal remains. Non-lacustrine resources were also utilized. Plants are not rep-

Figure 39. Stratigraphic distribution of ceramics by temper, 21CE5.

resented in the excavated sample (except by a few pieces of charcoal). Terrestrial animals represented include bison, coyote, beaver, wapiti, whitetail deer and cottontail rabbit. Routine tool maintenance is indicated by the lithic remains. There is also evidence for the gathering, probably opportunistic, and reduction of local lithic raw materials.

It is interesting to note the occurrence of burials at a location believed to be a seasonal wild ricing camp. Burial practices in the Upper Midwest included transporting skeletal remains until they could be interred in a mound (e.g., Lofstrom 1987). The occurrence of burials at a seasonal camp, however, suggests that some of the deceased may not have been so transported. Regarding Sandy Lake populations, Birk (1977:29) notes that "Unpublished data suggest that a more ordinary method of inhumation may have been within shallow pits excavated in midden deposits or other areas within or close to habitation sites," and considers that mound burials "may represent some form of status interment rather than a common mortuary practice." Unfortunately, very little is known about the burials and their contexts at the Lower Rice Lake site; whether or not a mound was present at the site is not known. (Note that burials have been found on at least one other ricing camp, Petaga Point [21ML11; Bleed 1969]).

Site Seasonality

Based on the interpretation of the Lower Rice Lake site as being primarily a ricing camp, an interpretation of seasonality can also be advanced. However, because this interpretation of seasonality is dependent on site function, it is therefore subject to the same limitations. If or when the site was used for other purposes, it may also have been utilized in other seasons of the year.

Ethnographic evidence indicates that ricing was carried on at the end of August and beginning of September (Jenks 1901:1056-1057), the period during which the rice ripens. Edman (1975:83) notes that "Because the rice ripens unevenly, it must be reworked about every two days to obtain the maximum yield." The entire stand cannot be harvested once; it must be repeatedly harvested over this period of a few weeks in order to obtain a good yield. Jenks (1901:1059, 1061) states that the harvest lasts about one month, although the practice of tying the rice in bundles to protect it commences before the grain is ripe, and thus adds a few days to the season. Thus the seasonality of the site is established as late summer and early fall, from early or mid-August to the middle of September.

Site Chronology

The chronology of the Lower Rice Lake site must be estimated by reference to dates from other archaeological sites in the region. Most of the useful chronological information comes from a series of relative and absolute dates associated with ceramic types (Fig. 42). Lithic artifacts also provide some limited chronological information. In addition, recent reports indicate that intermittent utilization of the site has continued into the historic era. Although a radiocarbon date was obtained for Feature 15, it is not believed to accurately date the feature for reasons discussed below.

C-14 Date for Feature 15: An attempt was made to obtain an absolute date on Brainerd Ware at the Lower Rice Lake site; at the time that the date was obtained, there were no C-14 dates clearly associated with Brainerd contexts. Feature 15, a truncated pit, contained only Brainerd ceramics (net impressed and horizontally corded, including both body sherds and rims), and turtle bone. A charcoal sample was also collected from the feature. The fact that the feature contained a restricted set of artifacts, and that it contained no later artifacts, suggested a good association between the artifacts and the datable charcoal. The resulting AMS date was 710 $\pm$ 60 B.P. (A.D. 1240) (Beta-60259, CAMS-5372).

It seems unlikely that the results accurately date the Brainerd component at the site. There are now a number of radiocarbon dates associated with Brainerd Ware (Hohman-Caine and Goltz 1995:123-125). These dates are consistently earlier than the CE5 date: even the youngest date listed by Hohman-Caine and Goltz is 1700 B.P., and that date is treated as suspiciously recent. In addition, these other dates have strong association with Brainerd sherds or components.

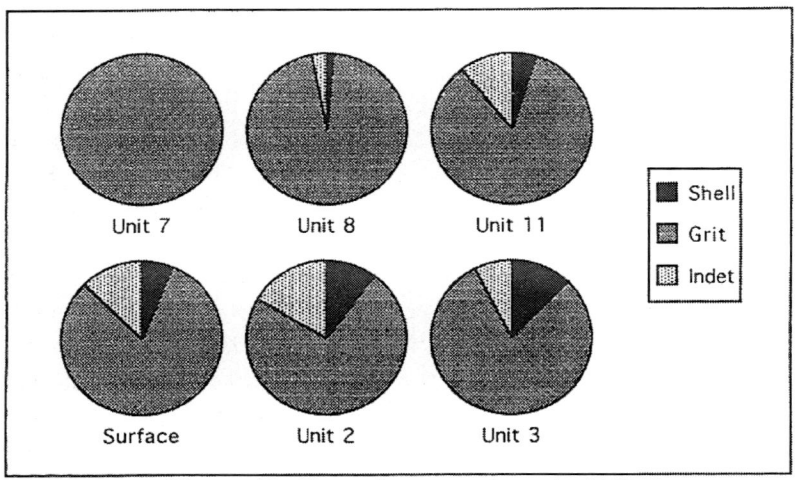

Figure 40. Ceramic temper by unit, 21CE5.

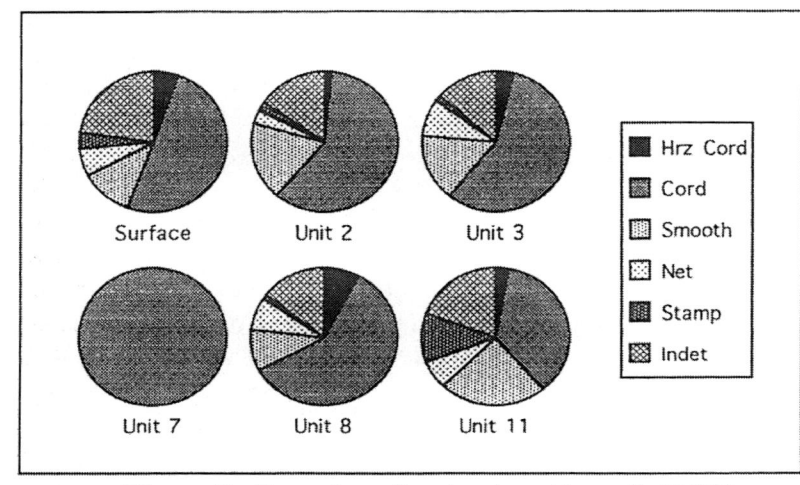

Figure 41. Ceramic surface treatment by unit, 21CE5.

The reasons for the late date from 21CE5 are not clear, but some possibilities can be suggested. As noted in the earlier discussion, there were a number of curious practices in the excavation of the site. Although there is no specific evidence of problems in the excavation of this feature, the possibility remains that the charcoal and the feature were not as clearly associated as the records make them appear. In addition, the sample was stored in the lab for almost 30 years. There is no record of how the sample was handled or curated over that period, and it is possible that the sample was compromised in some fashion. Finally, it is possible that the charcoal was simply intrusive and not actually a part of the feature.

Comparative Chronology. The earliest habitation of the site seems to be associated with Brainerd ware ceramics and corner-notched points. The chronology of Brainerd ceramics is still the subject of some discussion, mostly involving the interpretation of ceramic-residue dates.

In a regional context, ceramic wares with similar conoidal, wide mouthed forms and horizontal cord-marking as a surface treatment have a relatively early chronology. For example, roughly comparable wares discussed by Benn (1990) in a synthesis of ceramic period technology and chronology for the plains south and west of Lower Rice Lake include Crawford (ca. 2424 to 2021 B.P, corrected dates), Valley (ca. 2021 to 1684 B.P, first date corrected), and "middle" Fox Lake (within the period of ca. 2150 to 1450 B.P). Comparable wares discussed by Gregg and Picha (1989) for the Naze site (32SN246) in southeastern North Dakota include unnamed Early Plains Woodland (2780 $\pm$ 80 to 2388 $\pm$ 44 B.P) and Middle Plains Woodland (2035 $\pm$ 70 to 1760 $\pm$ 200 B.P) ceramics. In southwestern Minnesota, comparable Fox Lake ceramics were dated to 2050 $\pm$ 80 B.P. (100 BC) (Anfinson 1979a; Hudak 1976).

In any case, Hohman-Caine and Goltz (1995) present a series of radiocarbon dates associated with Brainerd ceramics. These range from 3180 to 1700 years B.P., including a wood charcoal date of 2480 $\pm$ 90 years B.P. Even if it was shown that the residue dates were too early by some factor of hundreds of years, they clearly place Brainerd early in the ceramic sequence for the region.

The corner-notched projectile point provides another point on the early end of the estimated site chronology. The point resembles the Besant points described by Kehoe (1974) for the northern plains and adjacent woodlands, except for a lack of basal grinding. In the Plains sites which Kehoe (1974:109) examined, points of this type were dated "from probably the time of Christ to about A.D. 400," or about 1950 to

1550 B.P. Similar points from Middle Plains Woodland sites in southeastern North Dakota (Gregg and Picha (1989:43, 51, 54) were found in components ranging in age from 2035 ± 70 to 1760 ± 200 B.P. (85 B.C. to A.D. 190). Similar points also occur in Laurel components in northern Minnesota, during the period of approximately 2000 to 1000 BP (see Anderson [1979:121], Lenius and Olinyk [1990:81-82], and Stoltman [1973:87, 133; 1974:80–83, 88-89]).

Onamia/St. Croix ceramics may be partly contemporaneous with the Brainerd ceramics, although they probably do not appear as early. The De Spiegler site (39RO23) in South Dakota contained two St. Croix vessels (Johnson 1973). Bone from a burial associated with the vessels was dated to 1350 ± 110 years B.P. (A.D. 600). At the Altern site in Wisconsin (47BT50), charred hazelnut shells associated with St. Croix ceramics were dated to 1610 ± 135 years B.P. (A.D. 340) (Cooper 1964; Johnson 1973:66; George 1979b:169). Note, however, that Caine (1983:219, 244), in an intensive analysis of St. Croix ceramics, views "the Altern site data [sic] with suspicion as dating the St. Croix component, [although] the assumption that St. Croix is earlier in the east than in the west may well be correct." She also states, based on a correlation of Blackduck, Clam River and St. Croix ceramics, that "the terminal dates for St. Croix should, then, be around A.D. 800 or slightly later" (Caine 1983:244). Onamia ceramics remain undated.

The chronology of Blackduck ceramics is better known. Lugenbeal, following a more traditional chronology and ware definition, says that

> The Blackduck ceramic tradition viewed as a whole probably spans the entire period from at least A.D. 800, if not earlier, to the period of historic contact. In Minnesota the Mississippi headwaters area sites appear to be limited to the first half of that temporal range. In the Rainy River drainage Blackduck sites seem to persist for a longer period of time, at least as late as A.D. 1400. [Lugenbeal 1979:23]

One of the more interesting aspects of Lenius and Olinyk's (1990) redefinition of Blackduck ware is a restricted chronological range for Blackduck, based on C-14 dates from "virtually pure Blackduck Horizon assemblages." These dates from sites in Manitoba, Ontario, and Minnesota range from 1440 ± 165 to 988 ± 80 years B.P. (A.D. 510 to 962). They propose that Blackduck "emerges at least by A.D. 700 and possibly as early as A.D. 500, and is not found much beyond A.D. 1000" (Lenius and Olinyk 1990:81-82). The date from the Dead River site (21OT51) Blackduck vessel, 1170 ± 120 B.P. (A.D. 780) (Michlovic 1979:9), fits into this range. Thus the chronological range for Blackduck in this region may be estimated as beginning between 1450 and 1250 B.P. (A.D. 500 to 700), and continuing to 950 B.P. (A.D. 1000) (Fig. 42).

The Sandy Lake and Northeastern Plains Village ceramics should represent the most recent prehistoric utilization of the Lower Rice Lake site. The chronological range of Sandy Lake ware is also relatively well known. A brief summary of the distribution and dates for this ware (Participants of the 1988 Lake Superior Basin Workshop 1988) indicates that Sandy Lake ranges from approximately 950 to 250 B.P. (A.D. 1000 to 1700). Dates For Sandy Lake at the Mooney site (21NR29) in the Red River Valley of northwestern Minnesota (Michlovic 1987:45) range from 1170 to 810 B.P. and average 940 ± 100 B.P. (A.D. 1010). Noted that these are thermoluminescence dates, and may not be directly comparable with radiocarbon dates. Two Sandy Lake sherds from the Femco Site (21WL1) were dated by thermoluminescence to 750 to 480 B.P. and 775 to 520 B.P. (A.D. 1200-1470 and 1175-1430) (Michlovic 1985:36). At the Shea site (32CS101), a fortified village in eastern North Dakota, Sandy Lake ware was found in association with Northeastern Plains Village ceramics. Six radiocarbon dates from the site ranged from 510 ± 50 to 350 ± 70 B.P. (A.D. 1440 to 1600) (Michlovic and Schneider 1993:124). At the Crosier Cemetery Habitation (21ML33), charcoal recovered in direct association with a broken but nearly complete Sandy Lake vessel was dated to 520 ± 110 years B.P. (A.D. 1430) (Mather 1991). Thus the chronological range of Sandy Lake appears to begin at about A.D. 1000 and continue until at least A.D. 1700 (Fig. 42). The co-occurring Northeastern Plains Village ceramics are judged to be contemporaneous with Sandy Lake. Small amounts of these ceramics are commonly found in sites which

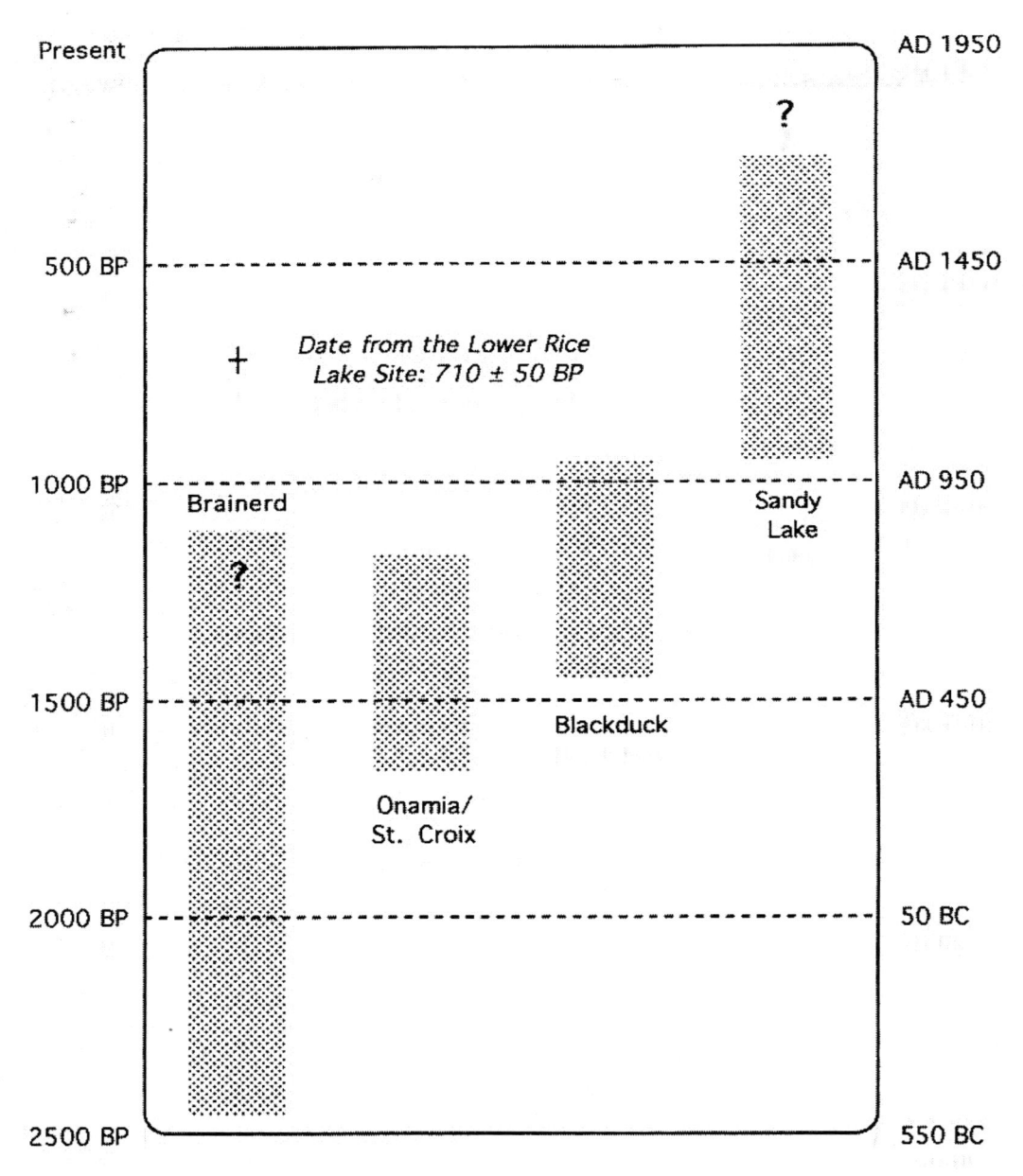

Figure 42. Estimated chronology of ceramic types found at the Lower Rice Lake site, 21CE5.

contain Sandy Lake, and their presence appears to be related to the Sandy Lake habitation. This includes sites with a restricted temporal duration (e.g., the Shea site), and sites where some stylistic blending occurs between the two types (e.g., Mooney).

The four small, triangular projectile points from the Lower Rice Lake site are of the kind commonly found in Late Woodland sites throughout Minnesota and the upper Midwest; examples are numerous. They are not otherwise more temporally diagnostic.

Utilization of the site continues up to the present. This includes recent (i.e., at least within the twentieth century) use of the site by Native Americans to continue the traditional practice of harvesting wild rice (Johnson 1969b:33; Schissel and Anfinson 1977). Presumably, this could also be taken to indicate that [prehistoric" utilization of the site for this same purpose continued until the end of the prehistoric period, i.e., until European contact or up to the period of Euroamerican settlement.

References Cited

Agricultural Experiment Station [AES]
1980 Minnesota Soil Atlas Project - Bemidji Sheet. Miscellaneous Report 168. Agricultural Experiment Station, University of Minnesota, St. Paul.

Anderson, Dean L.
1979 Laurel Ware. In *A Handbook of Minnesota Prehistoric Ceramics*, pp. 121-135, ed. by S.F. Anfinson. Minnesota Archaeological Society, St. Paul.

Anfinson, Scott F.
1979a Fox Lake Phase. In *A Handbook of Minnesota Prehistoric Ceramics*, ed. by S.F. Anfinson, pp. 79-86. Minnesota Archaeological Society, St. Paul.
1979b Orr Phase. In *A Handbook of Minnesota Prehistoric Ceramics*, ed. by S.F. Anfinson, pp. 157-161. Minnesota Archaeological Society, St. Paul.

Anfinson, Scott F., Michael G. Michlovic and Julie Stein
1978 *The Lake Bronson Site (21KT1): A Multi-Component Prehistoric Site on the Prairie-Woodland Border in Northwestern Minnesota*. Minnesota Archaeological Society, St. Paul.

Bakken, Kent
1985 Lithic Raw Materials in Northwest Minnesota. *The Minnesota Archaeologist* 44(1):34-46.
1994 *The Lower Rice Lake Site, 21CE5*. Masters thesis, University of Minnesota, Minneapolis.

Benn, David W.
1990 Woodland Ceramics. In *Woodland Ceramics on the Western Prairies: The Rainbow Site Investigations*, ed. by D.W. Benn, pp. 96-144. Office of the State Archaeologist, University of Iowa, Iowa City.

Birk, Douglas A.
1977 The Norway Lake Site: A Multicomponent Woodland Complex in North Central Minnesota. *The Minnesota Archaeologist* 36(1):16-33.

Bleed, Peter
1969 *The Archaeology of Petaga Point: the Preceramic Component*. Minnesota Historical Society, St. Paul.

Caine, Christy A.H.
1983 *Normative Typological and Systemic Stylistic Approaches to the Analysis of North Central Minnesota Ceramics*. Ph.D. dissertation, Department of Anthropology, University of Minnesota, Minneapolis.

Clark, Frances
1984 Knife River Flint and Interregional Exchange. *Midcontinental Journal of Archaeology* 9(2):173-198.

Clayton, Lee, W.B. Bickley, Jr. and W.J. Stone
1970 Knife River Flint. *Plains Anthropologist* 15(50):282-290.

Cooper, Leland R.
1964 A Preliminary Report on the Excavation of Two Late Middle Woodland Mounds in Northwestern Wisconsin. *Journal of the Minnesota Academy of Sciences* 32(1):17-23.

Cooper, Leland R. and Elden Johnson
1964 Sandy Lake Ware and Its Distribution. *American Antiquity* 29(4):474-479.

Edman, F. Robert
1975 *A Study of Wild Rice in Minnesota*. Minnesota Resources Commission Staff Report No. 14, 1975 reprint. Minnesota Resources Commission, St. Paul

Evans, G. Edward
1960 Upper and Lower Rice Lake Sites. *Proceedings of the Minnesota Academy of Science* 28:93-95.

Garland, William
1959 Memo on Survey of Ponsford Landing Area, Clearwater County, July 2, 1959. Handwritten notes on file, Wilford Archaeology Laboratory files, Minnesota Historical Society, St. Paul.

George, Douglas C.
1979b St. Croix Stamped Series. In *A Handbook of Minnesota Prehistoric Ceramics*, ed. by S.F. Anfinson, pp. 169-174. Minnesota Archaeological Society, St. Paul.

Gibbon, Guy E.
1976 The Old Shakopee Bridge Site: A Late Woodland Ricing Site on Shakopee Lake,

Mille Lacs County, Minnesota. *The Minnesota Archaeologist* 35(2):2-56.

Gregg, Michael L.
1987 Knife River Flint in the Northeastern Plains. *Plains Anthropologist* 32(118):367-377.

Gregg, Michael L. and Paul R. Picha
1989 Early Plains Woodland and Middle Plains Woodland Occupation of the James River Region in Southeastern North Dakota. *Midcontinental Journal of Archaeology* 49(1):38-61.

Hohman-Caine, Christy A. and Grant Goltz
1995 Brainerd Ware and the Early Woodland Dilemma. *The Minnesota Archaeologist* 54:109-129.

Hudak, G. Joseph
1976 *Woodland Ceramics from the Pedersen Site*. The Science Museum of Minnesota, St. Paul.

Jenks, Albert E.
1901 *The Wild Rice Gatherers of the Upper Lakes: A Study in American Primitive Economies*. In Annual Report of the Bureau of Ethnology 19(2):1013-1137, Smithsonian Institution Press, Washington, D.C. [Reprinted edition, 1977, J&L Reprint Company, Lincoln, Nebraska].

Johnson, Elden
1969a Archaeological Evidence for Utilization of Wild Rice. *Science* 163:276-277.
1969b Preliminary Notes on the Prehistoric Use of Wild Rice. *The Minnesota Archaeologist* 30(2):31-43.
1973 *The Arvilla Complex*. Minnesota Historical Society, St. Paul.

Jones, J. Knox, Jr. and Elmer C. Birney
1988 *Handbook of Mammals of the North-Central States*. University of Minnesota Press, Minneapolis.

Kehoe, Thomas F.
1974 The Large Corner-notched Point System of the Northern Plains and Adjacent Woodlands. In *Aspects of Upper Great Lake Anthropology: Papers in Honor of Lloyd A Wilford*, ed. by E. Johnson, pp. 103-114. Minnesota Historical Society, St. Paul.

Lenius, Brian J. and Dave M. Olinyk
1990 The Rainy River Composite: Revisions to Late Woodland Taxonomy. In *The Woodland Tradition in the Western Great Lakes: Papers Presented to Elden Johnson*, ed. by G.E. Gibbon, pp. 77-112. University of Minnesota, Minneapolis.

Lofstrom, Ted
1987 The Rise of Wild Rice Exploitation and Its Implications for Population Size and Social Organization in Minnesota Woodland Period Populations. *The Minnesota Archaeologist* 46(2):3-15.

Lugenbeal, Edward
1979 Blackduck Ware. In *A Handbook of Minnesota Prehistoric Ceramics*, ed. by S.F. Anfinson, pp. 23-37. Minnesota Archaeological Society, St. Paul.

MacNeish, Richard S.
1958 *An Introduction to the Archaeology of Southeast Manitoba*. National Museum of Canada Bulletin No. 157. National Museum of Canada, Ottawa.

Mather, David J.
1991 Toward a Cultural Landscape in the Mille Lacs Region: Trunk Highway 169 Corridor Survey and Site Evaluation in the Vicinity of Lake Onamia. *The Minnesota Archaeologist* 50(1):31-41.

Michlovic, Michael G.
1979 *The Dead River Site (21 OT 51)*. Minnesota Archaeological Society, St. Paul
1985 *Archaeological Studies Along the Upper Red River, Minnesota*. Report on file at the State Historic Preservation Office, Minnesota Historical Society, St. Paul.
1987 The Archaeology of the Mooney Site. *The Minnesota Archaeologist* 46(2):39-66.

Michlovic, Michael G. and Fred Schneider
1993 The Shea Site: A Prehistoric Fortified Village on the Northeastern Plains. *Plains Anthropologist* 38(143):117-137.

Murray, Robert A.
1962 A Brief Survey of the Pipes and Smoking Customs of the Indians of the Northern Plains. *The Minnesota Archaeologist* 24(1):4-1. [Reprinted in *The Minnesota Archaeologist* 42(1-2):81-100.]

Myster, Susan M.T.

1992 Report on the osteological analysis of the remains from Lower Rice Lake, University of Minnesota Accession Number 443. Manuscript in the possession of the author.

Neumann, Thomas
1978 Classification of Net Impressed Pottery from Central Minnesota. In *Some Studies of Minnesota Prehistoric Ceramics*, ed. by A.R. Woolworth and M.A. Hall, pp. 56-65. Occasional Publications in Minnesota Anthropology, No. 2. Minnesota Archaeological Society, St. Paul.

Participants of the 1988 Lake Superior Basin Workshop
1988 Desperately Seeking Siouans: The Distribution of Sandy Lake Ware. *The Wisconsin Archeologist* 69(4):347-353. Also published in *The Minnesota Archaeologist* 47(1):43-48.

Peterson, Leslie D.
1979 Blue Earth/Correctionville Phase. In *A Handbook of Minnesota Prehistoric Ceramics*, ed. by S.F. Anfinson, pp. 39-44. Minnesota Archaeological Society, St. Paul.

Ready, Tim and Scott F. Anfinson
1979 Ogechie Series. In *A Handbook of Minnesota Prehistoric Ceramics*, ed. by S.F. Anfinson, pp. 143-148. Minnesota Archaeological Society, St. Paul.

Romano, Anthony
1991 Northern Lithics. *The Platform* 3(1-4).

Schissel, Pat and Scott Anfinson
1977 National Register of Historic Places Inventory -- Nomination Form, for the Lower Rice Lake Site (21CE5). Copy on file in the Minnesota state site files, Office of the State Archaeologist. St. Paul.

Stoltman, James B.
1973 *The Laurel Culture in Minnesota*. Minnesota Prehistoric Archaeology Series 8. Minnesota Historical Society, St. Paul.
1974 An Examination of Within-Laurel Cultural Variability. In *Aspects of Upper Great Lake Anthropology: Papers in Honor of Lloyd A Wilford*, pp. 74-89, ed. by E. Johnson. Minnesota Historical Society, St. Paul.

Wilford, Lloyd A.
1953 Memo on Clearwater County, June 7, 1953. Typewritten note on file, Wilford Archaeology Laboratory file, Minnesota Historical Society, St. Paul.

Wilford, Lloyd A.
1970 *Burial Mounds of the Red River Headwaters*. Minnesota Historical Society, St. Paul

Wilford, Lloyd A., Elden Johnson and Joan Vicinus
1969 *Burial Mounds of Central Minnesota: Excavation Reports*. Minnesota Historical Society, St. Paul.

INVESTIGATIONS AT THE SUCKER LAKES SITE

Andrea K. LeVasseur and William J. Yourd
U.S. Forest Service
Chippewa National Forest Heritage Program

The Chippewa National Forest evaluated the National Register eligibility of the Sucker Lakes site with the help of students and volunteers. Testing demonstrated that artifact concentration features are present, including a rock concentration suggesting storage in a bag or basket container. Lithics were sparse and other artifacts included bone items and objects associated with red ochre or hematite. Ceramics are the predominant artifact category, and horizontal ceramic distributions indicate differential activity areas through time. Sucker Lakes may offer good potential for improving our understanding of Brainerd, Blackduck, and Sandy Lake affiliations. The presence of "Sandyota" Ware offers the opportunity to explore the poorly understood Oneota/Mississippian influence on Sandy Lake ceramics and Psinomani culture.

Natural Setting

The Sucker Lakes site (21CA50) was first recorded in 1979 in the Minnesota Statewide Archeological Survey. It was relocated in 1995 during reconnaissance survey of the area prior to a planned timber harvest. Thirty-seven positive shovel tests along the shoreline recovered Brainerd, Blackduck, and Sandy Lake ceramics, lithics, and faunal remains. In 2003 and 2004, The Chippewa National Forest evaluated the National Register eligibility of the site using forest Heritage Program personnel, students from the Cass Lake Alternative Learning Center, and volunteers in the Passport in Time program. A total of 36.25 square meters and eight shovel tests were excavated (Figure 2).

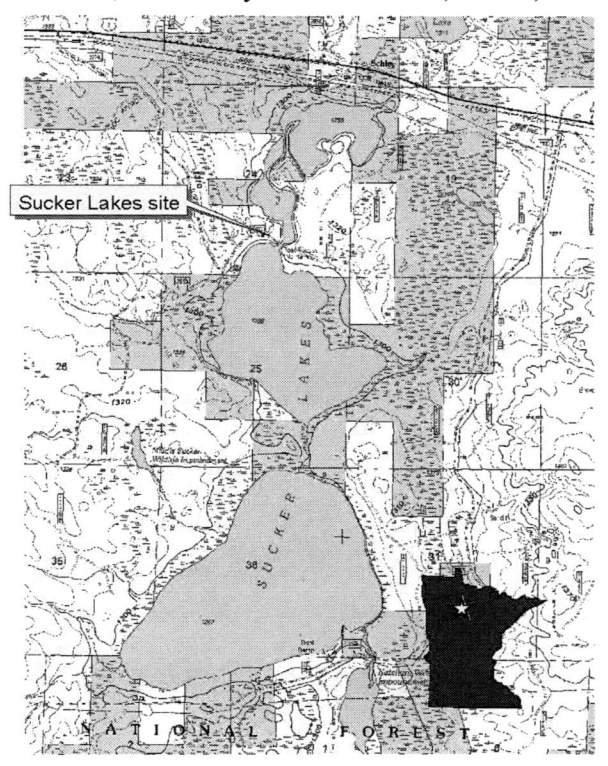

Figure 1. Site location.

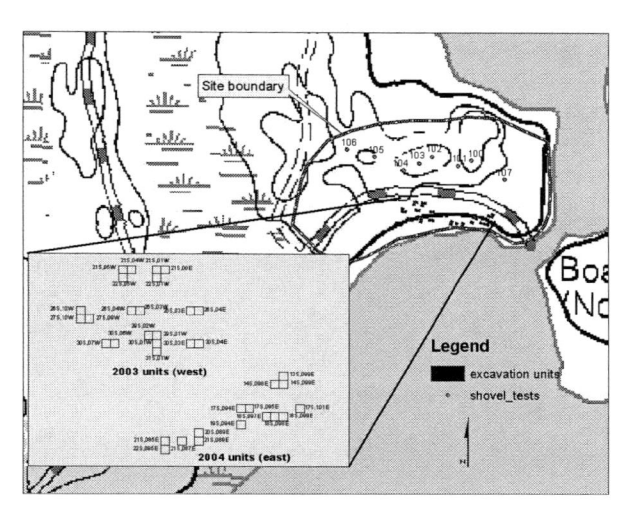

Figure 2. 2003-04 work.

Sucker Lakes is located about six miles east of Cass Lake. It is composed of three lake basins oriented north-south and connected by narrow channels. The Sucker Lakes site is located on the west side of the channel separating the northern and middle lakes. The area is accessed by a Forest Road that terminates at a minimally developed boat access.

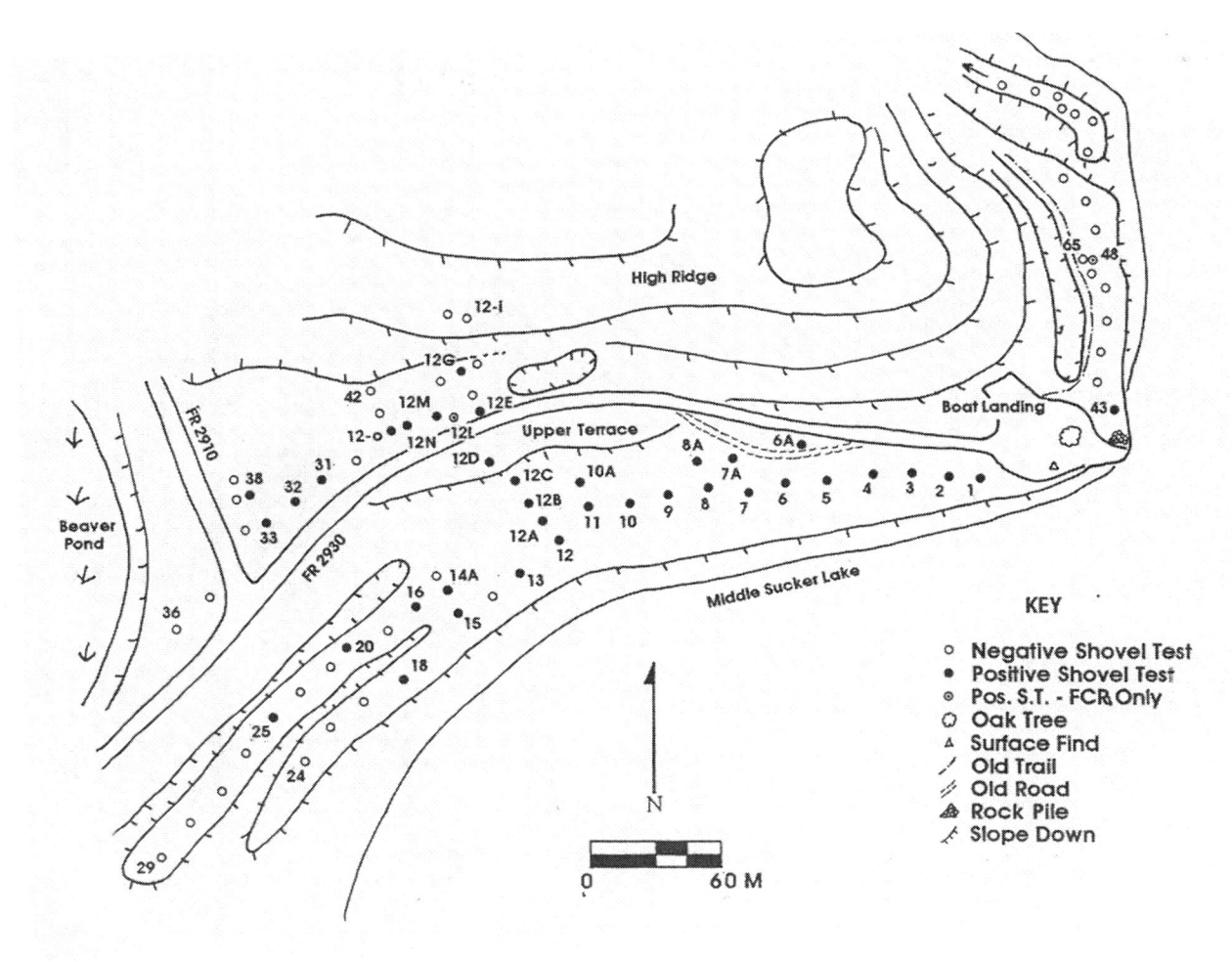

Figure 3. 1995 shovel tests.

The normal pool elevation of Sucker Lakes is about 1,300 feet. The highest uplands surrounding the lake are about 30 feet above lake level. At the Sucker Lakes site, as at many places along the shoreline, uplands are wave cut by water levels that were significantly higher than today. These wave-cut features form embankments that steeply rise about 20 to 30 feet above the lake. It is presumed that the high-water levels that cut these embankments were present during the early postglacial period. The beach ridges that form the lower terrace at Sucker Lakes were developed during periods of water levels closer to those of today.

Sucker Lakes is within the broader landscape unit known as the Bemidji Sand Plain, which is dominated by an outwash plain deposited by meltwaters of the last glaciation about 12,000 years ago. The unit is characterized by well-drained sandy soils supporting pine-dominated communities with occasional aspen and hardwood stands interspersed throughout. At Sucker Lakes the soils are sandy and the forested uplands are dominated by up to 80-year-old red pine with hazel shrub understory.

Within the archeological site area, the soils contain an atypical A horizon (anthrosol) of very dark "greasy" sand to about 40 CmBS. B and C horizons are brown glacial outwash sands to 140 CmBS with lacustrine sands beneath to at least 165 CmBS.

The site area extends north and inland from the shoreline about 200 meters, including the top of the ridge north of Forest Road 2930. Shovel tests on this ridge recovered additional artifacts and a concentration of Sandy Lake sherds. The site extends west from the channel between lake basins as far as the beaver pond wetland, a distance of about 350 meters. Total site area is about 17.3 acres (7 hectares).

The site retains excellent integrity. The timber stands in the site area were last harvested about 1910 and 1917. Methods used at that time included hand felling and log transport over frozen ground without the use of heavy vehicles, causing minimal soil disturbance. Major disturbance is confined to the roads, a small borrow area, and the parking area immediately around the boat access.

General Field Methods

Minimum test unit dimensions were 50 cm by 50 cm. Test units were generally excavated in 5 cm levels and all sediment screened through 1/8 inch hardware mesh, except for the top 10 cm, which was screened with ¼ inch mesh. Cultural and natural phenomena including features and distinct artifact concentrations as well as soil and sediment changes were documented on level forms. Cultural features were fully investigated through use of cross-sectional profiling and photography. Carbon from in situ feature contexts was collected for dating purposes, as appropriate.

Wall profiles, including graphic drawing of cultural and natural soil stratigraphy, were done on at least one representative wall from most excavation units to provide a north-south and east-west cross-section of the excavation area. Selected units were photographed prior to backfilling.

Shovel testing was used as necessary to assess site size. Shovel tests had a minimum diameter of 40 cm and all excavated materials were screened through hardware mesh with openings having a maximum dimension of ¼ inch. Shovel test profile forms were used to record basic soil profile description and the depth and nature of cultural materials recovered. Standard records were maintained, including field notes, field maps, photographs, and laboratory analysis records.

Figure 4. Rock concentration in unit 14S99E.

Artifacts were temporarily stored at the Chippewa National Forest offices until the collection was cleaned, catalogued, and analyzed. Original field notes were curated with recovered artifacts as part of that collection. Upon completion of analysis, the collection was delivered to the Chippewa National Forest curation facility at the University of Minnesota, Duluth.

Features

Owing to the very dark color of the cultural occupation soils, features that included soil discolorations and charcoal were extremely difficult to see. As a result, artifact concentrations were the predominant feature indicator. A feature in unit 14S99E included 31 racket- to baseball-sized rocks (Figure 4). These consisted of 15 granite, 11 basalt, one quartzite, and three limestone cobbles and one basalt fire-cracked rock (FCR). The cobbles were not modified and show no battering. The rocks were compressed into a single area, suggesting that they had been in some kind of container such as a bag or basket.

A second feature in unit 26S04W contained two thermally altered basalt fragments (FCR), one unidentified unburned bone fragment, 18 body sherds, and one Brainerd rim sherd. Sherds were grit/sand-tempered with 17 having a corded surface treatment consistent with horizontally corded Brainerd vessels. One sherd was smooth. Seven

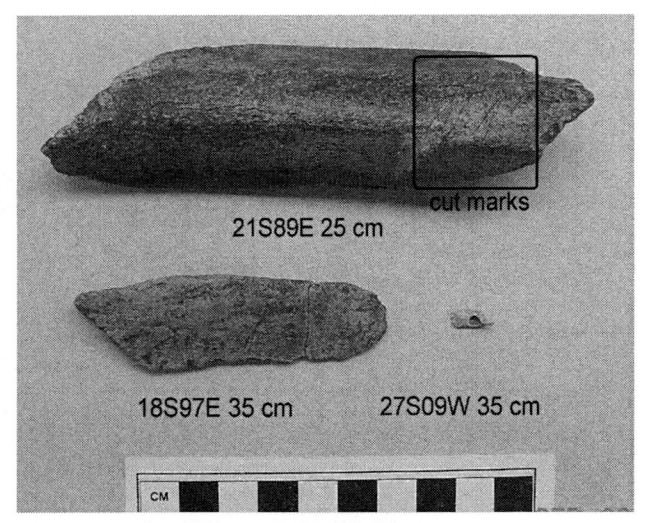

Figure 5. Bone objects.

of the sherds retained carbonized organic matter on the interior and were packaged for possible future radiocarbon dating.

Miscellaneous Cultural Materials

The faunal collection includes 6,263 bone fragments, 70 percent of which are calcined. In general preservation seems to be poor, although turtle carapace, fish remains, and some mammal bones can easily be identified. Detailed analysis has not yet been completed.

A large bone with cutmarks was found in unit 21S89E. It is a fragment of a long bone of a large mammal (e.g., wapiti or moose) that shows several cutmarks perpendicular to the axis of the bone. The bone has a spiral fracture, indicating that it was deliberately broken by humans (Figure 5). A second bone object was found in unit 18S97E. It also displays a possible spiral fracture. Unit 27S09W contained a small bone fragment with a shallow hole in it. The hole does not penetrate completely through the bone.

A single large mammal tooth with root was found in unit 17S101E at 40 CmBS. It appears to be the left premolar of an adult moose. No cultural modification is visible.

Seven units contained objects associated with red ochre or hematite (Figure 6). Three of these appeared to be raw red sandstone or hematite. There were also one granite cobble, two granite spalled fragments, and a siltstone fragment with what appears to be red ochre on the exterior.

Unit 22S01W contained a rounded piece of basalt with a flattened profile and may be a tool used to smooth or decorate pottery.

Lithics

Lithic waste was generally sparse. A total of only 2,181 waste flakes, cores, and discarded raw material were catalogued. This sample size is too small to show a meaningful distribution pattern, especially without stratigraphic identification of cultural components (see ceramic discussion below).

Twenty-eight hammerstones and two anvils were identified. Both anvils and most of the hammerstones (20) were located in the western excavation area in 11 units. Eastern units contained eight hammerstones in six units. Most of the hammerstones showed little wear, and no obvious lithic reduction areas were identified in the limited sample.

Figure 6. Ochre objects.

Figure 7. Projectile points.

At least three bipolar cores were identified out of a total of seven cores, three of chert and four of quartz.

Fourteen projectile points were recovered (Figure 7). Seven were triangular, one corner-notched, two side-notched, and the remaining were fragments. There were also five bifaces, 13 scrapers, three retouched flakes, and six utilized flakes. One ground stone tool resembling a mano was recovered. It has a flattened and polished surface that appears to have resulted from abrasion.

Ceramics

Ceramics are the predominant artifact category with a total of 13,008 sherds recovered, although the majority of the sherds are smaller than 1 cm in length and of more limited diagnostic value. The ceramics present fall into four broad ware categories: Brainerd (177 typed sherds, Figure 9), Blackduck and "Late Blackduck/Rainy River Composite-like" (71 typed sherds), and Sandy Lake (325 typed sherds). One vessel of Sandy Lake form bears a distinctive Oneota/Mississippian trailed decorative motif (labeled Sandyota in Figure 10). Some of the Late Blackduck/Rainy River Composite-like sherds are displayed in Figures 11 and 12.

Ceramic types do not clearly cluster stratigraphically and there are no sterile horizons separating occupation layers. However, in general, Sandy Lake rims seem to occupy mainly surface to 15 CmBS and Brainerd below 35 CmBS. Blackduck is mixed throughout, although the heaviest deposit seems to lie between 15 and 35 CmBS. This generalized stratigraphy would seem to fit well with evidence gained from other sites in northern Minnesota indicating a relative chronological distribution from oldest at depth (Brainerd) to youngest near surface (Sandy Lake).

A gross analysis of horizontal distribution of ceramics indicates that the Sucker Lake site has potential for allowing comparisons of different cultural components by location. The excavations of 2003 and 2004 were separated by about 80 meters. The western 2003 excavation contained Brainerd and Sandy Lake wares but no Blackduck or Late Blackduck/Rainy River Composite-like wares, whereas the eastern 2004 excavation area was dominated by Blackduck and the later affiliated

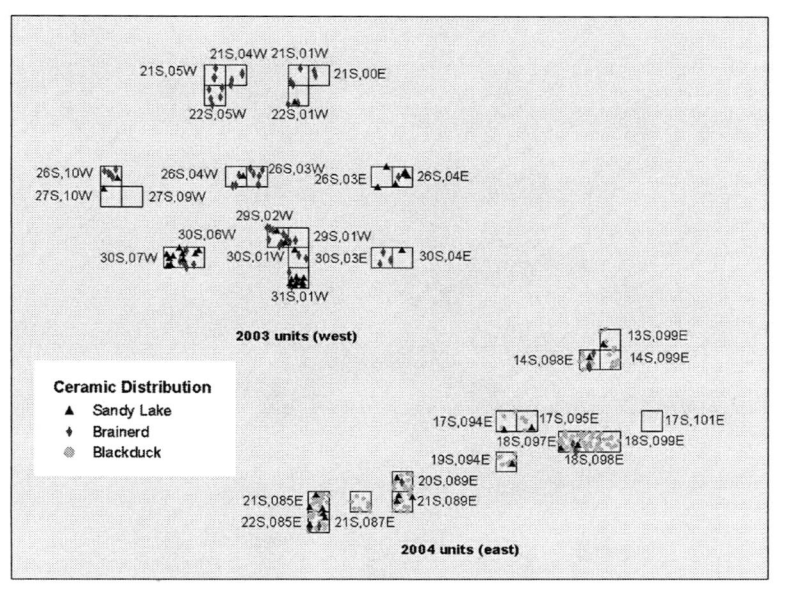

Figure 8. Ceramic distribution by type.

Figure 9. Brainerd ware.

Figure 10. Sandy Lake ware and "Sandyota" sherd (on right).

Figure 11. Blackduck/Rainy River Composite Ware.

ware(s) and Sandy Lake with very little Brainerd present (Figure 8).

The excavations of 2003 and 2004 allow limited conclusions regarding the cultural context. Ceramic types do not equal peoples, but to the extent that they may be correlated with cultural complexes observed by archeologists at a broader scale in northern Minnesota, the ceramics may offer insight into the identity of groups of people who chose to live at the site. Although the cultural affiliation of those who used Brainerd wares is unknown, they appear to have been the earliest inhabitants of the site based on evidence obtained from the site thus far. Elsewhere in the Mississippi Headwaters, the time depth for Brainerd or Elk Lake Culture has been shown to be as much as 2000-3000 B.P. (e.g., Hohman-Caine and Goltz 1995). The contrasting chronology and distribution of Late Woodland complexes of northern Minnesota indicates that Blackduck developed in the first millennium AD and seems more likely to represent an Algonkian affiliation that may be antecedent to the cultures such as the Cree and Ojibwe. Some researchers (e.g., Meyer and Russel 1987, Lugenbeal 1976, Lenius and Olinyk 1990) have hypothesized that Selkirk and Late Blackduck/Rainy River Composite ceramics may be of proto-Cree and proto-Ojibwe, respectively. Sandy Lake Psinomani Culture appears in the second millennium AD, has clear cultural connections to the south, and appears to represent affiliation with Siouan-speaking peoples.

Although other cultural components are almost surely to be present at the site, it is clear that Sucker Lakes has the potential to provide a greater understanding of the Woodland period in the Mississippi Headwaters region.

Figure 12. Blackduck/Rainy River Composite Ware.

Conclusion

The size and complexity of the site indicate it has the potential to contribute knowledge about poorly known historical patterns and contexts in northern Minnesota such as Brainerd, Blackduck, and Sandy Lake (Psinomani). Shovel testing indicates that the site is much larger than expected, including the large ridge north of the 2003-2004 excavation. (There are also ceramic materials that may be related on the east side of the channel connecting the lakes.) The fact that organic materials such as bone have been preserved adds to the significance of the site by increasing the potential information value of its data. Although bone preservation is relatively poor in the small portion of the site that was tested, it is nonetheless present and may offer additional insights as to the timing and nature of the occupations. Datable cultural features may also be present. Testing has demonstrated that artifact concentration features are present as well as horizontal ceramic distributions, and more discrete activity areas may be discernable with a larger sample size. Based on the available information, it appears that Sucker Lakes may offer good potential for improving our understanding of Brainerd, Blackduck, and Sandy Lake affiliations through the recovery of ceramic assemblages and lithic debris. Oneota/Mississipian influence is also present in the Sandyota Ware, whose appearance in the Mississippi Headwaters area is rare and poorly understood.

References Cited

Hohman-Caine, C. and G.E. Goltz
1995 Brainerd Ware and the Early Woodland Dilemma. *The Minnesota Archeologist* 54:109-129.

Lenius, B.J. and D.M. Olinyk
1990 The Rainy River Composite: Revisions to Late Woodland Taxonomy. In Gibbon, Guy E., ed. *The Woodland Tradition in the Western Great Lakes: Papers Presented to Eldon Johnson.*, ed. By G.E. Gibbon, pp. 77-112. University of Minnesota Publications in Anthropology No. 4, Department of Anthropology, Minneapolis.

Lugenbeal, E.N.
1976 *The Archeology of the Smith Site: A Study of the Ceramics and Culture History of Minnesota Laurel and Blackduck*. Ph.D. dissertation, Department of Anthropology, University of Wisconsin, Madison.

Meyer, D. and D. Russell.
1987 The Selkirk Composite of Central Canada: A Reconsideration. *Arctic Anthropology* 24(2):1-31.

Minnesota Archaeological Society

Playing with Prehistory

The Minnesota Archaeological Society is an organization that likes to see things, do things, and understand things. Our mission (to the best of our 21st Century ability) is to foster understanding of the past in Minnesota. We sponsor activities that invite everyone to participate in hands-on experiences with professionals along to explain things as they occur. We truly want to help Minnesotans know the thrill of uncovering that first artifact. Please join us in this endeavor. As a child you quite possibly enjoyed playing in the dirt, and we bet you will again!

Archaeologist Dave Mather digs in the dirt at Mille Lacs-Kathio State Park Archaeology Day in 2006. This excavation was a 1x1 meter demonstration of how archaeologists actually dig, slowly and carefully, for the many people who came to take in the activities and sites.

Flintknapper and current President of MAS Rod Johnson poses for the camera at Fort Snelling's Archaeology Fair 2005.

These big canoes, or ones like them, have been transporting humans on the rivers of Minnesota for hundreds of years. These young travelers were also at Archaeology Fair 2005.

Archaeology Fair 2005: Fort Snelling

Archaeology Fair was first held at the Ft. Snelling History Center on May 1, 2004, on opening weekend of Minnesota Archaeology Week. It was and is sponsored by the Minnesota Archaeological Society, the Council for Minnesota Archaeology, and the Minnesota Historical Society. The Fair was selected to be the theme event for the annual Open House at the Fort, which features free admission to the public and each year it has averaged close to three thousand visitors.

Archaeology Fair, which has become a yearly event, includes a wide range of hands-on activities, displays and lectures, and demonstrations such as flint-knapping, pottery making, a simulated excavation, an archaeology film festival, and "living history" performances. A main goal of the Archaeology Fair is to inform visitors about the nature of archaeology and of the activities in which archaeologists throughout the state are engaged.

89

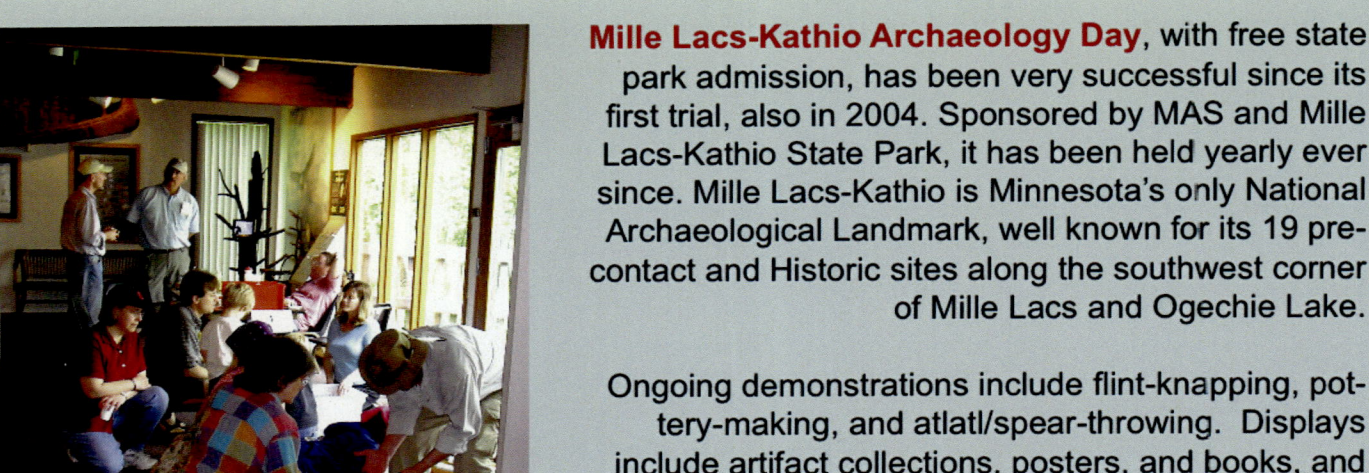

Mille Lacs-Kathio Archaeology Day, with free state park admission, has been very successful since its first trial, also in 2004. Sponsored by MAS and Mille Lacs-Kathio State Park, it has been held yearly ever since. Mille Lacs-Kathio is Minnesota's only National Archaeological Landmark, well known for its 19 pre-contact and Historic sites along the southwest corner of Mille Lacs and Ogechie Lake.

Ongoing demonstrations include flint-knapping, pottery-making, and atlatl/spear-throwing. Displays include artifact collections, posters, and books, and archaeologists are on hand to answer questions and identify artifacts. Tours of archaeological sites and rides are also offered in 10-person canoes on Ogechie Lake and the Rum River.

Archaeology Day 2005: Mille Lacs-Kathio State Park

MAS Mille Lacs-Kathio Archaeology Day 2005, when it was rainy and we were indoors, Sunday June 5

Archaeology Fair 2006: Fort Snelling

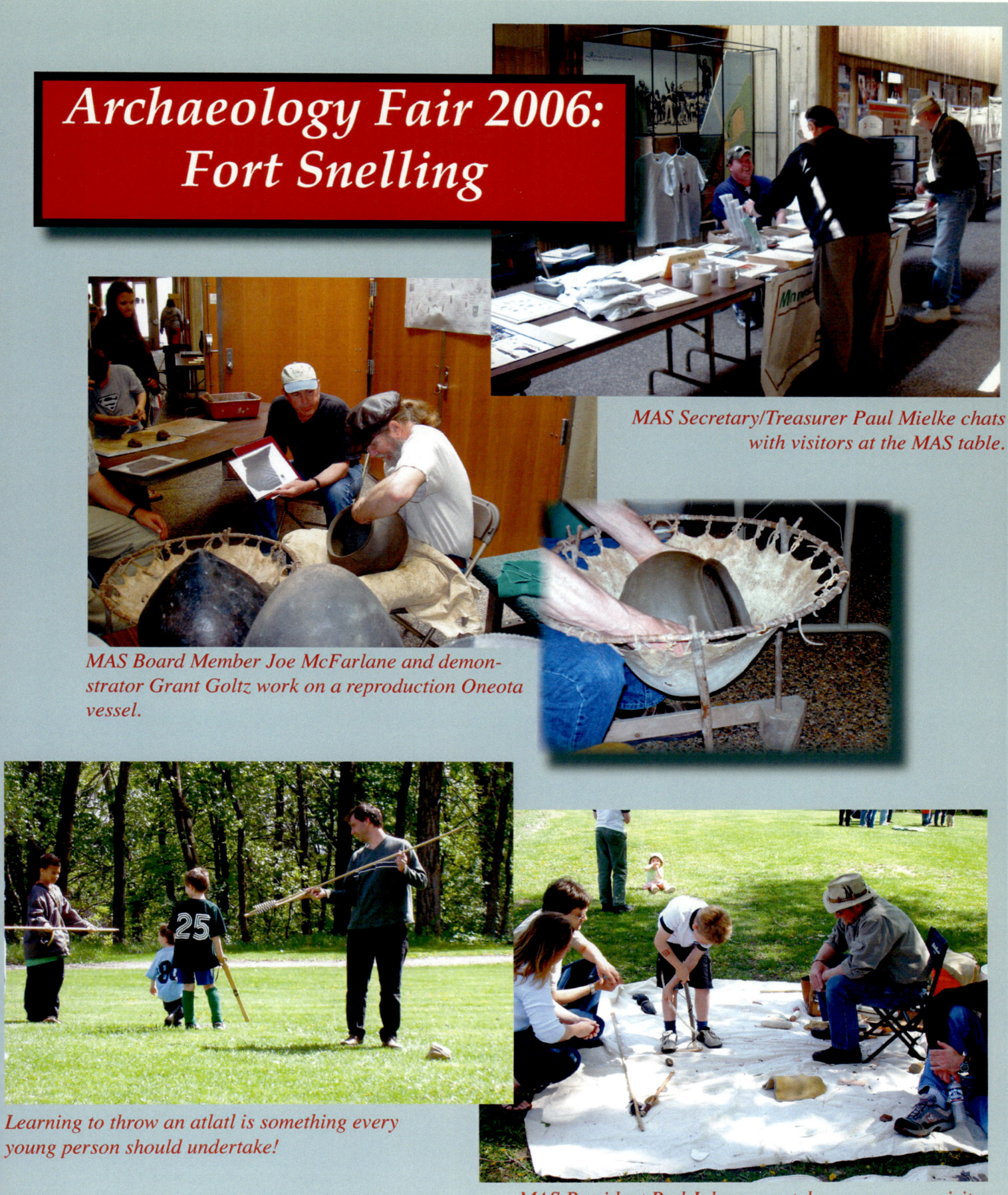

MAS Secretary/Treasurer Paul Mielke chats with visitors at the MAS table.

MAS Board Member Joe McFarlane and demonstrator Grant Goltz work on a reproduction Oneota vessel.

Learning to throw an atlatl is something every young person should undertake!

MAS President Rod Johnson watches as a young visitor learns to use a fire drill.

Animal Remains and Bone Tools From the North Twin Lake Site (21MH5), Mahnomen County, Minnesota

David Mather
Minnesota Historical Society

Zooarchaeological analysis of the Phase III assemblage from the North Twin Lake site (21MH5) reveals a diverse faunal assemblage dominated by bison, elk, and deer. Other important elements are fish, beaver, muskrat, and turtles, but these remains are thought to be underrepresented owing to taphonomic factors including scavenging by dogs. Two mandibles from domestic dogs and partially digested bone fragments are also present. The majority of the faunal assemblage was recovered from the western margin of the site, perhaps suggesting an activity area. An assemblage of six bone tools includes forms suggestive of woodworking or processing fiber and possibly one pressure flaker. The North Twin Lake faunal assemblage contributes to a growing body of data related to the human history and paleoecology of the prairie-forest ecotone.

Introduction

The interplay of ecology and culture across the transition from the Great Plains to the Eastern Woodlands is a significant issue in North American archaeology (e.g, Hickerson 1988; Michlovic 1980, 1983, 1990; Wood 1985). It is also a complicated one because the location and nature of the transition have changed dramatically during the course of the Holocene (e.g, Grimm 1985; McAndrews 1966; Shay 1971), through the combined effects of climate, vegetation, hydrology, fire, grazing animals, and human action. Within the last 150 years, the transition has been obscured or even eliminated through disruption of native vegetation by agriculture, logging, and other anthropogenic disturbance (Chapman, Fischer, and Ziegenhagen 1998; Tester 1995).

The North Twin Lake site is located at Minnesota's historical prairie-forest border, within a small area where the state's three major biomes are in closest proximity (Fig. 1). At the time of the U.S. General Land Office survey, the site area was only one mile east of the prairie edge (Trygg 1964). As such, it is an ideal case study regarding subsistence strategies and species representation in the ecotone during the Woodland tradition. Bison, elk, and deer are the prominent species within the assemblage. Domestic dog, beaver, muskrat, and turtles are also present, as is a wide array of fish species. Bird bone is present in trace amounts. Six bone tools are a particularly interesting aspect of the assemblage. Most were found at the western margin of the site (along with the majority of the other bone fragments). It is tempting to speculate that they may have been part of a toolkit for woodworking, processing fiber, or other tasks. One tool fragment may be the tip of a pressure flaker.

Zooarchaeology incorporates both the cultural and ecological aspects of ecotone studies. The primary prey animals along the prairie-forest border were bison, elk, white-tailed deer, and mule deer. Other grazing animals that may be present include moose, pronghorn antelope, and caribou. The varied representation of large grazing animals at archaeological sites across the prairie-forest border has been summarized by Shay (1985). Black and probably grizzly bears were also present along the ecotone, although they are less visible in the archaeological record. Fish species were also important resources, although they have not received the same level of analysis as large game species.

I have previously (Mather 2002) compared the North Twin Lake fauna to five other Minnesota sites along the prairie-forest border (Fig. 1): the Lake Bronson site in Kittson County (Anfinson, Michlovic, and Stein 1978), the Lake Lida, Maplewood, and Dead River sites in Otter Tail County (Mather 2002; Watrall 1985; Michlovic 1979); and the Washington Creek site in Meeker County (Mather et al. 1998). That discussion will not be repeated here. It is worth noting, however, that recent investigations have added new information relevant to the zooarchaeology of the ecotone (see below). A comprehensive review of faunal data across the prairie-forest border will be the subject of a future paper.

This article is adapted from a faunal report prepared for All Nations Cultural Resource Preservation (Mather 1996). The faunal catalog is included as an appendix in that report. Artifacts collected during the Phase III excavations were cataloged by All Nations staff under MHS Accession Number 96.1. The non-faunal artifacts and site data were later analyzed and reported by Michlovic and Sather (2000). The collection is currently housed at the White Earth Tribal Historic Preservation Office.

The North Twin Lake Site

The North Twin Lake site is a multicomponent shoreline village on the lake of the same name within the White Earth Reservation. The exact location of the site is not discussed here at the request of the White Earth Tribal Historic Preservation Office.

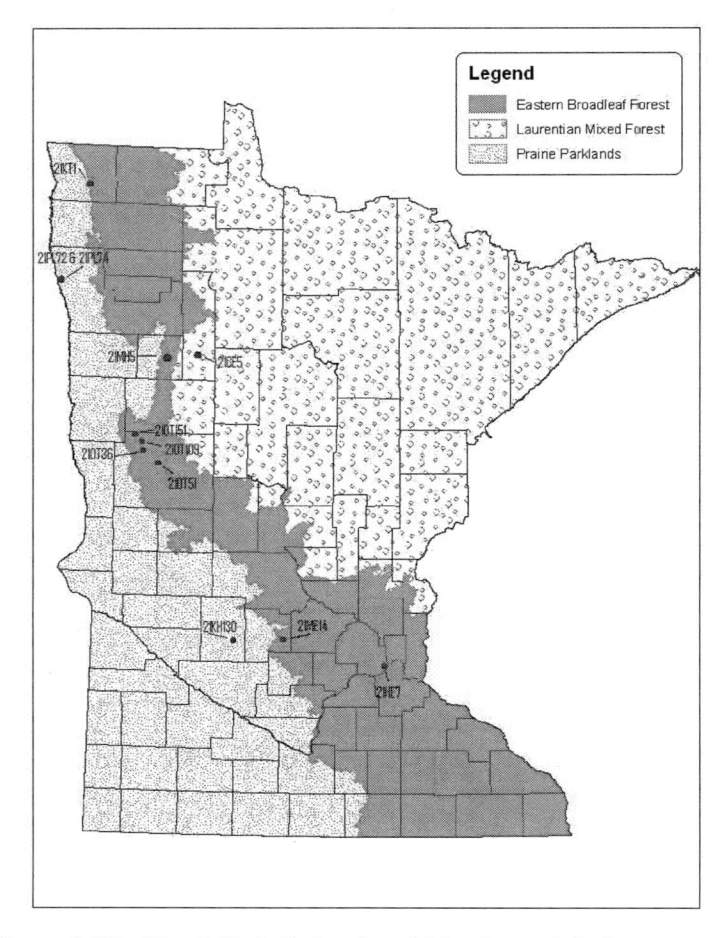

Figure 1. The North Twin Lake site within the prairie-forest ecotone, with other sites referenced in the text.

The faunal assemblage presented here was derived from Phase III excavations conducted by All Nations Cultural Resource Preservation in the winter of 1995-1996. There were five transects of shovel tests and 32 square meters of formal excavation (Fig. 2). A report of the site data and non-faunal artifacts was later completed by Moorhead State University (Michlovic and Sather 2000).

Although most pottery was found elsewhere in the site, diagnostic sherds in the western units include Laurel, Blackduck, and Sandy Lake wares (Michlovic and Sather 2000:36-41). This is the area that produced the majority of the faunal assemblage, so it is probable that most of the animal bone dates to the Middle and Late Woodland traditions. As will be discussed below, much of the bone from other areas of the site appears to be of recent origin, reflecting Historic or contemporary use of the site. The closest association for the faunal assemblage among the other artifacts is quartz debitage, for which the greatest concentration was also the western margin of the site. Swan River Chert and Knife River Flint were also present in lesser amounts (Michlovic and Sather 2000:55-57).

Other phases of investigation at the North Twin Lake site are reported by Navarre, McCauley, and Hagglund (1994), Berg (1995), and Berg and Beebe (2000).

Methods

The North Twin Lake faunal assemblage was sorted by taxonomic class and then to family, genus, or

21MH5: North Twin Lake

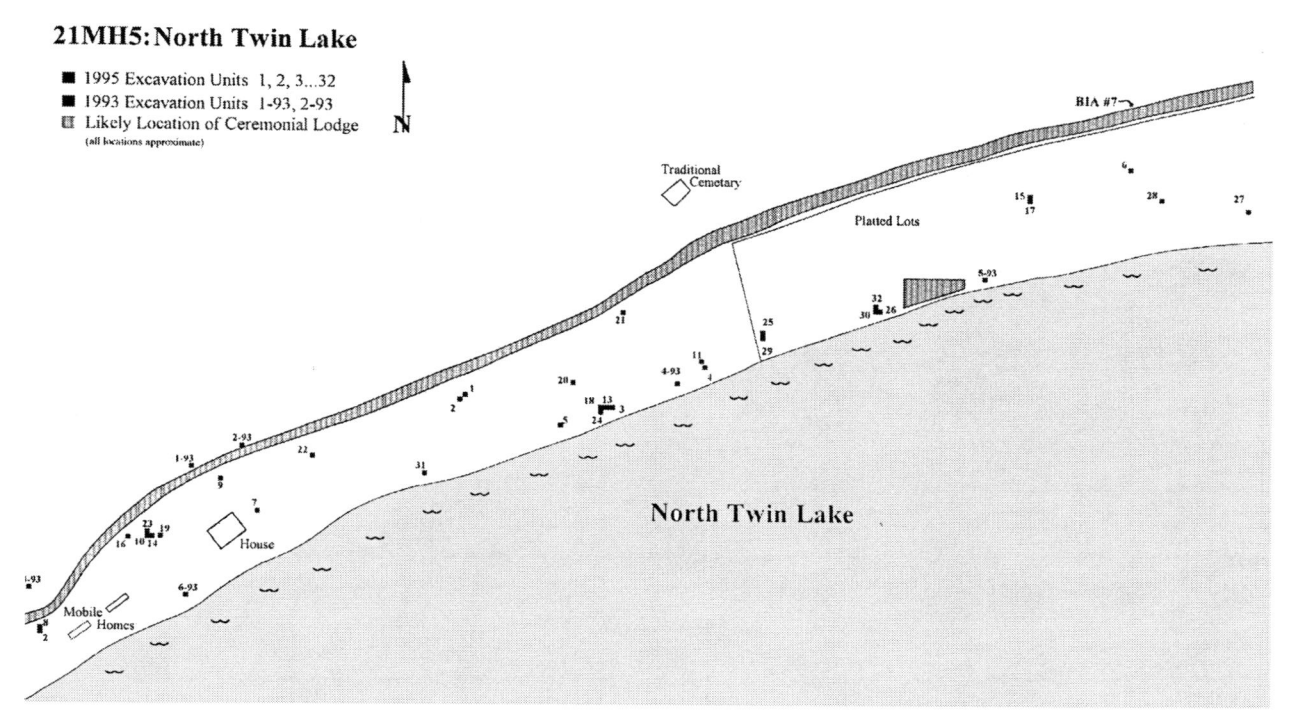

- 1995 Excavation Units 1, 2, 3...32
- 1993 Excavation Units 1-93, 2-93
- Likely Location of Ceremonial Lodge

(all locations approximate)

Figure 2. The North Twin Lake site excavations (from Michlovic and Sather 2000:15).

species through use of the vertebrate comparative collections at the Archaeology Department of the Minnesota Historical Society and the Department of Geology of the University of Iowa. Standard osteological texts were also utilized (e.g, Gilbert 1993; Gilbert, Savage, and Martin 1996; Olsen 1968; Brown and Gustafson 1979; Balkwill and Cumbaa 1992; Rojo 1991). The taxonomic nomenclature used here follows Hazard (1982) for the mammals, Oldfield and Moriarty (1994) for the reptiles, and Eddy and Underhill (1974) for the fishes. Dr. Holmes Semken kindly provided assistance with identification of selected micromammal fragments in addition to advice regarding the canid remains and other aspects of the assemblage.

The Faunal Assemblage

The animal bone recovered during the Phase III excavation is varied in terms of distribution, composition, and preservation. Perhaps most noticeable is the uneven distribution of faunal remains throughout the site. Total bone artifact counts for each test unit and shovel test transect are presented in Table 1.

The majority of the faunal assemblage was recovered from the western edge of the site. All Nations Test Units 8 and 12 (a 1 x 2 meter block) are the westernmost units (see Fig. 2). A short distance to the east is a larger concentration including Test Units 10, 14, 19, and 23 (one block) with single Test Units 16 and 19 nearby. Excluding the 789 bone fragments recovered from the shovel test transects, this relatively small area of the site accounts for 55 percent of the total assemblage. The same site area is covered by approximately the first eight shovel tests of Transects 1 through 5. The bone counts from those tests total 411 fragments. Combining the test unit and shovel test totals accounts for 85 percent of the total site faunal assemblage from less than 20 percent of the total site area. The only unit outside this area with bone counts exceeding 100 is Test Unit 15, which mainly consists of *Esox* (northern pike/ muskellunge) bone of recent origin. This skewed distribution limits intrasite comparison except at the most basic level, as the faunal assemblage of the western site margin is essentially the same as that for the site as a whole.

All bone was separated to the greatest degree possible between mammal, reptile, bird, and fish. Un-

Table 1: Identification to Class by Provenience.

PROV.	MAMMAL		FISH	BIRD	UNID.	OTHER	TOTAL
ST T-1	64	1	30	2	133	-	230
ST T-2	27	-	7	2	75	-	111
ST T-3	113	3	1	2	20	-	139
ST T-4	21	-	-	-	4	-	25
ST T-5	152	5	3	1	108	-	269
ST T-6	8	-	3	-	4	-	15
TU 1	3	-	-	-	14	-	17
TU 2	13	1	-	-	55	-	69
TU 3	4	1	-	2	6	-	13
TU 4	14	2	12	-	22	-	50
TU 5	15	4	4	1	30	-	54
TU 6	3	-	-	-	6	-	9
TU 7	2	-	6	-	12	-	20
TU 8	30	2	2	-	88	1 (snail)	123
TU 9	7	-	8	-	74	-	89
TU 10	48	17	3	-	90	-	158
TU 11	16	4	7	-	26	-	53
TU 12	104	-	7	-	125	-	236
TU 13	-	-	-	-	-	-	0
TU 14	21	30	3	1	43	-	98
TU 15	14	-	134	8	9	-	165
TU 16	-	-	-	-	-	-	0
TU 17	1	-	-	-	2	-	3
TU 18	4	-	-	-	1	-	5
TU 19	31	2	4	1	32	-	70
TU 20	-	-	-	-	-	-	0
TU 21	3	-	-	-	6	-	9
TU 22	12	-	-	-	26	-	38
TU 23	64	20	18	1	131	-	234
TU 24	12	-	-	-	1	-	13
TU 25	6	-	-	-	-	-	6
TU 26	2	-	-	-	6	-	8
TU 27	36	-	2	-	30	-	68
TU 28	2	-	-	-	2	-	4
TU 29	4	-	-	-	5	-	9
TU 30	4	-	-	-	21	-	25
TU 31	-	-	-	-	3	-	3
TU 32	2	-	-	-	10	-	12
TOTAL	862	92	254	21	1220	1	2450

identified remains (48 percent of the total) were generally small fragments that could not be placed in the other categories with certainty. Much of the unidentified bone consists of calcined fragments. Table 1 shows that, excluding the unidentified bone, mammal remains (35%) dominate the assemblage by count, followed by fish (10%), then reptile (4%), and finally bird (1%).

Taxonomic Identifications and Abundance

The faunal assemblage is quantified in Table 2 by Number of Identified Specimens (NISP) and Minimum Number of Individuals (MNI). The NISP is simply the number of identified fragments within a taxonomic category. The MNI is a calculation of the minimum number of animals within that category needed to account for the body part fragments present. As a hypothetical example, if three left dog jaw

Table 2. North Twin Lake Faunal Assemblage, NISP and MNI by Taxon

TAXON	NISP	MNI
Mammals		
Bison, *Bison* sp.	17	2
Elk, *Cervus elaphas*	7	1
Bison/ Elk, *Bison/ Cervus*	11	--
Deer, *Odocoileus* sp.	8	2
Hoofed mammal, undifferentiated (Order Artiodactyla)	54	--
Red fox, *Vulpes vulpes*	1	1
Domestic dog, *Canis familiaris*	2	1
Dog/ Wolf/ Coyote, *Canis* sp.	3	--
Beaver, *Castor canadensis*	13	1
Muskrat, *Ondatra zibethicus*	105*	8
Franklin's ground squirrel, *Spermophilus franklinii*	1	1
Short-tailed shrew, *Blarina brevicauda*	1	1
Large-size mammal, undifferentiated	22	--
Medium-size mammal, undifferentiated	6	--
Small-size mammal, undifferentiated	8	--
Micro-mammal, undifferentiated	7	--
Mammal, undifferentiated	596	--
Birds		
Bird, undifferentiated	21	--
Reptiles		
Turtle, undifferentiated (Order Testudinia)	91	--
Reptile, undifferentiated	1	--
Fish		
Northern pike/ muskellunge, *Esox* sp.	117*	10
White/ longnose sucker, *Catostomus* sp.	1	1
Brown bullhead, *Ictalurus nebulosus*	2	1
Bullhead/ catfish, *Ictalurus* sp.	3	--
Sunfish, *Lepomis* sp.	2	1
Crappie, *Poxomis* sp.	1	1
Walleye/ sauger, *Stizostedion* sp.	4	2
Yellow perch, *Perca flavescens*	1	1
Fish, undifferentiated	123	--
Mollusks		
Snail, undifferentiated	1	1
Unidentified	1220	--

* Counts strongly influenced by recent bone.

Table 3: Body Part Representation - Selected Mammals

	Beaver	Muskrat	Dog	Bison	Elk	Deer
Mandible	1 right	4 left, 1 right	1 left, 1 right	-	-	-
Incisor	3	3	-	1	-	-
Teeth	8 molars	1	-	-	1 left m1	1
Horncore	-	-	-	1 (?)	-	-
Scapula	-	-	-	-	1 right	-
Humerus	-	-	-	-	-	1 right immature
Radius	-	-	-	-	-	1 right
Femur	-	2 left, 1 right, 1 rt epiph	-	1 right px epiph	-	-
Tibia	-	3 left, 2 right	-	1 right	-	-
MetaT/C	-	-	-	1	-	2 (1 bone)
Astragalus	-	8 left, 6 right	-	1 left	-	-
Calcaneus	-	6 left, 5 right	-	1 right	-	2 right (1 bone)
Man./Pes undiff.	-	-	-	1	3	1
Carpal/Tarsal	-	28 undiff.	-	-	-	-
Phalanx	1 1st	-	-	6 2nd, 1 term.	1 1st, 1 2nd	-
Vertebra	-	34 caudal	-	2 cervical	-	-
Total	13	105	2	17	7	8

fragments are present in a group of seven dog bone fragments, the MNI for the *Canis familiaris* category is 3, and the NISP is 7 (Reitz and Wing 1999; Hesse and Wapnish 1985; Davis 1987; Lyman 1994).

Bison, elk, and deer are clearly the dominant mammals of the assemblage. Much of the undifferentiated mammal bone, and that able to be ascribed to the Artiodactyl category, is presumed to also have originated from these animals. Identified mammals also include domestic dog and other canids and beaver and muskrat. Turtles and a variety of fish species are represented. Bird bone fragments are present in trace amounts. The high counts of muskrat and northern pike/ muskellunge relative to the other taxa are owing to the presence of recent, intrusive specimens. That issue is treated in the discussion of assemblage taphonomy, below. Even if those counts were included, however, just one bison, elk, or deer would provide more usable meat than all of the other identifications combined.

Turtle and bird bone were too fragmented to allow species identifications, and calculation of MNI estimates was therefore not possible.

Hoofed Mammals: It is apparent that bison was the primary single animal resource for occupants of the North Twin Lake site. Herds of bison were characteristic of the western Minnesota prairies until the Historic era, and also occurred in the oak savannas and open deciduous woodlands reaching to the Mississippi River. Holocene-age bones of both modern bison (*Bison bison*) and the extinct *Bison occidentalis* have been recovered throughout much of Minnesota, south and west of a line extending approximately from Mille Lacs to the Headwaters region to Lake of the Woods (Hazard 1982; Lukens 1963). The diagnostic elements necessary for distinguishing between these species and the various subspecies are not present in the North Twin Lake assemblage (e.g, van Zyll de Jong 1986; McDonald 1981), but there seems little reason to suspect them to be other than *Bison bison*.

Table 4: Body Part Representation - Fish
R=Recent

	Northern	Walleye	Br. Bullhead	Crappie	Sucker	Perch
Maxilla	1 left	1 R	-	-	-	-
Dentary	2 right 1 undiff 4 left R 1 right R 1 undiff R	-	-	-	-	1 right
Articular	4 left R 1 right R 1 undiff R	1 left R 1 right	1 left 1 right	-	-	-
Palatine	1 1 R	-	-	-	-	-
Quadrate	1 1 R	1	-	-	-	-
Frontal	1 left R 2 right R	-	-	-	-	-
Preopercle		1 right	-	-	-	-
Opercle	1 left R 2 undiff R	-	-	-	1	-
Subopercle	1 R	-	-	-	-	-
Cleithrum	3 left 2 right 1 undiff 7 left R 3 right R	-	-	-	-	-
Parasphen.	1 R	-	-	-	-	-
Ceratohyal	2 R	-	-	1	-	-
Ectopteryg.	1	-	-	-	-	-
Vertebra	69 R	-	-	-	-	-
unid.	1 R	-	-	-	-	-
Total	117	4	2	1	1	1

Inclusive of tentative identifications, bison are represented primarily by phalanges (5 second and 1 terminal), one astragalus, and one calcaneus. An immature individual is represented by the proximal epiphysis of a right femur. Also present is the distal end of a right tibia. One tentative identification was made of a horn core fragment (Table 3). These identifications account for a MNI determination of 2. It should be noted that other bison elements are surely represented in the combined *Bison/Cervus* category, and within the broader categories of Artiodactyl and Large Mammal. Despite these combined categories, the greater role of bison compared to elk is suggested by the higher number of specific identifications (17 to 7), as shown in Tables 2 and 3.

The elk (*Cervus elaphas*) is osteologically similar to the bison (cf. Brown and Gustafson 1979), but in truth it is a closer relative to deer. Therefore, elk specimens are also assumed to be within the combined *Bison/Cervus*, Artiodactyl, and Large Mammal categories. Elk were once common in Minnesota on the prairie and along the prairie-forest border but have been absent except as managed herds since the early twentieth century (Hazard 1982). Elk are represented in the North Twin Lake assemblage solely by foot/ankle bones and dentition. One tentatively identified medial right scapula fragment is also present (Table 3). The *Cervus* NISP of 7 accounts for a MNI of 1.

Deer are represented by 2 animals (MNI) and a NISP of 8. The North Twin Lake deer could be either white-tailed deer (*Odocoileus virginianus*) or mule deer (*O. hemionus*). These species are generally associated with the forest or prairie, respectively, but

Table 5: Taphonomy by Provenience

PROV.	C	B	E	G	E/G	S	S/B	D	M	R	-	TOTAL
ST T-1	8	8	3	1	1	1	-	1	1	3	203	230
ST T-2	30	13	-	-	-	1	-	-	-	5	62	111
ST T-3	-	-	-	1	-	-	-	-	-	-	138	139
ST T-4	-	2	4	-	-	7	1	-	-	-	11	25
ST T-5	20	17	15	3	23	-	1	-	3	-	187	269
ST T-6	2	-	2	-	-	-	-	-	-	-	11	15
TU 1	9	-	2	-	-	1	-	-	-	5		17
TU 2	8	1	16	-	-	-	-	-	-	-	44	69
TU 3	2	1	3	1	-	-	-	-	-	-	6	13
TU 4	-	3	2	-	-	-	-	2	-	2	41	50
TU 5	6	-	-	-	-	-	1	-	-	-	47	54
TU 6	-	1	-	-	-	-	-	-	-	-	8	9
TU 7	-	-	10	-	-	-	-	-	-	6	4	20
TU 8	38	2	-	1	1	-	-	-	-	-	81	123
TU 9	73	3	-	-	-	-	-	-	-	3	10	89
TU 10	17	3	6	-	-	-	-	-	-	-	132	158
TU 11	5	6	-	-	-	-	-	-	-	-	42	53
TU 12	15	2	2	-	-	-	-	1	2	-	214	236
TU 13	-	-	-	-	-	-	-	-	-	-	-	0
TU 14	9	4	3	1	-	-	-	-	2	2	77	98
TU 15	25	-	-	-	-	-	-	-	-	133	7	165
TU 16	-	-	-	-	-	-	-	-	-	-	-	0
TU 17	2	-	-	-	1	-	-	-	-	-	-	3
TU 18	-	1	-	-	-	-	-	-	-	2	2	5
TU 19	3	2	-	1	-	-	-	-	3	-	61	70
TU 20	-	-	-	-	-	-	-	-	-	-	-	0
TU 21	2	1	1	-	-	-	-	-	-	-	5	9
TU 22	21	4	-	-	-	-	2	-	1	-	10	38
TU 23	107	4	3	1	-	1	-	-	1	-	117	234
TU 24	-	-	-	-	1	2	-	-	-	-	10	13
TU 25	-	-	1	-	-	-	-	-	-	-	5	6
TU 26	5	-	1	-	-	1	-	-	-	-	1	8
TU 27	2	-	5	1	1	-	-	-	-	1	58	68
TU 28	-	-	-	-	1	-	-	-	-	-	3	4
TU 29	2	1	2	1	2	-	-	-	-	-	1	9
TU 30	4	10	-	-	-	-	-	-	-	-	11	25
TU 31	3	-	-	-	-	-	-	-	-	-	-	3
TU 32	8	2	-	-	-	-	-	-	-	-	2	12
TOTAL	426	91	81	12	31	13	6	4	13	162	1611	2450

Key: C: Calcined   B: Burned   E: Eroded   G: Rodent gnawed   E/G: Eroded and Gnawed
S: Spiral Fracture   S/B: Spiral Fracture and Burned   D: Digested   M: Modified and Tools
R: Recent   -: None

both were once common along the ecotone (Hazard 1982). It should be noted that this analysis was completed before Jacobson's (2003) comparative osteology study of mule and white-tailed deer was available. As detailed in Table 3, deer are represented by one calcaneus, one radius fragment, and foot/ankle bones and dentition. An immature animal is indicated by a right humerus with unfused epiphyses.

Other hoofed mammals that might be expected at North Twin Lake include moose, caribou, and pronghorn (Shay 1985; Hazard 1982), but they were not identified in the Phase III assemblage. It should be noted that comparative specimens of caribou and pronghorn were not available during the analysis, but all Artiodactyl remains identifiable to element were consistent with the more expected taxa.

Beaver and Muskrat: Following the artiodactyls, large rodents are the most abundant mammal remains. Beaver (*Castor canadensis*) is most prevalent, with an NISP of 13 and MNI of 1. Muskrat is also present, but many bones of this species are suspected to be of recent origin. The MNI of 8 demonstrates that the high NISP count of 105 is from the remains of relatively few individual animals. Although the muskrat bone does not appear to be obviously recent, an intrusive origin is suspected owing to the concentration of remains. Beaver and muskrat would both be expected in North Twin Lake, as well as the surrounding area's wetland and drainages (Hazard 1982).

Dogs and Other Canids: Domestic dog (*Canis familiaris*) is of most interest among the North Twin Lake canids. These identifications (NISP 2, MNI 1) were possible owing to well-preserved mandible fragments with the close, "crowded" tooth spacing characteristic of the domestic species (e.g, Olsen 1985). These specimens appear to be from fairly large animals of approximately wolf-size. The domestic dog is of great antiquity in North America, with finds dating from the late Pleistocene. The morphology of extant *C. familiaris* archaeological remains suggests considerable variability in size and form, which potentially represent differing breeds. The largest of these are wolf-size (Olsen 1985).

In relative proximity to North Twin Lake, a domestic dog dating to approximately 7000 BP is reported from the Itasca Bison Kill site (Shay 1971). Dogs were also present at the Late Woodland village sites near Mille Lacs Lake (Whelan 1990). In addition, a necklace of canid teeth was associated with one of the Arvilla burials at the Lake Bronson site (Johnson 1973; Anfinson, Michlovic, and Stein 1978). Through ethnographic accounts, dogs are known to have been an important source of traction and food (Snyder 1991). No evidence of butchery is apparent on the relatively few canid remains from the North Twin Lake assemblage.

In addition to the domestic dogs, canids are represented by three fragments left at the genus level of *Canis* sp. These could be either domestic dog, wolf, or coyote. One carnassial from a red fox (*Vulpes vulpes*) is present in the assemblage.

Fish: *Esox* (northern pike/ muskellunge) are the most prevalent fish with an MNI count of 10 and NISP of 117 (Tables 2 and 4). The majority of the *Esox* remains are of modern origin, however, and were primarily recovered from Test Unit 15. "Old" specimens account for an MNI of 3 and NISP of 13. When also excluding recent bone, *Ictalurus* (bullhead) and *Stizostedion* (walleye/ sauger) are next most common. Two articulars were identifiable as brown bullhead (*I. nebulosus*) and three other specimens only to the generic level, for a total *Ictalurus* NISP of 5 and an *I. nebulosus* MNI of 1. *Stizostedion* total 5 NISP and 2 MNI, one of which is of recent origin. Crappie (*Poxomis*) and perch (*Perca flavescens*) each have an NISP and MNI of 1. Two specimens of *Lepomis* (sunfish) were identified, but both are of recent origin.

All of the fish identified in the North Twin Lake assemblage spawn in the spring, but northern pike and crappies are also particularly susceptible to being taken through the ice (Eddy and Underhill 1974). Although a limited sample, the Phase III assemblage suggests that North Twin Lake, at the time of site occupancy, fell between the classifications of "walleye lake" and "bass-panfish lake" as defined by Phillips, Schmid, and Underhill (1982). The former are generally large and shallow and well oxygenated. Classic examples are Mille Lacs and Red Lake. Other important fish in walleye lakes include pike, bass, perch, eelpout, and suckers. Bass-panfish lakes are typically smaller and more fertile. Panfish are most common in such lakes, but bass, pike, bullheads, perch, and walleye are also present.

Taphonomy

The taphonomy (Lyman 1994) of this assemblage is as important as the taxonomic identifications in interpreting past human behavior at the North Twin Lake site. The condition of the bone fragments is partly the result of human action (disposing of bones in the fire or feeding them to dogs) and partly owing to postdepositional influences such as rodent gnawing and decomposition. The assemblage as a whole is very well preserved, with the majority (66 %) bearing no clear indications of taphonomic processes. Table 5 presents the varied condition of the North Twin Lake bone. Recorded observations include calcination and burning of bone, spiral fractures, eroded and rodent-gnawed surfaces, digested bone, modified bone, and bone of recent origin.

Some issues of taxonomic abundance appear to be the result of taphonomic processes. Fish bone is particularly susceptible to postdepositional fragmentation. Wheeler and Jones (1989:151) point out that estimates of fish abundance are less reliable than those for mammals because of differential preservation. Recovery methods can also bias an assemblage. At the McKinstry site, for example, mooneye and goldeye were found to be important fish species but were only recovered from the fine-screen flotation samples (Morey, Falk, and Semken 1996). It is assumed that fish are underrepresented in the North Twin Lake assemblage, where a relatively large range of fish taxa were was identified in low quantities.

Burned and calcined bone combined are the most prevalent forms of bone alteration seen in the North Twin Lake assemblage. These are presumed to be the result of food refuse disposal, although food preparation could also be argued to be the case for the former. Other indications of foodways are seen in the spiral fractures, which are a classic sign of fractured green bone. Although there are numerous potential mechanisms for the breaking of green bone, a primary cause is the intentional breakage by people to extract marrow. One method documented ethnographically involves the heating of bones by fire to allow for easier breakage. This may account for the North Twin Lake bone fragments that exhibit both burning and spiral fractures, but the simpler explanation of food refuse disposal by fire is equally plausible (c.f. Brain 1981; Binford 1981; Bonnichson and Will 1993).

Modified bone includes bone tools (discussed below) and fragments with evidence of cut marks. Less than 1 percent of the assemblage was modified in these manners. Six of the 13 artifacts in this category are bone tools. While the concentration of the bone assemblage at the western edge of the site is suggestive of some sort of processing, the small numbers of modified bone suggest that it was not the location of bone tool manufacture. Likewise, it is surprising that more evidence of butchering is not evident in the assemblage. Perhaps most of the cut marks were obscured or destroyed by the other taphonomic factors discussed here, such as consumption by dogs or burning.

The combined categories of eroded, gnawed, and eroded/ gnawed account for 5 percent of the assemblage. These characteristics suggest the discard of food refuse in exposed areas, outside of fires or middens, where the bones were exposed to the elements and gnawed by rodents. It should be noted that eroded bone can be difficult to discern from bone that has been partially digested. In both cases the surface of the bone is etched. Further disfiguration, such as through pitting of the bone surface, is more indicative of partial digestion. Severely eroded bone is more likely to simply disintegrate after corrosive damage proceeds beyond modification of the surface. Less than 1 percent of the assemblage shows clear evidence of partial digestion. Some digested bone may be the result of human consumption, but dogs or other scavengers are considered to be the primary source owing to the size of the bone fragments (one partially digested elk metapodial condyle is approximately the size of a golf ball). The role of dogs is supported by the identification of the remains of domestic dogs and other canids, as discussed above.

Despite the small number of bones showing direct evidence of digestion, the behavior of dogs as co-inhabitants of the site is interpreted as having an impact on the faunal assemblage. An observation by Johann Georg Kohl about the habits of dogs in a nineteenth century Ojibwe village is instructive in this regard:

> Their great object of life is to crawl into the huts and carry off something edible; but they are continually driven out by the women and children, and recommended, by a sharp blow, to satisfy themselves with the fish and beaver bones thrown out for them. [Kohl 1985:37]

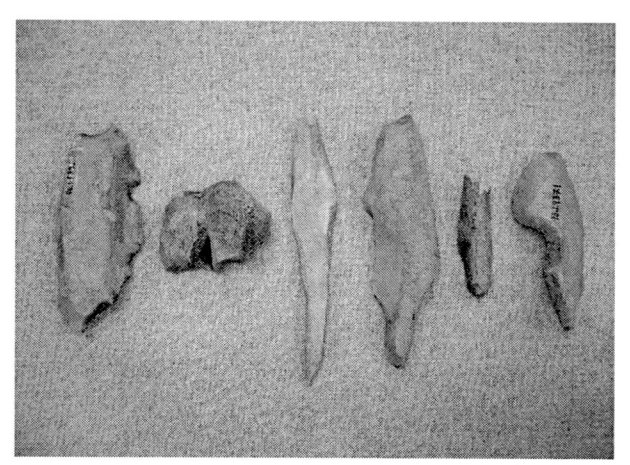

Figure 3. Bone Tools 1-6 (left to right), exterior bone surface (see text for tool measurements).

The amount of partially digested bone is not thought to reflect the amount actually consumed by dogs. Rather, it is presumed that the majority would have been entirely digested and thus destroyed. The few specimens of partially digested bone are all from large mammals and are therefore fairly robust and more likely to be preserved in general. Differential preservation of fish remains in particular was discussed earlier. It is doubtful that fish bone or bones of small mammals or birds would survive consumption by dogs. These animals can then be thought to have played a larger role in the North Twin Lake subsistence economy than is accounted for by the identifications alone.

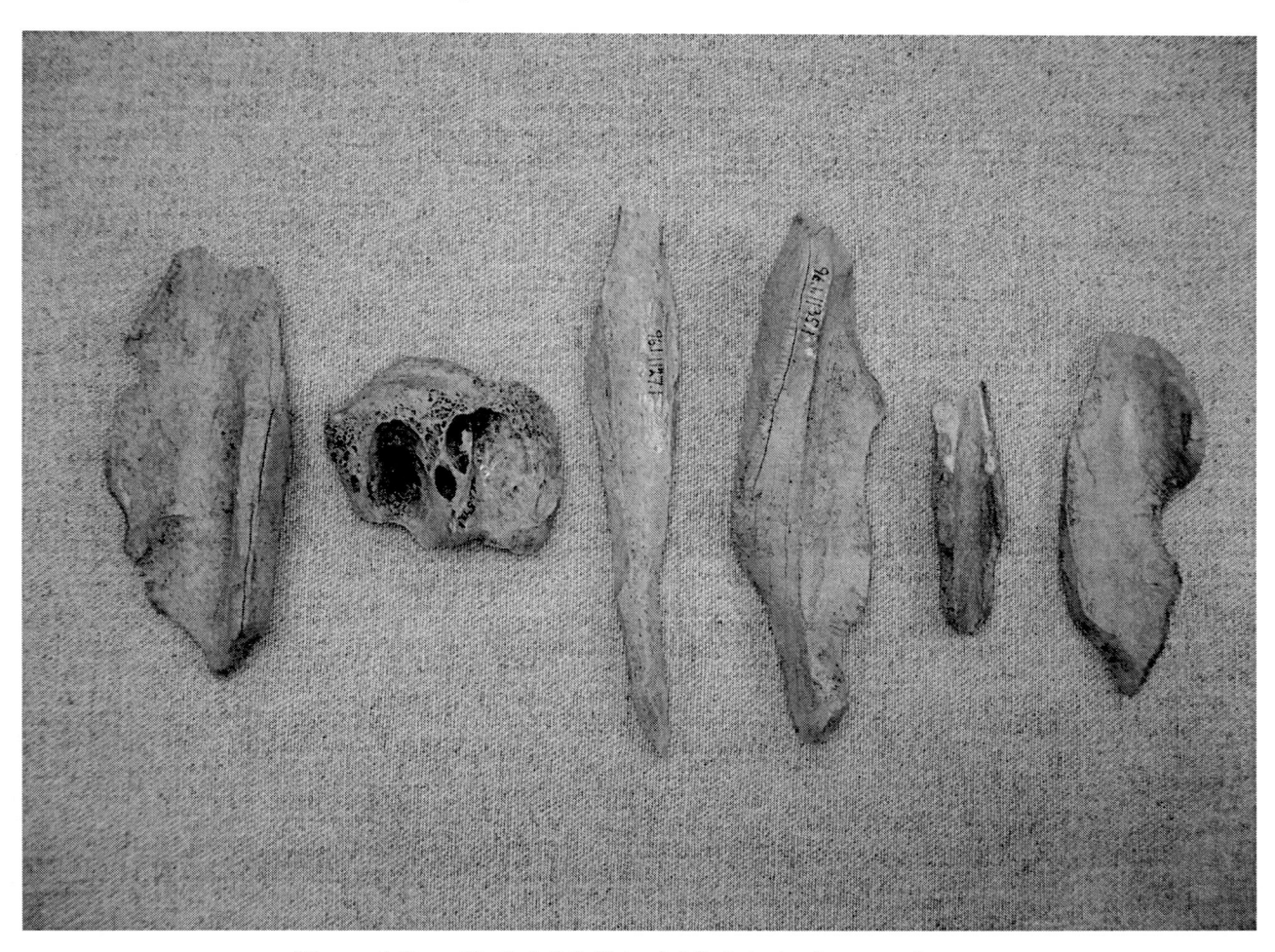

Figure 4. Bone Tools 1-6 (left to right), interior bone surface.

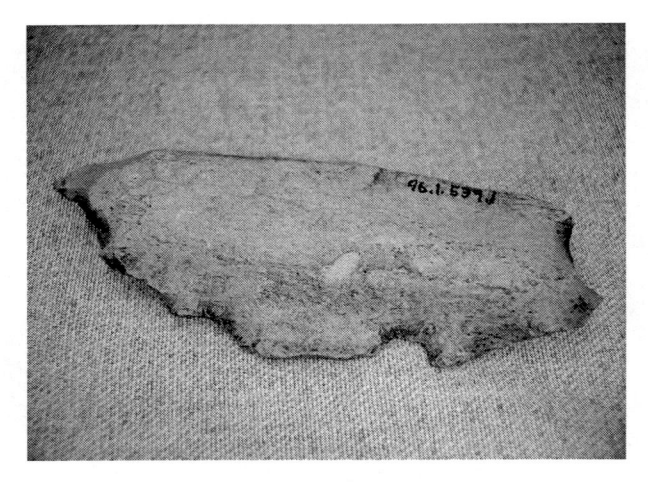

Figure 5. Detail of potential spokeshave features on Tool 1.

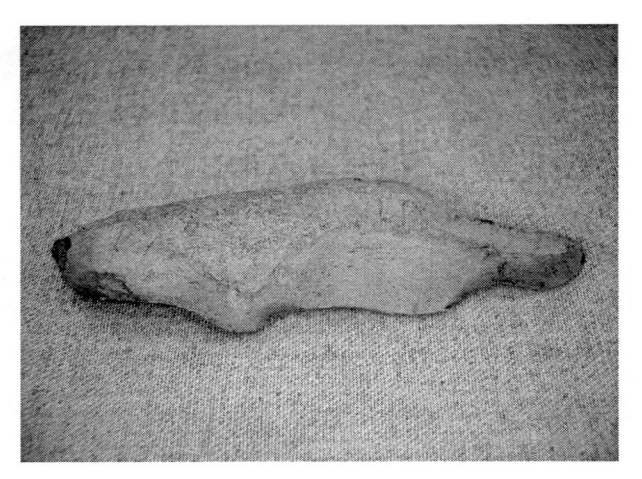

Figure 6. Detail of potential spokeshave feature on Tool 4.

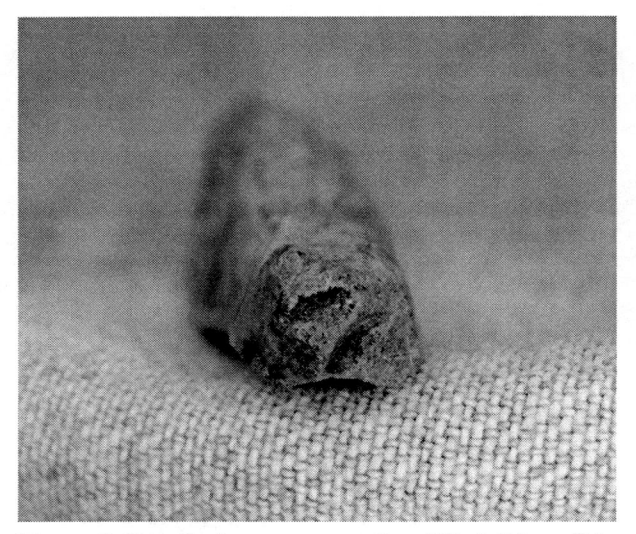

Figure 7. Detail of use-wear on tip of Tool 5 (possible pressure flaker).

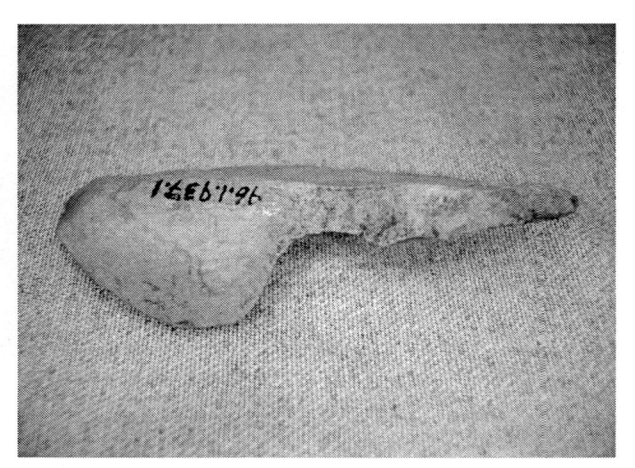

Figure 8. Detail of potential spokeshave feature on Tool 6.

Bone Tools

Six bone tools are present in the North Twin Lake assemblage (Figs. 3 and 4). All are fashioned from mammal longbone. Most bear evidence of manufacture from green bone, with opportunistic use of sharp point and edges resulting from spiral fractures.

Three of the tools have been retouched to create small, concave, round cutting surfaces. Tool 1 has four of these working edges, of varying size. I suspect that these may be spokeshaves used for working wood or fiber. The round (presumed) cutting edges would be a good size for stripping bark off twigs and small branches or shaving an arrow shaft, for example. Suggesting a function for the tools based on their morphology cannot be more than speculation, however. These tools would be an ideal study collection for microscopic use-wear analysis.

There are some small, linear grooves on some of the tools, including at least one of the round areas on Tool 1, that could be tooth marks from small rodents. I do not believe, however, that the unique shapes of the tools were formed by rodent gnawing. If these fragments of bone were modified by rodent gnawing alone, I would expect the marks to be more evenly distributed. Some of the grooves also appear to be the result of shaping the tool edges, or perhaps from use of the tools. Also, all six pieces still have sharp edges and polished surfaces.

The North Twin Lake assemblage does not include barbed harpoons and other patterned tools or decorated bone adornments such as have been recovered at the nearby Lower River Lake site (Bakken 1994) and at regional sites ascribed to the Arvilla Complex by Johnson (1973).

The distribution of the bone tools within the site mirrors that of the faunal assemblage as a whole in that four of the six are from near the western edge, concentrated in the excavation block consisting of Test Units 10, 14, 19, and 23. Two of the tools are from Test Unit 19. The other two are from shovel tests in Transect 5, immediately adjacent to the excavation block on the east and west sides. The bone tools are individually described as Tools 1-6 below. In the verbal descriptions, orientation of the tools is with the primary edge or point facing down, facing the exterior surface of the bone. Tools 1 through 4 are those concentrated in and around Test Unit 19.

Tool 1: *Accession Number 96.1.539.1, Test Unit 19, NE 35-40*
7.8 cm length x 3.2 cm width

This tool is fashioned from a robust segment of large mammal longbone. It is flaked to a tip at one end, apparently along the edge of a spiral fracture. The adjacent edge is thick (ca. 1 cm) and rounded, possibly as a result of the natural edge of the bone being carved or polished. The opposite long side is flatter but does not come to a sharp edge. Two probable spokeshave features are present on this edge. A third fills the short edge opposite the tip. A fourth possible spokeshave is present to the right and immediately adjacent to the tip (see Fig. 5).

Tool 2: *Accession Number 96.1.543.1, Test Unit 19, NE 45-50*
4.5 cm length x 3.4 cm width

The epiphysis of a large (possibly deer-sized) mammal is the basis for this tool, although the specific element could not be securely identified. It is flaked to a sharp edge along three of its four margins. The fourth edge is approximately 1.5 cm thick owing to the morphology of the bone. A natural foramen in the bone may have been a functional part of the tool, but it does not appear to have been enlarged.

Tool 3: *Accession Number 96.1.1127.1, Transect 5, Shovel Test 8*
10.0 cm length (broken) x 2.1 cm width

This tool is carved from a piece of mammal longbone that may have been opened when green, although the edges are modified to the point of obscuring the diagnostic spiral fractures. The working tip is carved down to a sharp point. The opposite end shows evidence of a recent break.

Tool 4: *Accession Number 96.1.1135.1, Transect 5, Shovel Test 9*
9.4 cm length x 2.7 cm width

This artifact is fashioned from a robust segment of large mammal longbone. The spatulate end measures approximately 2 cm in length by 1 cm in width. The opposite end has also been worked. The edges of the tool exhibit the classic spiral fracture pattern from breaking green bone. The function of the spatulate end is ambiguous, but similar forms have been documented at the Arvilla sites and the Washington Creek site (Johnson 1973; Mather et al. 1998). The curved side of the spatulate end may have functioned as a spokeshave. A natural depression in the bone below that feature may be polished from use (Fig. 6).

Tool 5: *Accession Number 96.1.1101.1, Transect 3, Shovel Test 3*
4.5 cm length (broken) x .5 cm width

Tool 5 was recovered from a shovel test a short distance west from the concentration described above. It is possible that this tool is a reworked version of Tool 3, resulting in a more blunt working tip. The tool is fashioned from a segment of mammal longbone. Little modification is evident other than at the end. Two short (ca. 1 mm) cuts are visible on the tip of the tool. The function of the tool and the source of the cuts are unknown. It is tempting to speculate that the tool may have been used as a pressure flaker during flint knapping (Fig. 7).

Tool 6: *Accession Number 96.1.937.1, Transect 1, Shovel Test 45 6.6 cm length x 2.6 cm width*
Recovered at the eastern edge of the site, this tool is far removed spatially from the concentration described above. It is most similar in morphology to Tool 1. There is a prominent tip and a relatively large spokeshave feature in the middle of one side. Little other modification is evident. The spokeshave may represent opportunistic use of a spiral fracture (Fig. 8).

Discussion

The North Twin Lake assemblage is reflective of a diverse subsistence economy within which big game hunting held an important role. The most prevalent animal resource was bison, followed by deer and elk. In preferred habitat, these animals span the prairie-forest border, but all can be present in the ecotone. Other animals represented in the assemblage include beaver, muskrat, turtle, bird, and fish. The muskrats and the fish remains include some specimens of recent origin. The turtles and birds were too fragmented to allow for more specific identification.

All of these animals, inclusive of the larger game, are thought to be underrepresented in the archaeological assemblage owing to consumption of food waste by dogs. The presence of dogs is confirmed by mandible fragments bearing the diagnostic traits of the domestic species. Their activities are suggested by the presence of partially digested bone fragments, and representation of the large mammal species is mainly by robust carpals, tarsals, and phalanges. Consumption by dogs of the remains of beaver, muskrat, fish, and other smaller animals is expected to have destroyed most of the bones entirely. Fragmentation of large mammal bone is also because of the intentional fracture of green bone by people for marrow extraction and potentially for bone-tool manufacture. Thus, analysis of taphonomic processes is equally important to taxonomic identifications in zooarchaeological interpretation of the North Twin Lake assemblage.

Consideration of bone taphonomy also found that after elimination of recent, intrusive bone, the majority (85 %) of the assemblage is clustered at the western margin of the site. Discussion of intrasite variability is therefore rather limited, except as the bone distribution may suggest some sort of activity area at that location. Four of the six bone tools were also recovered from this area, although the lack of other worked bone suggests that this was not primarily a place of bone tool manufacture. Likewise, clear evidence of butchery is scarce.

Zooarchaeology of the Prairie-Forest Border

As mentioned earlier, North Twin Lake is one of a series of archaeological sites along the historical extent of the prairie-forest ecotone. A previous article (Mather 2002) on the Lake Lida site (21OT109) fauna included comparison with the North Twin Lake assemblage as well as the Lake Bronson site (21KT1), the Dead River site (21OT51), the Maplewood site (21OT36), and the Washington Creek site (21ME14). That discussion will not be repeated here, except to reiterate that the nature of the ecotone differs among these site locations.

North Twin Lake is most similar in its faunal assemblage to Maplewood and Lake Bronson, with bison the primary meat source, supplemented by elk and deer. Complicating factors in these and any comparisons along the ecotone include the taphonomic biases imposed by dogs and other factors, the large span of time represented at the sites in question, and the relatively small amount of excavation conducted to date, inclusive of the North Twin Lake investigations. Thus, while North Twin Lake contributes to the regional data, many questions remain.

A future overview of faunal assemblages along the prairie-forest border will be more comprehensive than that presented in the Lake Lida article. Several recent studies add context to the discussion, and it is expected that the dataset will continue to grow.

Highlights of the recent studies include two bison kill sites, 21PL72 and 21PL74, in East Grand Forks (Harvey et al. 2005), adding to the context of previously known bison processing sites along the Red River (e.g, Michlovic 1986, 1987). Closer to the ecotone itself, an apparent bison kill site (21OT151) has been discovered in Otter Tail County (Hohman-Caine and Goltz 2004; Mather 2004).

The complex nature of the ecotone is highlighted by refugia of Big Woods vegetation at islands within the former extent of prairie in Little Kandiyohi Lake. One site there, 21KH130, produced hundreds of bone fragments from a single shovel test. The species represented were all small mammals, birds, and fish (McFarlane, Cummings, and Mather 2000:12; McFarlane and Mather 2001).

Another notable find is a grizzly bear metatarsal from the Lincoln Mounds (21HE7) in Hennepin County (Bakken et al. 2006). The grizzly is thought to be a prairie species, although very little is known regarding its presumed former presence in Minnesota. The Lincoln Mounds grizzly is mentioned here to highlight an alternative approach to exploring the time-transgressive nature of the ecotone. While the historical boundaries of the three major biomes (Fig. 1) provide a means to investigate relatively recent sites, the details of the boundaries are obscured with time, and some margin of error can be assumed even in the nineteenth century mapping efforts. A zoogeographical approach, in contrast, will focus on species representation across the state. Eventually, these data will be sufficient to compare across archaeological periods and will be a meaningful complement to other paleoecological sources.

Acknowledgements. I am grateful to Tom McCauley of the White Earth Tribal Historic Preservation Office for his continued interest in the North Twin Lake site and for his assistance in bringing this article to press. Thanks also to Lesley Kadish of the Geography and History Online Project at the Minnesota Historical Society for her help with Fig. 1. My original study of the North Twin Lake fauna was conducted at Loucks Associates in Maple Grove. Dr. Holmes Semken, Jr. of the University of Iowa provided helpful advice and encouragement with the identifications.

References Cited

Anfinson, S.F., M.G. Michlovic and J. Stein
1978 *The Lake Bronson Site (21KT1): A Multi-Component Site on the Prairie-Woodland Border in Northwestern Minnesota.* Occasional Publications in Minnesota Anthropology No. 3, Minnesota Archaeological Society, St. Paul.

Bakken, K.
1994 *The Lower Rice Lake Site, 21CE5.* MA Thesis, Center for Ancient Studies, University of Minnesota, Minneapolis.

Bakken, K., O. Elquist, A. Gronhovd, J. Jones, D. Mather, M. O'Brien, M. Regan, D. Ross, T. Ross and J. Williams
2006 *Mitakuye Owas, All My Relations: Authentication, Recovery and Reburial at the Lincoln Mounds for the Bloomington Central Station Project, Bloomington, Minnesota.* Summit Envirosolutions, St. Paul.

Balkwill, D.M. and S.L. Cumbaa
1992 *A Guide to the Identification of Postcranial Bones of Bos taurus and Bison bison.* Syllogeus 71, Canadian Museum of Nature, Ottawa.

Berg, R.E.
1995 *An Archaeological Reconnaissance Survey of Twenty-Four House Lots along the North Shore of North Twin Lake on the White Earth Reservation in Mahnomen County, Minnesota.* Bureau of Indian Affairs, Minneapolis Area Office. Report prepared for the White Earth Reservation Tribal Council.

Berg, R.E. and T.M. Beebe
2000 *Results of Monitoring Four Basement Excavations within Site 21MH5 in 1996 on the White Earth Reservation in Mahnomen County, Minnesota.* Bureau of Indian Affairs, Minneapolis Area Office. Report prepared for the White Earth Reservation Tribal Council.

Binford, L.R.
1981 *Bones: Ancient Men and Modern Myths.* Academic Press, San Diego.

Bonnichson, R. and R.T. Will
1993 Cultural Modification of Bone: The Experimental Approach in Faunal Analysis. In *Mammalian Osteology*, by B.M. Gilbert, pp. 7-30. Missouri Archaeological Society, Columbia.

Brain, C.K.
1981 *The Hunters or the Hunted? An Introduction to African Cave Taphonomy.* The University of Chicago Press, Chicago.

Brown, C.L. and C.E. Gustafson
1979 *A Key to Postcranial Skeletal Remains of Cattle/Bison, Elk and Horse.* Washington State University, Laboratory of Anthropology, Reports of Investigations No. 57, Pullman.

Chapman, K.A., A. Fischer and M.K. Ziegenhagen
1998 *Valley of Grass: Tallgrass Prairie and Parkland of the Red River Region.* North Star Press of St. Cloud, Inc., St. Cloud.

Davis, S.J.M.
1987 *The Archaeology of Animals.* Yale University Press, New Haven.

Eddy, S. and J. Underhill
1974 *Northern Fishes*, third edition. University of Minnesota Press, Minneapolis.

Gilbert, B.M.
1993 *Mammalian Osteology.* Missouri Archaeological Society, Columbia.

Gilbert, B.M., H.G. Savage and L.D. Martin
1996 *Avian Osteology.* Missouri Archaeological Society, Columbia.

Grimm, E.C.
1985 Vegetation History along the Prairie-Forest Border in Minnesota. In *Archaeology, Ecology and Ethnohistory of the Prairie-Forest Border Zone in Minnesota and Manitoba*, edited by J. Spector and E. Johnson, pp. 9-30. Reprints in Anthropology, Volume 31. J&L Reprint Company, Lincoln.

Harvey, J.H., K. Guidi, E. Hajic and D. Mather
2005 *Archaeological Data Recovery at 21PL72 and 21PL74, Polk County, Minnesota.* Report of Investigation 559, Great Lakes Archaeological Research Center, Milwaukee. Report prepared for the US Army Corps of Engineers, St. Paul District.

Hazard, E.B.
1982 *The Mammals of Minnesota.* The University of Minnesota Press, Minneapolis.

Hesse, B. and P. Wapnish
1985 *Animal Bone Archaeology.* Taraxacum, Washington D.C.

Hickerson, H.
1988 *The Chippewa and their Neighbors: A Study in Ethnohistory*, revised and expanded edition. Waveland Press, Prospect Heights, IL.

Hohman-Caine, C.A. and G.E. Goltz
2004 *Phase II Archaeological Evaluation: Fish Lake Development, Ottertail County, Minnesota.* Soils Consulting, Longville. Report prepared for Homeland Development.

Jacobson, J.A.
2003 Identification of Mule Deer (*Odocoileus hemionus*) and White-tailed Deer (*Odocoileus virginianus*) Postcranial Remains as a Means of Determining Human Subsistence Strategies. *Plains Anthropologist* 48(147):287-297.

Johnson, E.
1973 *The Arvilla Complex.* Minnesota Historical Society Press, St. Paul.

1985 The 17th Century Mdewakanton Dakota Subsistence Mode. In *Archaeology, Ecology and Ethnohistory of the Prairie-Forest Border Zone in Minnesota and Manitoba*, edited by J. Spector and E. Johnson, pp.

154-166. Reprints in Anthropology, Volume 31. J&L Reprint Company, Lincoln.

Kohl, J.G.
1985 *Kitchi-Gami: Life Among the Lake Superior Ojibway* [originally published in 1885]. Minnesota Historical Society Press, St. Paul.

Lukens, P.
1963 *Some Ethnozoological Implications of Mammalian Faunas from Minnesota Archaeological Sites.* PhD Dissertation, Department of Anthropology, University of Minnesota, Minneapolis.

Lyman, R.L.
1994 *Vertebrate Taphonomy.* Cambridge University Press.

Mather, D.
1996 *Zooarchaeological Analysis of the Phase III Faunal Assemblage from the North Twin Lake Site (21 MH 05), Mahnomen County, Minnesota.* Loucks Project Report 96503. Loucks & Associates, Inc., Maple Grove. Report prepared for All National Cultural Resource Preservation, Inc., Cass Lake.

2002 Zooarchaeology of the Lake Lida Site (21OT109), Otter Tail County, Minnesota. *The Minnesota Archaeologist* 61:9-22.

2004 *Faunal Summary and Recommendations: Bison and other Animal Bone from The Point Site (21OT151), Otter Tail County, Minnesota.* Mather Heritage Group LLC, Report M22, Minneapolis. Report prepared for Soils Consulting, Longville.

Mather, D., T. Olmanson, K. Gragg-Johnson and L. Schuster
1998 The Washington Creek Site (21ME14) and the Archaeology of the Prairie-Forest Border. *The Minnesota Archaeologist* 57:97-133.

McAndrews, J.H.
1966 Postglacial History of Prairie, Savanna and Forest in Northwestern Minnesota. Memoirs of the Torrey Botanical Club 22:1-72.

McDonald, J.N.
1981 North American Bison: Their Classification and Evolution. University of California Press, Berkeley.

McFarlane, J., J. Cummings and D. Mather
2000 Phase I Archaeological Reconnaissance Survey of Two Islands (Kandiyohi 005 and 006) in Little Kandiyohi Lake, Kandiyohi County, Minnesota. Loucks Project Report 00518. Loucks Associates, Maple Grove. Report prepared for the Bureau of Land Management, Milwaukee Field Office.

McFarlane, J. and D. Mather
2001 Stinking Lake and the Promise of Island Archaeology in Minnesota. The Minnesota Archaeologist 60:131-136.

Michlovic, M.G.
1979 *The Dead River Site (21 OT 51).* Occasional Publications in Minnesota Anthropology No. 6, Minnesota Archaeological Society, St. Paul.

1980 Ecotonal Settlement and Subsistence in the Northern Midwest. *Midcontinental Journal of Archaeology* 5(2):151-167.

1983 The Red River Valley in the Prehistory of the Northern Plains. *Plains Anthropologist* 28(99):23-31.

1986 The Archaeology of the Canning Site. *The Minnesota Archaeologist* 45(1):1-36.

1987 The Archaeology of the Mooney Site (21NR29). *The Minnesota Archaeologist* 46(2):39-66.

1990 Northern Plains-Woodland Interaction in Prehistory. In *The Woodland Tradition in the Western Great Lakes*, edited by G.E. Gibbon, pp. 45-54. University of Minnesota

Publications in Anthropology, No. 4, Minneapolis.

Michlovic, M.G. and D.T. Sather
2000   *Analysis of Cultural Materials from the North Twin Lake Site (21MH5), Mahnomen County, Minnesota.* Archaeology Laboratory, Moorhead State University, Moorhead. Report prepared for the White Earth Indian Reservation, Mahnomen.

Morey, D., C. Falk and H. Semken, Jr.
1996   Vertebrate Remains from the McKinstry Site. In *The McKinstry Site (21 KC 2): Final Report of Phase III Investigations for Mn/DOT S.P. 3604-44, Replacement of Bridge 5178 over the Little Fork River, Koochiching County, Minnesota*, by M.M. Thomas and D. Mather, pp. 15.1-15.56. Loucks Project Report 93512. Loucks & Associates, Inc., Maple Grove. Report prepared for the Minnesota Department of Transportation, St. Paul.

Navarre, G., T. McCauley and K. Hagglund
1994   *Phase I Archaeological Survey of the North Twin Lake Road Reconstruction Project and Phase II Evaluation of Site 21MH05, White Earth Indian Reservation, Mahnomen County, Minnesota.* Roads Archaeology Program, Bureau of Indian Affairs, Minneapolis Area Office.

Oldfield, B. and J.J. Moriarty
1994   *Amphibians & Reptiles Native to Minnesota.* University of Minnesota Press, Minneapolis.

Olsen, S.J.
1968   Fish, Amphibian and Reptile Remains from Archaeological Sites: Part 1 – Southeastern and Southwestern United States. *Papers of the Peabody Museum of Archaeology and Ethnology* 56(2).

1985   *Origins of the Domestic Dog: The Fossil Record.* The University of Arizona Press, Tucson.

Phillips, G.L., W.D. Schmid and J.C. Underhill
1982   *Fishes of the Minnesota Region.* University of Minnesota Press, Minneapolis.

Reitz, E. and E.S. Wing
1999   *Zooarchaeology.* Cambridge University Press, Cambridge.

Rojo, A.L.
1991   *Dictionary of Evolutionary Fish Osteology.* CRC Press, Boca Raton

Shay, C.T.
1971   *The Itasca Bison Kill Site: An Ecological Analysis.* Minnesota Historical Society Press, St. Paul.

1985   Late Prehistoric Selection of Wild Ungulates in the Prairie-Forest Transition. In *Archaeology, Ecology and Ethnohistory of the Prairie-Forest Border Zone in Minnesota and Manitoba*, edited by J. Spector and E. Johnson, pp. 31-65. Reprints in Anthropology, Volume 31. J&L Reprint Company, Lincoln.

Snyder, L.M.
1991   Barking Mutton: Ethnohistoric, Ethnographic, Archaeological, and Nutritional Evidence Pertaining to the Dog as a Native American Food Resource on the Plains. In *Beamers, Bobwhites and Blue-Points: Tributes to the Career of Paul W. Parmalee*, edited by J.R. Purdue, W.E. Klippel and B.W. Styles, pp. 359-378. Illinois State Museum, Springfield.

Tester, J.R.
1995   *Minnesota's Natural Heritage: An Ecological Perspective.* University of Minnesota Press, Minneapolis.

Trygg, J.W.
1964   *Composite Map of United States Land Surveyors' Original Plats and Field Notes: Sheet 11, Minnesota Series.* Trygg Land Office, Ely.

Van Zyll de Jong, C.G.

1986 *A Systematic Study of Recent Bison, with Particular Consideration of the Wood Bison (Bison bison athabascae Rhoads 1898)*. Publications in Natural Sciences 6, National Museums of Canada, Ottawa.

Watrall, C.
1985 A Structural Comparison of the Maplewood, Stott and Lake Midden Sites. In *Archaeology, Ecology and Ethnohistory of the Prairie-Forest Border Zone in Minnesota and Manitoba*, edited by J. Spector and E. Johnson, pp. 65-72. Reprints in Anthropology, Volume 31. J&L Reprint Company, Lincoln.

Wheeler, A. and A.K.G. Jones
1989 *Fishes*. Cambridge University Press, Cambridge.

Whelan, M.K.
1990 Late Woodland Subsistence Systems and Settlement Size in the Mille Lacs Area. In *The Woodland Tradition in the Western Great Lakes: Papers Presented to Elden Johnson*, edited by G. Gibbon, pp. 55-76. Publications in Anthropology Number 4. University of Minnesota, Minneapolis.

Wood, W.R.
1985 The Plains-Lakes Connection: Reflections from a Western Perspective. In *Archaeology, Ecology and Ethnohistory of the Prairie-Forest Border Zone in Minnesota and Manitoba*, edited by J. Spector and E. Johnson, pp. 1-8. Reprints in Anthropology, Volume 31. J&L Reprint Company, Lincoln.

Lead Round Ball and Shot from a Fur Trade Post on Horseshoe Bay, Leech Lake

Mathew J. Mattson
Leech Lake Heritage Sites Program

Analysis of size, application, method of formation, and distribution of lead round ball and shot has offered insight into occupational sequences and cultural applications. Manufactured versus chewed ball differences reflect varied economic conditions at different times. Lack of access to manufactured ball forced re-use and/or local formation of ball from cutting lead and chewing it into a sphere. An unusual amount of .51 to .52 caliber ball suggests a regional variant in the use of smaller-gauge smooth bores than commonly seen elsewhere. This may reflect availability of small game or cultural preferences in hunting practices. Analysis of ball and shot has also contributed to understanding the sequence and duration of occupation within the site. Earlier smooth bore guns are associated with the north structure, while later rifled bores are associated with the south structure. Distribution of ball is also consistent with this sequence. At least seventeen different muzzle-loading arms are represented at the site.

Introduction

Evaluation and data recovery excavations of the Horseshoe Bay site (21CA201) were completed in 1989-90 to mitigate the effects of transferring a parcel of land out of federal ownership. A total of 711 square meters were excavated. The site produced a tremendous volume of data, the analysis of which has been undertaken in small, focused segments spread over subsequent years.

Located on the south shore of Leech Lake (Fig. 1), six major components spanning the totality of human occupation of the Mississippi Headwaters are present: Paleoindian, Archaic, Initial Woodland, Terminal Woodland, Fur Trade, and eighteenth- and nineteenth-century Ojibwe (Goltz 1993).

The Fur Trade era is the dominant component on the site. Although some Euroamerican artifacts suggest a possible late eighteenth-century occupation, most of the materials indicate the major occupation was from the 1820s to the 1860s. While there is no positive identification of who inhabited the site (George 1999), they had access to large quantities of imported trade goods. Artifacts are numerous and include beads, buttons, trade silver and other jewelry, pipes, and ornaments. Trade muskets are represented by elements from all parts of the weapons. Gunflints are mostly British blade style of dark Brandon flint with a few blond flints of French style and a few of chert, which may have been locally made. Trap parts and muskrat spears make up most of the metal hardware, though trade axes, files, awls, and other small tools are present. Ceramics are numerous and varied, with at least 64 vessels represented. Most are of early to mid-nineteenth century manufacture.

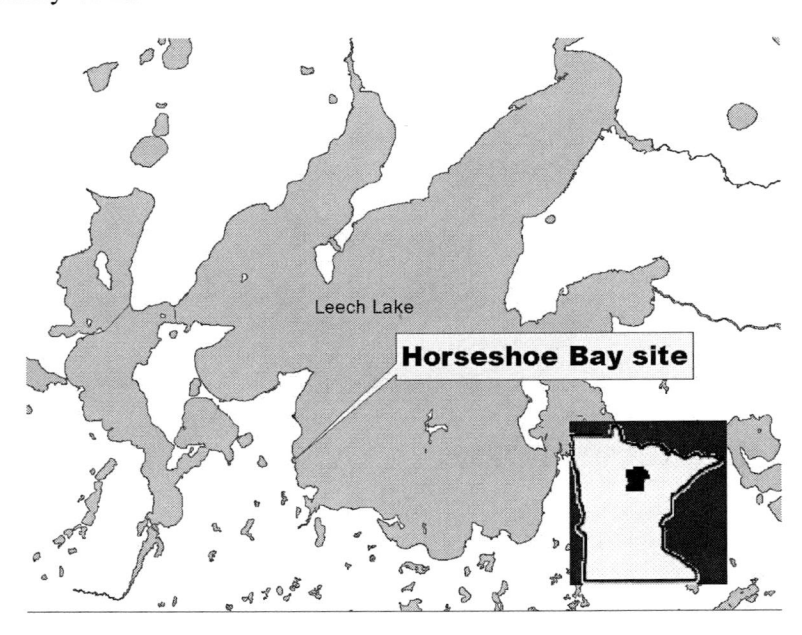

Fig. 1. Horseshoe Bay site location.

Table 1. Round Ball Distribution, Measurement, and Production Assignment

BUILD-ING	TYPE	MIN CAL	MAX CAL	AVG CAL		PRODUC-TION
South	Buckshot	.24	.26	.25	20	Factory
South	Rifle ball	.36	.38	.37	76	Chewed
South	Rifle ball	.37	.44	.40	99	Indeterminate
South	Rifle ball	.41	.45	.43	108	Chewed
South	Rifle ball	.38	.59	.48	164	Chewed
South	Rifle ball	.47	.51	.49	170	Indeterminate
South	Rifle ball	.48	.51	.49	179	Indeterminate
South	Musket ball	.51	.54	.53	198	Chewed
South	Musket ball	.51	.52	.51	199	Factory
South	Musket ball	.51	.57	.54	199	Chewed
South	Musket ball	.52	.52	.52	202	Factory
South	Musket ball	.50	.54	.52	202	Chewed
South	Musket ball	.50	.60	.55	205	Chewed
South	Musket ball	.52	.52	.52	208	Factory
South	Musket ball	.50	.54	.52	210	Hand mold
South	Musket ball	.51	.56	.53	211	Chewed
South	Musket ball	.52	.54	.53	215	Factory
South	Musket ball	.54	.58	.56	230	Chewed
South	Musket ball	.53	.57	.55	231	Factory
South	Musket ball	.53	.57	.55	236	Hand mold
South	Musket ball	.55	.57	.56	250	Chewed
South	Musket ball	.55	.63	.59	253	Chewed

Table 1 cont. Round Ball Distribution, Measurement, and Production Assignment

BUILD-ING	TYPE	MIN CAL	MAX CAL	AVG CAL		PRODUC-TION
North	Musket ball	.47	.52	.49	187	Chewed
North	Musket ball	.51	.54	.53	196	Chewed
North	Musket ball	.51	.54	.53	218	Factory
North	Musket ball	.54	.56	.55	221	Chewed
North	Musket ball	.52	.55	.54	225	Factory
North	Musket ball	.53	.56	.55	228	Chewed
North	Musket ball	.52	.56	.54	235	Factory
North	Musket ball	.57	.59	.58	278	Factory
North	Musket ball	.57	.59	.58	281	Factory
North	Musket ball	.57	.58	.58	281	Factory
North	Musket ball	.57	.58	.58	282	Factory
Exterior	Buckshot	.27	.28	.27	25	Factory
Exterior	Buckshot	.32	.32	.32	34	Chewed
Exterior	Buckshot	.28	.34	.31	35	Chewed
Exterior	Buckshot	.32	.33	.33	49	Factory
Exterior	Buckshot	.32	.33	.33	49	Factory
Exterior	Buckshot	.31	.35	.33	52	Chewed
Exterior	Buckshot	.34	.37	.36	62	Chewed
Exterior	Rifle ball	.38	.38	.38	79	Factory
Exterior	Rifle ball	.40	.45	.42	88	Chewed
Exterior	Rifle ball	.43	.45	.44	116	Factory
Exterior	Rifle ball	.42	.45	.44	122	Chewed
Exterior	Rifle ball	.47	.49	.48	137	Chewed
Exterior	Rifle ball	.50	.51	.51	174	Indeterminate

Fig. 2. Well-formed lead ball.

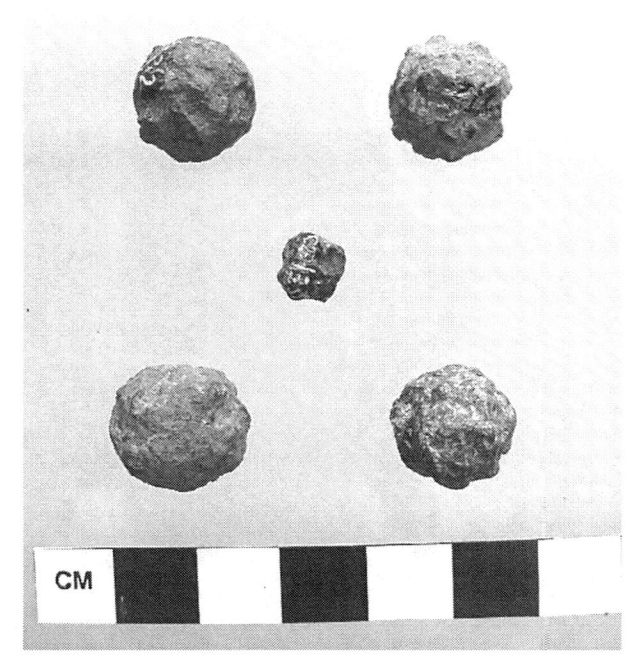

Fig. 3. Poorly formed lead ball and shot.

Post mold patterns that may represent Ojibwe lodges are associated with French Fur Trade artifacts from about 1760 to 1780. Two major Euroamerican structures associated with the Fur Trade component represent the remains of clay-chinked houses with stone fireplaces. The north structure was rebuilt and enlarged, while the south structure seems to have been occupied during a later period of abandonment of the north structure.

Faunal remains are abundant and well preserved. Shane (1996) analyzed fish remains from the two structures and found evidence of both normal fish consumption and large scale processing of 200-400 individual fish. He also notes differences in the nineteenth century fishery compared with the present. Hannes's (1994) faunal analysis compared Horseshoe Bay faunal remains with lists of Fur Trade species and compared the actual dietary remains with an idealized model based on historic and ethnographic records of Ojibwe subsistence practices.

Methodology

A total of 49 lead round ball and shot plus one #6 shotgun pellet were recovered from the Horseshoe Bay site. Initially ball diameters were measured with a dial caliper accurate to .001 inch at three to four places on the ball excluding the mold line (where present). The ball and shot were measured in such a manner as to determine maximum and minimum diameters while avoiding such obvious incongruities as flattening at the sprue (a protrusion on the surface of the ball that is a remnant from the hole in the mold into which the molten lead had been poured), mold ridges, and surfaces distorted by impact. The results of these measurements appear in Table 1. Owing to the deformities of many of the ball, discussed in more detail below, the ball were also weighed in an attempt to produce a more accurate reflection of possible caliber. This was performed with an Ohaus electronic balance accurate to 0.1 gram. The resulting weights were then converted to grains and appear in Table 1. Surface examination of the ball was performed under magnification of 3x to 10x as the situation required. Depth of surface imperfections was measured using a probe and the dial caliper. English measurements were used, as this was the system in use during the era of manufacture and it is still common in the arms field.

Volumetric evaluation of the ball was not undertaken. In the case of the mass-produced ball, weight and diametrical measurements were consistent in regard to caliber assignment. In the case of the chewed ball, volumetric measurement would have been pointless because of the varying degrees of asymmetry and presence of voids in the surface. Precise caliber determination is impossible with poorly formed ball, and minor differences in caliber would not alter the analysis based on weight and diameter measurements.

Analysis of Deformed Ball

As noted above, diametrical measurement of the ball proved to be problematic. Twenty-three of the ball (47%) exhibited moderate to extreme roughness, pocketing, and spherical distortion (see Fig. 2 and 3). The extent of roughness and pocketing was grouped into three categories: severe = depths of .035 to .090 inch with projections to .080 inch; moderate = depths of .010 to 035 inch; light = depths less than .010 inch. While it was impractical to measure every imperfection of every ball, detailed measurement of selected examples showed visual assignment to be acceptably consistent. It was initially suggested that this was the result of human chewing. Owing to the large number of such specimens and the degree of treatment, experiments were undertaken in an attempt to replicate these features by chewing and other means.

The first experiments involved the molding process. Using an open fire, melting ladle, and single-cavity mold of a design reflective of the era, attempts were made to deliberately produce "bad" ball. These attempts included varying the temperature of the molten lead, using cold and pre heated molds, introducing slag like impurities and wood ash into the molten lead, and various combinations of the above. The author even went so far as to contaminate the mold with water prior to the pour, with the expected violent (and hazardous) reaction. While these efforts yielded numerous imperfect specimens, none matched the recovered ball.

The second experiments were based on the concept of repeated pedestrian traffic in an area where ball had been lost and subsequently walked upon. This action was replicated on two soil types similar to those found on the site: sandy with sparse small gravel and a coarser soil of heavy small-gravel content. The ball being placed in the above matrices, it was walked on, kicked about, scuffed about, and generally abused. It was noted that when a ball was dropped and stepped upon it tended to stay imbedded in the soil and was only moved about by rather deliberate action. Again, this generally did not result in surfaces that matched ball from the site. However, upon comparative examination, it did result in the reclassification of one ball initially included in the pool, reducing the original number of 24 to the current 23.

The final experiments involved replicating an actual chewing process. Of the available maxillary/mandibular specimens available, those of a wild boar (Russian) were chosen as being sufficiently similar to human dentition to yield worthwhile comparison. With the ball being secured in a forceps, hand pressure was applied to the jaws imitating a crushing bite. The ball was frequently rotated and the crushing action repeated. Last, a ball was secured in plastic wrap and tightly clenched between the author's molars (followed by a flushing of the oral cavity with hydrogen peroxide.) The results of these last attempts produced ball with surfaces very similar to those found on the site, though the alterations to the surface were not as pronounced as some of the more extreme examples.

These experiments have led to the conclusion that the majority of ball deformations were, in fact, caused by chewing and the large proportion of chewed ball indicates that it was a common practice among the inhabitants of the site. It should be noted that substantial pressure was required to achieve the depth of indentation found on ball from the site. Also, many of the dentition marks are quite pointed. Given what is known of the dental practices and care of the nineteenth century, this may indicate the age and condition of those who formed the ball.

The chewed ball have generated a number of questions. Chewed ball have been reported from other sites and numerous explanations have been proffered. Sivilich (1996), working on a site "possibly associated with the (British) retreat from the Battle of Monmouth" (Revolutionary War), analyzed

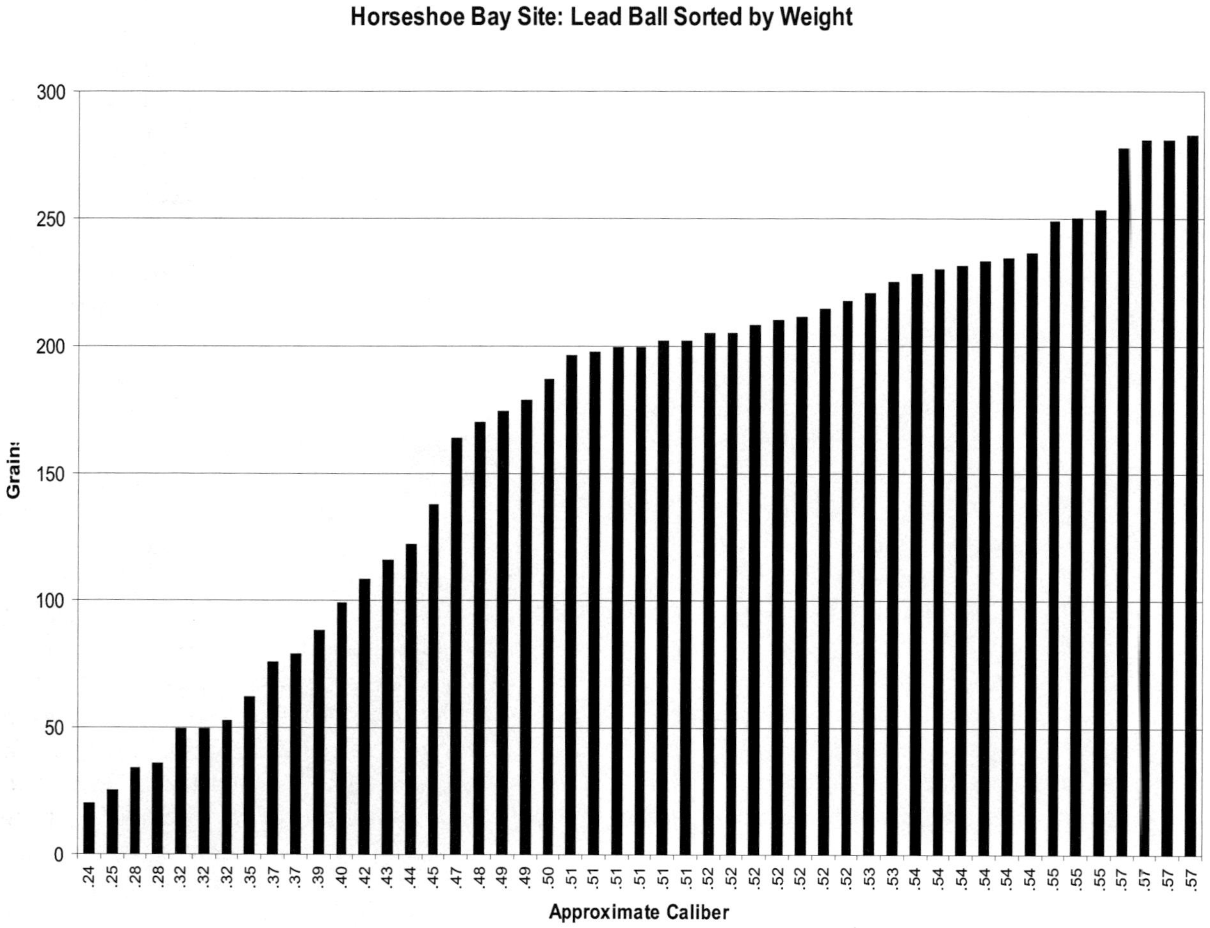

Horseshoe Bay Site: Lead Ball Sorted by Weight

Fig. 4. Lead ball sorted by weight.

52 ball, five of which (9.6%) showed evidence of chewing. Two showed deep impressions postulated to have been clenched between the jaws during field surgery. The remaining three were more lightly chewed and "attributed to pain or boredom, or possibly to promote salivation on a hot, arid day." Pratt (1995) examined 265 ball and shot from the site of the Battle of Fallen Timbers in 1794. Eight (3%) showed signs of chewing. Pratt deems it "a likely explanation" that some of the ball may have been carried in the mouth as a back-up round or to promote salivation in a " hot and stressful situation." Bailey (2001), writing in England on the English Civil War, attributes chewed ball to battlefield surgery, possibly reforming of oversize ball, or the creation of "dum-dum" rounds.

Most of the above explanations do not seem applicable to the Horseshoe Bay artifacts. Given the proximity (20-30 m) to Leech Lake, thirst was not a likely problem. Examination of photographs of ball believed to relate to field surgery (Sivilich 2005) show a notable (and expected) flattening not apparent in this site's ball. The above noted percentages (9.6%, 3.0%) do not compare well to the 47 percent chewed ball recovered at Horseshoe Bay.

Other explanations have been offered. One is the reforming of recovered ball. Tanner, in his Narratives (1830), relates an account of taking twenty moose and elk with his 7 remaining ball, noting "often times in shooting an elk or a moose the ball does not pass quite through and may be used again." Personal hunting experience has shown that even ball that only contacts soft tissue suffers deformation.

An experienced hunter like Tanner would naturally try for a rib cage shot whenever possible, especially on game of this size. Ball so used would almost assuredly require re-shaping.

Another explanation may lie in the initial forming of the ball without the benefit of a bullet mold. An account in Campbell's Travels in the Interior Inhabited Parts of North America in the Years 1791 and 1792 (n.d.) quotes his traveling partner, David Ramsey: "After killing the first Indians, I cut lead, and chewed about thirty balls and about three pounds of goose shot, for I thought it a pity to shoot an Indian with a smooth ball." While the specific implications of the above statement are unclear, the method of ball formation is obvious.

There are also anecdotal accounts of molten lead being poured into a narrow groove carved in wood, cooled, cut into sections, and chewed to form. Numerous irregularly shaped pieces of melted lead were recovered during excavation. At least three of these, found in close association with ball (including chewed ball), were in the range of 2 - 3 cm in length, up to 1 cm wide, and averaged .46 cm thick. The edges of these pieces display clear evidence of having been cut or chiseled. Also recovered were two pieces of long, narrow form. One piece from the south structure is 75 mm (2.95 inches) long, averages 7.5 mm (.30 inch) in width, and is triangular in cross-section with rounded corners. The other is hexagonal in cross-section and not likely related to ball formation.

The chewed shot could be reflective of fluctuating economic conditions during certain periods of the Fur Trade era at this locality. While the research on this site is still in progress, there are numerous indications that the Fur Trade component spanned a greater length of time here than is usually associated with such sites. Ball and shot were standard items of trade and at least 17 ball recovered are of the premanufactured form. Individually owned bullet molds were also a common item and are represented by two ball (see Table 1). The high percentage of chewed ball could indicate lack of access to either of the above sources. This lack of access could have occurred, for example, during periods when traders were not actively working in the area or even when extended severe weather prohibited travel to supply points.

Four ball were classed as indeterminate in regards to formation. While there is uncertainty here, it is suspected that these ball might have been initially formed by chewing and then further refined by gentle tapping and/or rolling between two hard surfaces. These are all of rifle caliber (.40, .45, .49) and modified to a level at least serviceable in patched ball/rifled bore application. Experiments to replicate this have not been conducted.

The four ball classed as lightly chewed are likely mass-produced trade fare that, for some reason, were rolled around in the mouth. The surface treatment does not reflect the amount of pressure required to form a ball with the jaws.

Among the 12 ball more firmly placed into the rifle class, all four ball classed as indeterminate are of rifle caliber, three from the South structure and one from the exterior. Two mass-produced ball .38 and .42 caliber were from the building exterior. One lightly chewed ball of .44 caliber is also from the exterior. The other lightly chewed ball (.37 caliber) is from the south building interior. These fall rather nicely into Shumway's eastern long rifle classification (Shumway 1970, 1998). Three classed as moderately chewed are of .39, .42, and .49 caliber. One ball, weighing 161 grains, would appear (by weight) to be of roughly .48 caliber. However, it is severely chewed with a maximum diameter of .587 inch.

The maximum diameter of the ball is a critical factor in determining caliber assignment for the chewed specimens. Personal experience in repairing the muzzle-loading arms of others has shown that an improperly sized ball lodged in a barrel (known as "short-starting") can be most problematic. If available, a screw like device known as a ball puller may successfully remove the ball. If this device is unavailable or unsuccessful, the breech plug must be removed. The tooling needed to dismantle the breech and remove the obstruction was not commonly present at smaller trading posts. The other option for dislodging the ball-firing the gun-would likely lead to a burst barrel and ruined firearm. As noted below, only two barrel sections were recovered

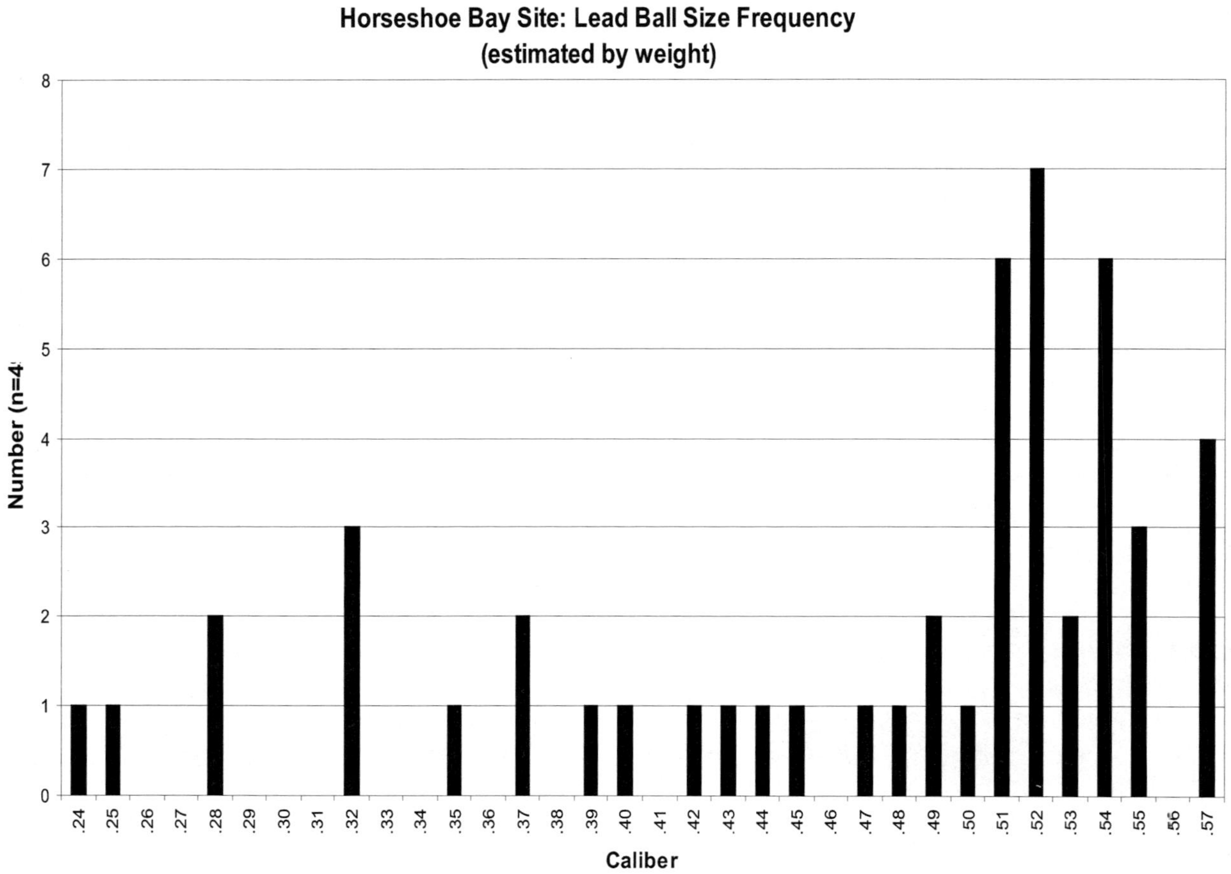

Horseshoe Bay Site: Lead Ball Size Frequency (estimated by weight)

Fig. 5. Lead ball size frequency by weight.

from the site. A Northwest gun barrel was recovered from the shallows of Pelican Island, Leech Lake, 4.5 miles east-northeast of Horseshoe Bay (Olmanson and Wells 2006). Its broken breech plug tang mates nicely with a damaged tang screw/trigger assembly from Horseshoe Bay. It has a burst barrel.

Sizes of Lead Round Ball and Shot

As demonstrated by Figure 4, a wide spread of ball and shot sizes were recovered. These have been grouped, somewhat arbitrarily, into three categories: buck shot .24 caliber to .36 caliber; rifle shot .37 caliber to .50 caliber; and smooth bore or musket shot .51 caliber and above. Potential areas of overlap occur in the .32-.36 and the .50-.53 ranges.
Ball in the .32-.36 caliber range can serve in two capacities. .32 is classed as "0" buck shot, .34 as "00", and .36 as "000" buck shot. One of the reasons for the sustained popularity of the Northwest gun and similar large smooth bores was their versatility. They could be loaded with small shot ("bird shot"), buck shot, or ball depending on the need, be it game size or defense. A combined load, known as "buck and ball" was also used, primarily in warfare. This usually consisted of one ball and three or four buck shot. General George Washington specified such a load in 1776. Personal experience on target ranges has shown this to be a most effective anti personnel load at sub-75 yard distances. Trade guns, as noted by Hamilton (1982), "were as often used with shot as with ball."

The term "Northwest gun" refers to a type of gun developed during the Fur Trade era in response to the requirements of the Native Americans. It was typified by an octagonal tapering round barrel fre-

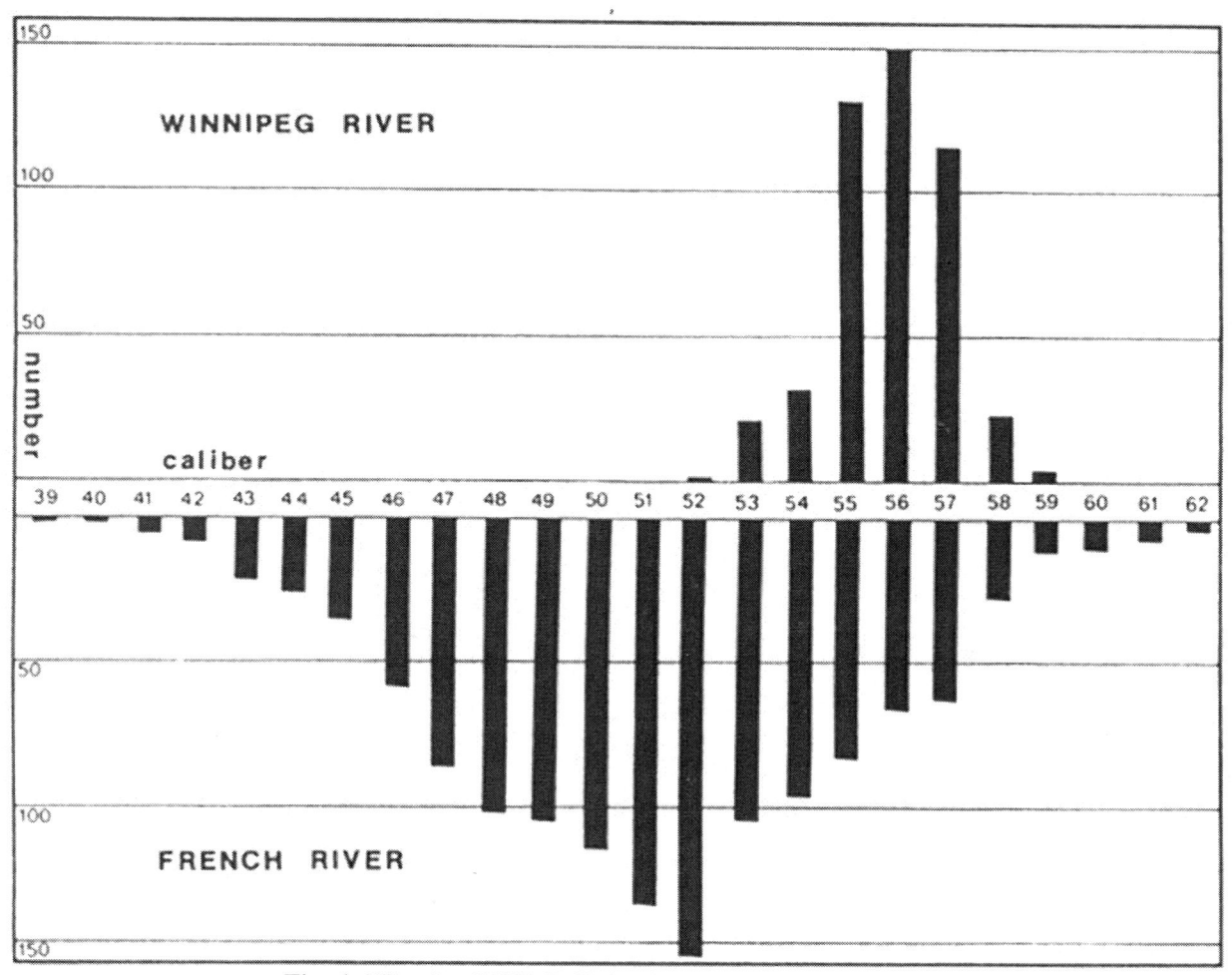

Fig. 6. Wheeler (1975) Ball size frequency graph.

quently of 24 gauge, two ribbed ramrod thimbles, over-sized trigger guard bow, and serpentine side plate. The earliest extant Northwest gun (held by the Museum of the Fur Trade, Chadron, Nebraska) was produced by Wilson in 1751 for Hudson's Bay Company. The evolution of this gun began during the early 1700s and was finalized by about 1775. It remained popular for the next century and beyond. This type of gun was handled by numerous trading companies, independents and the government.

Smaller rifled bores (.32-.36), often referred to as "squirrel guns," were certainly produced during the period involved but tend to have been most commonly used in the eastern United States and southern Appalachians, reflective of the size of some of the available game in those regions at this time. No documentation of rifled barrels in these calibers in association with fur trade activity in Minnesota has come to light during the current research.

Ball in the .50-.53 caliber range could have also been used in smooth bore or rifled guns. Smooth bores in these calibers were considered on the small side for effective use of bird and buck shot. During the era in question, the greatest use of ball in these calibers in rifled barrels was the result of westward expansion, a response to the game and distances thus encountered. American rifled arms had their birth primarily during the second and third quarters of the eighteenth century, blending features of the larger-bore Germanic Jaeger with the English fowler (Hanson 1980). The resulting rifle was generally of a medium bore, "typified as having a caliber of about .42" (Buchelle et al. 1998). British Colonel George Hanger, who served as captain of Hessian jaeger corps during the Revolutionary War, observed that the American long rifle carried "a ball no larger than 36 to the pound" (.506 caliber) (quoted in Hanson 1980). By the 1820s makers such as Deringer in Philadelphia (Hanson 1980) and the Hawken brothers in St. Louis (Russell 1967) were producing the larger-bored rifles more suitable for the taking of bison and coping with grizzly bear. With all of the above said, Hamilton's work on five Osage sites in what is now Missouri identified smooth bore barrels of .453-.526 caliber. These were initially considered to be of French origin, but it is now belived they are of English or Spanish manufacture. They date from the late seventeenth and early eighteenth centuries (Hamilton, 1982). In addition, the Museum of the Fur Trade, Chadron, Nebraska is in possession of a French trade gun ca. 1700 in .51 caliber (Hanson 1987). Note that the above examples predate the presumed period of fur trade activity on Horseshoe Bay.

Using the above classifications and referring to Figure 4, one can make some observations. Eight examples (16.3%) can be assigned as buck shot and 13 (26.5%) as likely rifle shot. The 13 ball in calibers .51 and .52 make up the single largest caliber grouping (26.5%) in the sample. The 15 ball (30.6%) of larger caliber are generally recognized as suitable for use in smooth bore trade guns.

In comparing Figure 5 with the graphing of the ball recovered by Wheeler et al. (1975, Figure 6) from the French River, it can be seen that while no buck shot were recovered, they did recover numerous shot in the rifle calibers and also had a strong representation in the .51-.52 range with a similarly declining curve in calibers above these sizes.

The assignment of the ball from the Horseshoe Bay site to specific barrel sizes is complicated by three factors.

1. The scales available at the time are not as finely graduated as one would prefer. While more accurate weighing would not significantly alter the general profile it might fine tune some of the categories. Impurities in the lead may affect the weight to caliber calculation, which was based upon the weight of pure lead.

2. The materials available for patching the ball are not known. One of the most commonly used materials was pillow ticking. Measurements of currently reproduced ticking show a thickness of .017 to .020 inch, with .017 to .018 inch being most common. Ticking as thin as .010 inch has been observed. Tanned doeskin was another available material. Measurements of suitable skin ranged from .012 to .017 inch. There is also the question of whether Native Americans actually or consistently patched the ball. At least two experienced observers, Osborne Russell and Henry Boller, related cases of Native Americans using fabric "over ball" wads (quoted in Hanson 1987). The compression capabilities of the patching material allow for some latitude in ball-bore fitment. As an example, one of the author's personal arms utilizes the following combination: a .62 inch smooth bore barrel, a .60 caliber ball, and a .017 inch pillow-ticking patch. .015 inch patching has been used, though with slightly reduced accuracy. Thus, depending on the selection of patching material or use of wadding, it would be possible to use ball (as an example) of .51, .52, and .53 caliber in a .54 caliber barrel.

3. The asymmetrical form of the chewed ball complicates specific assignment. In reality, their imperfect form and high percentage of representation probably negate any advantages gained by more-accurate weighing.

For a number of decades researchers maintained that the standard Northwest gun was of 24 gauge (.58 caliber) and utilized a 28 gauge (.55 caliber) ball (e.g. Hanson 1955, 1980, 1987). Ball of 30 gauge (.537 by calculation or essentially .54 caliber) were also a common trade item. The Hudson Bay Company sold ball in both 28 and 30 gauge (Hanson 1987). The ledgers of Francois Malhiot, a trader for the Northwest Company working south of Lake Superior in 1804, lists "1 pound of musket balls (30)", or 30 gauge (Gilman 1982). (Gauge is a commonly used standard to calibrate barrel bore size or ball. It is based on the diameter of the number of spheres derived from one pound of lead, i.e. 24 gauge indicates 24 ball to the pound, the bore being the diameter of one of these ball.)

Based on arms parts recovered, specifically butt plates, there are a minimum of eight Northwest guns represented at Horseshoe Bay. These butt plates plus numerous other Northwest gun parts compose the largest arms type grouping (83%). Two barrel sections were recovered. One cut-off muzzle end, approximately 1 inch long, is of .58 caliber. The other, a 4 inch muzzle end, is of .69 caliber and is probably from a former military arm. Northwest guns of larger than .58 bore are known. Russell (1967), addressing the Northwest gun, notes such "universal characteristics as the approximately .60 caliber part octagonal, thin-walled barrel." Hanson (1987) describes Belgian made Northwest guns in the Museum of the Fur Trade that have barrels ranging from .59 to .65 and refers to government contract Northwest guns made by Henry Leman in .60, .65, and .70 caliber. Compared to the ball recovered by Wheeler et al. (1975) from the French River, the ball from Horseshoe Bay has a notable representation of ball in the .51-.52 caliber range associated with fur trade activity and presumably Northwest guns. Dependent on patching, these would have been used in barrels in the .54 caliber (29-30 gauge) range. It should be noted that the bore of even a standardized caliber varied slightly because of manufacturing methods of the time. If the smaller ball are indeed tied to use in Northwest guns, it could represent a regional variant of the more-common 24 gauge. Lead and powder were valuable commodities. The balance between efficient use of materials and effectiveness on the game available in a given region has been briefly referred to above in regards to other arms applications. The use of smaller-gauge smooth bores in this area could be a similar adaptation.

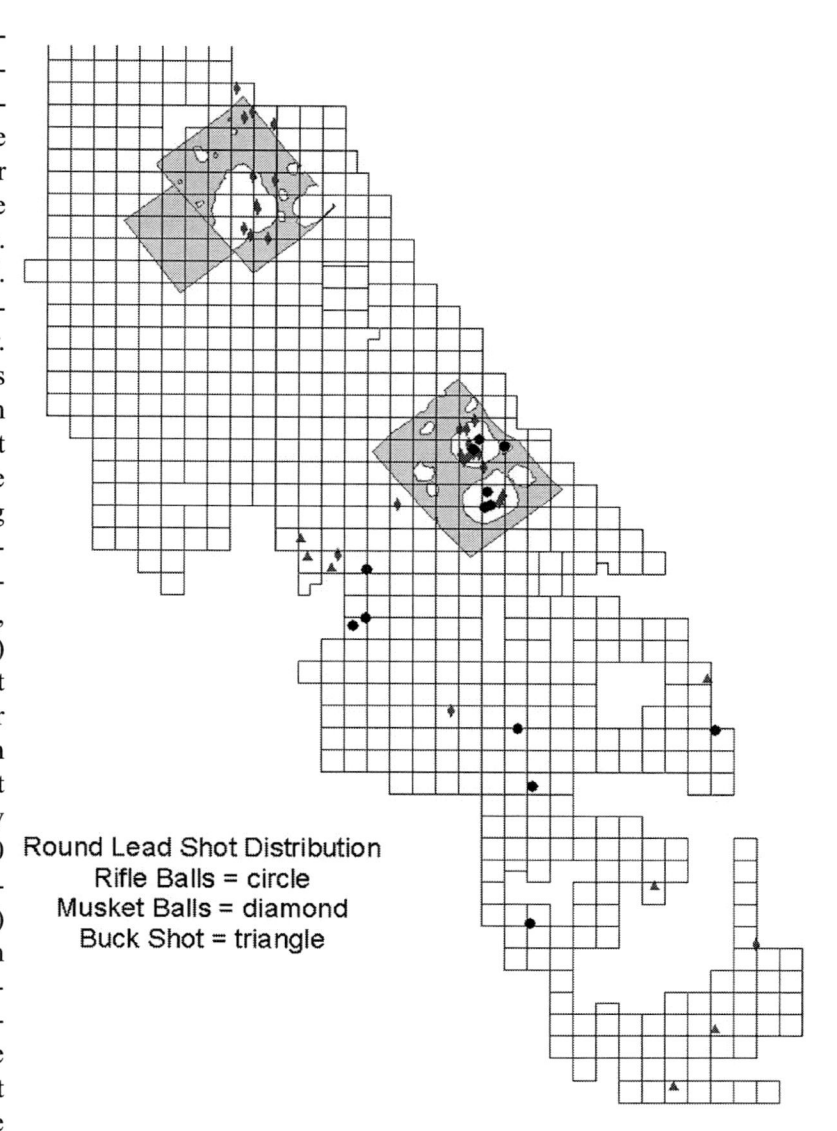

Round Lead Shot Distribution
Rifle Balls = circle
Musket Balls = diamond
Buck Shot = triangle

Fig. 7. Horseshoe Bay round lead shot distribution.

The 13 ball classed as rifle caliber come primarily from the south building (six) and the southern area exterior (six). The 186 grain ball from the north structure falls into a rather nebulous category on the boundary between smooth-bore and rifle use. As this ball shows moderate chewing, has a maximum diameter of .523 inch, and is associated with larger ball it could just as easily be assigned to smooth bore application.

The inherent advantage of a rifled bore over a smooth bore is its improved accuracy at longer ranges. This improved accuracy is contingent upon the ball-patch combination fitting snugly in the bore, as the fit must

Table 2a. Percent of Ball Above .50 Caliber by Location and Weight

	0.51	0.52	0.53	0.54	0.55	0.56	0.57	0.58
Sayer post	0	9	12	15	38	18	9	0
North bldg	9	18	27	9	0	0	36	0
South bldg	33	33	13	20	0	0	0	0

Table 2b. Percent of Ball Above .50 Caliber by Average Diametrical Measurement

	0.51	0.52	0.53	0.54	0.55	0.56	0.57	0.58	0.59
Sayer post	0	9	12	15	38	18	9	0	0
North bldg	9	0	18	18	18	0	0	36	0
South bldg	7	27	13	7	20	20	0	0	7

be tight enough for the patching to "grip" the rifling and thereby develop a spiral spin as it passes down the barrel. Modern muzzle-loading rifles often use a ball .010 inch smaller than the bore in combination with a patch of .010 or .015 inch, the thinner patches working best in smaller bores (see Fadala 2001). Given the necessity of a proper fit in rifled bores and the wide range of rifle-size shot recovered, it would appear that a number of rifles are represented.

Smooth-bore guns of the versatile Northwest type were a popular staple of the fur trade for over a century and were often the preferred arm of Native Americans, while rifles were frequently favored by Euroamericans. Rifled arms did, however, enter the trade arena. By the late 1790s the U.S. Office of Indian Trade was selling rifles by Dickert and De Huff at their "factories" (trading posts) (Hanson 1980). None of these factories were located in the Leech Lake area. The American Fur Company was selling rifles of English manufacture in the Great Lakes region in 1820, with American manufactures coming into play as the 1820s went on (Hanson 1980). In the 1830s numerous rifles were distributed to Native Americans in connection with treaty and relocation activities (Russell 1967). During the late 1830s and into the 1840s, the U.S. government alone procured at least 11,000 "Indian rifles" (Russell 1967). Numerous other references indicate a general increase in the use of rifled arms by Native Americans as the nineteenth century progressed, particularly in the south and west. While there appears to be little research regarding this topic in this immediate area, the presence of small- to medium-caliber rifle ball is likely indicative of later occupations " since the light calibered rifles did not make their appearance until after the frontier, with its larger game animals, had passed a given area" (Hamilton 1982). The distribution of these rifle ball would support the occupational sequence proposed at Horseshoe Bay.

Ball and Shot Distribution

The excavations at Horseshoe Bay revealed two structures of Euroamerican design. These have been simply designated the North and South structures. Eleven ball were recovered from the North building, 10 from the interior of the walls and one from the exterior in close proximity to the northeast wall (see Fig. 7).

One ball is of .50 caliber by weight with a maximum diameter of .523 inch. The other 10 ball all fall between .51 caliber and .57 caliber, with one at .51 caliber, one at .52 caliber, three at .53 caliber, one at .54 caliber, and four at .57 caliber (all by weight). Seven of the ball were classed as well formed, four as chewed, one of which was slightly flattened as a result of impact after firing. The ball classed as well formed represent mass-produced ball used as a trade item. The 10 ball in the .51-.57 range are consistent with smooth-bore trade gun application. The one ball (.53 caliber) that appears to have been fired shows no sign of rifling marks. The North structure also contained the single #6 bird shot. This shot is well formed. Records of the Ermatinger family, trading in Mackinac in 1782, list this size shot (Hanson 1987). However, this shot could also relate to post-Fur Trade activity as center-fire shotgun shell bases were also recovered. In referring to Figure 7, it can be observed that the ball recovered from the North building represent a rather isolated component, horizontally separated from the rest of the ball and shot by a minimum of over 12 meters.

The South building interior and immediate exterior yielded a total of 22 ball and shot with a much more diverse range of size and condition than the North structure. This data is summarized in Table 1 and Figure 8. Calibers range from .24 to .55, with four ball falling into the rifle category and a strong representation (10, 48%) of .51-.52 caliber. Five ball are of .54-.55 caliber. One buck shot (.24) is present. Only five of the ball are classed as well formed, while 11 show evidence of chewing. The two ball formed in hand molds, one in .52 caliber and one in .54 caliber, are from this building. Three were classed as indeterminate as to method of formation. Sixteen ball and shot were recovered from outside the structures, generally south and southeast of the South structure. These are, again, diverse, but with a different patterning than the South building (see Table 1). This area held the greatest number of buck shot (eight, 50%) and the greatest number of rifle ball (six), with only three falling into the smooth-bore category. Once again, eight show chewing, while five are well formed and one flattened. One was classed as indeterminate in formation.

In comparing the ball from Horseshoe Bay to a regionally proximal fur trade post of known short-term occupancy, interesting points can be noted. From the fall of 1804 through the spring of 1805, John Sayer of the North West Company (Fond du Lac Department) built and traded from a post on the Snake River in Pine County, Minnesota. This site was excavated by the Minnesota Historical Society in the 1960s and 1970s (Birk 2006). The Minnesota Historical Society and the surface collection of Joseph Neubauer recovered a total of 46 smooth-bore size ball. In addition, one "0" size buck shot, 173 birdshots ranging from #3/#4 to #7 (American sizing) and 222 #T shot (American sizing) were also recovered. Of the smooth-bore ball recovered, 34 were deemed to be in suitable condition for categorization. Table 2 is derived from the analysis of those ball by Birk. His analysis demonstrates that while the "typical" Northwest gun of 24 gauge and taking a 28 gauge (.55) ball was in common use at this post, both smaller and larger ball were also being utilized.

Table 2a compares the ball from the Sayer post with those of the North and South buildings based upon weight. Using this standard, it can be noted that while ball frequency varies, especially in the .55 and .56 calibers, the range of ball associated with the North Building falls into the same general brackets with a notable preference shift to the smaller .52 and .53 caliber ball. Comparison with the South building shows yet another shift to even smaller ball of .51 and .52 caliber with ball above .54 caliber falling out of favor.

Table 2b compares the same ball based on average diametrical measurement. While the general trend toward smaller ball is still evident, it becomes much less distinct. This is the result of the asymmetry of the chewed ball skewing the diameter readings and is reflective of the difficulties these ball have presented during the analyses. A number of the chewed ball weigh virtually exactly what a manufactured ball of a given caliber weighs. These ball likely represent used ball that have been reformed. It is possible that some of these "reforms" were discarded because of an inability of return them to serviceable shape. The weight of these ball would still relate to their original caliber.

The ball distribution may be a notable clue to the sequence of Fur Trade era habitation. During initial excavation it became apparent to the primary investigators that the North structure had been erected, in some manner razed, and then remodeled and rebuilt (Goltz 1993). The ball recovered from this building

Horseshoe Bay Site: Lead Ball Distribution by Location and Size (n=49)

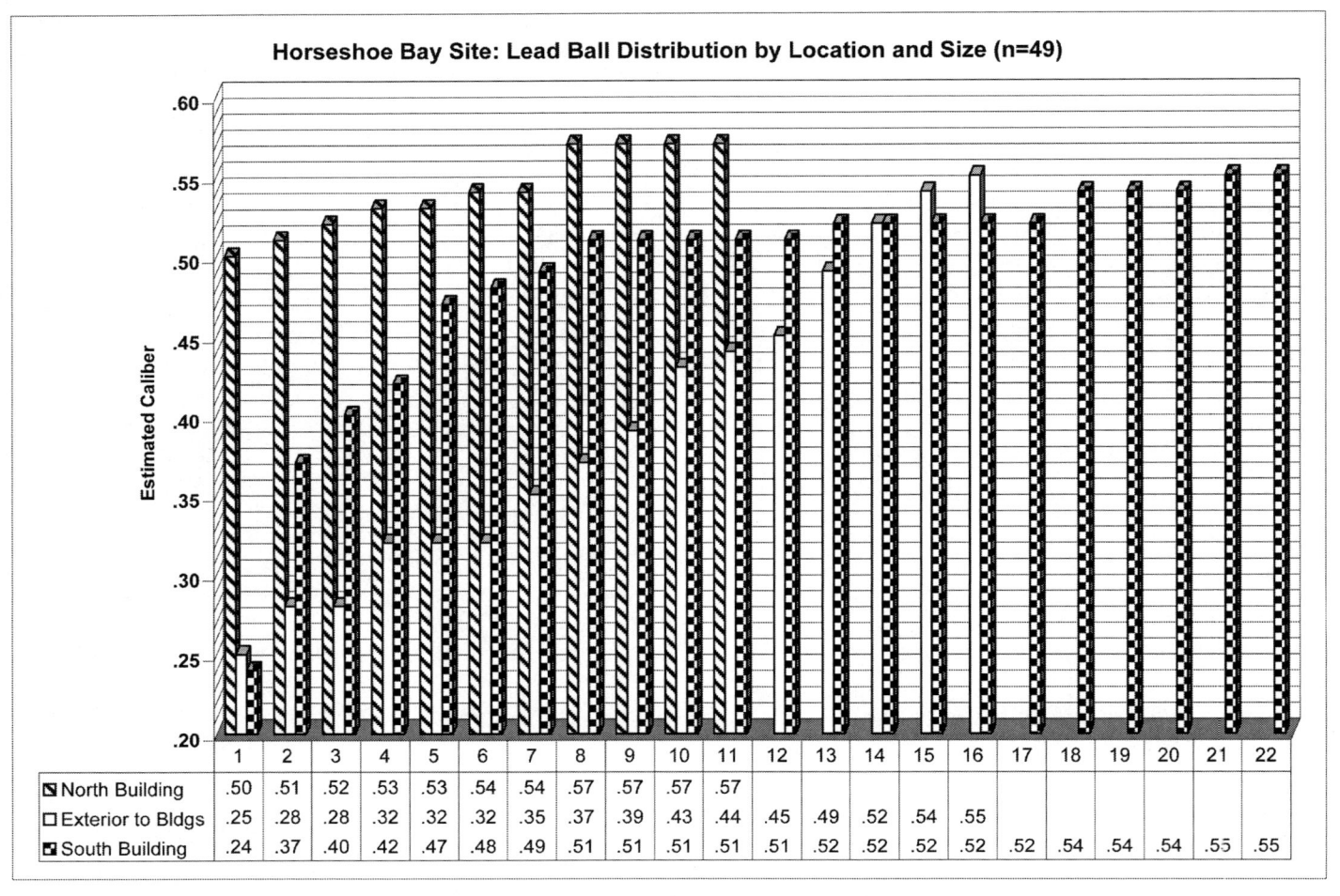

	1	2	3	4	5	6	7	8	9	10	11	12	13	14	15	16	17	18	19	20	21	22
North Building	.50	.51	.52	.53	.53	.54	.54	.57	.57	.57	.57											
Exterior to Bldgs	.25	.28	.28	.32	.32	.32	.35	.37	.39	.43	.44	.45	.49	.52	.54	.55						
South Building	.24	.37	.40	.42	.47	.48	.49	.51	.51	.51	.51	.51	.52	.52	.52	.52	.52	.54	.54	.54	.55	.55

Fig. 8. Lead ball distribution by location and size.

are spatially isolated from the other ball recovered and are of a more consistent caliber range. Four of these ball (36%) are the only representatives of the larger .57 caliber. As demonstrated in Table 5, the South structure has a strong representation of ball in the .51-.52 caliber range, along with rifle ball and buck shot. The percentage of chewed ball also increases. The ball and shot recovered from exterior areas south and southeast of the South building show yet another pattern. Post molds in this area may be evidence of traditional Ojibwe lodges. The highest percentage of buck shot comes from these areas and could be related to Native American hunting practices. The comparison of ball and shot patterns from the North and South structures lead one to suspect that the North building was the first one erected and that there was a temporal separation between its use and the construction of the South building. The ongoing analysis of the Fur Trade artifacts will hopefully assist in further defining the occupational sequence.

Conclusion

Analysis of lead ball and shot have proved valuable in understanding the Fur Trade and later occupations at Horseshoe Bay. The chewed ball and shot classed as moderate, severe, and indeterminate appear to be the result of initial formation from small cut blanks or reformation of used ball. They occur in buck, rifle, and smooth-bore calibers, demonstrating a wide range of application. Such formation implies a lack of access to mass-produced products resulting from fluctuating economic conditions. The high percentage of these ball recovered indicates this practice was not uncommon, especially in regards to the inhabitants of the South structure and exterior.

The ball recovered from the North structure consistently fall into the smooth-bore category, are of generally larger caliber, and have the highest percentage of mass-produced ball. They are spatially isolated from the rest of the assemblage. This is consistent with an earlier habitation temporally separated from the South structure.

The high percentage of buck shot recovered from the exterior areas and in association with probable lodge structures may be indicative of preferred Native American hunting practices.

The high percentage of .51 and .52 caliber ball indicates common use of arms of smaller caliber than the "standard" .58 caliber (24 gauge) Northwest gun. Ball in these calibers are particularly associated with the South structure. While the chewed ball complicate some of the assignments in this category, the presence of factory and hand-mold ball in these calibers is undeniable. These smaller-bore arms could be a later regional variant of the Northwest gun produced to meet the requirements of the area in regards to both efficient use of powder and lead and the available game resources.

The ball firmly classed as rifle caliber are exclusively associated with the South structure and exterior areas. This implies increased availability of rifled arms and a possible shift in both Native American preferences and hunting practices. This is also consistent with these being the areas of later habitation. The distribution and changing assemblage patterns support the contention that the Fur Trade era at Horseshoe Bay is represented by a series of occupations and was of longer duration than commonly found on such sites.

Based on the analysis of the ball, the author believes that at least 17 different muzzle-loading arms were utilized during the period of occupation.

While the lead ball and shot from the Horseshoe Bay site represent a numerically small percentage of the Fur Trade era artifacts, their analysis has revealed a number of interesting aspects. Among these are size and application, method of formation, and distribution. From such data one can theoretically gain insight into factors ranging from occupational sequences to cultural applications. The continuing analysis of the Fur Trade artifacts will, hopefully, either confirm or disaffirm the points presented above and thereby determine the usefulness of such analysis on other Fur Trade era sites, particularly sites where other data are sparse or lacking. Investigation by specialists into dentition patterns and chemical signature of the lead could prove interesting.

Acknowledgments. The author wishes to extend his sincere thanks to Andrea LeVasseur and William Yourd of the Chippewa National Forest and to principal investigators Grant Goltz and Dr. Christy A.H. Caine. Their on going assistance, support, and guidance is deeply appreciated!

References Cited

Baily, G.

    2001 Troubled Times. *Treasure Hunting*, May, p.29

Birk, D. A.

    2006 Firearms and Ordinance from 21-PN-11: An 1804-1805 North West Company Wintering Post Site in East Central Minnesota. Unpublished manuscript. Minnesota Historical Society, Archaeology Dept., St. Paul.

Buchele, W., G. Shumway and P. Alexander

    1998 *Recreating the American Longrifle*. George Shumway, Publisher: York, Pennsylvania.

Campbell, P.

    n.d. The Story of David Ramsey, In *Travels in the Interior Inhabited Parts of North America in the Years 1791 and 1792*, Eddited by H. H. Langdon, p.199. Champlin Society, Toronto. http://www.nyhistory.net/drums.

Dixie Gun Works

    2003 No. 152. Appendix. Note: Appendix data used throughout this paper for evaluation of ball.

Fadala, S.

    2001 *Lyman Black Powder Handbook and Loading Manual.* Lyman, Middletown, Connecticut.

George, D.C.

    1999 *Historical Context for the Horseshoe Bay Site (21CA201).* Paper prepared for USDA Forest Service, Chippewa National Forest.

Gilman, C.

    1982 *Where Two Worlds Meet – The Great Lakes Fur Trade.* Minnesota Historical Society, St. Paul.

Goltz, G.E.

    1993 *Horseshoe Bay Site 09-03-05-351, Preliminary Field Report Vol. I.* Soils Consulting, Longville, Minnesota.

Hamilton, T.M.

    1982 *Indian Trade Guns.* Pioneer Press, Union City, Indiana.

Hannes, S.M.

    1994 *The Faunal Analysis of the Horseshoe Bay Site: A Subsistence Study of a Nineteenth-Century Fur Trade Post.* M.A. Thesis, Department of Anthropology, University of Iowa, Ames.

Hanson, C.E., Jr.

    1955 *The Northwest Gun.* Nebraska State Historical Society, Lincoln.

    1980 *The Guns.* In *Book of Buckskinning,* Scurlock, Texarkana, Texas.

    1982 *Indian Trade Guns.* Pioneer Press, Union City, Indiana.

    1987 *Smooth Bores on the Frontier.* In *Book of Buckskinning IV* Scurlock, Texarkana, Texas.

Olmanson, T. and C. Wells

    2006 *Annual Report of Incidental Investigations Conducted by the Heritage Sites Program in 2004 and 2005 on the Leech Lake Reservation, Minnesota.* Heritage Sites Program, Cass Lake.

Pratt, G.M.

    1995 *The Archeology of the Fallen Timbers Battlefield: A Report of the 1995 Field Survey.* Paper prepared for the Maumee Valley Heritage Corridor.

Russell, C.P.

    1967 *Firearms, Traps and Tools of the Mountain Men.* University of New Mexico Press, Albuquerque, New Mexico.

Shane, O.C. III

    1996 *Identification and Analysis of Fish Remains from the Horseshoe Bay Site: North and South Buildings.* Paper prepared for USDA Forest Service, Chippewa National Forest.

Sivilich, D.M.

    1996 Analyzing Musket Balls to Interpret a Revolutionary War Site. *Historical Archeology* 30(2).

    2005 Revolutionary War Musket Ball Typology – An analysis of Lead Artifacts Excavated at Monmouth Battlefield State Park. *Southern Campaigns of the American Revolution* 2:(1).

Tanner, J.

    1830 *The Falcon – A Narrative of the Captivity and Adventures of John Tanner.* Reprinted 1994, Penguin Group: Putnam, New York.

Wheeler, R.C., W.A. Kenyon, A.R. Woolworth, and D.A. Birk

    1975 *Voices From the Rapids.* Minnesota Historical Society, St. Paul.

ARCHAEOLOGICAL REMAINS OF TWO MID-NINETEENTH-CENTURY DAKOTA HOMES ASSOCIATED WITH THE RIGGS HAZELWOOD MISSION SITE (21YM11/YM-MNF-007)

Richard E. Berg and James E. Myster
Bureau of Indian Affairs

The Bureau of Indian Affairs and the Upper Sioux Indian Community conducted Phase I and II archaeological investigations of a portion of the Riggs Mission site (21YM11/YM-MNF-007). It is believed that two homes constructed for two Dakota families during the mission period (1854-1862) at the Upper Sioux Agency were found during the investigations. Historic artifacts also were found out of context in three widely spaced Concentrations (2, 3/7 and 4). They may be associated with a short term Dakota encampment near the mission in September 1862 or as a result of decades of farming. There is also evidence for one or more prehistoric components present within the boundary of the mission site. No prehistoric non-mound features were found. The prehistoric component(s) were located in the plowzone and disturbed by nearly 150 years of farming. This paper discusses archaeological work on the historic components found at site 21YM11/YM-MNF-007.

Introduction

The Bureau of Indian Affairs, in cooperation with the Upper Sioux Community, surveyed and excavated several artifact scatters on land proposed for trust acquisition and development by the Upper Sioux Community (Fig. 1). Six artifact scatters (Concentrations 1-6) were found within the boundaries of the former Riggs Hazelwood Mission site (YM-MNF-007) and site 21YM11, a mound complex (Fig. 2). The investigations identified Historic and pre-Historic components at all six artifact scatters. The focus of this paper is to discuss the Historic components and the identification of two features believed to be Dakota home sites associated with the Stephen R. Riggs Hazelwood mission (1854-1862) at the Yellow Medicine, or Upper Sioux, Agency.

The archaeological survey and excavations for these two sites were Section 106 compliance-driven projects for proposed trust acquisition and planned development of lands acquired by the Upper Sioux Community. The archaeological survey of the property that identified the six Concentrations was carried out in 2002 (Berg and Myster 2002). Phase II evaluation excavations were conducted on four of the Concentrations (nos. 1-4) the following year (Berg and Myster 2005). Two of the Concentrations (nos. 5 and 6) that would not be affected immediately by development were not evaluated.

The BIA and the Upper Sioux Community provided funds for the Phase II evaluation in the summer of 2003. Several Community members and anthropology students were hired to work under the supervision of the BIA's Regional Archaeologist and Assistant Regional Archaeologist to make surface collections, shovel test, and excavate Concentrations 1-4.

Environmental Setting

The Riggs Hazelwood Mission site (21YM11/YM-MNF-007) is located on a broad ridge between the Minnesota River Valley (to the northeast) and Hazel Creek (to the southwest) in Minnesota Falls Township in Section 15, Township 115 North, Range 39 West in Yellow Medicine County, Minnesota. A private farmstead, the Doncaster Cemetery and an abandoned sand and gravel quarry encompass several acres near the center of the section. At the time of the Phase II evaluation the land was bare ground and had not yet been planted in crops.

In this part of Minnesota Falls Township, the soils are dominated by Ves-Canisteo-Spicer loamy and silty soils that are "well drained and poorly drained, undulating and nearly level soils formed in glacial till and lacustrine deposits" (Hokanson 1981: General Soil Map). Hokanson writes that the soils in the

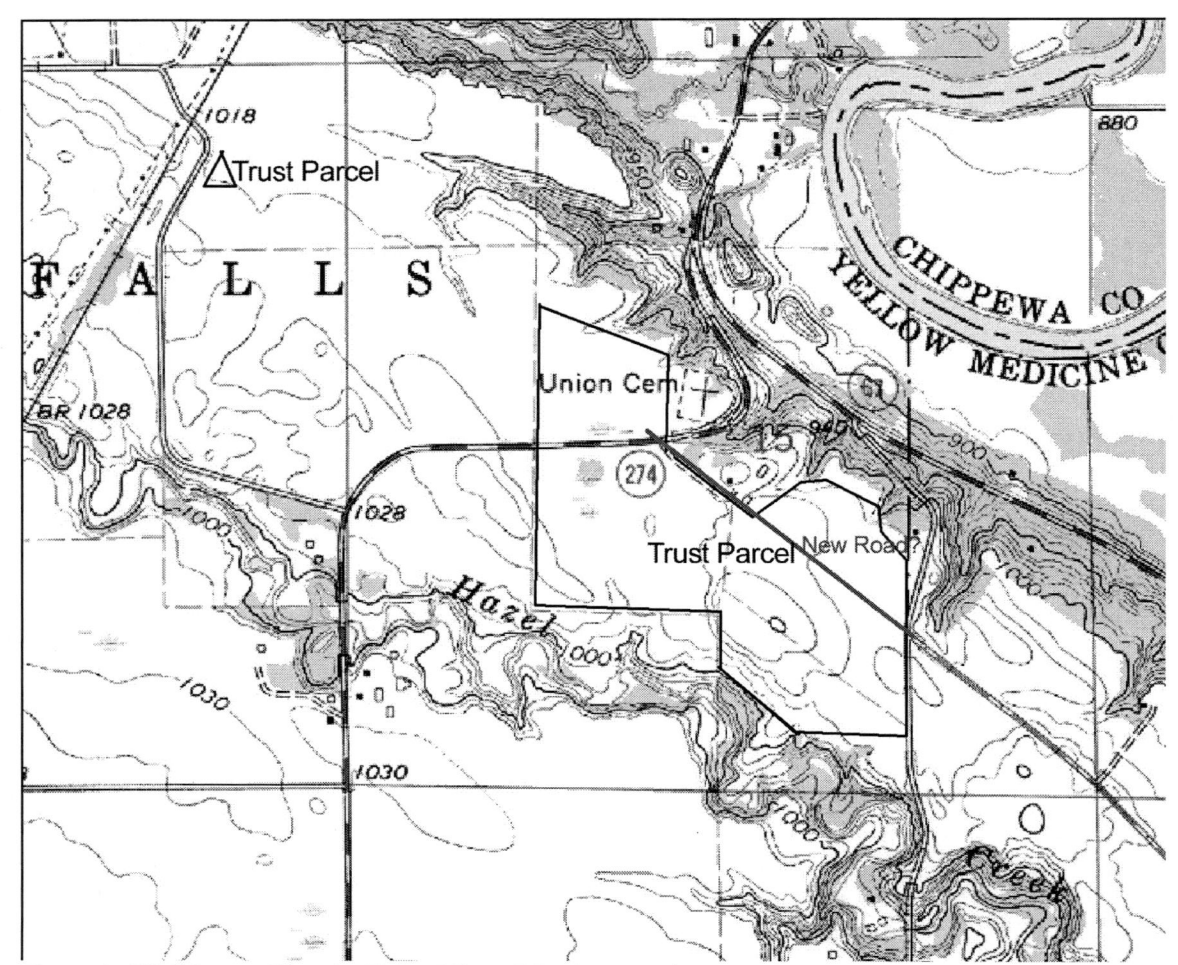

Figure 1. USGS map (Granite Falls, Minn. 7.5 minute series) showing the two trust parcels covered by Phase I and II archaeological investigations.

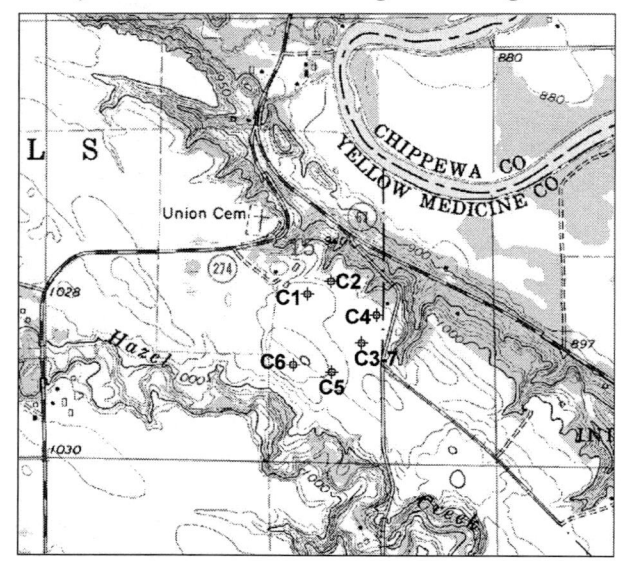

Figure 2. USGS map showing the Concentrations (C1-C6) centroids located during the Phase I archaeological survey.

county are young; they began forming 8,000-12,000 years ago. The native grasses here were mid and tall prairie grasses (Hokanson 1981). Farming was initiated in this section in 1854 or 1855 after the Riggs mission was relocated here from Lac qui Parle. Today most of the parcel is still farmed.

Archival Research

Archival information obtained for the Phase I and II archaeological investigations was acquired from the Wilson Library at the University of Minnesota, Minneapolis; the Minnesota Historical Society in St. Paul and Fort Snelling; the Minnesota State Historic Preservation Office (SHPO) and State Archives in St. Paul; the Yellow Medicine County Historical Society and county courthouse in Granite Falls; and the Center for Western Studies at Augustana College

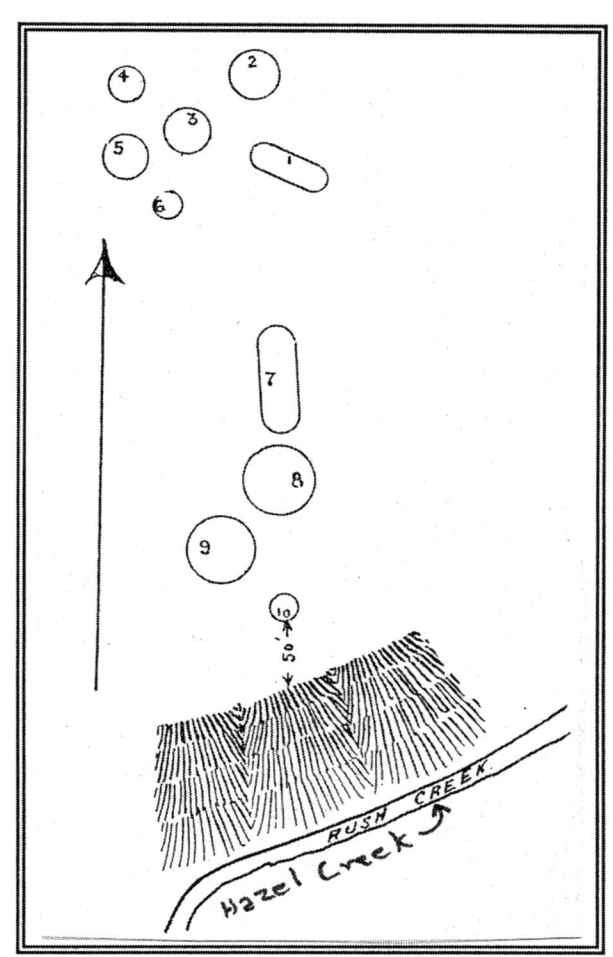

Figure 3. Mound site 21YM11 (from Winchell 1911: 117).

site 21YM11 is reported to be situated in the W½, SE¼ of Section 15 about 60 feet above Hazel Creek and 50 feet from the edge of the creek channel (Fig. 3). At that time the mound group extended northward several hundred feet from the creek edge. Two of the 10 mounds were elongated; the rest were circular. When Lewis mapped the complex, two of the circular mounds were 50 feet in diameter and between 4 and 5½ feet in height (Winchell 1911). This site has been subjected to cultivation since the 1850s. It is questionable whether there are still visible remnants of this complex present.

It wasn't until the 1950s that University of Minnesota Archaeologist Lloyd Wilford visited the site (Wilford 1954). Wilford made a site visit in May 1954, and he was shown rocks behind the extant farmhouse (presumably on the Minnesota River side) that might be a building foundation from the Riggs mission. Summing up his visit he wrote,

> Hunting for mounds at the Riggs Mission site, presumably very close to the point where the new state highway 274 leaves 67, at about the center of Sec. 15, T. 115-39. Hy 274 runs uphill from the junction and at the top is a cemetery [Doncaster/Union Cemetery] at the right. Here the road turns left to the house now owned by a Mr. Markman of Granite Falls, whose married daughter lives there. Her name may be Beck. At the foot of the hill behind the house is Highway 67, and here the Historical Society has placed the Riggs Mission Plaque. This was formerly the Dibble farm. The son-in-law showed me some rocks behind the house and at the top of the bluff, which he said formerly looked like foundations. Is this the Riggs site? In the field south of the house is a high mound in a plowed land. This may be the survivor of the group of 10 listed by Winchell . . . as mounds at the former Riggs Mission, . . . More likely the present mound represents the union of mounds 8 and 9, said to have been 4 and 5½ ft. high, respectively. They were close together and probably have been united by plowing. On the east side of the mound, the son-in-law [of William Markham in 1954] plows up bricks and

in Sioux Falls, South Dakota. Additional historical information regarding the Riggs mission was also obtained from John LaBatte, a member of the Upper Sioux Community.

21YM11/YM-MNF-007 (Hazelwood Mission)

This is a site complex that comprises two previously recorded sites: 21YM11 and YM-MNF-007. Archaeological site 21YM11 is a group of 10 earthen mounds recorded in the 1880s (Winchell 1911). The other site, YM-MNF-007, is the Hazelwood (also known as the Riggs) Mission (Granger 1985). The boundary of site 21YM11 also incorporates part of the Riggs (Hazelwood) Mission site.

Site 21YM11 was originally recorded as a complex of mounds by T.H. Lewis in the late 1880s. Surveyed by T.H. Lewis on October 17, 1887 mound

Figure 4. The Riggs' Mission circa 1860 (Photo courtesy of the Minnesota Historical Society).

mortar and ran into a wall. I had thought this might have been a remnant of a Riggs house, but, Alben Johnson, the neighbor to the south can remember when a brick house stood here. [Wilford 1954: 481]

In the Fall of 2001, the Upper Sioux Community contracted archaeologists with the Red Lake Band of Chippewa Indians to conduct a survey of the 80 acres (identified by Lewis as containing site 21YM11) in order to both relocate the mounds and discover other cultural properties in the area (Hohman-Caine, Peterson and Goltz 2002). Their investigation places the mound site in the southeastern corner of their project area. If this is true, the southern four mounds (nos. 7-10) are on private property and the six northern mounds (nos. 1-6) are on the Upper Sioux Community land (Dallas Ross, personal communication 2002).

Two years later the Upper Sioux Community made a second effort to locate the mounds by contracting for a geophysical survey and an additional study of early aerial photographs (Kluth and Fromm 2003). The survey identified a number of unknown anomalies that do not correspond to the mound centers as mapped by Lewis. The anomalies could either be Historic or pre-Historic features that would require excavation to identify. Kluth and Fromm place the mounds south of the area where their remote sensing was conducted. They placed seven (nos. 1-7) of the 10 mounds on Community land and three (nos. 8-10) on private property.

Subsequent to the geophysical survey, an additional reference to one of the mounds was found in the Riggs papers at the Center for Western Studies, Augustan College, Sioux Falls, South Dakota. It seems to support Wilford's memo regarding the presence of a mound next to one of the Dakota homes built

Figure 5. Group of Sioux Indians at Chaska's house near Pajutazee (Williamson) mission (Photo courtesy of the Minnesota Historical Society). House in the background is an example of the brick homes constructed for some the Sioux in the early 1860s at the Upper Agency.

while the Hazelwood mission was still in operation. In 1860 Stephen Riggs wrote his son Alfred about a photographer who came to take pictures of the mission. Reverend Riggs wrote,

> Monday morn. July 23. Saturday after I had written the above and while I was out hoeing rutabagas, Mr. Hill the artist, who has been here at Yellow Medicine since before the payments "reaping golden honors" by making light pictures of almost every body, drove up with Mr. Freniere. He had come to take the likeness of our mission premises. After trying from various points he finally placed his camera on the little mound back of Simon's. We gathered quite a company, perhaps too many, a mixed multitude, for the fore ground. The wind blew considerably which was rather against the result. He tried several times. His first and last negatives were he thought tolerably good. He took one ambrotype which was beautiful of the buildings, the trees back of the church showing very finely, but some of the crowd were rather blurred. It was half past two oclock before we got ready to eat dinner.[Riggs 1860 :1-2]

Reverend Riggs is probably referring to the photograph of the mission, taken about 1860, now in the archives of the Minnesota Historical Society (Fig. 4). The "Simon" that Riggs mentions in his correspondence is very likely Simon Anawangmani (1808?-1891). Simon is reported to have been the first full-blood Dakota converted through the proselytizing efforts of the Reverend Riggs in the early 1840s (Riggs 1880:65). Riggs writes that for many years Mr. Anawangmani had difficulty following his new faith. He later became a church elder at the mission and eventually received a license to preach in the latter third of the 1860s. He and a number of others protected those who fled the Riggs and Williamson missions at the outbreak of hostilities. He also served as a scout for the Sibley expedition (Anderson and Woolworth 1988:128; Riggs 1880).

The Riggs Hazelwood mission (YM-MNF-007) was established in 1854 after the Riggs mission at Lac Qui Parle accidentally burned to the ground. The American Board of Foreign Missions decided to consolidate the Riggs and Williamson missions at the same locality. After Riggs relocated to this area, the mission was first called New Hope, later the name was changed to Hazelwood. Construction first began on a house for the Riggs family and a framed building to be used as a multipurpose school and dwelling (boarding house). Riggs also broke ground for a mission field and built several log cabins for the Indians that were later replaced with wood-framed, then brick homes (Fig. 5) within the next several years. The U.S. government supplied the brick in 1860 after it had constructed a kiln (Riggs 1856, 1880; also see Appendix A with newspaper advertisements for building construction). But before then, in 1855, floors for nine log cabins were cut. Mrs. Riggs wrote that there was sufficient flooring cut for a one room cabin (Riggs 1996: 213). Further, Mr. Riggs reported that Simon Anawangmani had a frame house measuring 24 ft by 16 ft and 10 ft high. It had enough room for storage and a sleeping room upstairs. Mr. Anawangmani cut the shingles, sills, and sleepers and dug the cellar. The government furnished most of the window sash frames, glass, and nails (Riggs 1856). Work was started on the chapel in 1855, but no progress was made on building additional houses. Potatoes and corn were planted (Riggs 1856). The Riggs also had a chicken house north of the house (?) (Riggs 1996).

In August of 1862, during the initial phase of the Dakota War, the mission was abandoned. The Upper (Agency) Indians encamped in the vicinity of the mission on August 28 and stayed until September 9. Everyone then moved upriver to Chief Red Iron's camp, which would become known as Camp Release (Brown 1988). While at the Riggs Mission, the Indians and the Whites that were with them also occupied the houses and camped around the mission (Crawford 1998, Renville 1988). In early September 1862, Reverend Riggs was informed that all of the buildings at the mission except the church had been burned (Riggs 1862a). Within a week's time he was told that the church had also been burned (Riggs 1862b). Later in the same month, Riggs visited the mission while he was attached to the Sibley expedition. He identified the burned buildings as the ward house (the Riggs home?), stable, church, and schoolhouse. He also wrote that a photographer (Adrian J. Ebell) who was with the Sibley expedition took at least one photograph of the house remains in a stereoscopic view (Riggs 1862c). Unfortunately, the photograph was not found in the Minnesota Historical Society Archives. Most likely, either the photograph no longer exists or it is in an unknown collection back east where Mr. Ebell came from and later returned.

Decades later S. L. Riggs, son and T. F. Riggs, grandson of Stephen and Mary Riggs, visited the area in 1923 to see the Hazelwood and Williamson missions, the Upper Sioux Agency, and the Lac qui Parle mission. The grandson, T. F. Riggs, wrote the following description of the Hazelwood mission site to Doane Robinson in 1928:

> My father wanted to see if he could find the place without help so we drove south (from Granite Falls) on the "Sioux Historic Trail" and had passed several Indian houses when at a point about three miles south of town where the road leaves the river bottom and climbs up a ravine to the plateau on the west side my father began to recognize "the lay of the land." He thought he remembered this ravine as having been part of his father's pasture and sure enough as we came to the top there was the little slough where, on one occasion as a boy, he had tried to shoot ducks with a gun minus stock or lock and which he had attempted to fire by striking the cap with a carpenter's hammer! Needless to say it was fortunate that the powder did not ignite. To our right beyond the slough and toward the west he recognized the ridge along which the northern Indians used to travel on their way to the agency on the Yellow Medicine. It did not take him long to find the site of the house of the Hazelwood mission even though a modern farm house is now located there and then followed the (road?) locating southeast of the house the site of the school building in a slight hollow and the site of the church

on the little knoll further to the southeast. He showed me where the garden had been located northeast of the site of the house and the big field to the southwest and beyond the breaks of the little creek called by my grandfather "Hazel Run" because of the dense growth of hazel bushes, but originally called "Rush Brook" or "Rush Creek" by the Indians. We spent perhaps an hour looking about the place and then drove along the trail, crossing Hazel Run, to hunt for the site of Dr. Williamson's mission buildings of the second mission. [Riggs 1928:3-4]

During or shortly after the trip, Mr. Riggs also made a map of the old mission area and sent it along with the letter to Doane Robinson. If it still exists, the map may be somewhere with the Doane Robinson records in the South Dakota State Archives.

Another letter written by Thomas L. Riggs to his daughter Anna shortly after the visit to the old mission site by the Riggs and others, says, in part,

Theodore, Katherine, the little one, Thomas L. Riggs, Louisa and I and Harry Morris, have been this afternoon at Hazelwood and seen what is there. The frame house, where the house was, built over our cellar, where the large cottonwood trees that father and Mr. Cunninham must have planted straight along in front of our houses up towards the chapel up on the low range running north and south to trees and our houses, and other things that bring to our own childhood days— where Tatticorn, [undecipherable name], Pedoma, Buck and Bright figured so largely (horses names). Last objective Theodore and I made a flying trip to Lac que Parle. [Montevideo, Minn, July 2, 1924] [Riggs papers at the Center for Western Studies].

The 1923 trip by the Riggs was also reported on by the Granite Falls Tribune and in an article the following year in The Word Carrier of Santee Normal Training School. The newspaper story mentions the various stops and visitations that Riggs made while in the Granite Falls area. The news account also states that "the Riggs mission was at that time [1862] located at the top of the Doncaster hill, in fact, the present house is on the foundation of the mission" (Granite Falls Tribune 1923:1). The *Word Carrier* mentions the people who were on the trip and that the trees planted by Reverend Riggs "are great tall ones now; they ought to be marked (Anonymous 1924: 1).

The rock foundation shown to Wilford in 1954 behind the extant farmhouse may indeed be some of the architectural remains belonging to the Hazelwood Mission. Wilford speculated that the mission is located immediately north of the mound site. A circa 1860 photograph of the mission in the SHPO files shows several buildings near the terrace edge (see Fig. 4). The brick foundation beside the mound (Concentration 5) might be an upgraded brick home built for Simon Anawangmani. The mission site was eventually purchased by Joseph Doncaster and became a farm. By 1890 the plat map for Minnesota Falls Township shows a house occupied by Mr. Doncaster and may be the building mentioned above by T. F. Riggs in 1924. Today (2006) a farmstead is still present and the land around it is farmed (Fig. 6). The large trees also mentioned above may be the tall cottonwood trees on the left side of Figure 6. The current farmhouse is located behind the trees to the right of the tall trees. The location of Concentration 1 is also indicated in the figure.

As a side note to the above, Sibley's trench (21YMo) is reported to be about a mile to the west of the Upper Sioux Community property. This is an earthwork Sibley had his men build for protection in 1862 as the expedition traveled north after the battle with the Sioux at Wood Lake which is located several miles to the south. At least one historical record (Rose 1914:71) places the earthwork in the southern half of Section 15 somewhere along Hazel Creek.

Research Design and Methods

The primary purpose of the Phase I and II archaeological investigations was to identify and evaluate the cultural resources that would be placed into trust status and possibly affected by development pro-

Figure 6. Location of the former Riggs (Hazelwood) Mission viewed to the north.

posed by the Upper Sioux Community. Phase II focused on the field northeast of a new road leading to the Community's casino (see Fig. 1). Approximately one-half of the trust property lies within the recognized site boundary of the Riggs Hazelwood mission (21YM11/YM-MNF-007). The Hazelwood mission played an important part in the history of the Dakota during a very brief period of time (1854-1862). The missionaries here and at the nearby Williamson mission made intensive efforts to convert the Indians to Christianity and transform their culture to the extent that it would merge completely within the dominant nineteenth-century Euroamerican concept of civilization. In addition to the mission, six artifact concentrations containing Historic and pre-Historic artifacts were identified during the Phase I archaeological survey. These concentrations may represent the mission or other Historic occupations and one or more pre-Historic components.

The field methods in Phase I involved walking the parcel in transects spaced 10-20 meters apart. Artifacts observed on the ground surface along each transect were flagged. After the survey was finished, the surveyors returned to the flagged areas to look for evidence of artifact concentrations (possible activity areas). A total of six areas where there were artifact concentrations were identified. Once all of the observable artifacts were located, the dimensions of each concentration were measured with a metric tape and their centroids were recorded in 1983 NAD UTM coordinates using a Global Positioning System (GPS) instrument. All six areas were then surface collected. A 1 x 1 m unit was excavated in Concentration 5. Another walkover was conducted for Phase II, but it was confined to the field northeast of the road that divides the parcel.

Ten meter grids were then set up over four concentrations (C1, 2, 3/7, and 4) on the northeast side of the road (see Figs. 2, 7, and 8). This was followed by further surface collecting and shovel testing at all grid intersections. Positive shovel tests and shovel tests showing "deep" soils were used to place 1 x 1 m excavation units in a particular grid. All excavated soil was passed through a ¼ inch screen. All artifacts or questionable artifacts from each concentration were retained for analysis. Upon collection, the artifacts were placed in paper bags and labeled with the site number; concentration number; date; investigators; and applicable grid, ST number, or excavation unit and level. Soils were described for every shovel test and excavation unit. Munsel color designations were employed to identify soil color. At least one wall of every excavation unit was drawn and planviews of excavation unit floors were drawn when possible features were being uncovered or changes were observed in soil characteristics. Photographs were also taken of each unit, trench segments, features, or possible features.

Artifacts obtained in the field for this investigation were brought to the BIA Regional Office for cleaning, identification, recording, and cataloging. The

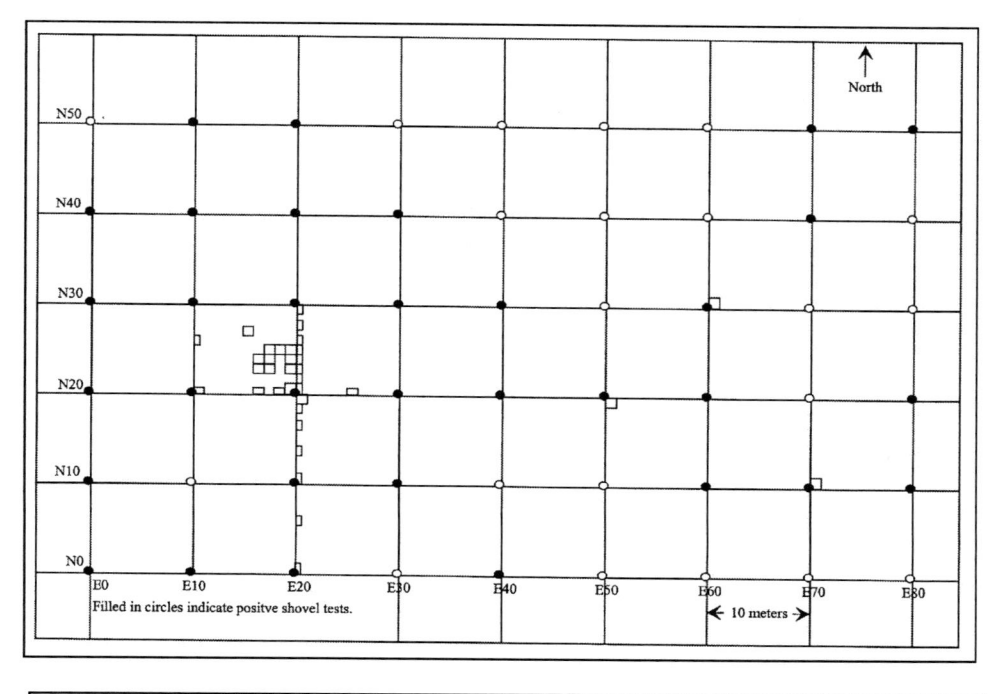

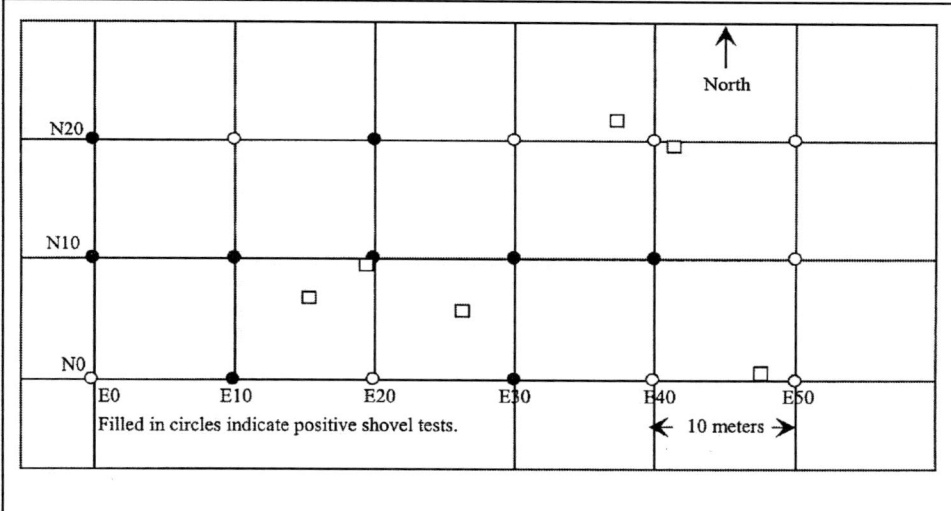

Figure 7. Concentrations 1 and 2 grids.

artifacts were catalogued using BIA accession numbers. Some Historic artifacts such as nails were also measured (in inches) for length, because such artifacts were manufactured and used by people working in this system of measurement. Organic materials were also weighed on a triple-beam balance. Historic artifacts were identified with the aid of various reference materials cited in the text. Diagnostic artifacts and recognizable tools were photographed for inclusion in this report.

The Phase I investigation indicated that six areas of the field northeast and southwest of the road had noticeable artifact concentrations. Each concentration was viewed as a separate entity. It was not known if these concentrations were separate sites or features belonging to a single site or were a result of over a century of farming. Although the methods employed at all four areas were similar, the amount of formal testing at each differed in intensity by the productivity of the surface collection and subsurface shovel testing.

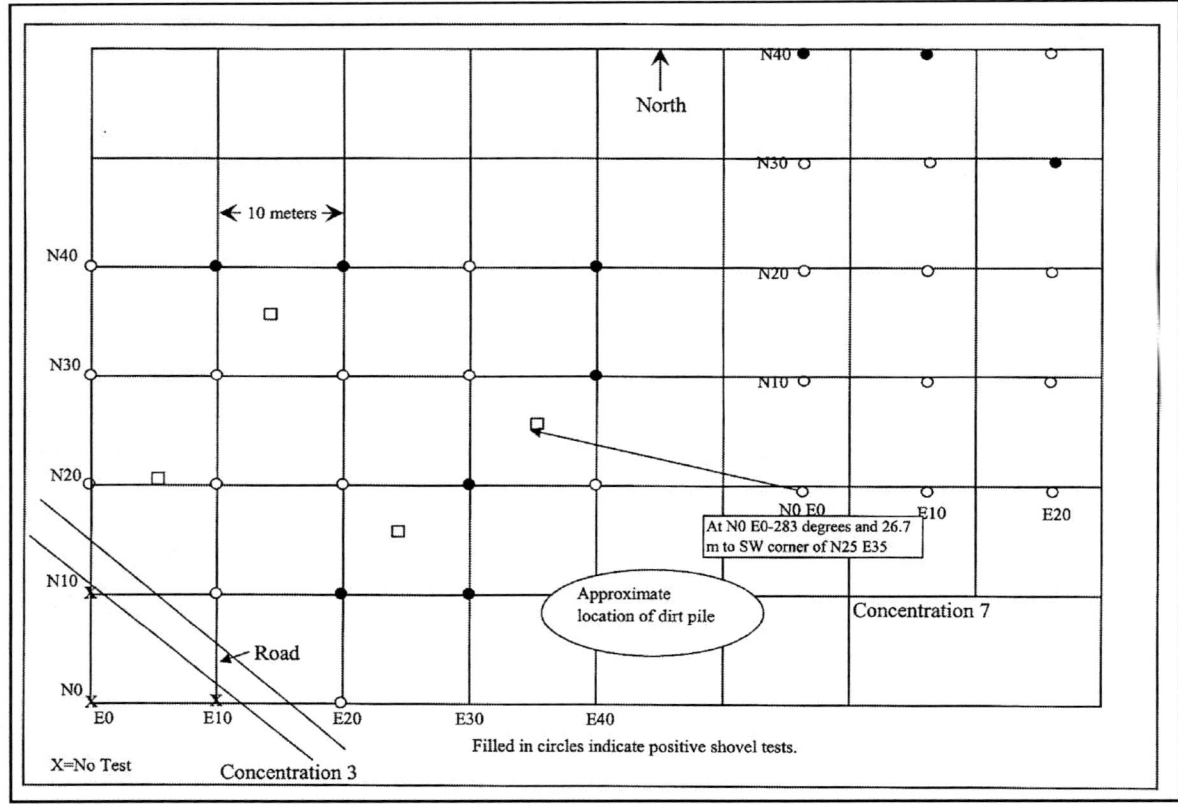

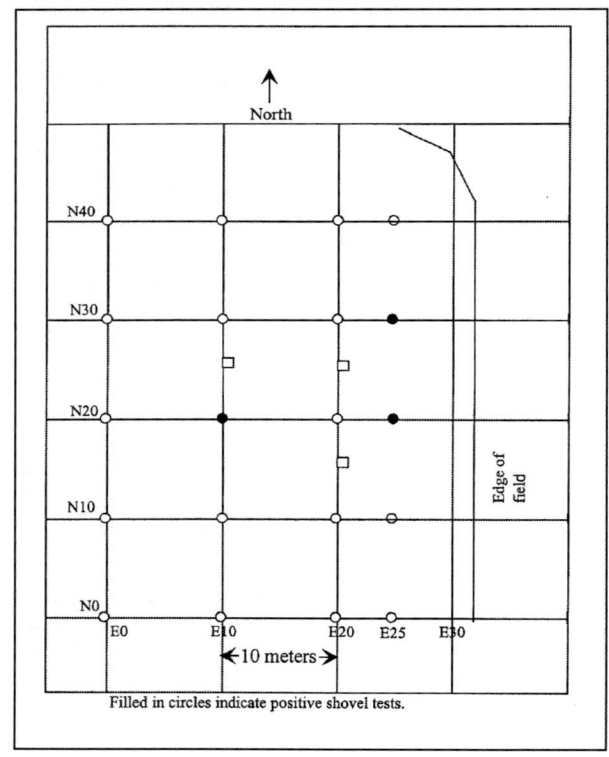

Figure 8. Concentrations 3/7 and 4 grids.

The Phase II investigation was directed by the BIA's Midwest Regional and Assistant Regional Archaeologists. They supervised three Community members and four anthropology students hired by the BIA and Upper Sioux Community to work on this project over a period of 25 days from May 20 to June 20 and August 11-14, 2003. A second transect survey was conducted in the field where Concentrations 1-4 are located including shovel testing and excavating within the four concentrations. All seven hires worked 21 days in May and June. They also cleaned and sorted artifacts on rain days. In August, two Community members assisted the BIA archaeologists in finishing the testing of an area where a buried Historic pit feature was found in Concentration 1.

Before the Phase II work commenced, the field was tilled in preparation for planting. The farmer who rented the field from the Community was informed that no planting was to occur until the excavations were over. In June he was allowed to plant crops in all of the concentrations except Concentration 1. He left the concentration untouched even after our work there was ended.

A series of grids were set up over five different areas (Concentrations 1, 2, 3, 4, and 7) (Figs. 7 and 8). Concentrations 3 and 7 were later combined as a single concentration: 3/7. The grids were oriented to magnetic north. The center of each grid was the centroid identified by GPS during the Phase I survey. The five grids were of varying sizes based on the extent of each surface concentration. For example, Concentration 1 had a grid of 50 x 80 m, and Concentration 3 had a grid of 40 x 40 m. Stakes were placed at 10 meter intervals across each grid. The southwest corner of every grid was used for the N0/E0 reference point. Each stake was then identified as point north and east of the grid reference point. All units were excavated by shovel skimming and troweling. The basic level depth was 10 cm but varied more or less depending on changes in soil characteristics and noticeable artifact clustering.

Concentration 1

This is the only concentration found on elevated ground on the northeast side of the road. A 50 x 50 m grid was set up to encompass the entire surface scatter and was later expanded another 30 m east to a grid 50 x 80 m in size. A total of 54 grid intersections were then shovel tested.

This area turned out to be the most intensively studied of the four concentrations. Initially we thought that this was the area where either the Riggs chapel was located or possibly a home was built for one of the Dakota families. If there was a home here, it may have been built some time after the 1860 photograph (Fig. 4) was taken. The quantity of buried artifacts and finding a buried feature on this hill eventually resulted in creating two discontinuous north-south trenches and a single east-west trench. Units excavated along the trench alignments were 1 meter in length and 0.5 meter wide. Fifteen of these half units were excavated along Trench 1 (north-south), which was set up to be 30 meters long between points N0-N29 and E20. One of the half units (N19 E 20) on this trench was expanded into a 1 x 1 m excavation unit. Trench 2 (east-west) was set up at N20 and went east from E15 to E25. Five half units were excavated along this line. One unit (N19 E19) on this alignment was expanded to a 1 x 1 m excavation unit. The third trench was actually a single partial unit placed north to south at points N20-N30 along E10. No other partial units were added on this alignment, because we encountered a buried feature to the southeast of this excavation and further testing was abandoned along the alignment. Thirteen 1 x 1 m units were also excavated in Concentration 1. Three were placed along the east edge of the grid with the other 10 clustered around the buried feature.

Concentration 2

A 20 x 40 m grid was set up in this concentration with the centroid at the center of the south edge of the grid because the surface collection in 2003 had found more artifacts north of the centroid and none to the south. Fifteen shovel tests were dug at the grid points and five 1 x 1 m excavation units were opened here near artifact clusters and a possible buried feature (post mold or rodent burrow?). Four units were placed within the grid and one was placed just to the north of the grid.

Concentration 3

A 40 x 40 m grid was set up in this concentration. The southern part of the grid extended into the road and a dirt pile. Nineteen shovel tests were dug 10 meters apart on the grid, avoiding the road and a dirt pile. Four 1 x 1 m units were placed in the vicinity of positive shovel tests. Concentration 3 was later combined with Concentration 7 because of their proximity to each other.

Concentration 4

A 40 x 25 m grid was set up in this concentration. The east side of the grid was shortened because it would not fit within the fence line bordering the field. A total of 19 shovel tests were dug on the grid points. Three 1 x 1 m units were excavated near the only three positive shovel tests in this concentration.

Concentration 5

Since this area was not part of the later Phase II evaluations, no grid was set up over this area. A

Table 1. Artifacts Recovered from Concentrations 1, 2, 3/7, 4, and 5

Materials	C1	C2	C3/7	C4	C1-C4*	C5	Total
Brick Fragments	2875	0	6	3	0	4	2888
Glass Shards	667	17	28	11	7	59	789
Metal	446	7	3	5	4	56	521
Prehistoric Lithics	(187)	(203)	(157)	(60)	(80)	(15)	(702)
Historic Ceramics	49	52	2	49	25	110	297
Historic Lithics	17	4	1	0	2	1	25
Flora	+11	0	0	0	0	0	+11
Fauna	5	0	0	1	0	2	8
Mortar/Plaster	3	1	0	1	1	2	7
Synthetic	1	0	1	0	0	0	2
Geode	0	0	0	1	0	0	1
Total	4261	284	198	131	119	249	5252
Total (minus Lithics)	4047	81	41	70	39	234	4550

*Artifacts/items collected between the concentrations.

single 1 x 1 m test unit was opened here during the Phase I survey.

Concentration 7

A 40 x 30 m grid was set up in this concentration found during a transect survey of the field during the Phase II investigation. It was relatively close to Concentration 3. For this reason, no excavation units were put within this concentration. There were 15 shovel tests dug in Concentration 7. Three of the shovel tests were positive. It was decided to add this concentration to Concentration 3.

General Surface Collections

Several surface collections were made between concentrations during the duration of the project. A second complete walkover of the field was done and the artifacts observed during the walkover were flagged and later collected. Periodically finds were made during the work at the various concentrations and those were also bagged separately.

Results

The four artifact concentrations found in 2002 northeast of the road were surface collected and below-ground cultural materials were recovered by shovel testing and more formal excavation. A total of 4,550 items (minus pre-Historic lithics) were recovered from two seasons of investigation on the field northeast of the road and Concentration 5 (Table 1). Each concentration and the general surface collection is presented separately. Only the Historic materials are discussed in this paper. Within these presentations, the surface finds are addressed before the subsurface finds.

Concentration 1

This concentration is in the southwest corner of the field on a hill crest and its upper slopes (Fig. 2). All of this concentration is situated on eroded Ves-Storden loam on 3-6 percent slopes. Ves soil has about a 23 cm surface soil of black loam with small masses of dark grayish brown subsoil. It can be deeper on lower slopes and shallow swales. Below the surface layer is approximately 43 cm of dark brown to dark yellowish brown friable clay loam in the upper part and the lower part has a calcareous friable loam. Below this layer to about 152 cm is an olive brown calcareous loam glacial till. Storden soil has a surface layer approximately 23 cm thick consisting of a dark grayish brown calcareous loam. Below the surface layer to about 152 cm is a calcareous loam glacial till of different shades of olive brown.

Figure 9. Selected historic artifacts from Concentration 1.

Frost action sometimes pushes stones to the surface (Hokanson 1981:65). Shovel testing and unit excavation identified three parts. The upper is clay silt loam ranging in color from black to very dark gray to very dark grayish brown to very dark brown, an olive to dark olive brown and dark yellowish brown. The depth from the surface of the upper part was recorded between 16 and 51 cm, averaging 22.7 cm. Four shovel-tested areas in this concentration seem to have a middle stratum between 7 cm and 48 cm in thickness, all of which are at or adjacent to the south edge of the grid, where a slope exists. The middle part is a clay loam that is black to a very dark grayish brown. The lower part is a silt clay loam that is olive or olive brown to dark yellowish brown and brown.

The surface artifact distribution is oriented roughly west to east (60 x 40 m). Concentration 1 was, by far, the most intensively investigated of the four concentrations identified northeast of the road. From this concentration, a total of +4,047 historic artifacts including floral and faunal remains were recovered in 2002 and 2003 (Table 1). Of this number, 71.2 percent (n=2,878) is made up of brick and mortar fragments that range in size from 0.4 to 7 cm. These architectural elements far outnumber any recovered from the other concentrations on the northeast side of the road. Concentration 5 also had a large quantity of brick and mortar fragments that were not collected from the ground surface in 2002 because diagnostic materials were being sought.

A small number of floral and faunal remains comprising corn kernels, charcoal, and a wood dowel segment plus burned and unburned bone were found in this concentration. The calcined bone is in small fragments and the unburned bone is a cortex portion of an unidentified mammal long bone (deer?).

Surface Collections

A total of 268 historic ceramic, glass, metal, and stone artifacts including coal and clinkers were collected from the ground surface over two field seasons.

Ceramics: Manufactured pottery includes 32 sherds comprising 20 whiteware sherds--one is blue spongeware and the other is blue with a circle within a diamond (Fig. 9,C and D); five coarse earthenware sherds--four have a dark brown salt glaze, the fifth has a reddish glaze; four stoneware body sherds--two have a brown glaze and one has an orangish glaze; one porcelain cup rim and attached handle fragment; and one possible redware sherd with a reddish glaze. The different sherds may represent at least seven separate containers. Besides these ceramic containers there is a refined earthenware sherd, one round door knob fragment, and four brick fragments. The broken door knob (Fig. 9A) has a Bennington glaze.

Glass: There are 202 glass shards, a number of which come from containers that include 16 aqua (two are melted) three amethyst, two pale blue one colorless, one green; two milk-glass jar lid liners; 61 melted aqua glass shards and eight unidentified aqua colored shards; 106 flat aqua glass window shards; one milk-glass button; and one colorless glass shard that may be part of a candlestick base. The container glass shards include at a minimum six separate bottles or vials. One of the aqua glass-container fragments is embossed ("...OR...N..." or "...OH...NV..."), but the word(s) cannot be identified. Another of the aqua glass-container shards has an embossed checkerboard pattern. The three amethyst-colored glass shards may belong to a single bottle. One of the shards is a vertical bottle neck with a two-part straight finish. The button (diameter=7/16") has four holes situated within a circular recess on the top surface. It has a lens-shaped cross-section.

Metal: A total of 24 metal items were collected from the ground surface. They are identified as 17 cut nails, one three-hole door hinge, three metal bars, one fence staple, one broken horse shoe, and one bolt (length=6") with a square head. Complete cut nails range in length from 1½ to 4 inches. The metal bars are rather short fragments of longer pieces of hardware. One has two bolts attached to it; another has a rivet attached and the third has a single hole. They are all different widths and thicknesses.

Stone: There are five Historic items derived from lithic materials. One is a nearly square (34.5 x 35.5 mm) piece of pipestone (catlinite) that appears to have been cut with a saw and is considered to be a Historic artifact (Fig. 9B). In profile it is a right-angled wedge the base is slightly convex, and the opposite surface is flat as is the back of the wedge. The top and back have a slight polish. Numerous crisscrossing striations are present on the top, sides, and bottom of the wedge. On the angled top portion of the stone, several millimeters of stone was removed to create a roughed-out V shape. A similar V shape is also present on the base at the same general location. There are no other recognizable patterns to be seen on the pipestone. The second lithic artifact is a broken gunflint (l=>½", w=ca. 1", thickness=⅜") represented by one end and part of two right-angled edges (Fig. 9E). The platform on the dorsal surface is concave; the striking edges are angled between 40° and 55°. The ventral surface is slightly sinuous. It was manufactured from a dark gray mottled flint. Finally, there are two pieces of coal (wt=4.8 gm) and one coal clinker (wt=53.2 gm).

Synthetic: One modern brown transparent plastic button (diameter=11/16") was recovered from the ground surface at Concentration 1. It has two holes and one surface is recessed, and it has a lens-shaped cross-section.

2003 Subsurface Investigations

Fifty-four shovel tests were excavated at intersecting corners 10 meters apart within a 50 x 80 m grid set up across the top and slopes of the hill where most of the surface artifacts were collected (see Fig. 7A). The depth of the plowzone at this concentration is 16-51 cm thick above the subsoil, and a midlevel stratum was found at some of the grid points. The topsoil depth averaged 24.8 cm. Four of the shovel tests that located the intermediate strata sandwiched between the plowzone and subsoil found it to be from 19 cm to 66 cm below surface depth (bsd). In 32 of the 54 shovel tests, 110 artifacts and several grams of charcoal and coal including a corn kernel were recovered from the plowzone; 15 shovel tests (46.9%) contained only Historic materials, another 10 tests (30.3%) contained just pre-Historic materials, and the other eight shovel tests (25%) had both Historic and pre-Historic materials present. The only potential diagnostic Historic artifact to come out of the shovel tests is a featheredge rim (Fig. 9F) from ST N10 E0.

In addition to shovel testing, 15 1 x 1 m, 18 1 x 0.5 m (half units), and one 1 x 0.3 m units were excavated in Concentration 1. Three excavation units (N10 E70, N19 E50, N30 E60) were initially set up at three locations where the soil appeared to have some depth. These were located in the eastern half of the grid on the hill slope. Two intersecting trenches 50 cm wide were placed at two locations where a quantity of Historic artifacts were recovered that could indicate the location of one or more features. One was oriented north-south (Trench 1) and the other oriented east-west (Trench 2). A third north-south alignment (Trench 3) was set up and one partial unit was excavated. The trenching effort resulted in finding the only buried feature (Feature 1) northeast of the road. Feature 1 is an Historic pit. A minimum of two and a maximum of 11 levels were excavated in 34 whole (1 x 1 m) and partial (1 x <1 m) units. From these excavation units, 3,916 artifacts, including coal and charcoal pieces, ocher, animal bone, wood, and a corn kernel were recovered.

Units N10 E70, N19 E50, N30 E60: A shovel test at N10 E70 identified a deep plowzone and a mid-strata plus a yellow ware body sherd. Unit N10 E70 was excavated in six levels (ranging 6-11 cm) to a depth of 65 cm bsd. Artifacts were encountered in the top 39 cm of the excavation. A whiteware sherd and a piece of coal were found in Levels 1 and 2. A shovel test at N20 E50 recovered a utilized flake and exposed a portion of a granitic rock. Unit N19 E50 was excavated in three 10 cm levels. The rock (ca. 30 x 35 cm) was fully exposed at the bottom of Level 3. Besides the rock and some rodent activity, no cultural features were found in this unit. A large mammal (deer?) bone fragment and a flat glass shard were found in Level 2. An aqua colored glass container shard was recovered in a shovel test at N30 E60. Unit N30 E60 was excavated in three levels of about 10 cm each to a depth of 34 cm bsd. No Historic artifacts were recovered in the excavation.

Trench 1: After no features were found or confirmed by the shovel tests and the three eastern excavation units, it was decided to set up a trench oriented north-south along the E20 line of the grid. (Figs. 7A and 10). This trench was divided into 1 m long by 50 cm wide segments starting at station N0 and ending at station N50. Eventually, 15 half units were excavated. Seven of them were noncontiguous and one partial unit was expanded to a 1 x 1 m excavation unit. The eight contiguous units will be discussed as a group. Profiles of the units that comprised Trench 1 are illustrated in Figure 10.

Units N0-N50 E20-20.5 of Trench 1: An aqua flat glass shard was found in a shovel test at N5 E20 of the grid. When Half Unit N5 E20-20.5 was opened here, three 10 cm levels were excavated to reach the subsoil. The depth of topsoil at this location is 22-24 cm. A slight undulation is present at the contact point with the Ap-horizon and subsoil. No Historic artifacts were recovered from this partial unit.

Half Unit N5 E20-20.5 was excavated in three 10 cm levels to a depth of 30 cm. The undulation seen

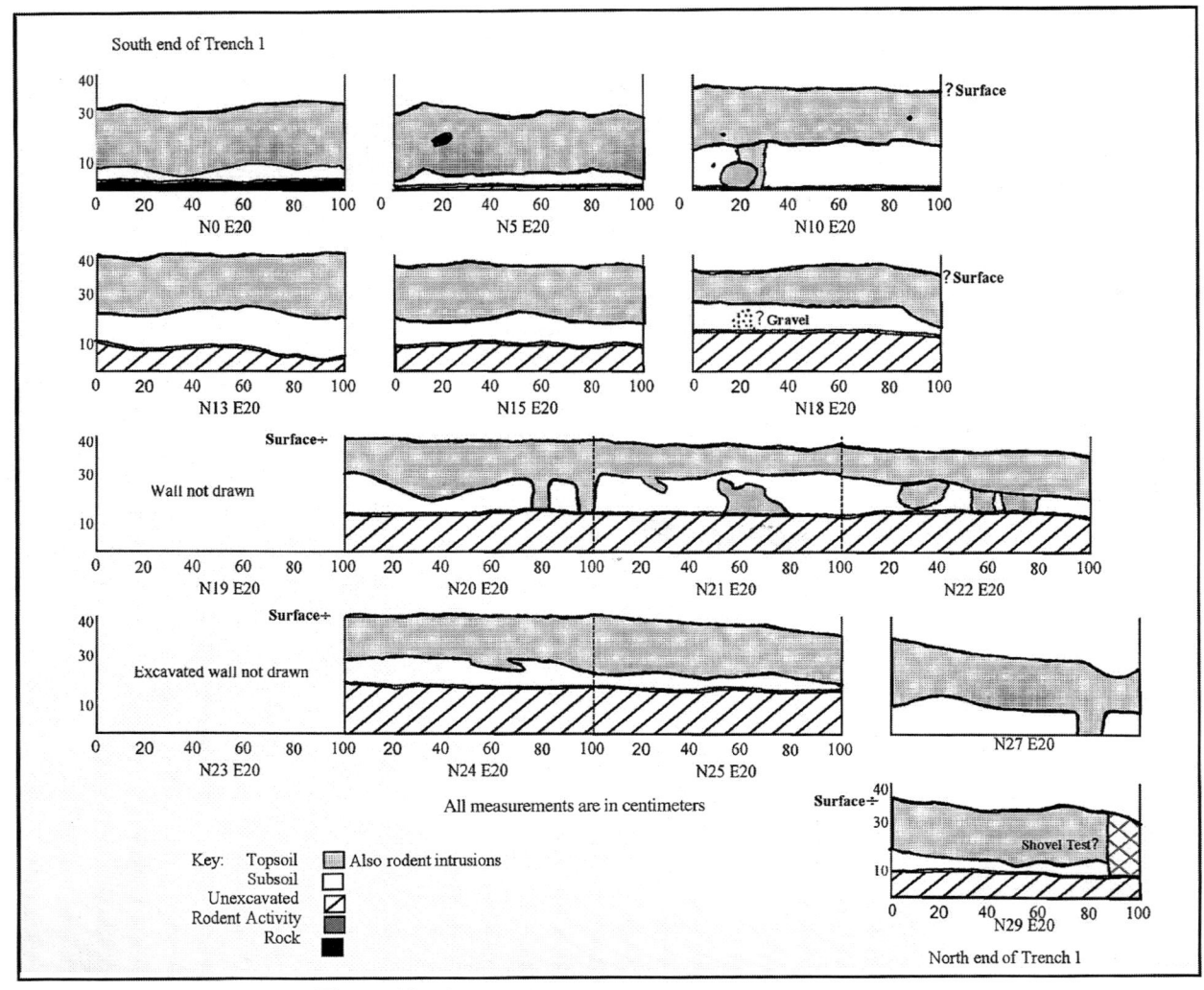

Figure 10. Composite west wall profiles of Trench 1.

in the previous unit is present at this location. No artifacts were recovered from this unit.

Half Unit N10 E 20-20.5 had four excavated levels. The top three were 10 cm while the bottom level, Level 4, was 9 cm thick. The same undulating profile is also present at the plowzone and subsoil interface. In the west wall of the unit is an intrusion from the plowzone, however, at this same spot is a rodent burrow partially obscuring the intrusion. Historic glass and metal artifacts came from Level 1 of this partial unit.

Half Unit N13 E20-20.5 has a similar soil profile to that seen in N5 and N10 E20-20.5. Four 10 cm levels were removed from this partial unit. Historic metal, brick, and glass were recovered from Levels 1-3 at this location.

Again, the soil profile in Half Unit N15 E20-20.5 is similar to profiles observed in the three previous units. This partial unit was excavated in three 10 cm levels. Glass and metal Historic artifacts were found in Levels 1 and 2 of this half unit.

Eight half units (N18-25 E20-20.5) in Trench 1 were contiguous. Half Units N18, 19, 21, 22, and 24 were excavated in three 10 cm levels (N22 had a Level 4 at 30-35 cm). Half Units N20, 23, and 25 varied somewhat from this by varying 0-3 cm in Level 1, 1-2 cm in Level 2, and 1-8 cm in Level 3. N19 was originally a half unit but later was expanded into a full 1 m² after two soil stains were observed in Level

Table 2. Historic Artifact Distribution by Level (L) in Eight Contiguous Units of Trench 1

Materials	N18	N19	N20	N21	N22	N23	N24	N25
Brick Fragments	L2	L1-2	L1-3	L1-3	L1-3	L1-3	L1-3	L1-3
Glass Shards	L1-2	L1-2	L2-3	L1-2	L1-2	L1-2	L1-2	L1-2
Metal	L1	L1-3	L1-3	L1-3	L1-2	L1-2	L1-2	L1-2
Historic Ceramics	--	L1-2	--	--	--	--	--	--
Flora	--	L1-2	--	--	--	--	--	--

2. The unit was excavated in two levels. Level 1 was originally 10 cm but with the expansion, Level 1 became 20 cm. So the materials in the two 10 cm levels of the half unit were combined with the expanded 20 cm level. The soil stains turned out to be ephemeral discolorations.

The west walls of six of the eight units were profiled. Two walls (N19 and N23) were not drawn because the adjacent units were excavated. The combined profiles for the six units indicate soil disturbance in all but possibly N22 and N25. The disturbed subsoil in N21 may be rodent den and part of a tunnel to the den. Rodent activity is probably evident at N24 with a shallow, angled cut into the subsoil. The plowzone above is similar to what is present in several of the above-mentioned Trench 1 units. Unit N18 has topsoil in-filling of a slight depression on the north end that extends into the excavated unit N19. This disturbance does continue in N22, which has two vertical intrusions (rodents or postmolds?) on the north end plus a shallow V shaped interface between the plowzone and subsoil. The depression and shallow V may be ruts and indicate that a wagon trail ran close to Feature 1. One such road was located somewhere in the vicinity in the early 1900s (Anonymous 1900). This disturbance might also be associated in some other manner with Feature 1, such as construction, occupation/use, and/or building demolition as discussed below.

Artifacts were found in all of these eight partial units. Table 2 lists what categories of Historic artifacts were encountered for each unit and at what levels. A wood dowel segment (Fig. 9G) was found in Unit N19 E20 (0-20 cm bsd). No Historic artifacts were found below Level 3 in this part of the trench.

Half Unit N27 E20-20.5 was 2 meters north from the north end of the eight contiguous half units. It was situated just past the top of the hill. Three levels were excavated in irregular depths of 10 (Level 1), 14 (Level 2), and 8 cm (Level 3). An intrusion from the plowzone into the subsoil was seen on the west wall. It appears to have vertical walls, but it is not possible to state conclusively whether it is a post mold or a rodent burrow. The number of artifacts from the unit decreased in numbers with depth. All three levels contained Historic glass, ceramic, metal, lithic, and brick artifacts.

Half Unit N29 E20-20.5 was the last partial unit of Trench 1, and it was situated 2 meters further down the slope to the north from N27. Three 10 cm levels were excavated here. The number of artifacts from this unit increased in number with depth, then dropped off in Level 3. Historic ceramics, glass, brick, and metal were found in all three levels.

Trench 2: Although quantities of Historic artifacts found in Trench 1 appeared to indicate that there once was a building somewhere on this hilltop, excavation along Trench 1 found no definite features (foundation, builders trench, or angular/symmetrical soil stains). It was decided to put a second trench perpendicular to Trench 1 on the N20 line of the grid. Four half units were excavated along a 16 meter segment between stations E10 and E26 (N20-20.5 E10, E16, E18, and E25) (see Fig. 6A). Included with Trench 2 is a 1 m² unit at N20 E19.

Units N20-20.5 E10, E16, E18-20 of Trench 2: Half Unit N20-20.5-E10 was opened at a shovel test where 18 brick fragments were found. At least one of the fragments appeared burned. Maximum depth of the topsoil here is approximately 20 cm. A bifurcated intrusion extending below the excavation was observed in the north wall. It may be a split rodent burrow with two tunnels. Two 10 cm levels were excavated in this partial unit. The number of artifacts increased with depth at this location before declining in number. Historic metal, brick, and glass were found in one or both levels.

Half Unit N20-20.5 E18 was excavated in two 10 cm levels and one 5 cm level (Level 3). The topsoil in this unit is about 18 cm thick and its contact with the subsoil is relatively uniform. The number of artifacts increased with depth at this location before decreasing in numbers. Glass, metal, and brick items were found in one or more of the three levels excavated.

Three 10 cm levels were excavated at Half Unit N20-20.5-E18. The north wall shows three intrusions into the subsoil from the plowzone. They could represent rodent or human activity, although no artifacts were encountered in Level 3 where these intrusions are better exposed in the profile. They may predate human activity since Level 3 was sterile. The number of artifacts increased with depth at this location before disappearing completely in Level 3. From Levels 1 and 2 were found a corn kernel (Level 1), glass, metal, and brick.

Unit N20 E19 was excavated to explore further the intersection of Trenches 1 and 2. The topsoil in this unit decreases in thickness from about 20 cm on the west side of the unit to approximately 14 cm on the east side. The interface between the topsoil and subsoil is somewhat undulating. This unit was excavated in three levels of 18 (Level 1), 12 (Level 2), and 6 cm (Level 3). The number of artifacts also dramatically drops as depth increases. The majority of Historic ceramics, glass, metal, and brick were recovered in Level 1. More brick was found in Level 2, and glass was uncovered in Level 3.

The furthest east half unit of Trench 2 was N20-20.5 E25. It was excavated in three 10 cm levels. Topsoil here is about 26-28 cm thick. The north profile exhibits similar intrusions as described in the previous partial unit. Artifacts were found in all three levels; their numbers increase into Level 2 before dropping significantly in Level 3. Historic glass, metal, brick, and ceramics were encountered in Levels 1 and 2. A brick fragment was located in Level 3.

Trench 3: This trench was laid out along the E10 line to intersect with Trench 2. Just a single 1 x 0.3 m unit (N25 E10-10.3) was excavated on this alignment to look for a suspected Historic feature. This third of a unit was excavated in two levels: a 10 cm Level 1 and an 8 cm Level 2. Some type of intrusion with a rodent burrow within it was discovered in the west wall of the unit below the plowzone (see Fig. 6A). The plowzone here is about 10 cm thick. The edge of the intrusion was indistinct, although the drawing indicates vertical edges. It could have been an older, larger burrow or possibly a post mold. Artifacts found in this partial unit decrease in number with depth. All of the artifacts are Historic materials that include metal, glass, and brick. This trench was abandoned after Feature 1 was found about 5 meters to the east where block excavations were conducted.

Block Area (Feature 1): Exploration of this area was prompted by the soil irregularities observed in Trench 1. Several 1 x 1 m squares were opened to the west of the trench to determine what the irregularities were possibly indicating. The edge of a semicircular stain was found in Unit N23 E16 (Fig. 11). Eventually nine 1 x 1 m units were excavated in the vicinity of this unit in order to determine the horizontal extent of what was identified as Feature 1 a buried pit. Feature 1 was found in portions of five units (N22 E16, N23 E16, N23 E17, N24 E17 and N24 E18) (Figs. 12-14). The full extent of the feature could not be determined because it was found near the end of the fieldwork phase. An inventory of Historic items found in these five units is also provided below.

Unit N22 E16 (Feature 1): Part of the edge of Feature 1 was located in the northwest corner of the unit at about 20 cm bsd. This edge remained present in all three levels excavated in this unit. Level 1 was the plowzone 20 cm deep. Levels 2 and 3 were each 5 cm in thickness. Level 1 contained nine flat glass fragments, six unidentified melted aqua glass shards, 18 complete (length=1½"-3") and broken cut nails, and four brick fragments (size=0.7-1.8 cm). Level 2 had one brick fragment (size=3 cm), and Level

Figure 11. Southeast edge of Feature 1 (lighter soil on right) in Unit N23 E16.

3 was sterile. Deeper excavation was not accomplished to show the pit wall.

Unit N23 E16 (Feature 1): In all, 11 levels were excavated in 10 cm increments within this unit. At 23 cm bsd (Level 3) the edge of a linear feature was observed between the SE and NW corners of this unit (see Fig. 11). Subsoil outside the feature was much different in color and texture and resembles the county soil survey description presented above. All artifacts that were recovered below 30 cm came from the feature fill. This unit was the deepest excavated in order to reach the bottom of Feature 1. A large rock was encountered outside the feature at about 50 cm. It is about 12 feet south of another rock found at the same depth in Unit N26 E15, almost due north. Charcoal flecks began turning up between 50 and 70 cm bsd. The charcoal was found in loose soil in the northeastern portion of Feature 1. Below 70 cm bsd the feature slowly retreated to the northwest until the excavation went below the bottom of the feature at 118-119 cm bsd. The southeast wall of Feature 1 was nearly vertical until a rounded corner was observed at the bottom of the pit in the south wall. The west wall combined with the previous unit shows a rising floor toward the center of the feature. Charcoal and a cut nail were present in the bottom of the feature.

Level 1 had three aqua glass container shards, seven flat glass shards, four unidentified melted aqua glass shards, seven complete (l=1½-2½ inches) and broken cut nails, and 88 brick fragments (size=0.5-1.5 cm). Level 2 contained one whiteware sherd, one possible ironstone sherd, nine aqua glass container shards, eight flat glass shards, four unidentified melted aqua (n=3) and colorless (n=1) glass shards, 16 complete (l=1¼-4 inches) and broken cut nails, and 224 brick fragments (size=0.4-3.5 cm). In Level 3 there were one possible aqua glass container shard, one unidentified melted aqua glass shard, three broken cut nails, and 28 brick fragments (size=0.8-1.9 cm). Level 4 held one 4½ inch long cut nail and a medial fragment of cortex from a mammalian long bone (wt=4.3 gm). In Level 5 were found two flat glass shards. Level 6 contained one flat glass shard, one 1½ inch long cut nail and a pencil lead 1 3/16 inch in length (Fig. 8H); and Level 7 was sterile. In Level 8 there were one 2½ inch long cut nail and charcoal fragments (wt=2.8 gm). Level 9 had one colorless glass hurricane lamp chimney shard, three badly corroded complete (l=3") and broken cut nails, two brick fragments (size=1.6 cm), and one piece of charcoal (wt=0.2 gm). A small amount of charcoal (wt=0.6 gm) was found in Level 10, and in Level 11 a badly corroded cut-nail fragment was recovered.

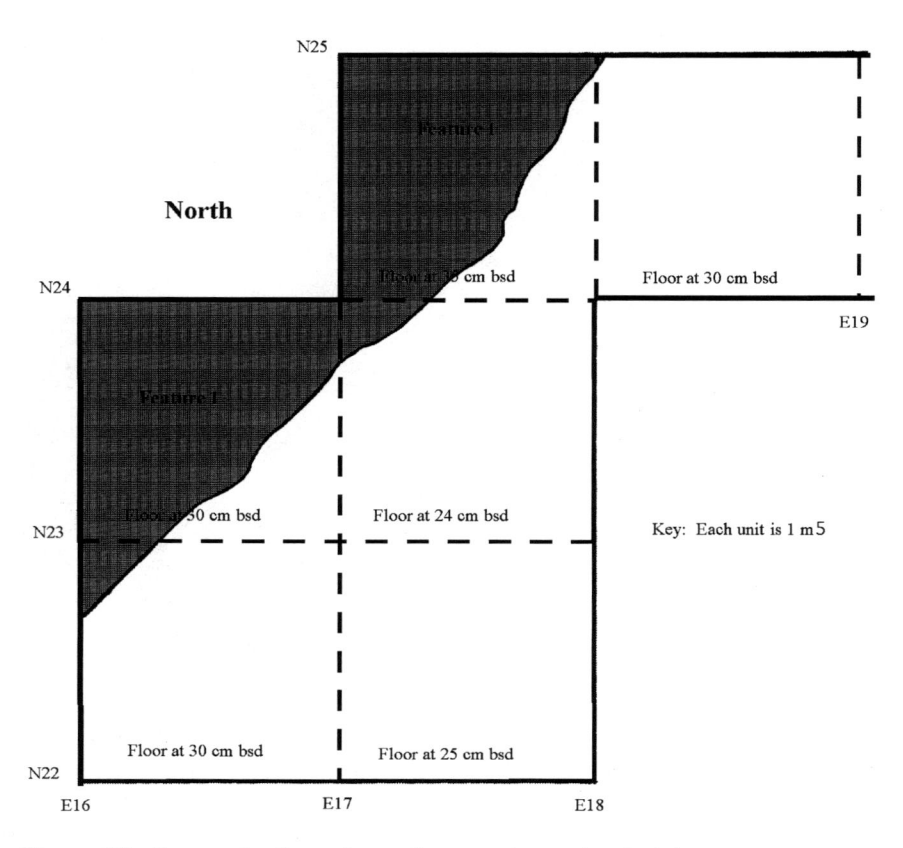

Figure 12. Composite floorplans of excavation units showing the southeast edge of Feature 1.

Unit N23 E17 (Feature 1): This unit was excavated in two levels. Level 1 was 20 cm and included the plowzone. Part of Feature 1 was found in Level 2 (20-24 cm bsd) in the very northwest corner of the unit. Level 1 contained two whiteware sherds (possible blue transfer ware and possible pearlware), one aqua glass container shard, nine flat glass shards, 17 unidentified melted aqua glass shards, 30 complete (l=1-3 inches) and broken cut nails, one broken wire nail, and 195 brick fragments (size=0.5-2 cm). One of the whiteware sherds has a blue featheredge decoration. In Level 2 were five brick fragments (size=0.8-1 cm). The bottom of the feature was located at a shallower depth (100 cm bsd). The upper two-thirds of the wall was vertical before curving inward.

Unit N24 E17 (Feature 1): Eight levels of varying thickness were excavated in this unit. Another edge of Feature 1 was located below Level 1. A sinuous line was observed at the northeast corner and arcing around to the southwest, disappearing into the south wall at about 30 cm east of the southwest corner. As the excavation went into deeper levels, the edge line retreated toward the northwest. A darker band also appeared between the original subsoil and the inside of the feature. This band had an area with black soil containing charcoal in the northeast corner. Once the edge of the feature was clearly defined, all of the artifacts were found in the feature from Levels 2 to 8. The east wall of the feature started to curve inward at about 60 cm bsd. A thin dark lens (charcoal) was located at 68 cm bsd in the western third of Level 4 (63-72 cm). The bottom of the feature was reached at 106 cm bsd.

Artifacts were found in all levels of this unit. Level 1 contained one whiteware sherd; 24 flat glass fragments; 13 unidentified aqua glass shards, eight of which are melted; 40 complete (l= 1-3 inches) and broken cut nails, 303 brick fragments (size=0.5-2 cm), and one piece of charcoal (wt=0.1 gm).

Level 2 had one aqua glass container shard and one cut nail 1¼ inch long. In Level 3 there was one

Table 3. Artifact Distribution by Level Outside of Feature 1 Within Block Area

Materials	N22 E17	N22 E19	N23 E19	N24 E19
Brick Fragments	L1-2	L1-3	L1-2	L1-3
Glass Shards	L1	L1-3	L1-2	L1-3
Metal	L1	L1-2	L1-2	L1-3
Historic Ceramics	L1	--	--	--
Historic Lithics	--	L2	--	--
Mortar/Plaster	--	L1	--	--

straight pin (l=1¼ inch) (Fig. 8I), five badly corroded complete (l=1½->2¼ inches) and broken cut nails, one wood screw, and one brick fragment (size=1.7 cm). From Level 4 came five badly corroded complete (length=1-3 inches) and broken cut nails. Level 5 possessed one colorless glass hurricane lamp chimney shard and one piece of red ocher. Level 6 contained one piece of charcoal (wt=0.1 gm) and one piece of red ocher. One badly corroded cut nail 2½ inches long, two pieces of charcoal (wt=5.2 gm), and one piece of red ocher were found in Level 7, and one badly corroded cut-nail fragment and one piece of red ocher were encountered in Level 8. The ocher is considered to be Historic, since it was found along with the Historic artifacts and probably has an association with the Dakota presence at the Riggs mission.

Unit N24 E18 (Feature 1): Two levels were excavated in this unit. Level 1 (0-20 cm) contained the plowzone and it was removed in order to find more of Feature 1. The subsoil was encountered in Level 2 (20-30 cm). A small sliver of Feature 1 was located on the northwest corner of the unit in Level 2. From Level 1 came one green glass circular bottle base, 27 flat glass shards, 16 unidentified melted aqua glass shards, 27 complete (l=1-3 inches) and broken cut nails, and 223 brick fragments (size=0.5-2.5 cm). Level 2 was sterile.

Portions of five wall profiles showing the southeast wall of Feature 1 were combined in Figure 14. The pit walls are more vertical and the depth of the pit is deeper to the southwest. The general soil characteristics within the feature show a broad plowzone over the interior fill. The fill is redeposited subsoil used to fill in the depression. Below the fill is another broad dark band of soil. There are several indistinct lenses containing charcoal with the fill and in the bottom band. The charcoal probably came from walls and beams of a structure above the pit as the structure burned. Some old rodent burrows are also present in Feature 1.

Units N22 E17, N22 E19, N23 E19, N24 E19: Four units excavated in this Block Area did not find any evidence of Feature 1 or other construction features. Old rodent tunnels were observed in all four units. Each of these units ended up having different depths for levels, because as excavation continued, any change in soil characteristics could signal the presence of Feature 1 or some other nearby feature.

Artifacts were found in all four of these units (Table 3). Table 3 lists at what levels Historic and pre-Historic artifacts were encountered for these four units. All of the brick, glass, ceramic, and Historic lithics are fragmentary. There are some intact metal artifacts such as nails.

Unit N26 E15: A unit was excavated to the northwest of Feature 1 in order to determine the northern extent of the pit feature. Fifty-seven cm of soil were removed in two levels in this unit before work here was terminated because no evidence was found for the north edge of Feature 1. Before work was terminated here, the floor was cored in two places to 35 cm and 38 cm with no change in the subsoil. A large stone was encountered at 53 cm bsd. Another stone of about the same size was found about the same depth in Unit N23 E16. The two stones are about 12 feet apart oriented north-south. From Level 1 came 12 flat glass shards, 11 unidentified melted aqua glass shards, 24 complete (l=1¼-3 inches) and broken cut nails, 63 brick fragments (size=1-2.3 cm), and three unidentified calcined bone fragments (wt=0.7 gm). Level 2 contained a single cut nail 2½ inches long and six pieces of red ocher.

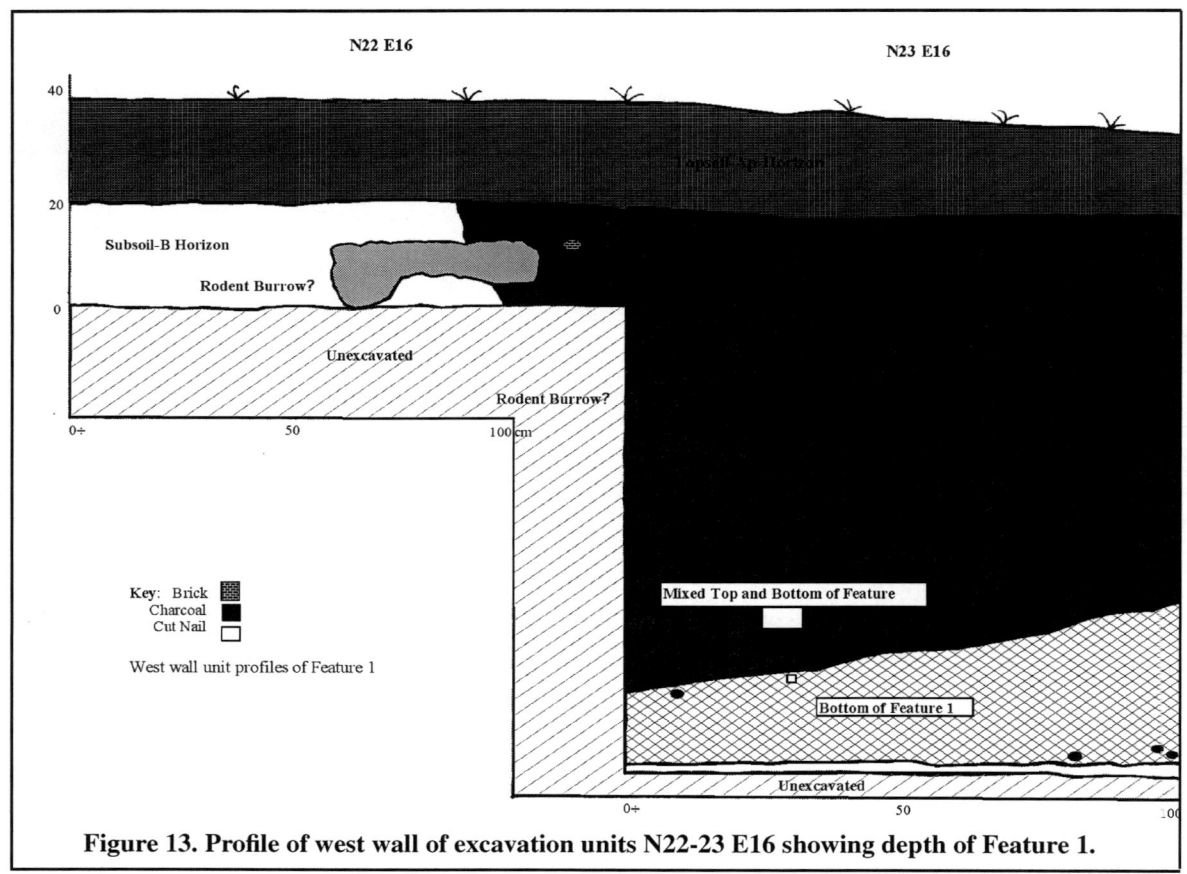

Figure 13. Profile of west wall of excavation units N22-23 E16 showing depth of Feature 1.

Concentration 1 Historic Component: The large amount of nails, brick fragments, Historic window glass shards, and the pit feature indicate that this concentration is a remnant of some kind of structure. The Historic artifacts in this concentration do seem to date to sometime between 1850 and 1900. Several artifact groups are present associated with architecture, furniture, kitchen/subsistence, clothing, personal/hygiene/pharmaceutical, arms, activities/entertainment, miscellaneous hardware, fauna, and flora. The architectural group (nails, brick fragments, and flat glass shards) clearly show that there was a building at this location. The presence of kitchen/subsistence, clothing, personal/hygiene/pharmaceutical, arms and activities/entertainment artifacts especially point to a domestic context. We know that brick was used to build homes for some of the Dakota in 1860 and later. If there was a brick building closer to the mission, it was not present when the mission was photographed in 1860. Such a building could very well have been built between 1860 and the 1862 Dakota War. There is also evidence of fire. Melted glass shards, some darkened brick fragments, and the presence of charcoal within the soil deposits in Feature 1 indicate that a fire occurred here.

Seven artifact distribution maps (Figs. 15-21) were created in order to define the location for a building at Concentration 1. Total artifact counts by whole and partial units were used to show the distribution of brick fragments (Fig. 15), cut nails (Fig. 16), flat glass shards (Fig. 17), melted glass shards (Fig. 18), ceramics (Fig. 19), and personal items and container glass (Fig. 20) as well as bone, ocher, wood, and corn (Fig. 21). All of the distribution maps show a trend in the number of these artifacts increasing in quantity from southeast to northwest. These quantities may either peak or begin dropping to the north and west of Feature 1.

Brick fragments were found in all but one (N10 E20) of the western units (Fig. 15). Some of the fragments appear to show the effects of fire not derived from routine kiln firing. Between 108 and 342

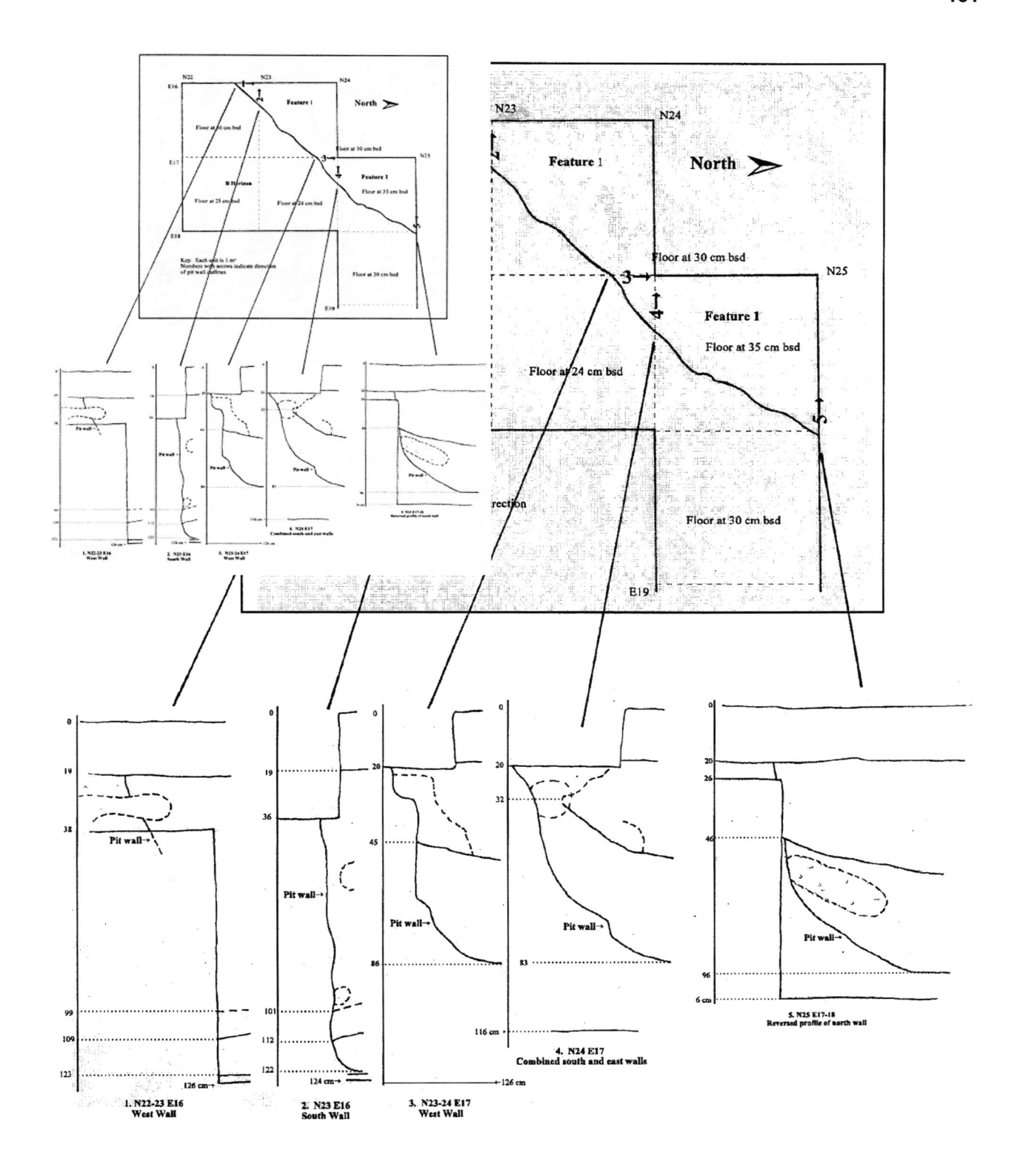

Figure 14. Southeast wall of Feature 1 as recorded in six excavation unit profiles.

brick fragments were recovered in nine units (N19 E20, N22 E17, N22 E19, N23 E16-17, N23 E19, N24 E17-19, and N29 E20-20.5). Two clusters are apparent. One is within and adjacent to Feature 1, which is located in the northwest corner of the Block Area and where Trenches 1 and 2 intersect (N20 E19). No brick was found below Level 3 in the units that were excavated beyond Level 3. This observation includes the pit feature. Most brick fragments were generally found in Levels 1 and 2. Over the two field seasons, no complete bricks were found in Concentration 1. They may have been scavenged for use elsewhere after the site was abandoned.

Cut nails were recovered in all of the units excavated in the western half of the grid (Fig. 16). Also found in this area were two wire nails, a single wood screw, and a bolt. The nail distribution shows the same southeast to northwest pattern as observed for the brick fragments. Eleven units (N19 E20, N20 E19, N22 E16-17, N22 E19, N23 E16-17, N22 E19, N24 E17-19, and N26 E14) had between 15 and 52 cut nails. Again there are two clusters of cut nails. One was in and around Feature 1 and the other at the intersection of Trenches 1 and 2. Cut nails were found as deep as Levels 8, 9, and 11 in the two units (N23 E16 and N24 E17) that explored the pit feature. These nails were badly corroded.

The third architectural group examined was flat glass shards that undoubtedly represent window glass (Fig. 17). Two units in Trenches 1 and 2 were devoid of window-glass shards. The same distribution pattern observed for the brick and nails is also present for window glass. There may be a shift to the north and northwest of the Block Area and southeast of the Trench 1 and 2 intersection. There were eight units (N19 E20, N22 E17, N23 E16, N24 E17-19, N26 E14, and N27 E20) that contained at least 11 and as many as 27 window

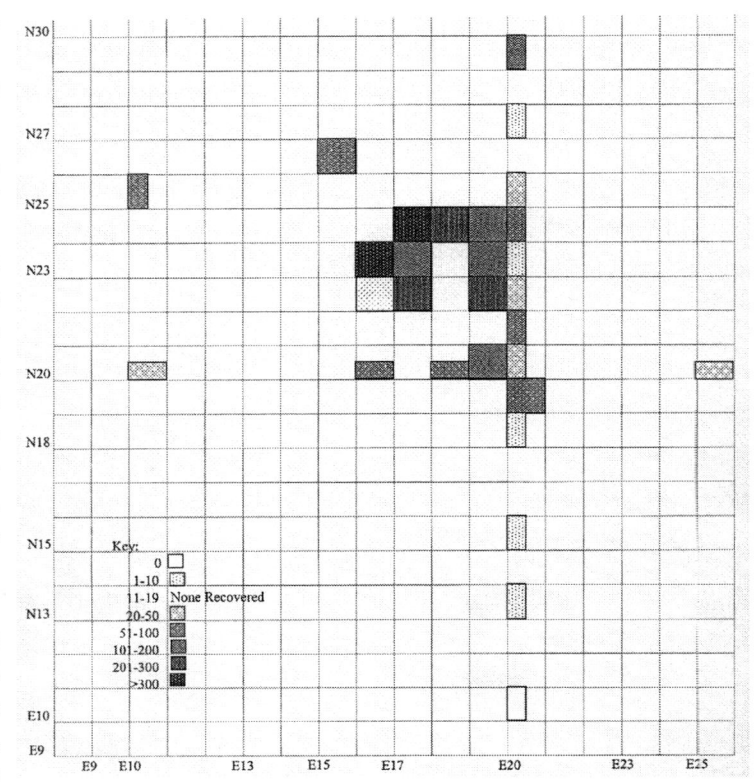

Figure 15. Distribution of brick fragments from the western excavation units of Concentration 1.

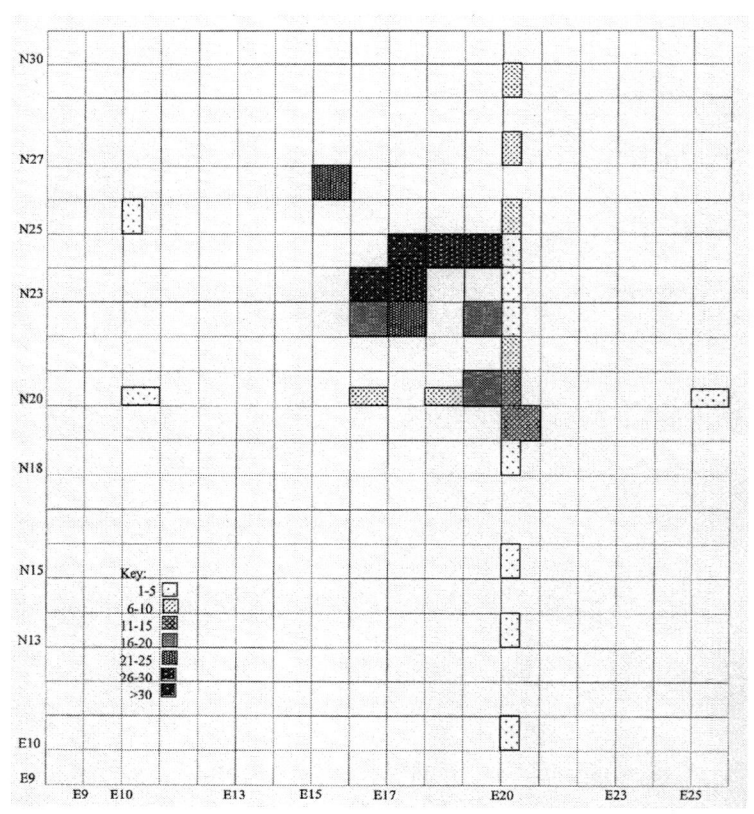

Figure 16. Distribution of cut nails from the western excavation units of Concentration 1.

glass shards. The largest quantities were still found in an around Feature 1. Flat glass was found no deeper than Level 5 in Unit N23 E16.

The collection contains 185 pieces of melted glass as evidence for an intense fire in Concentration 1. They are concentrated around Feature 1 and the intersection of Trenches 1 and 2 (Fig. 18). No melted glass was found in six of the units. However, six or more melted glass shards were recovered from 14 units (N19 E20, N20 E24, N21 E20, N22 E16-17, N22 E19, N23 E16-17, N23 E19-20, N24 E17-19, and N26 E14). A maximum of 22 pieces were encountered in Unit N22 E17. No melted glass shards were found deeper than Level 3 and most came from Level 1.

The presence of several architectural groups in Concentration 1 leads to a logical conclusion that there was a brick building on top of this hill somewhere around Feature 1. Assuming that it was a home occupied by a Dakota family, ceramics, personal items, and container glass found in the excavation units may also have a pattern associated with the architectural groups or something entirely different.

Ceramic sherd distribution in the western portion of Concentration 1 centers around Feature 1 and the intersection of Trenches 1 and 2 (Fig. 19). Nine (N19 E20, N20 E19, N20 E25, N22 E17, N23 E16-17, N24 E17, N27 E20, and N29 E20) of the 29 units here contained one to two sherds totaling just 12 examples. Half of the sherds were located in the vicinity of Feature 1. Most of the excavated sherds were found in Level 1; none were located below Level 2. Their location is consistent with the architectural groups discussed above.

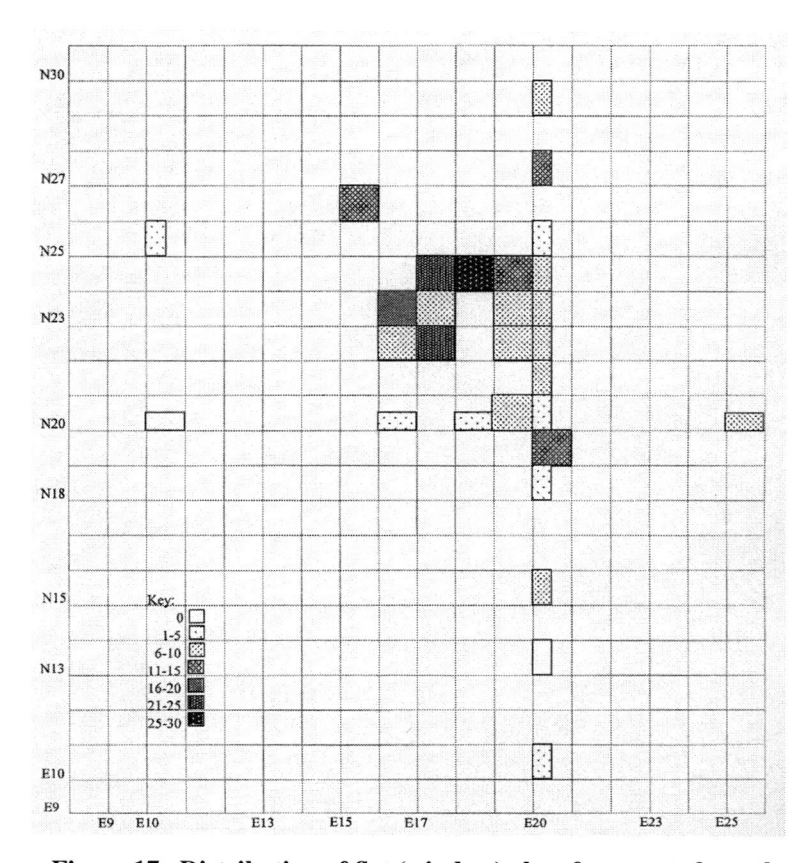

Figure 17. Distribution of flat (window) glass fragments from the western excavation units of Concentration 1.

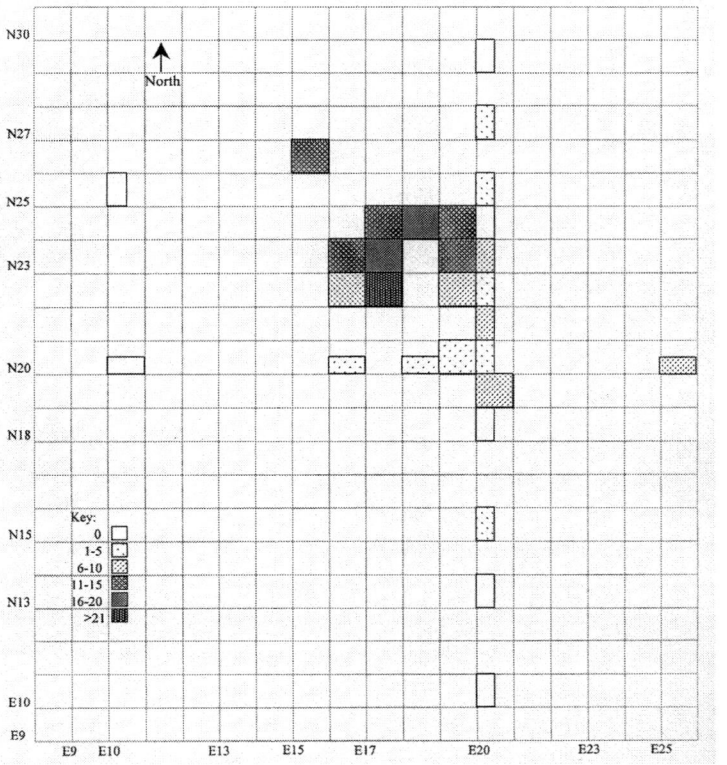

Figure 18. Distribution of all melted glass shards from the western excavation units of Concentration 1.

Two personal items and two lamp-glass shards along with 52 aqua (n=49), colorless (n=1), green (n=1), and white (n=1) container-glass shards were excavated from units in the western portion of Concentration 1 (Fig. 20). Some of the shards were partially deformed from melting. Seventeen of the units had glass-container shards. Only two had personal items and lamp glass. A pencil lead was recovered from Level 6 (50-70 cm bsd) of Unit N23 E16. A straight pin was found in Unit N24 E17 at Level 3 (35-63 cm bsd). Hurricane lamp-chimney shards also came from both of these units at Level 9 (90-100 cm bsd) and Level 5 (72-80 cm bsd), respectively. Container-glass shards again show quantities in and around Feature 1 and the intersection of Trenches 1 and 2. There seems to be a shift to the southwest corner of the Block Area and near the middle of Trench 1. There is an anomalous area containing three aqua colored shards at the north end (N29 E20) of Trench 1. In fact, the aqua colored glass was found in all but one (N24 E18) of the units where container-glass was encountered. None of the container glass was found deeper than Level 3.

The last distribution map created shows animal bone, red ocher, mica, coal, charcoal and wood, and corn excavated from the western units of Concentration 1 (Fig. 21). The weights of coal, charcoal, and bone were used to demonstrate density. Eight units had one or more of these items present. Four of the eight items plotted were found in and around Feature 1 and Unit N26 E15 that was excavated in an attempt to find the opposite wall of Feature 1. There appears to be no cluster of artifacts at the intersection of Trenches 1 and 2 as there were for the previously discussed groups. The wood dowel, corn kernel, coal, and mica were located in Levels 1 and 2. A small amount of

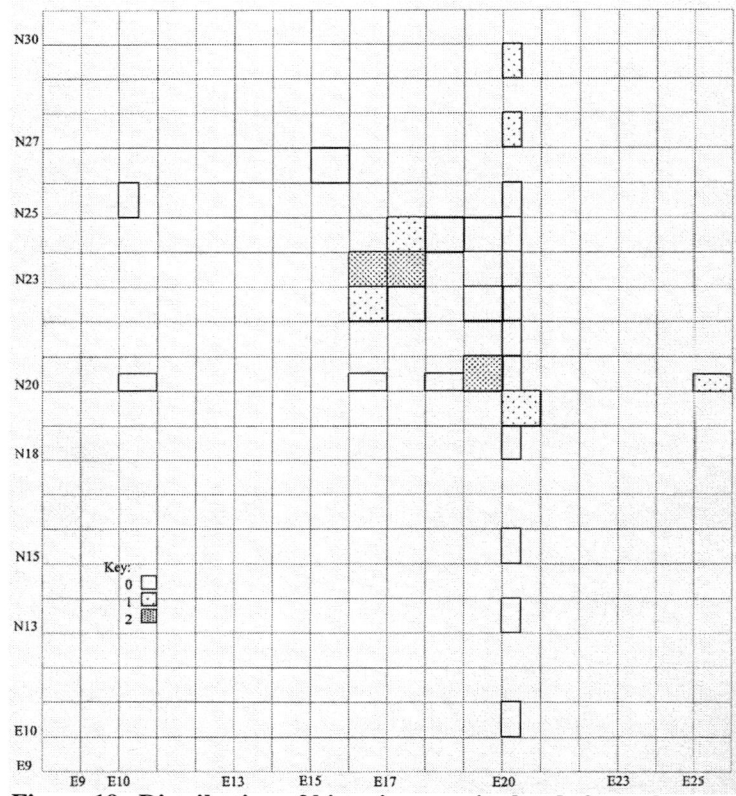

Figure 19. Distribution of historic ceramic sherds from the western excavation units of Concentration 1.

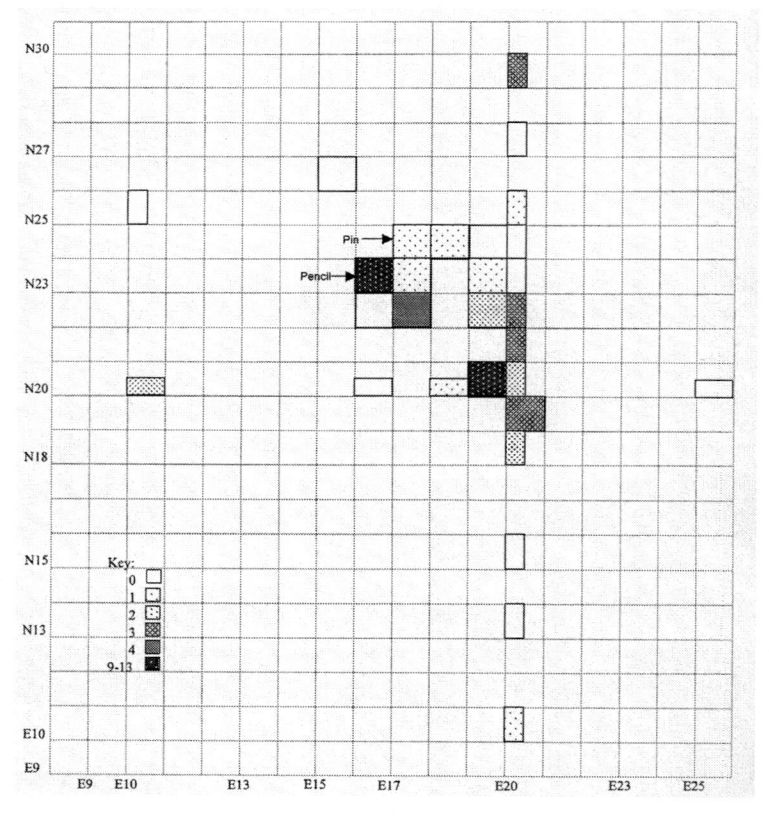

Figure 20. Distribution of personal items and container glass shards from the western excavation units of Concentration 1.

charcoal was found away from Feature 1 in Unit N20 E19. Ocher, charcoal, and bone were found at several levels in Feature 1. In Unit N23 E16 there were 4.3 gm of bone in Level 4 (30-40 cm bsd), and several grams of charcoal came from Levels 8-10 (70-110 cm bsd). Six pieces of ocher came from Levels 5-8 (72-110 cm bsd) in Unit N24 E17. In the same unit several grams of charcoal were recovered from Levels 1 (0-23 cm) and 6-7 (80-102 cm bsd). The corn kernel is probably a recent intrusion. Coal was probably used to heat the building. Mica was used in stoves as transparent or translucent windows that could stand up to the heat of a fire. Bone may be remnants of meals, or possibly one or more animals died in the vicinity without an association to the building occupants. The charcoal in the pit could be additional evidence for this structure burning, or, just as likely, wood was used to heat the building along with the coal. The presence of ocher in the pit points to the possibility that it may have belonged to a Dakota individual/family that lived here or that other individuals who may have occupied the home at the time of the Upper Agency Indians camped here in August-September 1862.

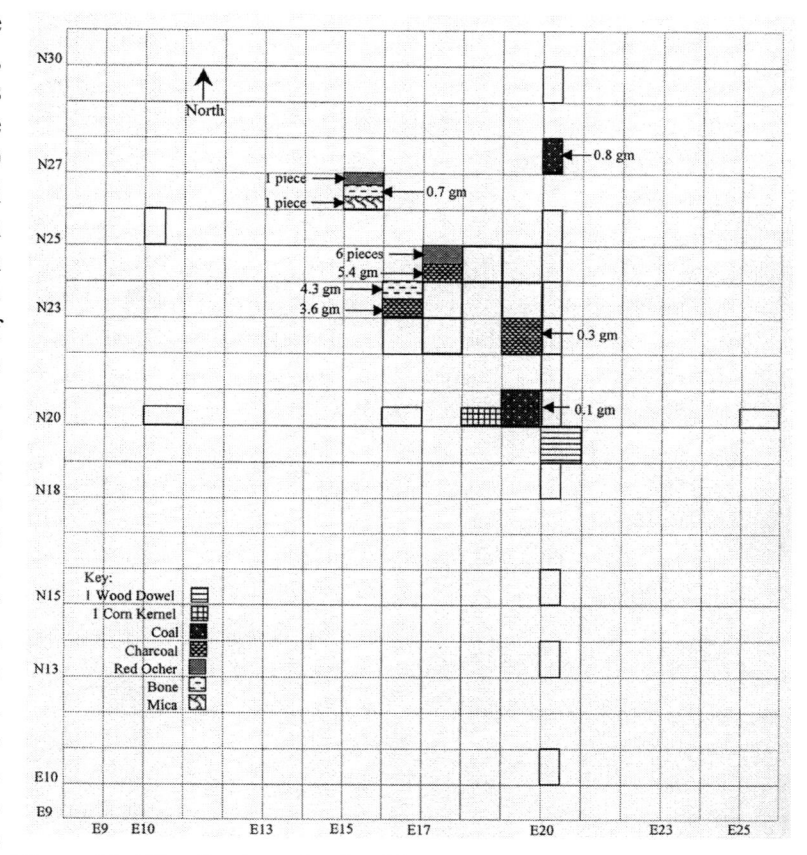

Figure 21. Distribution of animal bone, red ocher, coal, charcoal, wood and corn from the western excavation units of Concentration 1.

Concentration 2

This concentration is located below the hill to the northeast of Concentration 1. Artifacts found on the surface of this concentration were more or less distributed equally on eroded Ves-Storden loam on 3-6 percent slopes (50%) and Ves loam on 1-4 percent slopes (50%). Ves-Storden is described in Concentration 1 above. Ves loam on lesser slopes has black and very dark gray loam some 30.5 cm thick. The subsoil from 30.5-76 cm is a dark brown and dark yellowish brown friable clay loam in the upper part and for the lower part it is an olive brown calcareous soil, friable loam. From 76 to ca. 152 cm is an olive brown calcareous loam glacial till. Shale fragments are common in the subsoil and below. There are locations containing sand and gravel and surface

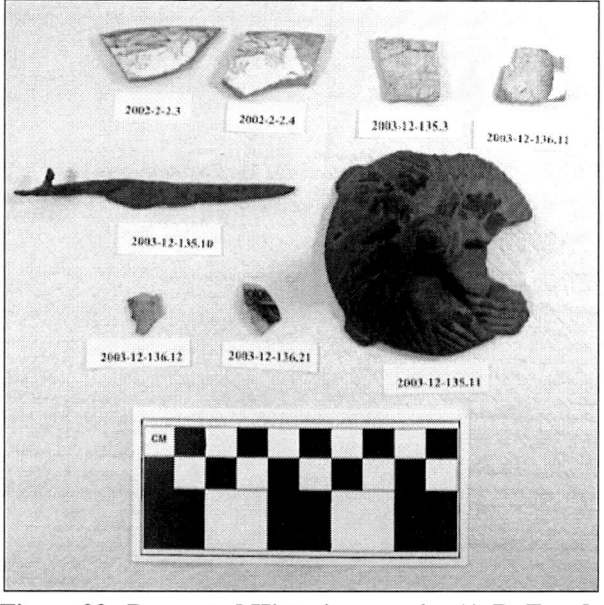

Figure 22. Decorated Historic ceramics (A-D, F and G), scissor blade (E) and coffee grinder part (H) from Concentration 2.

layers of Ves soils may contain silt loam, sandy clay loam, or sandy loam (Hokanson 1981:46-47 and 114). Shovel testing and unit excavation identified a top part of silt, clay, and loam soil gray-to-black to very dark brown in color. Depth of the upper strata varies in thickness between 19 and 25 cm. The average thickness of the upper strata is 22.7 cm. One shovel test showed a middle stratum 25-53 cm in depth. A silt loam middle part is a very dark grayish brown and dark yellowish brown. The lower part has a silt, clay, and loam soil of olive brown, dark yellowish, or grayish brown or brown.

Artifacts were clustered in a north-south (72 x 52 m) orientation. In 2002 and 2003, 81 Historic artifacts were collected from the ground surface and excavated from Concentration 2 (Table 1). Concentration 2 was also investigated below the ground surface. A rectangular grid was set up within the concentration that was 40 x 20 m (see Fig. 7B). Fifteen shovel tests were then excavated at 10 m intervals across the entire grid. The depth of the plowzone varied from 19 cm to 28 cm averaging 22.7 cm. One of the shovel test locations (N10 E0) contained a mid stratum 25-53 cm bsd. A typical excavation unit in this area contained rodent activity and an occasional rock in one or more levels. Six excavation units were set within and outside of Concentration 2 (see Fig. 7B). Three units were placed near the center of the grid (N7 E16, N9 E19, and N19 E21) and three (N0 E48, N6 E26, and N21 E28) were placed to the north and east. All of the units were excavated in two levels 17-23 cm deep in order to get below the plowzone. Level 2 was used to explore the subsoil for features. Level 2 in three units (N7 E16, N19 E21, and N21 E28) was sterile.

Surface Collections

The 57 Historic artifacts picked up on the surface in 2002 and 2003 include a variety of ceramic, glass, and metal items.

Ceramic: Ceramic artifacts consist of nine coarse eathernware- and stoneware-container sherds and 29 whiteware sherds. Six of the earthenware/stoneware sherds have brown glazed interiors and exteriors and another one has a orange glazed interior. Of the whiteware sherds, two are decorated with blue transfer print patterns (Fig. 22, A and B), two have a green stripe on the rim (Fig. 22, C and D), yet another sherd has a blue castle turret design on the body (Fig. 22F), and one is a possible flow blue with curvilinear design (Fig. 22G). The extant portion of the transfer print pattern present is located along the rim. It is a outdoor floral scene with five-petaled flowers, grass, leaves, and landscape. It resembles the Willow Pattern, but there isn't enough of the decoration present to make a definite identification. At a minimum, there are parts of 12 different ceramic containers and dinnerware items.

Glass: Glass artifacts include nine flat glass shards, one unidentified melted aqua glass shard, four aqua glass-container fragments (one is a base of an embossed medicine bottle), and one green glass-bottle shard. Two or three separate bottles and window glass may be represented by this collection of glass shards.

Metal: Metal artifacts include one tapered scissor blade (Fig. 22E), an iron umbrella-shaped object (Fig. 22H), a wide U-shaped iron handle, and one piece of coal (13.7 gm). The umbrellalike object has a circular skirt surrounding a circular rod. The skirt has three tabs with at least 11 sets of angled lines on each tab. The top of the rod (umbrella end) has a square end surmounted with a small nipple. The opposite end of the rod has a roughly square impression set off-center. This object was part of the coffee grinder.

2003 Subsurface Investigations

Just two of the nine shovel tests (see Fig. 7B) produced two Historic artifacts. These are a single wire nail and a coarse earthenware sherd. A few Historic artifacts (n=20) were located in five of the six excavation units. All but one were found in Level 1. A single whiteware sherd came from Level 2 (20-29 cm bsd) of Unit N9 E19. The other 19 items found in the first levels include 11 whiteware sherds, one colorless bottle glass shard (third or forth container), one flat glass shard, one broken cut nail and one wire nail (l=4¼ inches), one mortar fragment, and three coal clinkers (wt=5.8 gm).

The Historic component may represent a deposit of materials from a nearby domestic context (Concentration 1 or other Dakota home sites). They can be placed within kitchen (ceramics and container glass), architectural (window glass and nails), activities (scissors), miscellaneous hardware (coffee grinder), and energy (coal and coal clinkers) groups. No evidence of a structural remnant is indicated. Dating is problematic but an embossed medicine-bottle base found in 2002 may indicate that part of this component dates to sometime around or before 1900 from possibly the mid 1800s.

Concentration 3/7

The next concentration of artifacts was located in the southeast corner of the field (Figs. 2 and 8A). Normania clay loam on 1-3 percent slopes encompasses all of this concentration. The top 33 cm contains a clay loam. The upper part is black and the lower part is a very dark grayish brown. Worm casts are evident in the lower part. The subsoil below is a friable clay loam about 63.5 cm thick. The upper part is dark brown and grayish brown and the lower part is a calcareous mottled olive brown. From 96.5 to ca. 152 cm below the surface is a mottled olive brown calcareous loam glacial till and the surface soils and C horizon can contain silt loam, sandy clay loam, or sandy loam (Hokanson 1981:51 and 105). Field observations recorded silt clay loam soil that is mostly black and a dark grayish brown or dark brown or dark gray for the upper part. It ranges from 23 cm to 57 cm in thickness above the lower part and averages to be 36.2 cm in depth. The lower part is a silt clay loam with olive brown, shades of grayish brown, dark brown, and black.

In 2003 another artifact concentration (Concentration 7) was thought to have been found near Concentration 3 (Fig. 8A). However, owing to their close proximity, a decision was made in the laboratory to combine Concentration 3 and Concentration 7 for analysis. Before Concentrations 3 and 7 were combined for analysis, two separate grids were set up over each area in the field. This elongated concentration is oriented northwest to southeast (132 x 24 m). Within Concentration 3/7, a total of 41 Historic items were collected and excavated in 2002 and in 2003 (Table 1).

Thirty-four shovel tests were eventually dug in these two concentrations (Fig.8A). Topsoil depth ranged from 17 cm to 51 cm in thickness and its depth generally increases to the west; average topsoil depth here is 35.2 cm. One of the shovel tests (N30 E0) in this concentration located a mid stratum at 24-45 cm bsd. Four 1 x 1 m excavation units were placed within the combined concentration between positive shovel tests and adjacent to positive shovel tests. All were excavated in two levels of varying depths. The plowzone was considered a single level resulting in depths ranging between 24 cm and 30 cm. Finishing depths reached 40-50 cm bsd.

Surface Collections and 2003 Subsurface Investigations

Historic artifacts were recovered from both surface collection and unit excavation. However, no Historic artifacts were located during the shovel testing. Thirty-seven ceramic, glass, metal, stone, and synthetic items were collected from the ground surface over two field seasons. Just four Historic artifacts were found in the first levels of three of the four excavation units. They comprise one colorless glass container body shard, one flat glass shard, a fence-post staple, and one brick fragment.

Ceramic: This category includes one yellow-ware sherd, one stoneware sherd with a brown glaze interior and exterior, and four brick fragments (one burned).

Glass: There are five aqua glass container shards, three amethyst glass-container shards, eight colorless glass-container shards (one shard may be from a tumbler), two amber glass-bottle shards, and five flat glass shards. There are also two melted unidentified aqua glass shards. One of the amber glass shards is a bottle rim with a two-part finish (height=1") and a down-tooled lip. The container glass may represent four bottles/tumblers.

Metal: The metal artifacts are an iron ring (diameter=3¼ inches) and a possible iron hinge/strap fragment. The metal ring may be part of a grain drill (ca. 1899-1928) or a wagon fitting (Wendel 1997). The possible metal strap or hinge has a rounded end and an off-center hole drilled through it. Red paint may be present on one edge of this artifact.

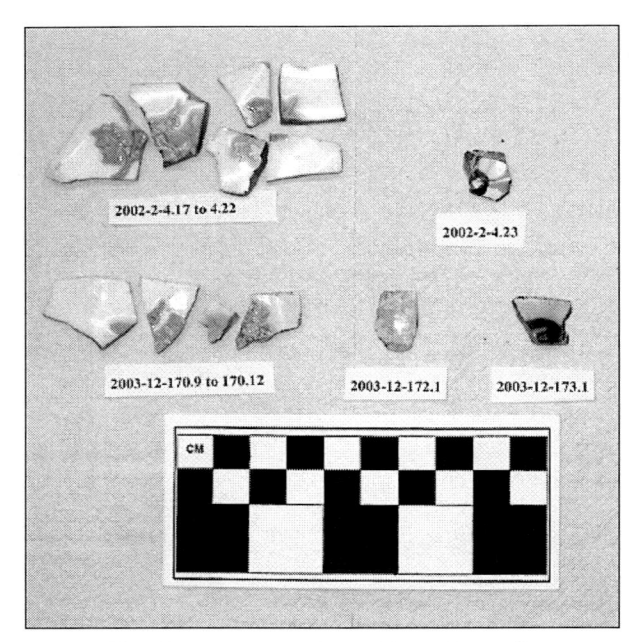

Figure 23. Historic ceramic artifacts from Concentration 4.

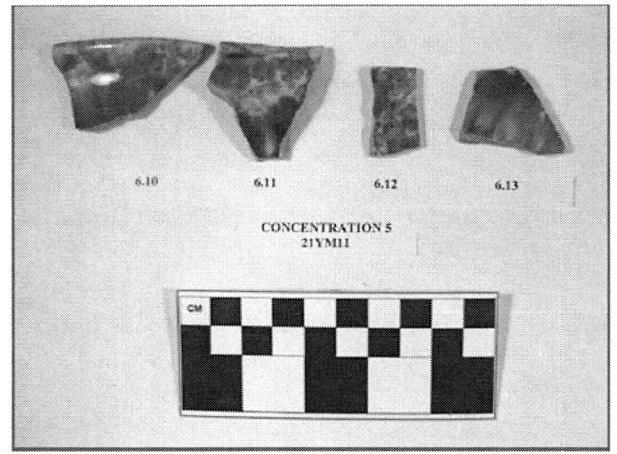

Figure 24. Bennington glazed sherds from Concentration 5.

Stone: A single chunk of coal (wt=7.9 gm) was found on the surface of this concentration.

Synthetic: A piece of white plastic picked up off of the ground surface could not be identified.

All 41 Historic artifacts can be placed into several functional categories that include kitchen (ceramics and container glass), architecture (strap/hinge, flat glass, and brick), machinery (iron ring), synthetic (plastic), and energy (coal). No evidence of an Historic structure was found in Concentration 3/7. The Historic artifacts seem to represent a variety of scattered deposits originating from nearby domestic contexts such as the Riggs mission or a Dakota home from the same 1854-1862 time period, later farming (1899-1928), or modern contexts (post 1940s).

Concentration 4

The fourth concentration of artifacts was found in the northeast corner of the field in 2002 (Figs. 2 and 8B). All of Concentration 4 is located in Ves loam on 1-4 percent slopes. This soil is described in Concentration 2 above. Subsurface testing yielded a clay loam in the upper part that ranged from black to a dark brown or dark gray to a dark yellowish brown. The upper part in this concentration is observed between 20 and 32 cm in depth, averaging 24.3 cm. The lower part was generally identified as a silt loam of an olive brown, dark yellowish brown to a dark brown color.

The artifacts were distributed in a narrow oval area oriented roughly north to south (58 x 18 m). During the Phase I and Phase II investigations, 68 Historic artifacts, a mollusk shell fragment, and a geode were recovered from Concentration 4 (Table 1). Sixty-nine artifacts (52.7%) come from at least one Historic component. The geode could have been brought here by humans, but the mollusk shell may or may not have been left here by people. Quantities of mollusk shells were unearthed at the pre-Historic Gillingham site (21YM3/15) about a mile to the east (Williamson 1880).

Nineteen shovel tests were excavated at points 10 meters apart within a grid pattern set up for this concentration. The depth of the plowzone in this area is 20-30 cm thick above the subsoil. Four artifacts (all Historic ceramics) were recovered in the plowzone of three of the 19 shovel tests. Three 1 x 1 m excavation units were placed in the vicinity of the positive shovel tests. All three units were excavated in two levels. Level 1 was essentially the plowzone (0-20 and 21 cm bsd); Level 2 removed the rest (ca. 5-7 cm) of the plowzone to reach the subsoil below (5-7 cm deeper). Twenty-four artifacts were recovered from the excavation units. Two (N15 E20 and N25 E20) of the three units contained Historic artifacts. The third unit (N25 E10) contained no Historic artifacts.

Surface Collections and 2003 Subsurface Investigations

In 2002 and 2003, 69 Historic artifacts were recovered through surface collection, shovel testing, and unit excavation. Fifty-five (80.9%) of those came from the ground surface. This number includes 38 ceramic fragments comprising one stoneware body sherd five possible pearlware sherds and 21 undecorated and 11 decorated whiteware sherds. The stoneware sherd has a gray glazed interior and exterior. Ten of the decorated sherds come from one or more individual pieces embossed and decorated with blue "grapes and leaves" (Fig. 23, A and C). The eleventh decorated sherd is a hand-painted blue and red floral (?) pattern (Fig. 23B).

Besides the ceramics, there is an aqua colored pill-bottle base three aqua colored glass-container shards five flat glass shards, and one colorless glass hurricane lamp-chimney body shard. Metal artifacts consist of a container rim and one broken cut nail. Four brick fragments and a piece of mortar are also in this collection of artifacts.

Four artifacts were recovered in the plowzone of three shovel tests. All of the artifacts are Historic ceramics: two whiteware sherds and two yellowware sherds. The two whiteware sherds are decorated. One is a rim with a thick black (?) curved line (Fig. 22E), while a body sherd is a blue flower transfer print (Fig. 23D).

Another nine historic items come from the two excavation units. These items are five whiteware sherds, one flat glass shard, a fence-post staple, one wire nail, and an unidentifiable piece of rusted metal.

All of the Historic artifacts can be organized into kitchen (ceramic sherds and container glass), personal/hygiene/pharmaceutical (bottle shard), architectural (flat glass and nail), and miscellaneous hardware (staple) functional groups. The Historic component may represent materials from a nearby domestic context such as Dakota homes or the Riggs mission (with some modern intrusions). Other than the few brick and mortar fragments, no evidence of a structure is indicated in Concentration 4. The possible pearlware and decorated whiteware (especially a possible hand-painted polychrome sherd) can be assigned to the mid 1800s. If so, these particular sherds and the brick and mortar fragments may be contemporaneous with the Riggs mission period.

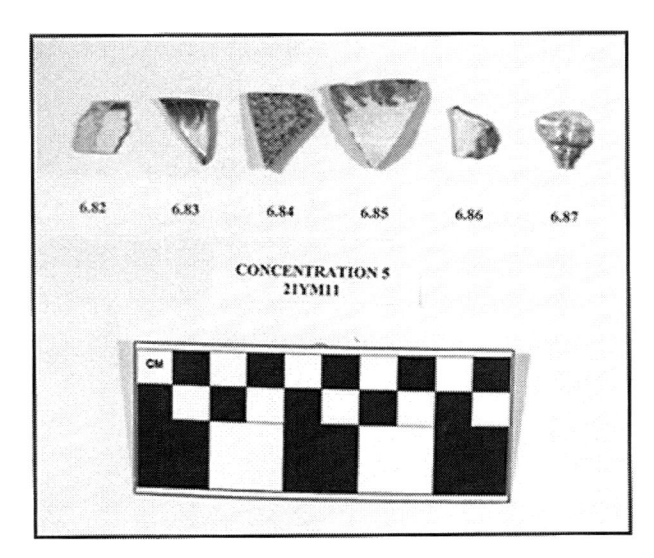

Figure 25. Six decorated Historic sherds from Concentration 5.

Generalized Field Scatter

General surface collections also were made in 2002 and 2003 that covered the field between the four concentrations. The surface collections resulted in a total of 119 Historic and pre-Historic artifacts (Table 13) and two possible manuported objects. Over two-thirds (67.2%) of the items are pre-Historic lithics. Just under one-third (32.7%) are historic materials.

Ceramics: The 25 Historic ceramics include six coarse earthenware, three stoneware, two ironstone, and 14 whiteware sherds. The coarse earthenware is brown glazed; one has a possible Albany slip interior and another has a salt glaze. One of the stoneware sherds has a brown glaze.

Glass: Seven glass artifacts consist of two colorless bottle-glass shards; an amethyst glass-container body shard; three window-glass fragments; an unidentified thick, flat colorless glass shard. The thick colorless shard appears to have some unifacial modification on one end and along part of the fractured

Figure 26. Pipe bowl fragment (left) and gunflint from Concentration 5.

edge. It is not known what or who caused this modification. The unbroken edge of this shard was mechanically ground to remove two 90- degree corners and the flat edge. This shard probably came from a covered vehicle with windows such as a buggy or automobile (?).

Metal: The four metal objects comprise a partial disc from an iron corn sheller, a T-strap iron hinge, a wood rasp file, and a broken cut nail. The corn sheller machine part is a section of a larger cast-iron disc with multiple teeth. It fit within a box into which ears of corn were fed, and opposing discs were turned to remove the kernels from the husk. Hand-operated and machine-operated shellers were in existence from the 1850s to the late 1950s (Wendel 1997). The file has a coarse or rough spacing of single cut tooth pattern with a broken tang handle. In cross section it is half round. It could have had multiple uses to finish wood items (Ross and Light 2000).

Stone and Mortar: The last two Historic artifacts are one mortar fragment (size=6.8 cm) and two pieces of coal (wt=20.0 gm). The Historic artifacts can be placed within kitchen (ceramics and container glass), architecture (flat glass, hinge, cut nail), miscellaneous hardware (file, corn sheller), and mineral (coal) groups. These groupings are consistent with what was found in the other four concentrations north of the road.

Concentration 5

On the southwest side of the new road is another Historic artifact concentration (Concentration 5) (see Fig. 2).

This concentration is a dense scatter (68 x 52 m) of Historic materials located on an east facing hill slope. This could be the site mentioned by Wilford in his 1954 memo cited earlier. It revealed a plowzone with a very dark brown silt loam over a yellow brown clayey silt loam. The excavation unit and shovel tests were all placed in Normania clay loam on 1-3 percent slopes and Storden-Ves loams on 5-12 percent slopes.

Surface Collection

A total of two molluscan shell fragments along with 188 Historic artifacts were collected from the surface of this concentration. Of the 188 Historic artifacts, 94 are ceramic, 51 are glass, 38 are metal, and five are nonorganic items not included in the above catagories.

Ceramics: The 94 ceramics are a mixture of six coarse earthenware, one possible pearlware, four unidentified refined earthenware, one stoneware, 76 whiteware, and six yellow-ware sherds. The unidentified refined earthenware sherds are all decorated in Bennington glaze, dating to the mid-to-late 1800s (Fig. 24). Five of the whiteware sherds are embossed with a rope or wheat design. Six are decorated in various motifs including red annular ware, blue featheredge, blue spongeware, and generalized blue transfer print (Fig. 25).

Three of the whiteware sherds have makers' marks. Two of them are printed with royal arms designs. It is suspected that they are from imported vessels from England. Unfortunately, both are too fragmented to completely identify the name and year of the maker(s). The third makers mark is an impression (not printed) of a diamond seal and another figure that has within it a partial anchor and the word "Davenport". This mark is likely from the Davenport (Henry and William era) Company of Longport, Staffordshire, England and dates sometime in the 1850s (Kowalsky and Kowalsky 1999:167-169).

Glass: The 51 glass artifacts include one amethyst, 10 aqua, and three dark green bottle fragments; one aqua flatware (plate?) fragment; one clear hurricane lamp fragment; one cobalt blue faceted hexagonal bead; 32 window fragments; and two unidentified colorless glass shards.

Metal: The 38 metal artifacts are a variety of nails, closures, flatware, machine parts, miscellaneous hardware, and tools. Twelve cut nails are present. Five latch or hinge closures, a knife flatware fragment, and two unidentified machine parts are also present. The eight miscellaneous hardware pieces include a key hole, a hook, a threaded hollow tube, a solid tube, and four objects that could not be identified. Two axe-head tools are also present, one of which is identified as a shingling hatchet (Association for Preservation Technology 1980).

Non-organic: The five nonorganic artifacts in this portion of the surface concentration include a kaolin pipe bowl fragment and gun flint (Fig. 26) and samples of both brick and mortar.

The surface collection of this concentration shows strong evidence of burning as eleven artifacts are either burnt or melted.

Shovel Testing

A pair of shovel tests (ST) were dug at 5 m intervals proceeding north (ST1 and ST2) and west (ST3 and ST4) of the northwest corner of Excavation Unit 1 (see below). They were dug through the plowzone. No artifacts were recovered from ST1 or ST3. However, ST2 yielded two cut-nail fragments, one whiteware ceramic sherd, one refined earthenware door-knob fragment (with brown glaze), one window-glass shard, and a brick fragment. ST4 had one cut nail.

Unit 1 Excavation

A 1 x 1 m unit was set up where the southeast corner of the unit was 4.5 meters from the center of the artifact concentration. It was excavated in two levels. Level 1 was excavated to the base of the plowzone and Level 2 was excavated from the base of the plowzone to 25 cm below surface (approximately 5 cm into the subsoil). The plowzone (Level 1) is a very dark brown silt loam over a yellow brown clayey silt loam. Twenty-two artifacts were recovered in Level 1. They were all Historic and included six ceramic sherds (one coarse earthenware, four undecorated whiteware and one decorated whiteware sherd), two glass window fragments, nine cut-nail fragments, three unidentified metal fragments, and two brick pieces. Four artifacts were also recovered in the subsoil in Level 2. These include one undecorated whiteware sherd and two cut-nail fragments.

Surface Outliers

A collection of artifacts immediately surrounding the concentration was also made. It is assumed that some of the Historic artifacts are directly associated with the concentration. The 31 artifacts recovered include one deer scapula fragment, 19 Historic materials, and 11 precontact lithics. The Hstoric material is comprised of eight ceramics, six glass fragments, four metal artifacts, and a concrete or mortar fragment. Ceramics include two coarse earthenware container fragments (one burned), one porcelain rim sherd, and five undecorated whiteware sherds.

Although the artifact assemblage is inconclusive owing to the lack of tightly dated diagnostics, it seems possible that Concentration 5 (including the outliers) represents the remnants of a brick house built around 1860 for the Dakota associated with the Hazelwood mission. Somewhat surprisingly, there is evidence of burning in the concentration. Wilford's 1954 local informant, Alben Johnson, around the area since 1880, remembered when a brick house stood in this area (Wilford 1954). Was the house burned during the 1862 Dakota uprising or did it survive only to burn later?

Discussion

The purpose of this archaeological investigation was to evaluate cultural resources documented during a Phase I survey of land later placed into trust status for the Upper Sioux Community. Historic and pre-Historic artifacts were found scattered across the entire field northeast of the road that now splits part the former Radunz property in two. In this field were four areas where artifacts were concentrated. Initially identified by field numbers (YM-BIAFN-#), they were later designated Concentrations 1, 2, 3/7, and 4. All four surface concentrations were subjected to shovel testing and more formal excavation in order to find buried features or evidence of intact subsurface artifact deposits (e.g. campsites, village sites, other activity areas). This exploratory work resulted in finding a single buried feature in Concentration 1 but no evidence of intact subsurface artifact deposits in any of the concentrations. All four concentrations possessed a variety of Historic and pre-Historic artifacts in 11 different categories (Table 1). When these numbers are placed together in a single table, Concentration 1 stands out by the sheer numbers of artifacts recovered on this hill top. This is where the Historic pit feature (Feature 1) was found.

There were several clues to indicate Feature 1's use. During the field work and artifact analysis this pit was considered to be a dugout or a cellar to the chapel or house, a privy pit, possibly one of Sibley's entrenchments, or even a submound burial pit from the mound complex 21YM11. A burial pit thesis can be excluded because there were no human remains, pre-Historic lithics, or other artifacts found within the pit, even though 195 lithic artifacts were found on the ground surface and upper excavation levels in Concentration 1. Red ocher pieces were found in the feature with Historic artifacts, but the ocher is considered to have been in the possession of one or more Dakota at this location during the Mission period. A recent study of mounds has tentatively indicated that all of the mounds investigated in this region of Minnesota have submound burials (Arzigian and Stevenson 2003:175-176). A few burials were also found on the original ground surface and the mound fill. Their average depth is about 1.62 feet (ca. 50 cm). The entrenchment thesis was eliminated because there were no military artifacts such as buttons. Records indicate that soldiers from the Sibley expedition poked around the burned out buildings, but Sibley's camp was probably south of Hazel Creek or somewhere west of the mission. A privy pit use for feature 1 was considered because only the nails found in Feature 1 were very corroded. Such corrosion has been observed by the authors on ferrous items recovered in outhouse contexts. However, the suspected length and width of the pit (>9 feet x >4 feet) is far too large for an outhouse associated with a brick house, and it would be too far away from the other mission buildings to make it practical for the students, teachers, and missionaries to use. The 1860 photograph shows a small building between the school and chapel that may be an outhouse. A dugout use for this feature may be possible, but it would seemingly have been situated too close to the summit. It would have been more logical to build a dugout further down the slope where there would be a better advantage of having higher walls to cover over. None of the records consulted for this project discuss building dugout homes here or at the Williamson mission. The chapel was briefly considered as the source of this feature, but it was a wood-framed building; the use of brick was not mentioned in the records. The large numbers Historic architectural materials found in Concentration 1 would best identify the feature as a cellar associated with a brick house built for a Dakota individual or family.

The Historic feature and artifacts in Concentration 1 are associated with events and patterns that are significant to the Dakota and the State of Minnesota during the years 1854-1862. This site reflects the pressures of acculturation and proselytizing efforts by missionaries that the Dakota people were experiencing in the mid-nineteenth century, culminating in the catastrophic events of 1862. This concentration has yielded information that has contributed to our understanding of the history of this area and those involved in making that history. There is still information in this concentration that was not recovered that is considered important. It is the BIA's determination that the Historic component of Concentration 1 qualifies for the National Register.

Regarding the other concentrations having Historic materials, most of the Historic artifacts encountered within and between the other concentrations could have come from Concentration 1, but the records indicate that there was at least one other brick building in the vicinity, on the southwest side of the road located in 2002, near which the mission was photographed in 1860. No other architectural features were found during the Phase II investigation that might have an association with the Riggs mission between 1854 and 1862. A few items (synthetics and corn sheller) represent farming or other activities that postdate the mission by decades. The number of Historic materials found at the other three concentrations generally pale in comparison, although comparable numbers of Historic ceramics were present at Concentrations 2 and 4. Nearly 150 years of farming has displaced these artifacts from their original locations; a few are quite probably parts to lost articles, clothing, containers, and equipment.

Concentration 5 is also another location where a homesite was built during the Riggs mission era at the Upper Sioux Agency. The Historic artifacts are located in the vicinity of a reported brick wall and the location where the 1860 photograph was taken of the mission buildings.

Acknowledgments. Funding to support Phase II fieldwork was provided by the Upper Sioux Community and the BIA's Central Office. Without such support it would not have been possible to field a crew or acquire such a substantial amount of information from the four areas that were investigated. We are very grateful for the work that Phyllis Littlcreek-Wilbanks, Ursula Stavne, Micha Sheppard, Leah Hedalen, Lora Kludt, Anthony Domencich, and Steven MacManion, Jr. contributed in the field to make this report possible. Our appreciation is also extended to Harry F. Thompson, Director of Research Collections and Publications at the Center for Western Studies, for providing access to the Riggs family papers. The Minnesota Historical Society gave permission to use the 1860 photograph of the Riggs mission. It is Figure 4 of this report.

References Cited

Anderson, G.C. and A.R. Woolworth (edits.)
    1988 *Through Dakota Eyes: Narrative Accounts of the Minnesota Indian War of 1862*. Minnesota Historical Society Press, St. Paul, Minnesota.

Anonymous
    1900 *Plat Book of Yellow Medicine County, Minnesota.* Northwest Publishing Company. No place of publication mentioned.
    1924 Visits his Birthplace. *The Word Carrier of Santee Normal Training School*, Volume 56(6):1.

Arzigian, C.M. and K.P. Stevenson
    2003 *Minnesota's Indian Mounds and Burial Sites: A Synthesis of Prehistoric and Early Historic Archaeological Data.* Publication 1. The Minnesota Office of the State Archaeologist, St. Paul, Minnesota.

Berg, R.E. and J.E. Myster
    2002 *Archaeological Reconnaissance of the Former Dora Radunz and Selmer Hildahl Properties Proposed for Trust Acquisition for the Upper Sioux Community in Yellow Medicine County, Minnesota.* Paper prepared for the Upper Sioux Indian Community, Granite Falls, Minnesota. Bureau of Indian Affairs, Midwest Regional Office, Fort Snelling, Minnesota. Prepared for the Upper Sioux Indian Community, Granite Falls, Minnesota.
    2005 *Phase II Evaluation of Historic and Prehistoric Components at the Riggs Mission Site (21YM11/YM-MNF-007) on Upper Sioux Community Lands in Yellow Medicine County, Minnesota.* Paper prepared for the Upper Sioux Indian Community, Granite Falls, Minnesota. Bureau of Indian Affairs, Midwest Regional Office, Fort Snelling, Minnesota.

Brown, S. J.
    1988 Samuel J. Brown's Recollections. *Through Dakota Eyes: Narrative Accounts of the Minnesota Indian War of 1862*, pp 169-176. Edited by G.C. Anderson and A.R. Woolworth. Minnesota Historical Society Press, St. Paul.

Cherveny, T.
    1988   Doncaster Cemetery: 100 Years of Area's History. *Granite Falls Tribune*, Thursday, December 8, 1988.

Crawford, C.R.
    1988   Charles R. Crawford's Testimony. *Through Dakota Eyes: Narrative Accounts of the Minnesota Indian War of 1862*, pp. 201-203. Edited by G.C. Anderson and A.R. Woolworth. Minnesota Historical Society Press, St. Paul.

Granger, S.
    1985   *Yellow Medicine County Historic Sites Survey, 1984-1985*. Minnesota State Historical Society State Historic Preservation Office, St. Paul, Minnesota, in cooperation with the Yellow Medicine Historical Society, Granite Falls, Minnesota.

Granite Falls *Tribune*
    1923   Missionary's Son Visits Landmarks. Granite Falls *Tribune*, November 7, 1923.

Hokanson, H.L.
    1981   *Soil Survey of Yellow Medicine County, Minnesota*. U.S. Department of Agriculture, Soil Conservation Service and Minnesota Agricultural Experiment Station. U.S. Government Printing Office, Washington D.C.

Hohman-Caine, C.A., L.D. Peterson and G.E. Goltz
    2002   *Field Re-Location of 21YM11 and Phase I Archaeological Reconnaissance of Surrounding Area, Yellow Medicine County, Minnesota*. Paper prepared for the Upper Sioux Community Board of Trustees. Red Lake Band of Chippewa Indians, Red Lake, Minnesota.

Kluth, D.W. and A. Fromm
    2003   *Geophysical and Archaeological Investigation of Mound Complex 21YM11, Yellow Medicine County, Minnesota*. Paper prepared for the Upper Sioux Community, Granite Falls, Minnesota. Foth & Van Dyke and Associates, Eagan, Minnesota.

Kowalsky, A.A. and D.E. Kowalsky
    1999   *Encyclopedia of Marks on American, English, and European Earthenware, Ironstone, and Stoneware (1780-1980)*. Schiffer, Atglen, Pennsylvania.

Renville, G.
    1988   Gabriel Renville's Memoir. *Through Dakota Eyes: Narrative Accounts of the Minnesota Indian War of 1862*, pp. 186-192. Edited by G.C. Anderson and A.R. Woolworth. Minnesota Historical Society Press, St. Paul.

Riggs, M.L. (edit.)
    1996   *A Small Bit of Bread and Butter: Letters from the Dakota Territory, 1832-1869*. Ash Grove Press, South Deerfield, Massachusetts.

Riggs, S.R.
    1856   No. 18, Hazelwood, Minnesota, September 30, 1855. Letter to Major R.G. Murphy, Dakota Indian Agent. In *Annual Report of the Commissioner of Indian Affairs*, pp. 61-62. A.O.P. Nicholson, Washington D.C.
    1857   No. 20, Hazelwood, Minnesota, October 21, 1856. In *Report of the Commissioner of Indian Affairs, for the Year 1856,* pp. 64-65. A.O.P. Nicholson, Washington D.C.
    1860   Letter to his son Alfred, Oomahoo, Minnesota, July 21, 1866. Center for Western Studies Box folder 4,11.
    1862a   S. R. Riggs letter to his wife Mary, September 8, 1862. In *Stephen R. Riggs and Family Correspondence*. Bound volume on file with the Minnesota Historical Society, St. Paul, Minnesota.
    1862b   S. R. Riggs letter to his wife Mary, September 11, 1862. In *Stephen R. Riggs and Family Correspondence*.

Bound volume on file with the Minnesota Historical Society, St. Paul, Minnesota.

1862c S. R. Riggs letter to his wife Mary, September 24, 1862. In *Stephen R. Riggs and Family Correspondence*. Bound volume on file with the Minnesota Historical Society, St. Paul, Minnesota.

1880 *Mary and I. Forty Years with the Sioux*. W.G. Holmes, Chicago, Illinois.

Riggs, T.F.
1928 Letter to Doane Robinson, Pierre South Dakota. Papers of Stephen R. Riggs. On file with the Minnesota State Historical Society, St. Paul.

Rose, A.P.
1914 *An Illustrated History of Yellow Medicine County, Minnesota*. Northern History, Marshall, Minnesota.

Riggs, T. L.
1924 Letter to daughter Anna. Papers of Riggs Family on file with the Center for Western Studies. Sioux Falls, South Dakota.

Ross, D.
2002 Personal communication. Office of the Environment for the Upper and Lower Sioux Communities, Redwood Falls, Minnesota.

Soil Survey Staff
1975 *Soil Taxonomy: A Basic System of Soil Classification for Making and Interpreting Soil Surveys*. Agriculture Handbook No. 436. U.S.

DeWendel, C.H.
1997 *Encyclopedia of American Farm Implements & Antiques*. Krause, Iola, Wisconsin.

Wilford, L.
1954 *Memo on Yellow Medicine County, May, 1954*. Copy on file with the Minnesota Historical Society, St. Paul.

Williamson, T.S.
1880 THE SIOUX OR DAKOTAS: A Sketch of Our Intercourse with the Dakotahs on the Missouri River and Southwest of that Stream. *Collections of the Minnesota Historical Society*, Vol. III: 283-294. Minnesota Historical Society Press, St. Paul.

Winchell, N.H.
1911 *The Aborigines of Minnesota: A Report Based on the Collections of Jacob V. Brower, and on the Field Surveys and Notes of Alfred J. Hill and Theodore H. Lewis*. Minnesota Historical Society, St. Paul.

Appendix A

TRANSCRIBED HISTORIC DOCUMENTS AND EXCERPTS RELATING TO THE RIGGS MISSION, DAKOTA HOMES AND THE YELLOW MEDICINE AGENCY

(Sources: *Minnesota Historical Society*, St. Paul, Minnesota and *Center for Western Studies*, Augustana College, Sioux Falls, South Dakota)

THE HENDERSON WEEKLY DEMOCRAT
VOL. 4—NO. 30   HENDERSON, SIBLEY COUNTY, MINNESOTA, SATURDAY, MARCH 3, 1860   WHOLE NO. 186

SIOUX AGENCY, YELLOW MEDICINE
February 21, 1860

Scaled Proposals will be received at the office of the
Sioux Agent,

Until twelve 0'clock, M,

On Saturday, the 17th day of March, 1860,

for the following work, vis:

For the plastering of the Agency Building as the Agent may prescribe. The Lime, Sand, Water and Hair to be furnished on the premises, and the Lathe nailed by the Department. Each proposal will state the price per square yard, openings not counted, for a single a coat, and also for two coats. The contractors will be required to complete the work previous to the first day of May, 1860.

Also-For Laying Brick on the Upper and Lower Reservations. The proposals to state the price per thousand, kiln measure, for one eight inch wall, and also for a twelve inch wall. The brick, lime, sand and water to be delivered by the Department at several locations where the work is to be done. The Agent will prescribe the size and shape of the buildings or other work required.

Bids will also be considered for Erection of Brick Houses of the following dimensions. Each house to be seventeen feet wide by twenty-one feet long on the outside, the foundations to be two feet high of twelve inch wall, and the walls to be twelve feet above the foundation and eight inches thick, the gables to suit a roof of one third pitch. Each building to contain such openings as the agent may direct. All the wood work to be done, and the Brick Lime, Sand and Water to be furnished on the premises at the expense of the Department. The bidder will state the price for which he will do the Brick work of each house, and will designate whether he proposes for the work to be done on the Upper and Lower reservations, or on both.

Also-For Breaking New Land, on the Upper and on the Lower Reservations at such points as the Agent may direct. The breaking will be required to be done on lots of five acres each, and all must be completed on or before the tenth day of June, 1860. Bidders will state the number of teams they will work, and will be required to work the number of teams designated. No bidder will be awarded a contractor for breaking to exceed fifty acres for each team he employs. The breaking will be required to be six inches deep, and the sod must be turned completely over.

The Agent reserves the right of limiting the quantities of each species of work to meet the requirements of the department and the interests of the Indians, and also of rejecting any and all bids that he may deem exorbitant or the guarantors irresponsible.

Bids for the plastering must be separate from any other proposals, but the same bids may contain proposals for the Breaking and Brick work on both Reservations, specifying the price proposed for doing work on each of the reserves, or may propose separately for either Breaking or Brick Work on either reservation.

No bid will be considered unless accompanied by a guarantee signed by two responsible persons that the bidder, if awarded the contract, will enter into bonds satisfactory to the Agent, conditioned for the faithful fulfillment of the contract awarded; and guarantors will understand that the neglect or refusal of any person or persons awarded a contract under any bid for the before-mentioned work, or any portion of it, will subject his or their guarantors to a prosecution of damages.

All bids will be endorsed "Proposals for work," and be addressed to the undersigned at Yellow Medicine, Minnesota.

JOSEPH R. BROWN
Sioux Agent.

(From page 3 of the newspaper)

AGENCY CONTRACT - [Mr. G.W. Piper to build Indian Houses, Wash to do, St. Peter Tribune, May 9, 1860

The Agency Contract–The contract of Mr. G. W. Piper of this place with the Government for breaking and at the Agencies, and building a hundred brick houses for the occupancy of such of the tribes as have devoted themselves to manly labor, and has been confirmed by the department at Washington, and the work will go on rapidly. Already the plow has turned the sod of the hunting ground, and many acres are ready for planting.

The houses will be 16 x 18 and two stories high. The brick and lime are made at the Agency, where we understand that both can be made of a very superior quality. The timber used in their construction, is sawed by the department mill. The work will all be completed before the fifteenth of June, and will necessarily require a large number of hands for its timely completion.

There will be a house on each surveyed tract of eighty acres, the ground having been laid out and platted by Mr. Leavenworth last fall. Many of the leading men of the tribe have declared for hard work, and there really seems to be some hope of the success of the civilization movement. Such men as Shakopee, Wabashaw (chiefs) and other "big Indians" have cropped their hair, mounted "atile," and dropped the blanket. "Soldier Clothes" is the promenade dress of a fashionable Sioux now, the lady Indians considering them perfectly irresistible.

CENTER FOR WESTERN STUDIES, SIOUX FALLS, SOUTH DAKOTA

    Box folder 3,6
    Mary to Miss Spooner   Hazelwood   February 1, 1855

    ... One of the principal (trials) has been counter with the sawmill. It has used up the timber too fast while it was sawing. Mr. Riggs has given each man who is building a house enough boards to floor one room, but they expected the sawmill would supply them any amount of boards without expense for sawing! .... Page 2, para 2

    Box folder 4, 11
    Thomas Riggs to his Brother Alfred   Hazelwood   December 5, 1859

    Papa has put a floor on the wagon house & put the calves in it & some corn put the cows in the log stable.   Paragraph 2

    Box folder 4,11
    Stephen Riggs to his son Alfred   Hazelwood?   December 14, 1859

    We sawed a week-of which I got two days and made about a thousand feet. The stable is weatherboarded-enclosed-except the sheeting stands as you and I left it last summer I could have put the sheeting on if I had felt it important. Amos N(?) Got about 1300 shingles made-used all the timber we cut up.

    Box folder 4,11
    Stephen Riggs to his son Alfred   Oomahoo, Minn   February 3, 1860

    Down in the woods below us where the two ravines join the river the greater part of the Hintahahkpanampi (sp?) are encamped. Page 3, para2

    Box folder 4,11
    Stephen Riggs to his son Alfred   Oomahoo, Minn   April 21, 1860

    Did I tell you that I had put a board fence around the church this spring? I have also ploughed a little piece beyond our garden and run a fence across the corner of Mr. Cs garden. This we shall plant in pumpkins this year, and perhaps next season take it, or a part of it, into our garden.   Page 4, para 3

    Box folder 4,8
    Mary A.C.L. Riggs to Alfred Riggs   Home (Hazelwood)   May 12, 1860

    ... I have just been out attending to the chickens. We have six very fine broods & we keep them in the part of the yard north of the house & chicken house. ...

Box folder 4, 11
Stephen Riggs to his son Alfred   Oomahoo, Minn   June 1, 1860

... that night before last our stable was broken into and all our horses stolen. The door was locked and bolted-that they did not disturb, but they pried off the boards from that part that was to be the door of the wagon part. They took all three horses and a colt. But instead of going out the lane below the school house, they took down the logs between the stables and going around the head of the hollow went out at the woods side of the calf pasture-thence we tracked them round by Eli's old stable and up by Renville's house. (...) And then as our big pasture fence had been blown down by a storm the other night, they crossed that diagonally and came out by Lorenzo's and so round our field crossing Rush Brook at the lower ford.   Page 1, para 1

Box folder 4,11
Stephen Riggs to his son Alfred   Oomahoo, Minn   July 21, 1860

Monday morn. July 23. Saturday after I had written the above and while I was out hoeing rutabagas, Mr. Hill the artist, who has been here at Yellow Medicine since before the payments "reaping golden honors" by making light pictures of almost every body, drove up with Mr. Freniere. He had come to take the likeness of our mission premises. After trying from various points he finally placed his camera on the little mound back of Simon's. We gathered quite a company, perhaps too many, a mixed multitude, for the fore ground. The wind blew considerably which was rather against the result. He tried several times. His first and last negatives were he thought tolerably good. He took one ambrotype which was beautiful of the buildings, the trees back of the church showing very finely, but some of the crowd were rather blurred. It was half past two oclock before we got ready to eat dinner.   Pages 1-2

They are now putting up brick houses for Indians. Two have gone up in this neighborhood–one for Mrs. Theresa Renville and one for Simon. But the same miserable policy is pursued-that of finishing them off in such a way as not to be comfortable-the floors are not ever jointed-for the carpentry work of a house they only pay $25-which Maj. Cable(?) says ought to have been $50 and that it could have been done properly. But so things are done in this Sham age.   Page 3

Box folder 4,11
Stephen Riggs to his son Alfred   Dakota Mission,
                                                   Pajutazee P.O., Minn
                                                   March 12, 1861

Discusses possible improvements for the church which was just replastered last fall (1860). The interior was lighted with four side lamps a one stand lamp. Improvements being considered are wall paper, more lighting and window blinds.   Page 3

Box folder 3,12
Stephen Riggs to Dr. Williamson   St. Anthony   November 28, 1862

My Dear Doctor,
     Today I wrote to you by Mr. Ketchum, but I forgot altogether the questions you asked about losses in making out bills for. Last week I made out an account of ours. Mrs. Riggs and the girls have been

calling to rembrance the various articles, while I was away, and putting them down. In this way I think we got the nine tenths of all at any rate. Though since we finished it up we occasionally think of things not put down.

I appended to mine in a different Schedule, the property of the Board at Hazelwood and estimated them as follows
Viz My own house $1000
Boarding School house 1000
Church 700
School House 150
The stables and other out houses
and improvements I estimated separately and also the crops-the whole amount was about $3500. Riggs goes on to discuss Williamsons losses.

Box folder 6,3
Thomas L. Riggs to Anna   Montevideo, Minn, July 2nd 1924

Dear Anna

Theodore, Katherine, the little one, Thomas L. Riggs, Louisa and I and Harry Morris, have been this afternoon at Hazelwood and seen what is there. The frame house, where the house was, built over our cellar, where the large cottonwood trees that father and Mr. Cunninham must have planted straight along in front of our houses up towards the chapel up on the low range running north and south to trees and our houses, and other things that bring to our own childhood days–where Tatticorn, (undecipherable name), Pedoma, Buck and Bright figured so largely. Last objective Theodore and I made a flying trip to Lac que Parle.

Box folder 6,5
Hazelwood Republic
by T.L. Riggs

Partial description of the church: "..., a neat framed building capable of accommodating about one hundred persons. At the front was a bell tower, which below served as a vestibule, and in which above swung a clear-toned bell ... The entire cost of the building was about seven hundred dollars. Page 5 no date on paper.

THE WORD CARRIER OF SANTEE NORMAL TRAINING SCHOOL
Volume LIII   Number 6
Nov-Dec. 1924
Visits His Birthplace

A very interesting party took place this summer when Dr. Thomas L. Riggs celebrated his 77th birthday at the place where the old Lac-qui-parle mission stood and where he was born on June 3, 1847. The only living survivors of that mission station are Dr. Riggs and the Rev. Elias Gilbert, an aged Indian pastor, who joined Dr. Riggs on this trip. The other members of the little party were Mrs. Thomas Riggs, Dr. And Mrs. Theodore Riggs, Mrs. Elia Gilbert, and Dr. Doane Robinson, state historian of South Dakota. The elder Dr. Riggs identified the various sites. The trees planted by his father are great tall ones now; they ought to be marked. Page 1.

Held in Captivity
by Benedict Juni
Liesch-Walter Printing Co., New Ulm, Minnesota
1926

Page 15. At Hazelwood there were three buildings still intact when we first formed camp there, a residence, a work shop and a two-story building swerving both as chapel and school house. It was the best equipped school house I had seen so far. The boys first ransacked the desks, scattered the books and other utensils and rang the large bell that hung in the belfry. When they tired of this window panes afforded targets for stone and arrows. Next the work shop was visited and some of the rod iron formed into spears and these hurled at fence posts. The days program was concluded by a monstrous bonfire in the evening. The white frame dwelling of Mr. Riggs and the Williamsons fell prey to the flames. Bear in mind that this was not done by adults but by boys not yet in their teens and elicited no applause from their parents.

"Samuel J. Brown's Recollections"
Upper Indians encamped west of the mission near a creek (Hazel Creek) on August 28th and stayed at this location until September 9th when they moved upriver to Chief Red Iron's camp which would become Camp Release. "Through Dakota Eyes" Pp. 169-176.

"Gabriel Renville's Memoir"
Friendly Indians occupied the houses about the Riggs mission, probably including his home. Renville camped near the buildings. Also mentions a large camp west of the mission buildings. They eventually moved to Red Iron's camp. "Through Dakota Eyes" Pp. 186-192

"Victor Renville's Account"
About 100 tents in the friendly camp. "Through Dakota Eyes" Pp. 192-194

"Charles R. Crawford's Testimony"
He and some others camped about one-quarter mile west of the village. Indians camped around the mission buildings. "Through Dakota Eyes" Pp. 201-203.

Appendix B

INVENTORY OF ITEMS MENTIONED, LOST, AND/OR RETURNED TO THE RIGGS

Mrs. Riggs discusses long distance purchases in portions of some of her letters while at Hazelwood, but it is unclear if everything she mentions is actually bought and sent to her.

Hazelwood August 1, 1860
Sewing machine
Oil lamp with glass chimney

Hazelwood May 5, 1862

Sitting room:
Stove made with metal plates and iron rod

> Saint Anthony October 3, 10, 13, 24, 29, 1862 Mary Riggs letters to her husband and December 2, 1862 Mrs. Riggs letter to Mrs. Blake.

In back room of house close to the stove:
5 Smoothing irons
Old tongs

In closet of Riggs bedroom:
2 Escritoires (Mrs. Riggs' was found by her husband)
Work box with breast pin and Daguerreotypes (Lucretia, husband, Mary, Ella, Mr. And Mrs Drake, brother Alfred and his wife, another of Alfred and several others not identified) inside
Spectacles were on the bureau
Senate clock
Britannia ware
Bedtick
3 plus several other bed quilts (2 quilts returned from Dakota friends)
Several comfortables
Several blankets
Sheets (3 pair of sheets returned from Dakota friends)
Pillow cases
Towels
Table linen
Framed Daguerreotype of Alfred, Isabella and Anna
Carpets
Underclothes
Wearing apparel (1 dress returned from Dakota friends)
Tea knives and forks
Small birds eye maple box

> Hazelwood September 24, 1862 Stephen Riggs letter to his wife Mary

Church bible (Recovered by Dakota friend)
Church bell (Recovered by soldiers)
Books (Partially recovered by soldiers)

The Rock Art of Big Room Cave

Rebecca Sprengelmeyer
University of Wisconsin-La Crosse

Big Room Cave is located near the headwaters of the Root River in southeastern Minnesota. It is along the western edge of an unglaciated region known as the Driftless Area and the eastern edge of the Great Plains. Big Room Cave is a sinkhole cavern formed out of New Richmond Sandstone. Preliminary investigations revealed possible Native American glyphs present within the cave. Building on earlier speleological and archaeological investigations, documentation of the rock art in Big Room Cave was carried out between October of 2005 and January of 2006 by a Mississippi Valley Archaeology Center staff member, University of Wisconsin--La Crosse students, and volunteers. The investigation discovered probable Native American glyphs overlaid by extensive modern and Historic graffiti. The prehistoric images included various elliptical shapes often interpreted as vulva forms, two boxy animals (possibly bison), several human figures, and a few abstract forms. This paper details the documentation of rock art found in Big Room Cave during the 2005-2006 investigation, regional manifestations of similar rock art motifs, and the possible temporal and cultural affiliation of these images.

Introduction

The purpose of this investigation is to record the Native American rock art at Big Room Cave, document the context, and offer insight that may aid in the interpretation of these images. Information about the prehistoric cultures that created the rock art in Big Room Cave can be gleaned from the documentation and study of these glyphs. Rock art is a unique cultural resource that is being destroyed at Big Room by the natural processes of water runoff, freezing and thawing, fading, and modern human graffiti. By documenting the rock art we are preserving this resource as part of the archaeological record of the Driftless Area.

Documentation of this site in 2005-06 included mapping the cave and locating potential Native American glyphs. Once the glyphs were found and differentiated from modern graffiti, recordation involved mapping the location, drawing, recording the condition, and photographing each glyph. This process resulted in the documentation of over 37 probable Native American glyphs the most prevalent being un-rayed elliptical forms with center dots.

Background

Rock art is often the only remaining form of communication left by prehistoric cultures. Rock art is not a form of writing to express the spoken language, but it is "a visible manifestation of the desire for early man to communicate some message in a tangible and permanent manner" (Sanger and Meighan 1990). Rock art provides unique insights into past cultures: "The figures and symbols painted and engraved on rock surfaces constitute documentation of the utmost relevance for the study and comprehension of the cultural roots of humankind" (Anati et al.1984:217).

Terms and Definitions

Rock art is a term referring primarily to carvings and paintings made by aboriginal peoples on natural rock surfaces. It also includes images made by scraping away gravel or earth from the surface of the ground to reveal the underlying soil, as well as placing rocks in patterned arrangements on the ground. Some rock art is found almost everywhere that rock surfaces are exposed, and it is absent only in areas of alluvium where no rocks with useable surfaces are to be found. Desert areas are particularly favored for rock art since there is plenty of exposed rock and little vegetation to cover it. Rock art also is found along jungle rivers and in heavily forested areas, on rocks along the ocean shore and at the top of mountains peaks [Sanger and Meighan 1990:19]

A rock art site may consist of a single image or an assemblage of hundreds of glyphs. There are three basic techniques that can be employed to make rock art: painting/drawing, carving, and geoglyphs. Pictographs are painted/drawn figures on rock surfaces; petroglyphs are figures impressed into the surfaces by pecking, scraping, or carving grooves with tools; and geoglyphs are land figures made by removing the surface material to create an image in relief (Sanger and Meighan 1990:21). "The terms 'pictograph' and 'painting' are interchangeable, as are the terms 'petroglyph' and 'engraving.' In some instances, a petroglyph can be painted or vice versa; if so, it is simply both a pictograph and a petroglyph" (Loendorf et al.1998:11). Both pictographs and petroglyphs are found in Big Room Cave.

Dating

Dating rock art is difficult at best and is virtually impossible in some instances using current methods. When an image was made by painting/drawing, as in the case of pictographs, organic material in the pigment can sometimes be dated. However, when the image was created by carving petroglyphs into the rock face, no such analysis is possible and, consequently, the vast majority of engraved images cannot be assigned reliable dates. The problem is further complicated by the common phenomenon of superimposed art from widely differing time periods occurring on the surface. Often earlier art is incorporated into the art of a later time period, making it very difficult to distinguish the images, and thus the periods, being represented. However, superimposed rock art provides stratigraphy and the opportunity to use relative dating. Despite these difficulties rock art can sometimes be dated based on style (especially if a specific animal, such as a horse, or a technology, such as bows and arrows, are depicted) or patination, which measures the amount of patina covering the image. Also, some rock art has been associated with specific cultures based on archaeological excavations in caves. This is beneficial because the rock art can be correlated with the cultural material found buried under floor deposits.

Rock Art Research in the Driftless Area

Description of the Driftless Area

The Driftless Area is a topographically rugged zone that includes portions of southeastern Minnesota, southwestern Wisconsin, northeastern Iowa, and northwestern Illinois (Fig. 1). The most unique aspect of the Driftless Area is the fact that it is an island of unglaciated terrain surrounded by glaciated zones. Advancing ice sheets were detoured around the Driftless Area by the highlands to the north, which shifted the flow of ice to both the east and the west, leaving the Driftless Area untouched. The absence of glaciation left this area with a varied topography including steep valleys, bluffs, numerous rock exposures, and caves. The Driftless Area occupies close to 15,000 square miles. The majority of this region, 13,360 square miles, is in Wisconsin. The Upper Mississippi River flows through the western part of the Driftless Area (Martin 1965:83).

The Upper Mississippi Valley includes a rich variety of landforms and ecological biomes, each supporting a variety of plants and animals that provided food and other resources for prehistoric people.

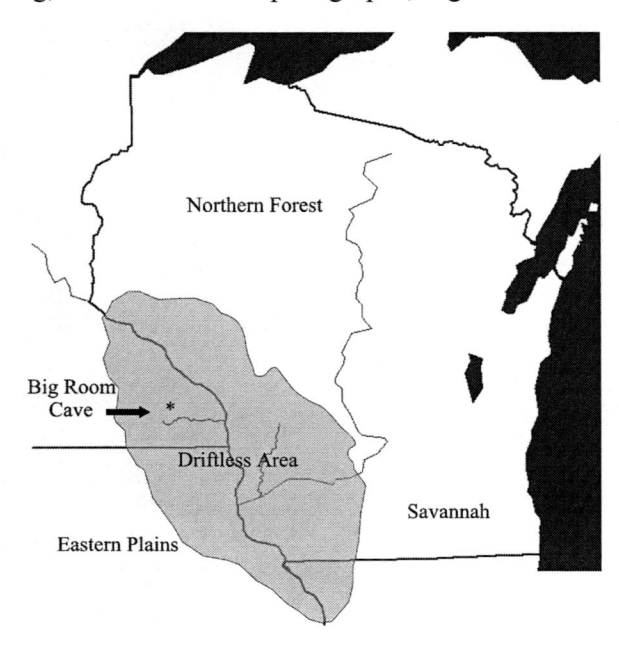

Figure 1. Driftless Area map.

Topographically distinct eco-niches "are therefore considered economic resource zones" (Theler and Boszhardt 2003:29). For the last 4,000 years the climate has been relatively similar to that of today. Most of the upland areas would have been covered by prairie while the river valleys would have been forested with willows, boxelders, maples, oaks, birch, white pine, and hickories. The variety of land and water resources within the Driftless Area provided the richest array of plant and animal species in the region. The Upper Mississippi River valley was a rich resource corridor that "offered a wealth of natural resources during the warm season, and supported human populations, including the regions first agriculturalists nearly 1,000 years ago" (Theler and Boszhardt 2003:32). Big Room Cave is located at the west edge of the Driftless Area. Prehistoric peoples could have used the strategic location of Big Room Cave to take advantage of resources from both the river and the plains through travel and trade.

Cultural History

Upper Mississippi River valley cultures represent 12,000 years of human occupation. Little evidence exists today of the earliest people to occupy the Driftless Area, known as Paleoindians. The only artifacts to survive are stone and bone objects. These peoples are believed to have been nomadic large-game hunters. By 8000 B.C. many of the large-game species had become extinct. Late Paleoindians adapted to the changing environment by hunting early forms of bison (Theler and Boszhardt 2003:58-68). There are no known Paleoindian rock art sites in the Upper Mississippi River valley; however, one glyph at Tainter Cave may represent a long-horned bison (Boszhardt 2003), now extinct.

Like that of Paleoindian cultures, the Archaic lifestyle involved hunting and gathering, but the smaller nonherd animals that Archaic peoples relied on, coupled with increasing human population, allowed these groups to develop social territories. Archaic people lived in small groups that sometimes utilized natural structures, such as rockshelters and caves during the winter months. The Archaic toolkit included ground stone axes and copper tools. Based on the presence of bannerstones toward the end of the Archaic, it is clear that these groups used atlatl spear throwers (Theler and Boszhardt 2003:69-95). Atlatls are depicted at the Jeffers Petroglyph site in southwest Minnesota and are interpreted as representing Archaic rock art (Callahan 2000). The Archaic culture lasted until 500 B.C., longer than any other tradition.

The Woodland tradition began around 500 B.C. and extended to A.D. 1200. Woodland peoples were hunter-gatherers who began to grow plants in small gardens. They are known for the construction of earthen burial mounds and the manufacture of grit-tempered pottery. The mound cemeteries, pottery, and horticulture suggest that Woodland peoples were developing a more sedentary life-style. Toward the end of the Woodland period it is believed that populations increased, possibly depleting resources and placing an increased strain on relationships with neighbors (Theler and Boszhardt 2003:99-139). It is assumed that some of the rock art in the Driftless Area is associated with Woodland cultures.

In the Driftless Area Woodland cultures were influenced by Middle Mississippian cultures around A.D. 1000. This Mississippian influence lasted only about 200 years and coincided with the end of the Late Woodland stage. The Mississippian tradition was centered around the site of Cahokia, located across the Mississippi River from the current city of St. Louis, Missouri. There Mississippian people lived in a hierarchical society with elaborate ceremonial centers surrounded by large permanent towns. Mississippians constructed sizable political and religious structures in the form of platform mounds. The large urban Mississippian population was supported by farming corn, squash, and other cultigens. Mississippian ideas spread from Cahokia to other areas. Mississippian sites are located up and down the Mississippi River, including two major sites in Wisconsin: Aztalan, between Milwaukee and Madison, and a platform-mound site near Trempealeau (Theler and Boszhardt 2003:141-156). The rock art at the Gottschall Rockshelter in southeastern Wisconsin is distinctly Mississippian in style. Other potential Mississippian rock art glyphs have been identified in the Driftless Area, including panel 1 at Tainter Cave, glyphs at La Moille Rockshelter near Trempealeau, and glyphs at Rainy Day Shelter at Silver Mound (Boszhardt 2003).

Mississippian culture influenced the Driftless Area in a unique way by blending new Mississippian ideas with existing Woodland traditions. The Oneota culture emerged around A.D. 1200 and lasted until around A.D. 1650. The Oneota were farming people who grew crops of corn, beans, squash, and tobacco. They made their home on the terraces along major rivers and lakes, harvesting wetland resources and hunting bison. The Oneota lived in large villages. Traces of their settlements have been found throughout the Upper Midwest. Archaeological remains of Oneota habitation sites include storage pits, refuse piles, cemeteries, shell-tempered pottery, stone tools, and floral and faunal remains. These people interacted with other groups, but they did not maintain as extensive trade networks as did the Mississippians. Several distinctly Oneota rock art sites have been identified in the Driftless Area, often on the basis of depictions of modern bison (Theler and Boszhardt 2003). The rock art found in the rock shelters of Allamakee County, Iowa and in Samuels Cave and Bell Coulee in La Crosse County, among others, have been attributed to Oneota groups.

The Oneota likely disseminated into various bands: "Among their present descendants are the Ioway, Otoe, Missouri, Winnebago, Osage, Kansas, and Quapaw Indians" (Blaine 1995:8). The primary Historic tribes associated with the Driftless Area are the Winnebago or Ho-Chunk, the Santee Sioux, and the Ioway: "Allamakee and Winneshiek counties are in the extreme northeastern corner of Iowa. Here what are very possibly the earliest known Ioway village sites may be found" (Blaine 1995:8). Early European explorers, traders, missionaries, and settlers in the Driftless Area were French. It is from their accounts that information from the early Historic tribes is gleaned. These records tend to emphasize problematic tribal relations as a number of eastern tribes moved westward: "Seventeenth-century French accounts describe extensive intertribal warfare in the Upper Mississippi Valley, largely between the Dakota Sioux and eastern groups" (Theler and Boszhardt 2003:180). Both the Ho-Chunk and the Ioway were said to be at war with the Sioux. Along what is today the border between Minnesota and Iowa, the Meskwaki also skirmished with the Sioux. While the Ioway shifted farther onto the prairies, the Ho-Chunk experienced resurgence in the late 1700s and their settlements spread. In the 1840s the federal government removed Ho-Chunk people from western Wisconsin and placed them in an agency complex first in northeastern Iowa, then on a reservation in Minnesota, and finally in Nebraska, where many Ho-Chunk formed the Nebraska Winnebago Nation. Some of the people filtered back to western Wisconsin, and in the 1870s the federal government recognized their homestead near Black River Falls as well as those along the Mississippi River between Trempealeau and De Soto (Theler and Boszhardt 2003).

Research History of Driftless Area Rock Art

The diverse topography makes archaeological research in the Driftless Area difficult in remote areas, particularly on steep valley slopes. Consequently, most archaeological investigation has taken place in valley bottoms and in easily accessible rockshelters. The first published account of archaeological findings within the Driftless Area was Richard Taylor's description of animal effigy mounds between Madison and Prairie du Chien in 1838. Most of the early reports focused on mounds that existed along the Mississippi River and its tributaries (Theler and Boszhardt 2003:39-52). In 1879 the first documentation of a rock art site in the Driftless Area took place at Samuels Cave (also called Picture Cave). The art work at Samuels included several images of bison, humans, birds, and abstract symbols (Boszhardt 2003:24). Theodore H. Lewis was employed by Alfred J. Hill in the 1880s to map mounds in southern Wisconsin, eastern Iowa, and southeastern Minnesota. Lewis also documented the presence of several rockshelters and caves, tracing rock art images at several sites, including La Moille and Samuels Cave.

In the 1930s Ellison Orr documented archaeological sites in northeastern Iowa, including several rock art sites (Stanley 1993). In the early 1900s crews sponsored by the Milwaukee Public Museum photographed rock art sites in western Wisconsin, which resulted in the identification of Indian and Larson Caves. Subsequently, Robert Ritzenthaler formally synthesized the known rock art sites in Wisconsin (Ritzenthaler 1950). Warren Wittry found rock art depicting bison as well as other animal and human forms in 1958 at Gullickson's Glen. Dean Snow published a synthesis of Minnesota rock art in 1960, which was later updated by Mark Dudzik in 1995 (Boszhardt 2003:24-25). During the 1960s several Wisconsin rockshelters and caves, including Preston Rockshelter, Brogley Rockshelter, Bard Lawrence Rockshelter, and Mayland Cave, were excavated, revealing stratified sequences containing Archaic and Woodland components, but no rock art was documented (Theler 1987). In the 1970s R. Clark Mallam from Luther College in Iowa conducted research to relocate rock art sites recorded by Lewis and Orr. After Mallam's death, Lori Stanley continued rock art research for Luther College (Stanley 1993).

In the early 1980s rock art studies and investigation of sites along the Root River in southeast Minnesota were conducted by the Mississippi Valley Archaeology Center (MVAC). MVAC launched an in-depth investigation into rock art of the Driftless Area that spanned the 1980s and 1990s. The result was the discovery of previously unrecorded art at Samuels Cave, Roche-a-Cri State Park, Viola Rockshelter, and Agger Rockshelter (Boszhardt 2003:25-26). This rock art study also led to the discovery of new sites, including Bell Coulee Rockshelter (Loubser 1995). In the 1980s Dave Lowe conducted a survey of rock art sites in Iowa and Dane Counties in Wisconsin (Lowe 1987). His survey identified 23 rock art sites. It was during this time that Robert Salzer initially investigated the Gottschall Rockshelter, which contains over 40 pictographs and petroglyphs in conjunction with stratified sediments that provided information on the chronological and behavioral contexts of the rock art (Salzer 1987:419). In the 1970s, there were fewer than 50 known rock art sites in Wisconsin. By 2003 there were nearly 200, and many less visible caves and rockshelters containing rock art remain to be documented. The vast majority of known rock art sites are located within the Driftless Area because of the thousands of sandstone and limestone outcroppings, shelters, and caves (Theler and Boszhardt 2003:39-52).

Research History of Big Room Cave

Preliminary speleological investigations at Big Room Cave were carried out by Dave Madsen and Jim Magnusson in 1983 and Dr. Calvin Alexander in 1984. Madsen and Magnusson drafted the initial map of Big Room Cave during their 1983 trip (Madsen and Magnusson 1983). Dr. Alexander reported the Cave to Robert Boszhardt from the Mississippi Valley Archaeology Center, who conducted an initial archaeological reconnaissance with Dr. Alexander in 2001. Documentation of the rock art in Big Room Cave was begun in October of 2005 by Robert Boszhardt, Katherine Stevenson, and two archaeology students from the University of Wisconsin--La Crosse, Chris Driver and Rebecca Sprengelmeyer. Greg Brick and Tim Stenerson from the Minnesota Speleological Society joined the investigation. This investigation was concluded in January of 2006 with a second trip into the cave. This time Robert Bozshardt, Katherine Stevenson, and Rebecca Sprengelmeyer were joined by rock art specialist Linea Sundstrom and Glen Fredlund (both of UW--Milwaukee), Andrew Jalbert, Chloris Lowe Jr. (former president of the Ho-Chunk Nation) and his son Chloris Lowe III, and David Alderman.

Description of Big Room Cave

Geology

Calvin Alexander's 1984 investigations indicated that Big Room is a sinkhole cave formed in the New Richmond Sandstone (Alexander 1984). The New Richmond is a member of the Shakopee Formation in the strata between Oneota Dolomite below and St. Peter Sandstone above. This sandstone formed in the Lower Ordovician period and is part of the Prairie du Chien group. The New Richmond is a 20-meter-thick, well-sorted and well-rounded quartz sandstone unit that forms the lower part of the Shakopee Formation (Ojakangas and Matsch 1982:75). New Richmond Sandstone is described on Minnesota bedrock geology maps as a "fine-grained sandstone with well-developed cross-bedding as much as 40 feet thick [overlying a] thin interval, 15-20 feet thick, of thin-bedded, sandy dolostone and dolomitic sandstone. Some basal beds are oolitic, stromatolitic, or contain interclasts" (Mossler 1995).

The Cambrian, Ordovician, and Devonian geologic periods are represented by the strata found in southeastern Minnesota. The Devonian and Upper Ordovician units have been eroded away in the lo-

Figure 2. Big Room Cave sinkhole.

Figure 3. Entrance to Big Room Cave.

cality of Big Room Cave: "Near the Mississippi River downstream from St. Paul, erosion has removed the soft St. Peter Sandstone and any younger units," (Ojakangas and Matsch 1982:234) exposing the Ordovician unit. In the Ordovician period (500-430 million years ago) carbonates in the form of dolomite and limestone were produced by debris from Paleozoic marine environments. Most caves in southeastern Minnesota have been formed in Ordovician limestones. According to Ojakangas and Matsch, "Wherever limestone and dolomite make up part of the bedrock, caves are likely to be found, because these rock types are susceptible to fairly extensive solution by ground water. Such is the case in southeastern Minnesota" (1982:241). Erosion left Prairie du Chien and Upper Carbonate rocks to form the current bedrock surface. The highest occurrence of karst topography such as sinkholes, caves, and extensive conduit systems is in the rocks of the Upper Carbonate and Prairie du Chien groups (Lively and Balaban 1995:16). The Cambrian units underlie the Oneota Dolomite and are primarily sandstones and shales.

Sinkholes occur sporadically throughout the Driftless Area. Sinkholes are circular depressions sometimes found in conjunction with ponds or caves. They are often recognizable in fields because of associated tree clumps and debris piles. Sinkholes are formed by the chemical action of underground water dissolving soluble portions of rock material below the surface. Water picks up carbon dioxide from decaying organic material in the soil making it more chemically active by producing carbonic acid that dissolves calcite, a mineral found in limestone. Water soaks into the ground through joints in the sandstone until it reaches a layer of limestone, which the water then dissolves. As long as the cavity remains full of water it continues to enlarge; thus, limestone caves develop best near the water table. When the water table drains, sandstone above the cavity can weaken with time and collapse. The ground above this cavity then slumps forming a depression. Sinkholes result from solution and collapse (Martin 1965:93). The large, open cavity of Big Room Cave probably formed in this fashion. Terrestrial deposits, washed in from above, are common inside sinkhole caves.

Location and Description

Big Room Cave is located south of Interstate 90 in Winona County in southeastern Minnesota, near the town of Fremont. The area surrounding Big Room Cave is within the Mississippi River basin and is on the western edge of the Driftless Area. The sinkhole entrance to Big Room Cave, located in the center of a farm field, is clearly indicated by a cluster of trees (Fig. 2). The entrance is 1,482 feet from Rush Creek, which feeds into the Root River, a tributary of the Mississippi River. Big Room Cave is located 22 miles from the Mississippi River.

A cluster of trees surrounds the sinkhole entrance to Big Room Cave. Soil has eroded to partially obscure the opening, but several large roots and rocks add stability to the cave entrance (Fig. 3). The eroded soil has formed a large debris cone that extends into the chamber of the cave, where the sediment flattens out and coats the floor. The surface entrance to Big Room Cave, as well as the subsurface floor, is lit-

Figure 4. Big Room wall with graffiti and probable Native American glyphs: Panel 7-12.

tered with animal bone and garbage, including modern beer cans and a full wine bottle. We observed three distinct types of animal scat and encountered several bats. The cavity of Big Room Cave is rectangular in shape, 36 meters long (northeast/southwest), roughly 8 meters wide (northwest/southeast), and 3 meters high. In cross-section, Big Room is square, with vertical walls and a flat floor and ceiling. There are several large rockfall slabs on the floor toward the back of the cave. The walls of the cave are composed of New Richmond Sandstone, which is yellowish brown (10YR 5-6) in color. There is visible cross-bedding, and there are ripples on the ceiling. A light deposit of white efflorescence is present on the walls. There are no calcite formations, such as stalactites or flowstone, and no fossils within the cave. The cave surfaces are damp. Most of the moisture was concentrated on the northwest wall. There is extensive graffiti on both the north and south walls despite the moisture along the northwest wall. The graffiti consists of numerous names and dates carved, drawn with pencil, drawn with charcoal, and spray-painted onto the walls. The earliest dates are from the 1860s. Symbol designs include a large blue and white spray-painted Star of David and several drawn characters (Fig. 4). Probable Native American glyphs are present on the southeast wall. They include charcoal elliptical images with central dots, elliptical images with central dots and extension rays, and carved versions of the elliptical motif (Fig. 5). These elliptical forms are often interpreted as vulva forms. There are also two drawings of large animals (possibly bison) associated with human figures (Fig. 6), several other human figures, and a few abstract forms. We identified over 37 probable Native American glyphs.

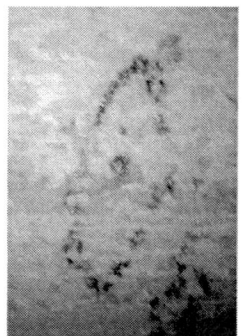

Figure 5. Big Room elliptical glyphs.

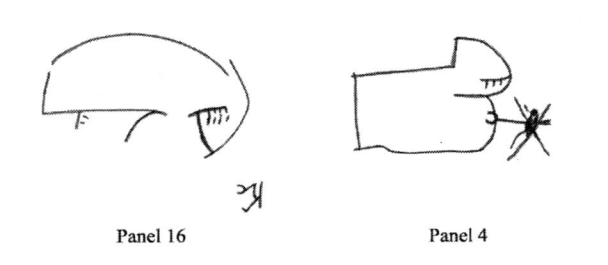

Figure 6. Big Room boxy animals with human figures.

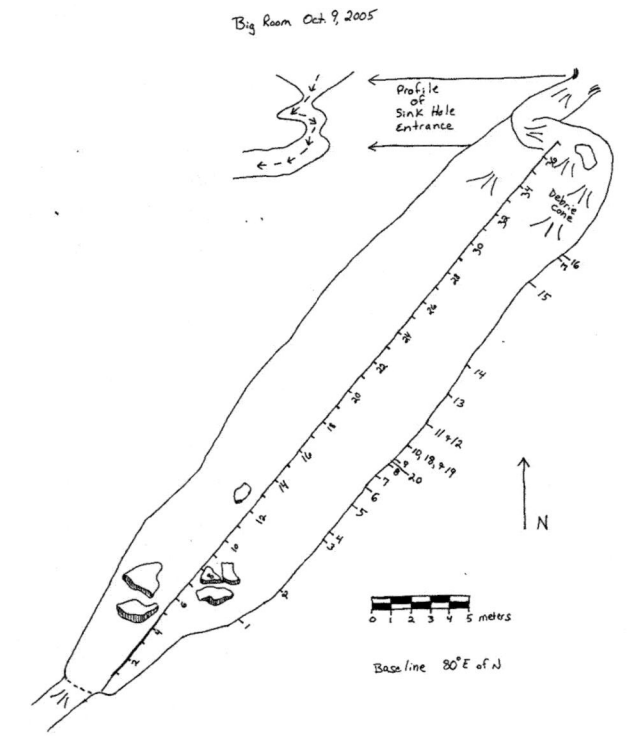

Figure 7. Map of Big Room Cave with location of panels.

Methods

Distinguishing Rock Art from Graffiti

The rock art at Big Room Cave has been partially obscured by graffiti. The graffiti on the north wall overlies much of the prehistoric art, making it difficult to discern modern images from prehistoric. Distinguishing these images is further complicated in Big Room because some of the graffiti artists used charcoal, the same medium used by the prehistoric artists. Graffiti displaying names, letters, and dates were identified as having an obvious Historic or modern origin and were omitted from further study. Graffiti consisting of symbols and figures were more difficult to discern. We then looked at the medium with which the image was created as an indication of antiquity. Graffiti created with spray-paint and pencil were easy to rule out as having a possible prehistoric origin, but the incised and charcoal images required further scrutiny. Indicators of antiquity such as weathering and patination needed to be considered to distinguish the modern figures from prehistoric ones. We also looked closely at each image to see whether it was interrupted by other art/graffiti. Most of the images, both modern and prehistoric, were overlapped by other images. By discerning which image was created first, we were able to determine which images were the oldest and most probably Native American. This was a particularly useful technique in the case of two caricatures that were determined to be relatively old only after it was discovered that they were interrupted by a carved date from the 1880s. The glyphs that could not be ruled out as modern graffiti were marked with flagging tape.

Mapping

Working from the 1983 speleological map of Big Room Cave, we redrew the map to facilitate our goal of documenting the rock art (Fig. 7). We established a baseline by placing a metric tape down the center of the floor, stretching it from southeast to northwest so that it spanned the longest dimension of the cave (36 meters). We then used another meter tape to measure the distance from the baseline to various points along the northwest and southeast walls. In this way we established the parameters of the cave. We then plotted major rooffall boulders to use as reference points. Once the cave map had been redrawn we began to map the glyphs.

After determining which glyphs were potentially Native American, we decided which images would be mapped individually and which to group together as a panel, based on the proximity to others. We identified 21 panels and numbered them from the back of the cave to the front. We plotted the location of each panel by measuring its position along the baseline and its distance from the baseline. We also measured the vertical distance from the floor to the center of the panel and took the measurements of each individual glyph. I sketched and noted the percent of deterioration of each glyph, with the exception of Panel 14. This panel was a complex of several images, and due to its complexity, we omitted it from our documentation on October 9 to properly document it on January 12. On the later trip into the cave, we finished documenting Panel 14 and recorded Panels 17 through 21. Each image was photographed with a digital camera, and most panels were also photographed with digital infrared photo equipment as described below.

Photography

During the initial trip into Big Room Cave on October 9, 2005 each image was photographed with a digital camera and the aid of a spotlight. On the January 12, 2006 trip a gas generator provided electricity to light up the cave with a series of halogen bulb floodlights. Once the cave was illuminated by four mounted floodlights and two portable lights, the drawings on the cave wall were much more visible. During this process, Glen Fredlund and Andrew Jalbert each took digital infrared photographs of all the panels using a Hoya R72 IR-Pass filter. This filter allows infrared waves to pass into the camera while blocking most of the visible light.

Infrared photography produces images that are not possible with conventional photographic films. The same cameras and processing can usually be used for infrared and normal photography. The difference lies in the ability of the camera to record what the eye cannot see: "Infrared light is invisible light found just below the red portion of the spectrum" (Newton's Apple 2005). The electromagnetic spectrum is made up of types of electromagnetic radiation like radio waves, microwaves, infrared radiation, visible light, ultraviolet radiation, X-rays, and gamma rays that transfer energy via waves of oscillating electromagnetic fields. What distinguishes them from each other are the frequency of the oscillation and the wavelength. Visible light has a range of wavelengths from red to violet light. Infrared light has a range of wavelengths just beyond red. Near-infrared light is closest in wavelength to visible light, and far infrared is closer to the microwave region of the electromagnetic spectrum (Infrared Information 2003). Many materials reflect and transmit infrared radiation in a different manner than the visible radiation of light. The visible spectrum ends at a wavelength of 700 nanometers. The infrared range of the electromagnetic spectrum lies beyond the red and is invisible to the human eye. Infrared includes all radiations between wavelengths just beyond those of the deepest reds of the visible spectrum (700 nm) and microwaves (100,000+ nm) (Davidhazy n.d).

When the average temperature of an object increases, its wavelength also increases and so does the intensity of the radiation. Infrared film detects differences in radiation intensity and then assigns different tones, or false colors, forming a picture that our eyes can interpret. Infrared photography is used in a large number of applications in various scientific fields including archaeology. Infrared photography has important applications for the documentation of rock art, because it can help researchers distinguish between pigments and detect pigment residue that cannot be seen with visible light. Infrared photography can be used to record two similar pigments as different, distinct colors because it records the absorption or reflection of infrared radiation that is characteristic of each pigment. Thus two pigments that seem to be the same color to the human eye can appear as different and often distinct colors in an infrared photograph. This type of image provides a different view from traditional visible-light photography as well as additional information about the subject, producing a more complete picture of the site.

Glen Fredlund shot regular images with a Nikor AF 18-70mm f/3.5-4.5G lens. He used manual focus and auto exposure with and without flash, manual-mode infrared with both high and medium resolution, and incandescent photos. He then processed some of the images, post-capture, in Adobe Photoshop. Photoshop procedures used included desaturation, using auto contrast, and converting the photos to black-and-white or gray-scale images. The resulting images were saved as high-resolution. jpg files, which are on file at the Mississippi Valley Archaeology Center.

Results and Glyph Summary

We documented 21 panels and over 37 individual glyphs. Of these glyphs, 33 were drawn in charcoal and four were incised. Of the carved images, all were elliptical, two had rays, one lacked rays, and one took advantage of an elliptical natural fracture. One of the rayed elliptical images was incorporated,

Rock Art Motifs Found Within Big Room Cave

Motif	Drawn Pictographs	Incised Petroglyphs	Total
Ellipticals		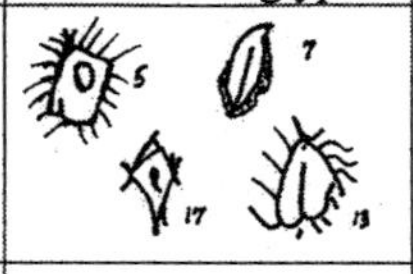	14
Humans			13
Humans with Animals			2
Animals	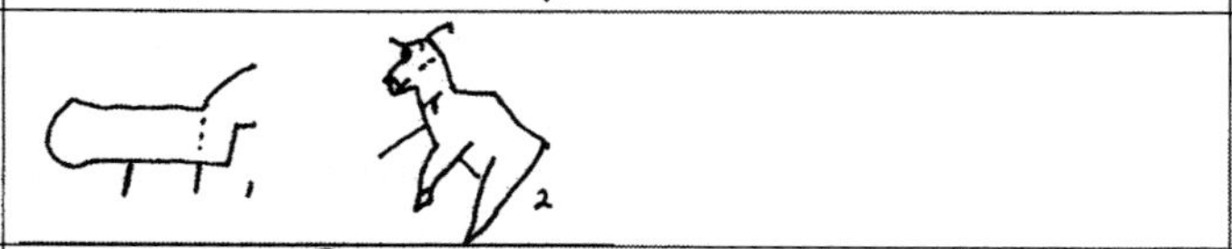		2
Abstract	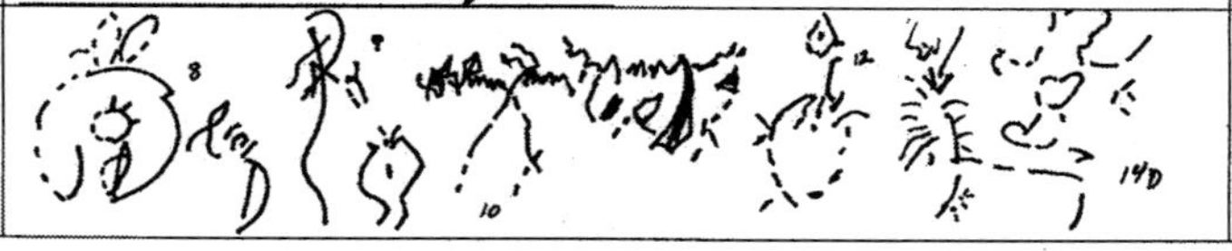		7

Figure 8. Rock art motif chart.

probably at a later date, into another image to form the head of a human figure with a drawn stick body. These carved elliptical glyphs may represent the oldest rock art at Big Room Cave. In total, we documented the following motifs: 14 elliptical glyphs, 15 human forms (two are attached to form one image, and two very similar human forms with X-shaped bodies are each associated with possible bison), two other animals, and seven abstract forms (Fig. 8). Some of the abstract forms share characteristics with the elliptical forms.

Within the elliptical motif there are several variants at Big Room: 10 unrayed, four rayed, eight with center dots, six with centerlines, and one with possible speech lines. Of the 10 unrayed elliptical images, six have center dots and four have centerlines. While two of the four rayed elliptical images have center dots, the other two have centerlines. One of the rayed elliptical images with a center dot also has a serpentine body. Additional possible elliptical forms exist in Panels 10, 12, 9, and 21. These images are too deteriorated to distinguish with certainty at this time.

There is also variation within the human figure motif. Of the 15 human forms, eight are drawn in profile facing north toward the cave opening, two are frontal drawings, and five are undistinguishable. Three images are just heads, two are of heads with triangular torsos, one is a headless body, and nine depict full human bodies. Some human bodies are drawn as stick figures, others are outlined, and some have abstract forms for bodies. Each human figure seems to have unique characteristics. This variation within the human form motif makes the elliptical motif by far more prevalent in Big Room than any other motif. Unrayed elliptical forms with center dots are the most common consistent form of rock art at Big Room Cave.

Interpretation of Glyphs

The specific purpose of most artifacts, such as tools, can often be discerned, but the original function and meaning of rock art often remain enigmatic. The most common art forms remaining in the archaeological record were constructed from ceramic and stone. Ceramic styles have been studied in depth and widely used to mark cultural changes through time. Rock art has not gotten the same attention, in part because it is difficult to date and interpret, making cultural affiliation hard to determine. Was it a form of communication like writing, a form of art for the sake of art, individual graffiti, or a spiritual ritualistic activity? If the latter is the case, then was the activity perhaps related to puberty rites, or vision quests, or other rituals? More than likely, some rock art was created for each of these reasons as well as others. Not all comparable rock art has to mean the same thing or have been created for the same purpose. Rock art may have been created for a number of reasons, which may have changed with time. It is possible to extract information about the behavior of the people who made and used art without necessarily knowing what it meant to them. As with all artifacts we have to look at context to gain clues that may help us interpret the significance of rock art glyphs: "Regional distribution studies can assist in estimating the age of rock art" (Theler and Boszhardt 2003:225). Ethnographic comparisons to abstract designs on other art forms offer insight. Interpretation of art meanings is an ongoing study that seeks to establish the cultural and temporal context of rock art sites by cross-dating styles and motifs using images of known context and origin.

Regional Manifestations of the Motifs Found Within Big Room Cave

Variations of the motifs found within Big Room Cave can be found throughout the Driftless Area. To place these images in regional context, my investigation into similar rock art styles has focused on sites located within the Driftless Area, Figure 9 shows the location of each site mentioned below. However, since Big Room is located on the eastern cusp of the Plains and only 22 miles from the Mississippi River, I have also explored connections to the west and south via the Mississippi River.

The elliptical motif, also known as a vulva form, is not only the most common motif in Big Room but is also the most commonly found motif at other area sites: "Petroglyphs classified as vulva forms range from ovoid or nearly round to triangular in shape, with the central feature being either a small round

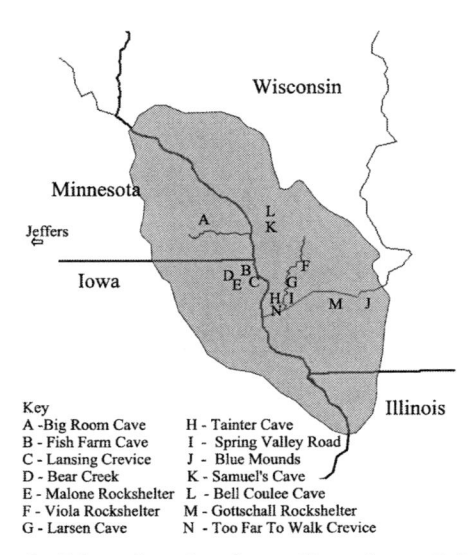

Figure 9. Map of regional manifestations of the motifs found within Big Room Cave.

depression or a vertical groove that bisects the ellipse" (Stanley 1993:117). Vulva forms have been found throughout the upper Midwest and Plains and are common at petroglyph sites in northeastern Iowa.

In Allamakee County, Iowa, along the Mississippi River, is an outcropping of Jordan Sandstone. A series of vertical crevices extend back into the rock along fissures on the face of the sandstone exposure. Carved on the walls of these crevices and overhangs are many petroglyphs depicting human, bison, bear, turtle, thunderbird, turkey track, and elliptical forms. These sites are considered to be late prehistoric and "it is likely that at least some of the petroglyphs can be attributed to Oneota authorship" (Stanley 1993:121).

Indian Cave/Lansing Enlarged Crevice

Indian Cave (13Am84), also known as the Lansing Enlarged Crevice, is located near the town of Lansing in east-central Allamakee County. Glyphs include whole animals, animal and bird tracks, human feet, human faces, canoes, and elliptical forms (Stanley 1993:113). The elliptical forms are similar to those at Big Room. Petroglyph C, on the north wall of the south crevice, depicts a human body that shares similarities with Panel 20C at Big Room. Petroglyph A, located on the north wall of the south crevice, is of a human head that has common fea-

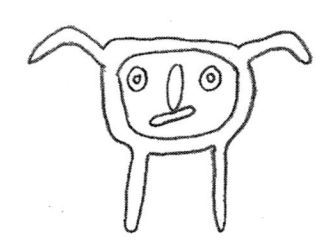

Big Room Panel 21   Indian Cave Petroglyph A

Figure 10. Indian Cave and Big Room Cave similarities.

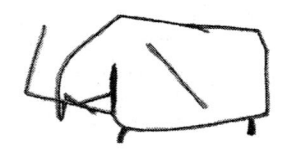

Figure 11. Bear Creek Rockshelter bison.

Big Room Panel 21   Fish Farm Glyph #3

Figure 12. Fish Farm and Big Room similarities.

tures with the human head depicted on Panel 21 at Big Room (Fig. 10).

Malone Rockshelter

The Malone Rockshelter (13Am125) is located along the east bank of Bear Creek in Allamakee County. There are two panels, each containing 29 elliptical designs of various sizes. Most of these designs are divided by a central dot or incised with a central line. Some glyphs were created individually, while others exist in rows or overlap each other (Stanley 1993:116). These glyphs are similar to the elliptical motif found at Big Room Cave.

Bear Creek Rock Shelter

Toward the east end of an exposure of Jordan sandstone in Allamakee County is an overhang that forms the Bear Creek Rockshelter (13Am127). The site is located downstream from the Malone Rockshelter. On the back wall of the southwest chamber are 12 subangular elliptical forms. Some occur singly, others are arranged in patterns. The elliptical motif is the prominent motif in the northeast chamber where the narrow passage is filled with rows of elliptical glyphs. Other glyphs include three bison, three bear paws, and a turtle (Stanley 1993:119). Of the three bison, two are stylized in a way similar to those found at Big Room Cave (Fig. 11).

Fish Farm Cave

The Fish Farm Cave site (13Am49) in Allamakee County consists of two enlarged sandstone crevices. Fish Farm Cave is located near Fish Farm Mounds State Preserve at the mouth of the Upper Iowa River. Glyphs at this site include several slashes or grid marks, human hands and feet, a human face, human forms, birds, elliptical forms, and elliptical forms with tails. In addition to the similarities between the elliptical forms at Fish Farm and Big Room, there is also a human head (No 3) at Fish Farm that is similar to the human head depicted on Panel 21 at Big Room (Fig. 12).

Bell Coulee Cave

Bell Coulee Cave (47Lc547) is a deep sandstone rockshelter located in La Crosse County, Wisconsin. Elliptical petroglyphs with center dots and slashes similar to those found at Big Room are found within this rockshelter. Other glyphs include parallel engraved lines, abstract designs, bird shapes, and animals. The presence of bison with heart-line arrows from the mouth into the chest at Bell Coulee suggests an Oneota origin. The heart-line motif is found in late prehistoric and Historic times from the Great Lakes across the Plains and down to the Southwest (Theler and Boszhardt 2003:170).

Larsen

Larsen Cave (47Cr619) is located in Crawford County, Wisconsin. There are nine panels at this site, composed of both petroglyphs and pictographs.

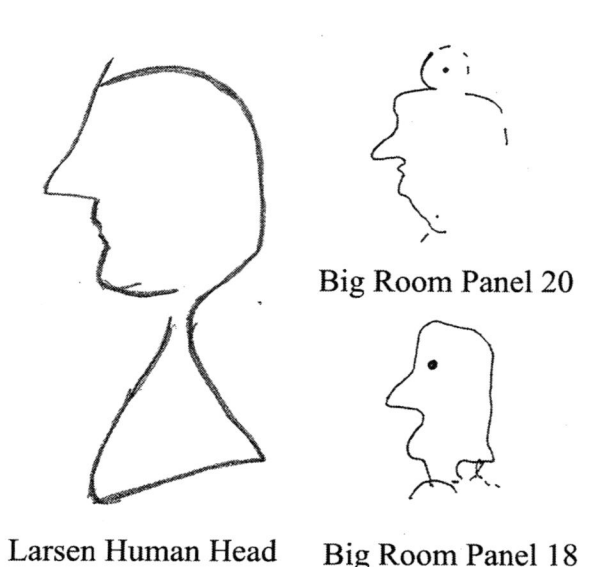

Figure 13. Larsen and Big Room similarities.

The pictographs were rendered in both black and red pigment. Glyph motifs include grids, grooves, geometric shapes, deer, birds, a human arm, and a human head. The human head was formed out of red pigment and drawn in profile, and it is similar in shape to the human head in Panels 18 and 20B at Big Room Cave (Fig. 13).

Tainter Cave

Tainter Cave (47Cr569) is located near the top of a ridge in Crawford County. There are over 100 glyphs inside the three chambers that make up Tainter Cave. The petroglyphs and pictographs include grids, zig-zag lines, abstracts, boxy deer, turkey tracks, thunderbirds, human forms, and diamonds with dots. Again, the diamond-and-dot motif is comparable to the elliptical motif found at Big Room. The glyphs at Tainter, some of which exhibit Mississippian affiliation, appear to correspond to Middle and Late Woodland dates (Boszhardt 2003:29).

Too Far to Walk Crevice

Too Far to Walk Crevice (47Cr639) is located in Crawford County, in the Kickapoo River Valley. This site is a shelter formed by the overhang of a sandstone exposure. Here again elliptical glyphs have been documented, similar to those found at Big Room. Vertical and basin-shaped grooves have also been recorded at Too Far to Walk.

Spring Valley Road Cave

The Spring Valley Road Cave (47Cr709) is a small crevice cave also located in the Kickapoo River Valley. The site consists of five petroglyphs that make up three panels on the south-facing slope of the cave wall. Panel 2B has an abstract vulva form, and 3A is a vulva with a central slash. Other petroglyphs include turkey tracks and a thunderbird (Georgeff 2004:42).

Viola Rockshelter

The Viola Rockshelter (47Ve640) is located on a tributary of the Kickapoo River in Vernon County, Wisconsin. Petroglyphs recorded at the south end of this shelter consist of three groups of figures depicting the upper torsos of human figures with headgear floating in a boat, a tree or mushroom, and a single diamond-shaped petroglyph. This latter petroglyph is two miles east of the others and contains a bisecting vertical line that gives it a strikingly similar appearance to the elliptical figures at Big Room. The floor area nearest to this panel was not excavated, but excavations of floor deposits near the other panel revealed occupation levels ranging in age from Late Archaic to Late Woodland (Stiles-Hanson 1987).

Blue Mounds Creek and Mill Creek Drainages

Blue Mounds Creek and Mill Creek are tributaries of the Wisconsin River. They are located in Iowa County, Wisconsin. There are 23 rock art sites located within the drainages of these two creeks. Glyphs at DNR #5 (47La168), Hole-in-the-Wall #1, and Hole-in-the-Wall #2 resemble the elliptical shape found at Big Room and the diamond-shaped petroglyph found at the Viola Rockshelter. The art at DNR #5 consists of two large diamond-shaped petroglyphs with oval marks in the centers. The Hole-in-the-Wall #1 Cave contains five separate clusters composed of 20 petroglyphs and one small pictograph. Identifiable images include zoomorphic figures, turkey tracks, a celt or axe, V-shaped images, and an almond-shaped petroglyph resembling an eye. Hole-in-the-Wall #2 is a fissure cave with a large overhang. On the west wall of the overhang several figures were recorded, including one diamond motif, a turkey track, a diamond-shaped fig-

Figure 14. Boxy animals at Samuels' Cave.

ure associated with several grooves, and an eyelike image (Lowe 1987).

Samuels' Cave

Samuels' Cave (47Lc5), located in the La Crosse River Valley in La Crosse County, was one of the earliest reported rock art sites in Wisconsin. There are both petroglyphs and pictographs found at Samuels'. Glyphs at this site include geometric abstract designs, slashes, turkey tracks, birds, deer, small mammals, bison, and human forms (Fig. 14). Among the human forms there are figures holding bows and figures with eight plums on the tops of their heads. The glyphs at Samuels' Cave have been attributed to the Oneota (Stiles-Hanson 1987:295).

Gottschall Rockshelter

The Gottschall Rockshelter (47Ia80) is a sandstone rockshelter located in Iowa county, Wisconsin. More than 40 pictographs and petroglyphs, most of them depicting human and animal forms, have been documented at Gottschall. Preliminary results have implied that these images were made after A.D. 900 by peoples familiar with Mississippian iconographic styles (Salzer 1987). Of interest here are human figures represented with rayed orbs on their heads. They are depicted in detail, with familiar diamond- and almond-shaped eyes containing a central dot. On the tops of their foreheads are curious rayed circular forms "that may represent an unusual hairdo or headdress" (Salzer 1987:443). These orbs have a similar appearance to both the rayed elliptical images and the circular object on the top of the head depicted in Panel 20B at Big Room (Fig. 15).

Another human figure located on the same panel as the Mississippian figures bears a strong resemblance to several human figures from Big Room. On the Gottschall panel an orange-red pigment was applied to create a human head and upper torso over an earlier human figure painted with a blue-grey pigment (Fig. 16). The orange-red human head was rendered in profile and faces left (north), as do those at Big Room, and is comparable to the silhouette of a red human head at Larsen Cave. The shape of the profile face with its prominent nose is similar to Panel 20B at Big Room. The use of a simple dot to represent an eye is a shared trait of Panel 18 at Big Room, while the earlier blue-grey body with partially flexed legs, horizontal lines representing feet, and an arm crossing the upper torso is drawn in the same style as the figure in Big Room's Panel 14A.

Possible Interpretations of the Elliptical Motif

Much of the art attributed to the Great Plains was disseminated by the movement of people and their

Gottschall Panel

Close up of Gottschall Head   Big Room Panel 20

Figure 15. Gottschall human figures with circular orbs.

interactions across ethnic boundaries. It is not possible at this time to convincingly relate rock art in the Eastern Woodlands and Great Plains to specific tribal groups, but ethnographic data does assist in ascertaining cultural identification and interpretation of rock art symbols. Pauketat and Emerson (1991) have conducted a study based on ethnohistoric and ethnographic data from the native cultural traditions of central and southeastern North America as a source of guidance into late prehistoric iconography. They claim that "among the themes that run through Native American cosmologies in the North American Plains, Prairie, Great Lakes, and Southeast is the notion that the cosmos included upper and lower 'Worlds' inhabited by distinctive beings" (1991:926), and that the sun/fire was central to southeastern Native American cosmologies and those of certain Plains groups as well. They also say, "Isolated circles or volutes, may have symbolized sun or fire. . . . However, most 'sun' symbols in the iconographies of late-prehistoric southeastern or midcontenental Native Americans are actually 'cross-in-circle' or 'quartered-circle'" (1991:926). The volute and associated elements have also been associated with serpentine and marine shell forms, symbolizing Under World themes.

Mississippian Influence--Southeastern Ceremonial Complex

These associations are based on motifs found in Mississippian art forms: "The design elements show important similarities with art depicted in a variety of other mediums including engraved shell cups and gorgets, engraved pottery and stone, painted and modeled pottery, repousse' copper items, chipped stone effigies and engraved bone" (Bostwick 2001:439) (Fig. 17). Designs on these objects have been associated with a widespread Southeast Ceremonial Complex, or Southern Cult. During the Mississippian period bird, human/bird composites, serpents, warriors, geometric circle-cross motifs, and other designs interpreted as bird-wing motifs are common. The Mississippian rock art style occurs on bluffs, rockshelters and faces, boulders, and the walls of limestone caves. Mississippian and Woodland art designs have been found in caves in Alabama, Arkansas, Illinois, Kentucky, Missouri, Tennessee, West Virginia, and in Wisconsin at Gottschall Rockshelter. Common motifs include the weeping eye, mace, cross-in-circle, diamond-and-dot, elongated bi-pointed oval or "blade," concentric circles, sun with rays, rayed semicircles, birds, anthropomorphic masks with weeping eyes, and bird-men (Bostwick 2001:441). The diamond-and-dot motif, similar to what is found in Big Room, has also been interpreted as an eye with possible Upper World or thunderbird symbolism. Conversely, it may be a stylized ogee, perhaps symbolic of vaginal or anal orifices or the *Ulunsu'ti,* a magical diamond-shaped crest in the middle of an Under World serpent-monster's forehead. Pauketat and Emerson admit that "aspects of Under World and Upper World symbolism may coexist within the bounds of a single motif" (1991:929). This is especially true of orifice symbols that are interpreted as a passage between earth and sky or Under and Upper Worlds. These images are simultaneously associated with feminine life or activities, earth, fertility, the Under World, and the masculine realm including the sky, the Upper World, and warfare (Pauketat and Emerson 1991).

Expressions of the elliptical images found at Big Room are similar to several other regional mani-

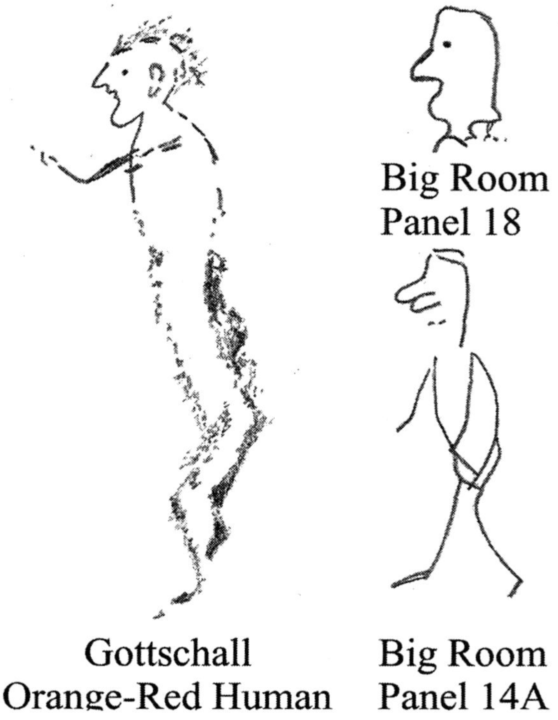

Figure 16. Gottschall orange-red human.

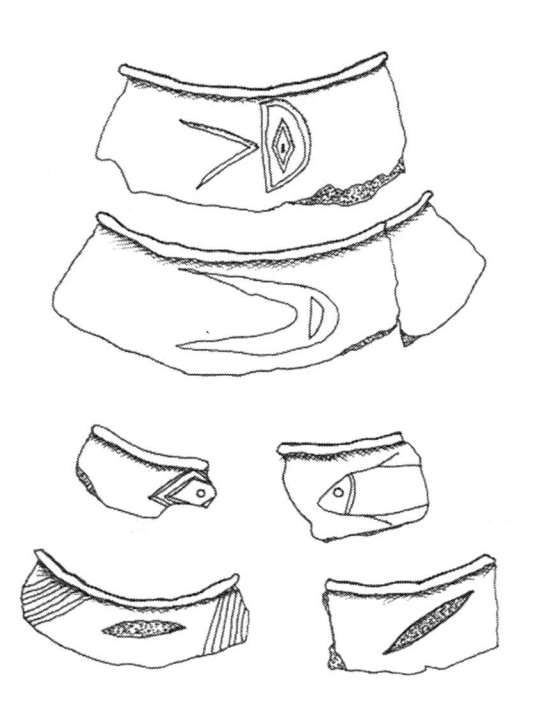

Figure 17. Mississippian elliptical art motifs.

festations of rayed and unrayed circular, elliptical, ovate, and diamond forms. They have been interpreted as sun symbols, masks, weapons, eyes, serpents, anuses, and vulvas. They have been linked with shamanic rituals, the sky or Upper World, masculinity, the Under World, femininity, and everything in between. Although the Big Room images are generally accepted as vulva forms, they are particularly similar to the open eye or ogee motif frequently found in Mississippian-styled art.

Plains Influence and the Hoofprint Tradition

Linea Sundstrom argues for a feminine association for the images found at Big Room. She states that

> in the Black Hills and Cave Hills, these designs (vulva motif) appear as part of whole figures of women, so they are not so ambiguous when they appear alone. These are not pornography. American Indian religious--at least in the Eastern Woodlands and Great Plains—are all about renewal. These designs really are openings--openings to caves, ceremonial grounds, and wombs, among others, places from which people emerge new or renewed. . . . The Hand-eye motif probably represents something similar--a doorway or passageway. Eyes are also doors or windows, and sometimes one design can mean several things (Sundstrom 2005).

Vulva motifs are common in the Plains and are often associated with footprint, hand prints, animal tracks, faces, bas-relief human figures, phallic designs, and grooves (Fig. 18). The consistent juxtaposition of female symbolism, such as vulva motifs, and bison is explained in the ethnographic record by myths and ceremonies that commemorate female reproductive power and the regenerative power of nature. "The emphasis on female fertility and bison fecundity may provide one possible explanation for the grooves so ubiquitous in North American rock art and commonly associated with vulvas" (Turpin 2001:396).

Figure 18. Selection of plains hoofprint images.

The association between elliptical glyphs and bison is often referred to as the Hoofprint Tradition. The Hoofprint Tradition is part of a widespread form of rock art common throughout the northwestern Plains and Eastern Woodlands. Northwestern Plains Hoofprint rock art is largely made up of glyphs in the shape of ungulate, cloven-hoofed animals like bison often associated with human forms (Keyser and Klassen 2001:184-185). Varying in size and concentration, sites sometimes include groups of hoofprints associated with carvings of bison, elk, humans, faces, and the elliptical images known as vulva forms. Keyser and Klassen state, "Representing the westernmost extension of a widespread rock art tradition common throughout the Eastern Woodlands, ethnographic evidence shows that these Northwestern Plains petroglyphs are related to themes of fertility, fecundity, and the sacred relationship between women and bison" (Keyser and Klassen 2001:177). The foremost abstract geometric designs associated with Hoofprint rock art "are circles or ovals, sometimes bisected by lines or with interior crosses. . . . Vulva forms at Hoofprint tradition sites suggest an emphasis on fertility" (Keyser and Klassen 2001:182). At sites in the states of Missouri, Iowa, Wisconsin, and Minnesota, related rock art motifs include bird tracks known as turkey tracks, thunderbirds, elliptical vulva forms, and bear tracks as well as human faces, handprints, and footprints.

Jeffers Petroglyphs

Another tie between the rock art of Big Room Cave and Plains rock art styles is the Jeffers Petroglyph site in southwestern Minnesota (Callahan 2000). The Jeffers Petroglyph site contains one of the largest concentrations of Native American rock art in the Upper Midwest. Animals, humans, hunting, warfare, geometric forms, dream symbols, and shamanic symbols have been recorded there. Atlatls, used by Archaic cultures dating back to 5000 B.P., are also represented at this site and have been used to ascribe a relative date to some of the petroglyphs at the site. The rayed elliptical petroglyph found at Big Room resembles a glyph that has been documented at the Jeffers Petroglyph site. At Jeffers this image is referred to as a Sun-Headed figure and as a stick man with feather headdress (Callahan 2000:48-49). The figure at Jeffers is completely incised, while at Big Room it appears that the petroglyph "head" was created first and the drawn black stick body was added at a later date, perhaps by someone familiar with the Jeffers glyph (Fig. 19). Even though regional manifestations of the rayed elliptical motif exist, this is the only other manifestation of this symbol being used in place of a human head.

Conclusion

Big Room Cave contains at least 37 probable Native American glyphs that can be divided into four motifs: elliptical, human, animal, and abstract. The most common rock art motif found at the cave is the elliptical motif. Manifestations of rock art motifs similar to those at Big Room Cave are found at several other rock art sites within the Driftless Area. The glyphs at Big Room Cave also share characteristics with Mississippian and Plains art styles believed to date to late prehistoric and early Historic times. The people who occupied the Driftless Area during that time frame are known as the Oneota. Several distinctly Oneota rock art sites have been documented in the Driftless Area. They are often interpreted as Oneota on the basis of depictions of modern bison. The rock art found in the rock shelters of Allamakee County, Iowa and in Samuels' Cave have been attributed to the Oneota. The Oneota likely disseminated into various Historic tribes, and among their present descendants are the Ioway, Otoe, Missouri, Winnebago, Osage, Kansas, and Quapaw Indians (Blaine 1995:8). The primary historic tribes associ-

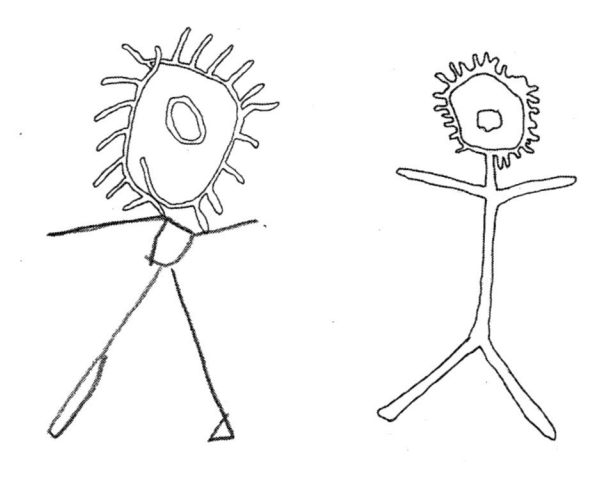

Big Room Panel 5   Jeffers Glyph

Figure 19. Jeffers Petroglyph site and Big Room Cave similarities.

ated with the Driftless Area are the Winnebago or Ho-Chunk, the Santee Sioux, and the Ioway.

The Upper Mississippi Valley includes a rich variety of topographically distinct eco-niches. Prehistoric and early Historic peoples could have used the strategic location of Big Room Cave to take advantage of resources from both the Mississippi River Valley and the Plains through travel and trade. There is strong evidence of Mississippian and Oneota interaction with groups to the west. Interaction networks spanned the Upper Midwest from Lake Michigan west to the Missouri River. There is evidence that the Oneota took advantage of plains resources, particularly bison (Theler and Boszhardt 2003). Bison images, believed to have been created by the Oneota, are depicted in several rockshelters throughout the Driftless Area. The realistic depictions of bison suggest that the Oneota had firsthand knowledge of bison hunts that took place to the west. It is believed that the Oneota did not use rockshelters as winter living spaces as Woodland and Archaic cultures did but used them for ritual purposes (Theler and Boszhardt 2003:170). The elliptical motif is widely believed to represent a spiritual opening. I believe it is fitting that this motif is the dominant motif found within Big Room, a sinkhole-entrance cave. This sort of cave entrance is undisputedly an opening between the surface and underground.

Acknowledgments. I would like to thank Robert (Ernie) Boszhardt for helping me document the rock art in Big Room Cave, suggesting related literature, proofreading my drafts, and acting as my project advisor. I am thankful for the help Kathy Stevenson provided as a proofreader and caver. We never would have made it in and out of the cave without her ropes. I would like to thank Calvin Alexander for sharing the information he had gathered on Big Room Cave and for proofreading the geology section of this paper. I am grateful to Linea Sundstrom for coming with us and lending her expertise to the project in spite of the treacherous descent into the cave. I would also like to thank Glen Fredlund and Andy Jalbert for their infrared photography work, Chris Driver for his digital photography, and Chloris Lowe Jr., his son Chloris Lowe III, and Dave Alderman for bringing the generator and lighting equipment. Thank you all for coming and for all your help.

References Cited

Alexander, C.
    1984 Troy Sink, Big Room Cave and Hiawatha Caverns. Unpublished manuscript on file, Mississippi Valley Archaeology Center, University of Wisconsin--La Crosse.

Anati, E., I. Wainwright, and D. Lundy
    1984 Rock Art Recording and Conservation: A Call for International Effort. *Current Anthropology* 25:216-217.

Blaine, M.R.
    1995 *The Ioway Indians.* University of Oklahoma Press, Norman.

Boszhardt, R.F.
    2001 Unpublished field notes and Minnesota Archaeological Site Form for Big Room Cave. Copy on file, Mississippi Valley Archaeology Center, University of Wisconsin--La Crosse.
    2003 *Deep Cave Rock Art in the Upper Mississippi Valley.* Prairie Smoke Press, St. Paul, Minnesota.

Bostwick, T.W.
    2001 North American Indian Agriculturalists. In *Handbook of Rock Art Research*, edit. by D.S. Whitley, pp. 414-458. Altamira Press, New York.

Callahan, K.L.
    2000 *The Jeffers Petroglyphs: Native American Rock Art on the Midwestern Plains.* Prairie Smoke Press, St. Paul, Minnesota.

Davidhazy, A.
    n.d. Infrared photography. Electronic document <http://www.rit.edu/~andpph/text-infrared-basics.html. March 13, 2006.

Georgiff, M.
    2004 An Analysis of Rock Art Motifs Within the Driftless Area of the Upper Mississippi River Valley. Unpublished manuscript on file at the Mississippi Valley Archaeology Center, University of Wisconsin--La Crosse.

Infrared Information. Electronic document.
    2003 http://imagers.gsfc.nasa.gov/ems/infrared.html. March 13, 2006.

Keyser, J.D., and M.A. Klassen

2001 *Plains Indian Rock Art*. University of Washington Press, Seattle.

Lively, R.S., and N.H. Balaban (editors)
1995 Text Supplement to the Geologic Atlas Fillmore County Minnesota. *Geologic Atlas Fillmore County, Minnesota*. County Atlas Series C-8, Part C. University of Minnesota Press, St. Paul.

Loendorf, L., L.A. Olson, S. Conner, and J.C. Dean.
1998 *A Manual For Rock Art Documentation*. National Park Service and the Bureau of Reclamation.

Loubser, J.H.N.
1995 *The Tale of Two Shelters: Recordation and Conservation Status of Bell Coulee and Fleming No. 1, La Crosse County, Wisconsin*. Technical Report No. 331. New South Associates. Copy on file, Mississippi Valley Archaeology Center, University of Wisconsin--La Crosse.

Lowe, D.
1987 *Rock Art Survey of the Blue Mounds Creek and Mill Creek Drainages in Iowa and Dane Counties, Wisconsin. The Wisconsin Archeologist, 68:341-375.*

Madsen, D., and J. Magnusson
1983 Cave Prospecting Update: Big Room Cave; Winona County, Minnesota. Unpublished manuscript on file, Mississippi Valley Archaeology Center, University of Wisconsin--La Crosse.

Martin, L.
1965 *The Physical Geography of Wisconsin*. The University of Wisconsin Press, Madison.

Mossler, J.H.
1995 *Plate 2. Bedrock Geology. Geologic Atlas Fillmore County, Minnesota*. County Atlas Series C-, Part A. University of Minnesota Press, St. Paul.

Newton's Apple infrared information. Electronic document.
2005 http://www.tpt.org/newtons/11/infrared.html. March 13, 2006.

Ojakangas, R.W. and C.L. Matsch
1982 *Minnesota's Geology*. University of Minnesota Press, Minneapolis.

Pauketat, T.R. and T.E. Emerson
1991 The Ideology of Authority and the Power of the Pot. *American Anthropologist* 93:919-941.

Radin, P.
1990 *The Winnebago Tribe*. University of Nebraska Press, Lincoln.

Rands, R.L.
1956 Southern Cult Motifs on Walls-Pecan Point Pottery. *American Antiquity* 22(2):183-186.

Ritzenthaler, R.E.
1950 Wisconsin Petroglyphs and Pictographs. The Wisconsin Archeologist 31: 83-129.

Salzer, R.J.
1987 Preliminary Report on the Gottschall Site (47Ia80). *The Wisconsin Archeologist* 68:419-472.

Sanger, K.K., and C.W. Meighan
1990 *Discovering Prehistoric Rock Art: A Recording Manual*. Wormwood Press, California.

Steinbring, J. and F. Farvour
1987 The Hensler Petroglyph Site, Dodge County, Wisconsin. *The Wisconsin Archeologist* 68:396-411.

Stanley, L.A.
1993 Rock Art. In *Archeological Investigations of The Bear Creek Locality Allamakee County, Iowa, Chapter 7. HCRC #155*, edit. by D.G. Stanley, pp. 105-122. Highland Cultural Research Center, Highlandville, Iowa.

Stiles-Hanson, C.
1987 Petroglyphs and Pictographs of the Coulee Region. *The Wisconsin Archeologist* 68:287-340.

Sundstrom, L.
1984 Rock Art of Western South Dakota: The Southern Black Hills. *South Dakota Archaeological Society Journal and Special Publications*, edit. by A. Hannus and L. Rossum. Sioux Falls: Sioux Printing.
2001 *Stories on Stone: The Rock Art of the Black Hills Country*. University of Oklahoma Press, Norman.

2005 Eyes have it. E-mail correspondence, May 5, 2005.

Theler, J.L.
1987 *Woodland Tradition Economic Strategies*. Report 17. Office of the State Archaeologist of Iowa, University of Iowa, Iowa City.

Theler, J.L. and R.F. Boszhardt
2003 *Twelve Millennia: Archaeology of the Upper Mississippi River Valley*. University of Iowa Press, Iowa City.

Turpin, S.
2001 Archaic North America. In *Handbook of Rock Art Research*, edit. by D.S. Whitley, pp. 361-413. Altamira Press, New York.